Feeding a Thousand Souls

Feeding a Thousand Souls

Women, Ritual, and Ecology in India—An Exploration of the Kōlam

VIJAYA NAGARAJAN

OXFORD
UNIVERSITY PRESS

June 15, 2019
Phil Rogers Station

To Robert,
to feeding 1000's souls all around the world
in admiration
Vijaya
NAGARAJAN@USFCA.edu

OXFORD
UNIVERSITY PRESS

Oxford University Press is a department of the University of Oxford. It furthers the University's objective of excellence in research, scholarship, and education by publishing worldwide. Oxford is a registered trade mark of Oxford University Press in the UK and certain other countries.

Published in the United States of America by Oxford University Press
198 Madison Avenue, New York, NY 10016, United States of America.

Library of Congress Cataloging-in-Publication Data
Names: Nagarajan, Vijaya, 1961– author.
Title: Feeding a thousand souls : women, ritual and ecology in India : an exploration of the Kōlam / Vijaya Nagarajan.
Description: New York, NY, United States of America : Oxford University Press, [2019] | Includes bibliographical references and index.
Identifiers: LCCN 2018012954 (print) | LCCN 2018033276 (ebook) |
ISBN 9780190858087 (updf) | ISBN 9780190858094 (epub) |
ISBN 9780195170825 (hardcover) | ISBN 9780190858070 (pbk.) |
ISBN 9780190858100 (online content)
Subjects: LCSH: Kolam (House marks) | Women, Tamil—Rites and ceremonies. |
Hindu decoration and ornament. | Hinduism—Rituals.
Classification: LCC GT470 (ebook) | LCC GT470 .N34 2018 (print) |
DDC 294.5/37—dc23
LC record available at https://lccn.loc.gov/2018012954

3 5 7 9 8 6 4 2

Paperback printed by Sheridan Books, Inc., United States of America
Hardback printed by Bridgeport National Bindery, Inc., United States of America

For Amma—Pichammal Nagarajan,
who has taught me and continues to teach me to practice unconditional love.

For my children, Jaya and Uma,
who teach me every single day and
who fill me with gratitude toward the wonder all around us.

For all the Tamil women who have ever practiced the kōlam,
For all the Tamil women who are practicing the kōlam,
and for all the Tamil women who will be practicing the kōlam.
For all of the Tamil women who taught me so much.

CONTENTS

LIST OF FIGURES

All photos not cited are by the author, Vijaya Nagarajan.
All figures cited to anyone besides the author have been used with permission from the copyright owner.

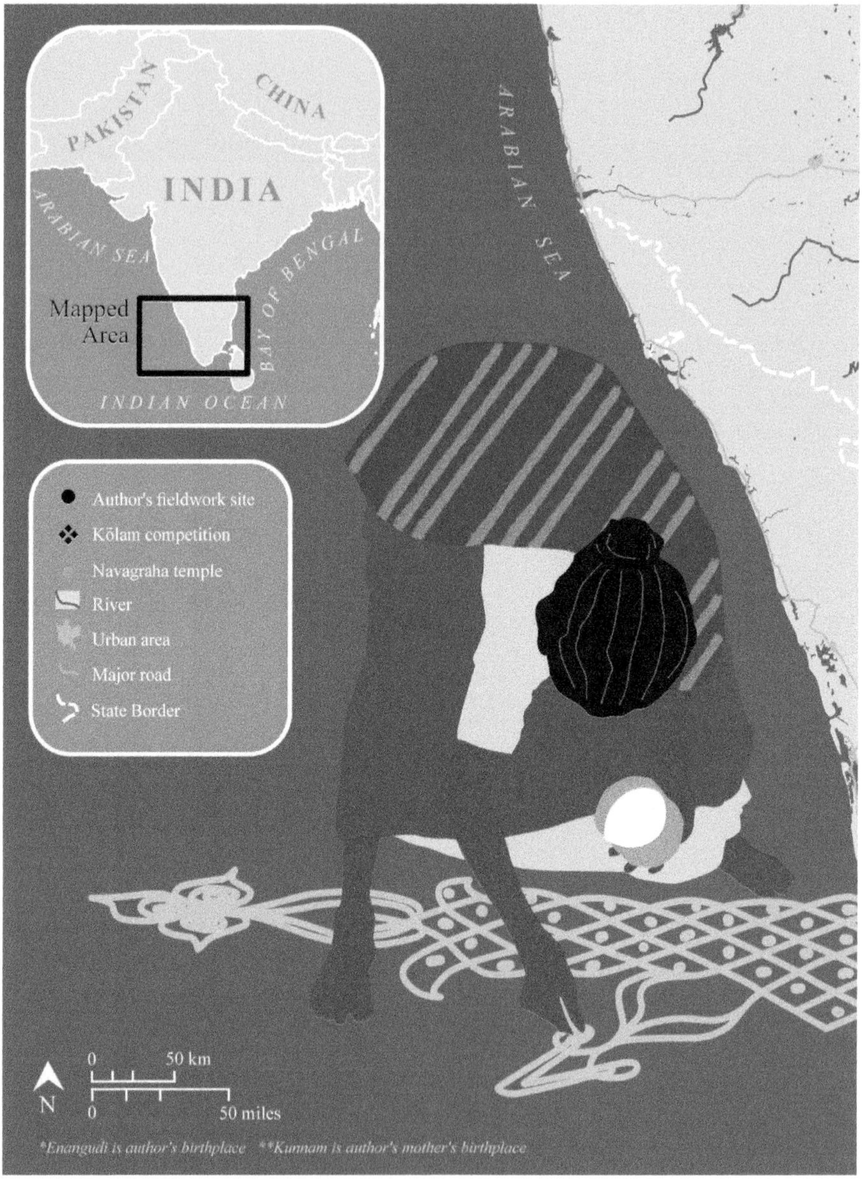

Map Tamil Nadu. Created by Molly Roy.

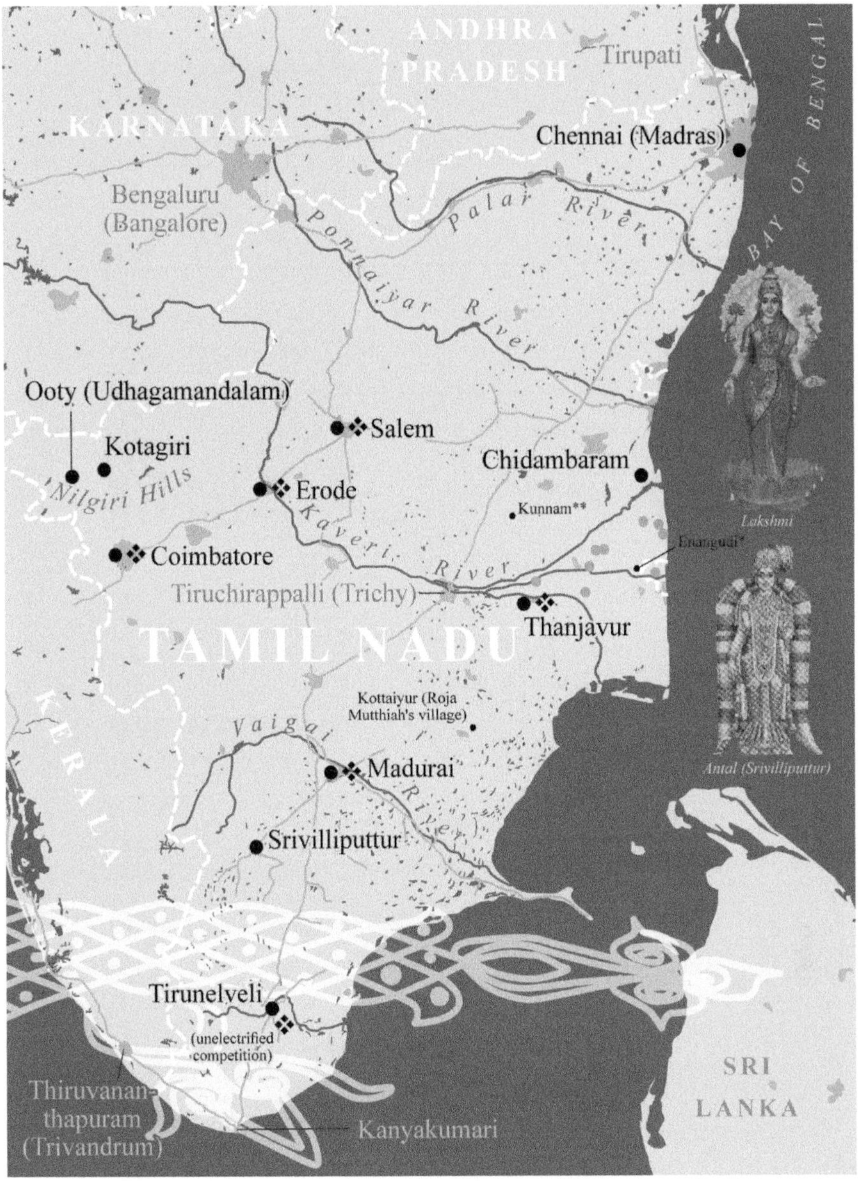

ANDHRA PRADESH
Tirupati
KARNATAKA
Chennai (Madras)
BAY OF BENGAL
Bengaluru (Bangalore)
Palar River
Ponnaiyar River
Ooty (Udhagamandalam)
Salem
Kotagiri
Chidambaram
Nilgiri Hills
Erode
Kunnam**
Kaveri River
Lakshmi
Enangudi*
Coimbatore
Tiruchirappalli (Trichy)
Thanjavur
TAMIL NADU
Kottaiyur (Roja Mutthiah's village)
KERALA
Vaigai River
Madurai
Antal (Srivilliputtur)
Srivilliputtur
Tirunelveli
(unelectrified competition)
SRI LANKA
Thiruvananthapuram (Trivandrum)
Kanyakumari

(a)

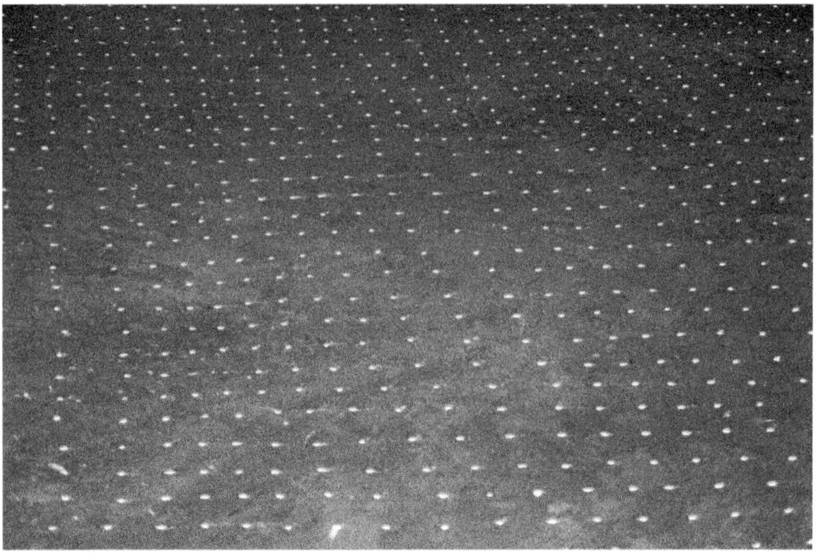

(b)

Facing Page 1a–d. Steps in making a grand kōlam in a village near Mayiladuthurai, Tamil Nadu.

(c)

(d)

ACKNOWLEDGMENTS

People, ideas, and institutions have helped me create this book; they are like the dots in a kōlam. They formed a broad canopy stretched across the United States, India, and Europe and acted not just as a point of reference, but also as an underground aquifer, nourishing my inspiration, conceptualization, researching, and writing. I have circled through and around these dots in interweaving loops. These kinfolk who have helped me with their generosity of time, abundant gifts, and enthusiastic support that were essential to its completion. I am grateful for each and every one of them. Their commitment and love has sustained me throughout.

I thank Amma, my beloved mother, whose loyalty and devotion embodies the Hindu bhakti tradition. A primary source of oral understandings of the nature and significance of women's ritual power and powerlessness in Hinduism, she provided me with a deeply meaningful counterpart to my father's literate understanding of Hinduism. She was a gratifying force during the writing process, and she eagerly color-coded my transcribed interviews, which ran more than 5,000 pages. My mother is also deaf, which made her reading of the Tamil transcripts even more poignant. She would say: "I get so much pleasure out of 'hearing' my daughter speak and listen in India." The sassy Zora Neale Hurston in my life, my mother's vernacular Tamil is sprinkled with much wit, humor, and insight. This book is a telling of women's lives to people who often did not understand or perceive people like her. Women—who did not have the equal opportunity of education because of their gender, class, rural background, family values, and historical moment of coming of age during World War II—often felt that educated people did not "see" them. My mother was taken out of elementary school in her south Indian village, Kunnam, at a very young age but taught herself Tamil, Hindi, and English, with great difficulty. This work, therefore, is an ode to hundreds of millions of women like my mother, who move in the worlds of orality, visuality, gestures, and ritual, but who, in the tidal waves of "modernity," are misjudged as "incompetent," "illiterate," or "ignorant." I can think of no other way to thank her than to dedicate this book to her and all the women like her.

I thank my children, Uma and Jaya, who have been lively and exuberant throughout the continual adventurous unfolding of this book. They have been at the center of my life and their living fully has taught me so much. This book is dedicated to them and to their vital, exciting generation. Lee, my husband and companion, has been an engaged and highly curious witness; there are no words to describe a multi-decade relationship that has maintained its tensile strengths with laughter, intelligence, and empathy, even as it has had to ride through huge obstacles.

My father's sharp intellect prodded my own, bolstering my sagging spirits in the midst of persistent waves of illnesses, accidents, and obstacles. In the last seven years of his life, I felt the enormous power of our mutual forgiveness from earlier battles; his surprising love at the end of his life glimmered. My sister Usha has been a steadfast, wise, and faithful companion along this journey. My other sister, Mala, drew me persistently into the task of recovering and learning Tamil as a scholarly language and was a catalyst for one of the foundations I stand on today.

My cheerful cousin-brother Srikanth (New Delhi) was a determined problem-solver; my cousin-sister Pattu and my manni were both eager storytellers. Bhuvana mami lived and breathed Chidambaram; she took me in as one of her own and hosted me in her natal village with Thandavamama and his wife. Relatives made me feel at home in India, providing a wonderful, generous bowl of affection and hospitality, critical for my work's flourishing.

The unstinting inspiration, collaboration, and excitement of hundreds of kōlam-making women throughout Tamil Nadu were centrally important. They spoke to me and answered my questions with intense joy and pride. I hope I have done justice and respect to our many conversations and insights and conveyed what I have learned with as much humility, clarity, and accuracy as possible. I thank each woman who gave me her time, knowledge, and generosity of spirit. This book is permeated with words, actions, and gestures gleaned from these countless dialogues. I ask all those who I have not been able to name individually to accept my deep gratitude for their help. The conventions of anthropology require that informants be protected by pseudonyms, so this prevents me from listing each person who helped me by name.

Friends and colleagues in India were also exceptionally generous. In Thanjavur, S. Chitra went to phenomenal lengths to actively help me. In Madurai, my extraordinary research assistant, V. Krishnaswamy, bolstered me continuously in my fieldwork from 1989 to 1994. S. Geetha, Leela Venketaraman, Saraswathi Venugopal, J. Rajasekaran, V. Fatima, Nagarajan Bhagavatar, and many others walked with me in this journey and shared their knowledge and time. The brilliant Tamil kōlam scholar V. Saroja, who had written her own dissertation on the kōlam in Tamil, took me on fieldtrips and shared her extensive insights. The scholar Jenny Springer kindly invited me to a nonelectrified village in Tirunelveli District. In Madras, Parimala Rao has embodied a marvelous, treasured friendship full of close conversations and love; she introduced me to Chandralekha, Bamini and Amrita Narayanan, and so many others. Chandralekha gifted me her gracious hospitality, riveting friendship, humor, deep love, and stimulating conversations from 1988 to 2006. Her best friends, Dashrath Patel and Sadhanand Menon, also became close friends and inspired me. Tapathi Guha Thakurti hosted me in Calcutta for 10 days to explore the ālpanā, organizing my visit to Shantiniketan, one of the most intellectually scintillating places I have ever been to. In Rajasthan, Komal Kothari, an incredible storyteller and a living vision of oral traditions, helped me understand better the māndana and the commons.

Throughout this project, I was fortunate to have lively friends who were also mentors, colleagues, and peers. I deeply honor and thank them. The late C. V. Seshadiri permanently sparked my imagination at his highly creative institution, Murugappa Chettiar Research Centre (Taramani, a village then outside of Chennai). His sudden disappearance and death in 1995 was a shock. In 1984, Ivan Illich asked the most important and vital questions of society, and his endless curiosity about the kōlam excited my own. Stella Kramrisch, in the 1980s, shared with me her perseverance, devotion, and love for Indian art. A. K. Ramanujan's encouragement, friendship, and guidance from 1985 onward came at crucial moments in my groping toward becoming a scholar. His unexpected death in 1993 was devastating to those in the middle of conversations left forever dangling. Richard Kurin's invitation to speak on the kōlam at the Smithsonian for the Festival of India sparked all that followed.

I am enormously grateful to the Recovery of the Commons Project and the Institute for the Study of Natural & Cultural Resources (ISNCR), two small nonprofits I cofounded with Lee Swenson, which helped sustain this project in innumerable ways. I founded the ISNCR in 1986 to support the study of the kōlam and other related Indian arts and environmental movements. It expanded quickly in 1990 to become a pulsing nerve center that organized countless workshops, conferences, and lectures for over a decade. Foundational supporters, activists, environmentalists, artists, and writers are entwined throughout the warp and weft of this book. They enlivened and encouraged my search for understanding the kōlam.

I am eternally grateful for two radiant and vital activists without whom this book would not have started or finished. Both saw the intrinsic and extrinsic value of this work. So much flourished with the seeds they provided. Marion

Weber, the godmother of seed-beginnings, first gave the research grants that allowed me to return annually to India from 1986 to 1990. Susan O'Connor, the godmother of closures, gave much-needed research grants so I could finish writing this book, from 2006–2009. I especially thank them for enabling me to have the time and support to braid stories into the book. Josh Mailman gifted a vital subvention toward the publication of the color photos and illustrations. His love rendered this book beautiful in yet a whole other way. The USF Faculty Development Fund also provided critical grant support toward the subvention of the illustrations and so much support throughout the last two decades. For awarding grants at critical junctures, I am deeply grateful to Margaret Schink, whose love and compassion stretched far and wide; Paul Strasburg, whose depth of commitment was rare and precious; Tyrone Cashman, whose friendship and remarkable intelligence run like a river alongside of me; Lexi Rome, whose dedication and loyalty were foundational; Kate Strasburg, whose timely gifts spurred me forward into my journeys; Bokara Legendre, whose tremendous curiosity matched my own; Joanna Macy, whose organizing skills and love know few parallels; and Mimi Buckley and Helen LaKelly Hunt, whose generosity came at significant crossroads.

Some friends pushed me to stretch in various directions; others were moved by the work itself; others' brilliant passions inspired my own. A huge gratitude to them: Elizabeth Weber, whose compassionate heart led the way; Malcolm Margolin, whose brilliant storytelling was always a marvel to witness; Maxine Hong Kingston and Earll Kingston, whose love and devotion to our family and whose sparkling humanity is a tremendous, unparalleled gift; Susan Griffin, who first exuberantly noticed the kōlam; Peter Matthiessen, whose tender, intelligent eyes I still can see; Grace Paley, whose own voice is the miracle; Gary Snyder and Carole Koda, whose conversations on the commons laid down so much groundwork; Barry Lopez, whose passion for ideas and the natural world have few limits; Richard Nelson, whose rare sensitivity raised a high bar; Ashis Nandy, whose gentle, probing questions were signposts; Vandana Shiva, who first told me about Chandralekha and changed my life; Terry Tempest Williams, whose tender voice is soul-catching; W. S. Merwin and Paula Merwin, whose love and wisdom I will never forget; Sadanand Menon, whose deep, wicked laughter accompanies me; Dashrath Patel, who had a rare and wise tenderness; Ramchandra Gandhi, Brooke Williams, Shiv Visvanathan, Smitu Kothari, Oren Lyons, Peter Buckley, Roy O'Connor, Tom Joyce, Amitav Ghosh, and Arundhati Roy whose courage moves me deeply; Rebecca Solnit, whose incandescence lights the way for all of us and who in some ways is a twin sister; Candace Falk, Jim and Jeannie Houston, Mayumi Oda, Wolfgang Sachs, Franco La Cecla, Stanley Crawford, Wendell Berry, Gurney Norman, and Peter Warshall, whose intelligence I still commune with; Diana Hadley, Chitra Divakaruni, Peter Nabokov,

Ramachandra Guha, Lakshmi (Ambai, Mumbai), Jay Harman and Francesca Bertoni, and T. M. Ravi and Francine Lejeune, whose gracious hospitality knows no bounds; Paul Hawken, George Lakoff, Manil Suri, Jerry Mander, Doug and Kris Tompkins, V. S. Naipaul, Daniel and Patricia Ellsberg, Rina Swentzell, Roxanne Swentzell, Al Young, Robert Haas and Brenda Hillman, David Abram, Kamini Ramini, Omar Khan, Mark Dubois, Anthony Appiah, Mark Dowie, Anil Agarwal, Pupul Jayakar, Kapila Vatsyayan, Howard Zinn, John Markoff and Leslie Terzian Markoff, Ann Markusen, Claire Greensfelder, Indu Krishnan, Ariella Hyman; John Gouldthorpe, Kate Levinson and Steve Costa; Ermila Moodley for her insights into Tamil life in South Africa and her deep, loving friendship and hospitality; Elizabeth Stark Powers, a master teacher and craftswoman, and her beloved community of writers, *Book Writing World*, without which this book may never have been finished; and M. Saravanan and Narmada of the California Tamil Academy, for presenting me with the Award for Extraordinary Service to the Tamil Community. All of these kinfolk have believed in me as a writer and had continued faith in me. Gloria Steinem, Virginia Woolf, Jhumpa Lahiri, Zora Neale Hurston, and Anand Coomaraswamy continuously inspire my life and work from afar.

At the University of California, Berkeley (UCB), I thank those who were my bedrock there: Usha Jain, who helped launch my journey into the academy; the multiple FLAS (Foreign Language Area Studies) fellowships in the Tamil language; Linda Hess, Frederique Apffel-Marglin, and Ann Gold, who read draft after draft and helped me with great advice along the way, all mentors exemplifying beacons of humane, feminist scholars; George Hart, who taught me the profound beauty of ancient, medieval, and contemporary Tamil language; Kausalya Hart, who helped unstintingly with translations in the Āṇṭāḷ chapter and so much more; Joanna Williams, who taught me art history and the multiple worlds of Indian beauty; Professor Alan Dundes, who moved me with his bountiful curiosity, unending enthusiasm, and intellectual generosity; these brilliant scholars girded my work. The American Institute of Indian Studies–The Advanced Tamil Language Program in Madurai (1989–1990) with K. Paramasivam, a Fulbright-Hays Doctoral Dissertation Research Fellowship, and the UCB Chancellor's Dissertation Writing Fellowship were all critical for my research and I owe them all many debts of gratitude. The Center for South Asian Studies, an intensely inspiring environment for over three decades, has been a continuous fountain of intellectual work that has watered this book.

My academic life at USF provided a patient, nourishing hospitable home and steady collegial, emotional, and intellectual support. This anchor was invaluable, critical, and necessary for the long and deep investigation this project demanded; they were colleagues and friends one can only wish for. Their hands of friendship, sisterhood, and brotherhood bridged many rising rivers along the path: Lois Lorentzen has been a fellow scholar-activist-writer, who welcomed and mentored me graciously and lovingly into the circle of USF faculty; Jennifer Turpin, whose clear, compassionate, nurturing feminism and life work were stimulating and strengthening; Pamela Balls Organista's insightful friendship, solidarity, Ethnic Minority Faculty Writing Retreats, and the College of Arts and Sciences Faculty Writing Retreats without which this work would not have had the sunlight necessary to grow; and Stephanie Sears, a brave and clear-eyed warrior. Others provided huge infusions of enthusiasm and support: the brief but impactful USF Faculty East Bay Friday Writing Retreats; Aparna Venketesan, my Tamil sister; Tanu Sankalia, Brian Weiner, Lilian Dube, Jorge Aquino, Eileen Fung, Candice Harrison, Kathy Nasstrom, Bernadette Barker-Plummer, Karen Bouwer, Dorothy Kidd, Keally McBride, Eveyln Ho, Gerardo Marin, Stanley Nel, Peter Novak, Dean Rader, Marcelo Camperi, Susan Prion, Tracy Seeley, Alice Kaswan, Elisabeth Friedman, John Pinelli, Aaron Hahn Tapper, and Pedro Lange Churion. I thank my home department of Theology and Religious Studies and the Program in Environmental Studies for their wonderful collegiality and extensive support. Students in my classes were always excited when they encountered the kōlam. I thank them for their depth of interest.

Many USF Faculty Development Fund Grants provided critical support for field research in India (1998–1999; 2005–2006; 2010–2011; 2014). All of my research assistants committed their immeasurable energy: Bethany Schmid (2008–2013), and Rachel Babcock, Syona Puliady, Sally Morton (2015–2017), Kaitlin Chassagne, and Lydia Lapporte. They were, above all, conversation partners, who helped me work through the countless tangled knots in the manuscript and kept up my spirits when they were sagging. Amanita Rosen, a brilliant editor, challenged me, word by word, helping me sharpen and polish.

Being selected as a Research Associate at the Harvard Divinity School was enormously stimulating. This teaching and research fellowship and my students' comments, critiques, and delight all were highly fruitful. Ann Braude, Emilie Townes, Michelene Pesantubbee, Joan Branham, Anne Lerner, and Arti Devarajan gifted unfaltering encouragement. In addition, I cannot wish for a more congenial academy than the American Academy of Religion. Its resources, its institutional weight, my election to the steering committee of Hinduism, and the co-chairship with Timothy Lubin all provided a continuous bracing to my work.

I thank the indomitable friends, scholars, writing groups, writing partners, and mentors who guided me over many bridges and crossings: Kirin Narayan, Sumathi Ramaswamy, and Kamala Visweswaran, who lit beautiful lamps of scholarship that guided me at each turn; David Shulman, who took the time to talk to a young woman for hours about the kōlam and Tamil culture decades ago, enthusiastically brought alive the multiple layers of Thanjavur District history, and introduced me personally to Roja Muthiah; Tracy Pintchman, Kimberley Patton, David Haberman, Diana Eck, Anne Monius, Christopher Chapple, Valentine Daniels, Eugene Irshick, Paula Richman, Mary McGee, Laurie Patton, Francis Clooney, Wendy Doniger, Arti Dhand, Deepak Sharma, Julia Leslie, Huston Smith, Barbara Stoler Miller, Jack Hawley, Joyce Flueckiger, Patrick Olivelle, Rajasekharan, Peter Nabokov, Mary Evelyn Tucker, John Grim, Donna Jones, Rakesh Bandhari, Saidiya Hartman, Aditya Behl, Charis Thompson, Richard Norgaard, Ann Markusen, S. Bharathy, Harsha Ram, Lawrence Cohen, Nancy Martin, Vasudha Dalmia, Raka Ray, Jennifer Beckman, Karen Bouris, Hyungsook Kim, Myra Paci, Jonathan Chester, Chandra Easton, Maureen Fan, Peter Vinella and Jeanette Jin, Asha Harikrishnan, Punam Thakran, Rachel Silvers, Camille Seaman, Kevin Parker, Reuben Margolin, Martina Kaller-Dietrich, Nagata Shojiro, Lewis Hyde, Marina Illich, Judith Ehrlich, J. Swaminathan, Gift and Rani Siromoney, Tami Spector, Robert and Sally Goldman, Vasudha Narayanan, Indira Peterson, Leslie Orr, Archana Venketesan, Davesh Soneji, Isabelle Nabokov, Shanti Sekharan, Barbara Metcalf, Nora Fisher, Lance Nelson, Eduardo Mendieta, David Batstone, Eliza Kent, Susan Seizer, Bernard Bates, Homi Bhaba, Stephen Huyler, and many others. There were friends whose spirit kept me going in the darkest and lightest of times, who poured out love every step of the way: Susan Moran, Jennifer Nauts French, Bernadette Ross Brockman, and Sharon Negri. I am grateful to each and every one of them.

Those who invited me to present my work to audiences as it was developing helped me sharpen my ideas: Elizabeth Collins, Conference on Religion in South India and the Annual Meeting of the American Academy of Religion; Western Region of the American Academy of Religion; Barbara Duden, Swiss Technical University, Geneva, Switzerland; Franco La Cecla, Gaia Conference in Palermo, Sicily; Carol Breckenridge, Department of South Asian Languages and Civilizations, University of Chicago; Shirley Ardener, Research Fellow, Center for Cross-Cultural Research on Women, Oxford University; Soraya Tremayne, International Workshop on Gender and Environment, Oxford University; Center for the Study of Women and Religion, Harvard University; Tracy Pintchman, South Asian Studies Conference, University of Wisconsin; International Folk Art Museum; Jennifer Burke, TedX Conference: Teaching Compassion, UC Berkeley and Prospect Sierra School; Carl Anthony and Paoloma Pavell, 22nd Annual Bioneers Conference; and Professors George and Kausalya Hart, the eight Annual Tamil Conferences. Pierro Scaruffi's infectious enthusiasm and constant advocacy of my ideas and exploration sustained me through uncertainties; Margot Knight, the Djerassi Fellowship; Aurogeeta Das, J. D. Talsek (National Academy of Sciences, Washington D.C.); Professor Jyothsna Sainath (University of Utah), and Professor Daryl Cooper (UC Santa Barbara) for carefully reviewing the mathematical chapter, all helped me push through my own doubts and gave me confidence, though I alone am responsible for any errors. Librarians, libraries, and independent bookstores all guided me: The USF Library (Joseph Campi and others), UC Berkeley Libraries, Roja Muthiah, Roja Muthiah Library, Giggles Book Store, The British Library (London), Point Reyes Books, Black Oak Books, Books, Inc., and others were key to major insights. This is the bedrock of mutual conviviality for deep, scholarly work.

I am grateful to Cynthia Read at Oxford University Press for her patient longstanding commitment and for the anonymous peer reviewers' comments, many of which I took, though I am responsible for any errors. I am enormously grateful to Marion Weber and Susan O'Connor for their deep love of me and the kōlam; without both of them, this book would not be in your hands. There are those I have not been able to name here: know that your help was invaluable at the time and place that you gave it. I feel enormous gratitude toward each and every one of you, without whom this book would not be in your hands.

Earlier drafts of some chapters were published in the following publications. I thank them all. They are reprinted here with the kind permission of the publishers. Aspects of Chapters 1 and 3 appeared in *Mud, Mirror and Thread: Folk Traditions of Rural India* (Grantha Corporation, Santa Fe, Museum of New Mexico Press, 1993). Portions of Chapter 4 appeared in *Women's Lives, Women's Rituals in the Hindu Tradition* (Oxford University Press, 2007). An earlier draft of Chapter 8 appeared in *Religions/Globalizations: Theories and Cases* (Duke University Press, 2001). A previous version of Chapter 9 appeared in *Purifying the Earthly Body of God: Religion and Ecology in Hindu India* (State University of New York Press, 1998) and in *Women as Sacred Custodians of the Earth: Women, Spirituality and the Environment* (Berghahn, 2001). Facets of Chapter 10 appeared in *Hinduism and Ecology: The Intersection of Earth, Sky, and Water* (Harvard University Press, 2000).

NOTE ON DIACRITICS AND TRANSLITERATIONS

This book mostly uses a standard scholarly transliteration, following the *Tamil Lexicon* (University of Madras). If the reader wishes to pronounce the Tamil words in the Tamil way, then use the following preliminary guidelines. Vowels are distinguished by length of sound; for example, the ā (as in bark) is twice as long as a (as in gut or hut); ī (as in tree or sleep) is twice as long as i (as in kit); ū (as in moon) is twice as long as u (as in should); ē (as in hay) is twice as long as e (as in let); ō (as in boat) is twice as long as o (as in oblique). Two diphthongs are ai (as in eye or bike) and au (as in cloud). For Tamil consonants, ṅ is pronounced with a nga sound (as in sing); ñ is pronounced with a nya sound (as in banyan); ḻ represents a unique Tamil sound, which is between an l and a retroflexive r. Most names of places, deities, and people are transliterated in the most common English pronunciation without diacritics.

1

Beginnings

Even one's own tradition
is not one's birthright;
it has to be earned, repossessed.
The old bards earned it
by apprenticing themselves to the masters.
One chooses and translates a part of one's past
to make it present to oneself and maybe to others.
One comes face to face with it
sometimes in faraway places, as I did.

—Ramanujan 1985, xvii

Introduction

Every day in southern India, millions of women wake up before dawn, dreaming of drawing designs filled with their desires for the well-being of themselves, their communities, and the world. These designs—*kōlams*—on the thresholds of homes, temples, and businesses are ephemeral; they are gone a few hours later, rice dust on the feet of passersby, blessing both the ritual drawers and those who see them (Figures 1.1–1.3). The kōlam is created by Tamil women in Tamil Nadu, the southeastern state in India, and wherever Tamils have migrated—northern India, Sri Lanka, Malaysia, Singapore, South Africa, England, the United States, and elsewhere. In the Tamil language, the other classical language in India besides Sanskrit, the word "kōlam" means beauty, form, play, disguise, and ritual design.

Figure 1.1 Typical neighborhood kōlam drawings, Thanjavur.

(a)

Figure 1.2a Typical village street on the day of Pongal, the harvest festival, Thirunelveli District.

(b)

Figure 1.2b Kōlams overflow the threshold like rice overflowing the Pongal pot.

(a)

Figure 1.3a–c Elderly woman drawing a continuous labyrinth kōlam before sunrise, village near Swamimalai.

(b)

Figure 1.3a–c Continued

This book is about these kōlam designs and what they mean to the women who draw them (Figures 1.4 and 1.5). Women taught me that kōlams are made to:

- Do something beautiful;
- Invite, welcome, and host Lakshmi, the goddess of wealth, good luck, wellness, and alertness;
- Banish, unwelcome, and dehost Mūdevi, the goddess of poverty, misery, bad luck, sickness, and laziness;
- Catch the negative effects of the evil eye, jealousy, and envy of those who intend harm, both those you know and strangers;
- Embody Ganesha, the elephant-headed god, the remover of obstacles;
- Indicate auspiciousness and well-being and prevent suffering and death;
- Play, with women competing among each other for the "best" design;
- Show one's intimate love for God to be like the ninth-century girl-woman saint, Āṇṭāḷ, who is thought to be one of the first kōlam-makers;
- Remember and ask for forgiveness to the earth goddess, Bhūdevi, for our walking and stepping on her;
- Feed a thousand souls;
- And so much more.

Throughout India, bright colors of red ochre vermillion, golden turmeric, and gray-white ash powders splash the surfaces of foreheads and bodies, stones and temples. These designs range from thin red U-shaped markings, to three parallel

(c)

Figure 1.3a–c Continued

Figure 1.4 Woman performing kōlam, village near Chidambaram.

horizontal lines, to a smudge of filled red circle. Hours later, these dabbed marks are worn down to a light tincture. Forehead marks on women are called *bindi* in the Hindi language, *pottu* in Tamil, and "red dot" in English. These particular ritual markings are often red and made of saffron and turmeric and are also called *kumkum* or *kunkumam*.

Figure 1.5 Grand kōlam in front of a medical shop, Thanjavur.

Along a similar vein, hundreds of millions of Hindu women draw ritual pattern designs on the thresholds of houses, businesses, trees, and temples. These threshold designs are created with ground white rice flour and are sometimes simple, sometimes elaborate. They are called by many names—*kōlam* in Tamil Nadu, *sathiya* in Gujarat, *māndana* in Rajasthan, *ālpanā* in Bengal, *muggū* in Andhra Pradesh, *chita* in Orissa, and *rangōli* in Karnataka, Gujarat, and Maharashtra. These Indian ritual designs are also in kinship with those farther away: Tibetan sand mandalas of ephemeral power in South Asia, Navajo sand paintings made by medicine men for healing illnesses in the southwestern United States, *sona* ritual drawings with parallel mathematical properties in Angola in the African continent. There are also *caums* (or *cauks*) drawn on thresholds by pre-Christian women to protect the household from harm in Wales and England, which were made even as late as the 1930s. Another related ritual tradition is *mahendi,* also known as henna, which is an ephemeral tattoo-like design drawn on the hands and feet of women to mark special occasions such as weddings and festivals.

Like the bindi and other women's ritual markings, the kōlam in Tamil Nadu is one of the many daily or calendrical rituals that evoke, host, and dehost the divine as guests, similar to markers of hospitality, as in the coming and going of important guests. These ritual blessing markings are some of the most ubiquitous signs of sacredness in Hinduism. The kōlam is designed as a way for a Hindu woman to invite, host, and maintain close relationships with the goddess Lakshmi and prevent her sisterly counterpart, Mūdevi, from entering the household. It is often placed in front of an altar in the *pūja* area of any natural or cultural space, including households, temples, trees, and stones. The pūja is part of the wider context of Hindu prayer customs that is commonly performed but not required. It is performed on a daily, weekly, or monthly basis, depending on the ritual intensity of the worshipper, and involves an offering of food, chanting, and a circling of the altar images with a lamp filled with oil or camphor and lit up with fire. So, the kōlam participates actively to indicate calling forth a divinity and then saying goodbye when the kōlam fades away.

Kōlam designs are many and varied. Most are geometric and involve dots, curved lines, squares, and triangles. There may be two opposing triangles facing each other, intertwined; one triangle is seen as male and the other as female—equal and opposing forces in tension and balance. Sometimes there are complex unbroken lines looping around a matrix of dots or flattened trapezoidal geometric structures facing the center. The center is an empty space imagined to be a pool filled with the sacred river Ganges. There are also figurative kōlams, which can range from a cobalt-legged Bharatanatyam dancer to a cartoonish Mickey Mouse, from a young figure of a Hindu saint to the sinking *Titanic*.

As a child, I watched my mother create kōlam patterns in front of the many houses we lived in, from India to America and back and forth again. Sometimes these blessing designs were simple; other times they were elaborate. They stretched to the edges of the threshold area, whether the threshold was in front of our ancestral village summer home in southern India, our government flat in New Delhi, or our suburban townhouse in the Washington D.C. area. The kōlam seemed to be one of the few constants in my family's nomadic, bicultural migratory life, which crisscrossed continents every few years.

The first time I participated in learning how to make this women's ritual art, I was nine years old in our ancestral village in Thanjavur District in central Tamil Nadu. My family had come to spend the summer there in 1970, returning from a four-year sojourn in Washington D.C. Our village was surrounded by bright parrot-green rice fields, fed by one of the many tributaries of the sacred Kaveri River and still moving in oxcart time. The green of the rice fields was so bright there against the full rays of the southern sun that sometimes I had to shield my burning eyes.

Each room in our home had a raised step at the entrance that was thought to be inhabited by the goddess Lakshmi, so it was marked by a kōlam during festive occasions. This made it essential to avoid stepping on the actual raised threshold. Stepping on her was a sign of disrespect and would cause her to leave the house, making it susceptible to misfortune and poverty. Although the kōlam was painted on each of these doorways during festive occasions, the most important entrance was called *vāsilpati* in Tamil, meaning "front threshold." This was a part of the wide veranda at the front of the house, the *thinnai* area, just large enough to hold two or three people. My grandmother or my mother, raised in orthodox Tamil Hindu families and communities, painted the thinnai daily with a kōlam. The kōlam primarily existed where the house met the outside world, where the private and familial realm encountered the community and the shared public commons; it held strangers and friends, agricultural workers and landlords, the invited and the uninvited.

The first day I tried to make the kōlam, I was squatting in front of the thinnai at our home, clenching white rice flour in my fist. Whenever I held rice flour in my hand, I was keenly aware of the importance of not spilling so much as a bit of it onto the recently swept ground. It was to be handled with the utmost delicacy and attentiveness. So often I had been told by my grandmother and my mother that if even a few grains of the precious rice were to fall on the ground in wastefulness or carelessness, then Lakshmi would stop entering the threshold of our home. The goddess Lakshmi was in charge of much that was good: rice, earth, good luck, good health, abundant wealth, alertness, and a lustrous quickening energy, or *shurushuruppu*. If neglected by the goddess Lakshmi, our family could become impoverished and hungry, and Lakshmi's infamous sister, Mūdevi, would befriend and even occupy our bodies, our homes, and our wills. Mūdevi was in charge of exactly the opposite characteristics as Lakshmi: bad luck, ill health, poverty, hunger, and laziness, or *sōmbērithanam*. The two opposing goddesses were constantly at war with each other and they could never be found in the same room.[1] Wherever Mūdevi was found, Lakshmi would not come.[2]

The hands of my mother and my grandmother, sometimes one, sometimes the other, curved lightly over my small right hand, gently guiding my trembling fingers as I sat crouched with anticipation. I tried to spread the rice flour with my fingers in an even flow, almost as if I were pouring "dry water" from my hand. My thumb repeatedly and firmly pressed down on my first and second fingers to guide the flow of rice flour onto the wet, cleansed earth. The rice flour fell in uneven clumps that in no way resembled the beautiful carpet-like drawings in front of the neighboring houses. At first I felt a sense of deep embarrassment and shame, but after a week or two of rough attempts I began to get the hang of it.

I was learning to make an elemental kōlam, one of the first a young girl may learn. It is formed by the intersection of two opposing triangles, with an added dot in the center. Sometimes it would be outlined in a subtle shade of burnt sienna red or ochre red with a material known as *kāvi*, a kind of red brick powder. Watching the other village girls my age do it with ease made me eager to catch on. As I became more adept, I vaguely sensed that making a kōlam was one of the signs of womanliness in traditional Tamil life.

I lived in that oxcart village for several months, and though I had been there many times as a very young child, daily life was a stark contrast to where I had just been, in the United States. Every time I did something inappropriate for that culture, my parents were scolded. It was as if each and every moment I experienced there was filled with a sense of the familiar cast in the barely understood and remembered. I grew up in New Delhi after my father left for America to go to graduate school. Even now, I can dip into that pail of memory without difficulty and bring up people I met and the experience of walking on that land, as if that past lived on in a time that is still jutted close to the one I live in now, as if the past were no longer the past but a room next door that I could walk into or just another kind of clothing I could drape myself in. Two years later, in 1972, when I was eleven, we stopped making those summer visits to Tamil villages: my mother's ancestral village, Kunnam, and my father's ancestral village, Rettakudi. When my father completed his education in America and got a job as an accountant in a public school system, my mother, sisters, and I then immigrated to Maryland, becoming permanent alien residents, green cards in hand.

As a teenager, some of my first memories of the United States involved were laced with the image of my mother making the kōlam every morning in front of the threshold of our suburban Maryland townhouse. I would wake up before sunrise to the sounds of my mother clearing and cleaning the ground surface, scraping the ice and snow off the gray slate slabs that made up the path beyond our modest home. Taking the ground dry rice flour out of a recycled Gerber's bottle that she kept at the household shrine, she would begin making the kōlam on the cold surface of the slabs in the predawn darkness. If it were a festival day, she would finish the design by outlining it with ochre red paste. Hours later, she would crack blessed coconuts onto the kōlam, catching the coconut milk in a round stainless steel mixing bowl for us to drink later.

My mother drew these ritual patterns almost daily. Sometimes she drew just a few strokes and was done, simply and quickly, seemingly unconsciously, as if it were just a part of housework. Other times she drew them over a long period, in a leisurely fashion, as if she were taking delight and pleasure in the process of making them. These were elaborate designs, since they marked ritual festive days: Krishnajayanthi (Krishna's birthday), Ganeshchatūrthi (Ganesh's birthday), Navarāthri (Nine Nights of the Goddess), Deepavali (Festival of Lights), Thai Pongal (Rice Harvest festival), Sivarāthri (Siva's night), the Tamil New Year, and *vratas* (special religious vows). Since wet rice flour was used on these special days, the designs were more permanent and therefore more likely to be visible still in the afternoon. Whenever I brought American friends home and they saw smudged traces of the drawings, they expressed curiosity. "Oh, just something my mom does every day," I would say a bit too quickly, and move on. These ritual patterns were as much a part of my life as the schools I went to, the beds I slept on, and the books I read.

I often wondered what these patterns were, what they meant, and why my mother drew them. I once asked her these questions when I was a teenager, and she replied instantly, "It is tradition. It is our custom." I was not satisfied with this answer, and asked her again, "But why?" She replied with teasing, sparkling eyes, "When I was your age, we as children did not dare to ask such types of questions to our elders. If we had to wake up at 3:30 in the morning, hours before sunrise to begin helping in the preparation of food for the offerings to the gods, then we would just wake up. It didn't occur to us to ask our elders why. You ask such a strange question. I don't know how to reply to you. Now that you have come to America, you ask me such questions, especially the question of why. Somehow, when I was young, these questions did not seem so important to ask." Her eyes looked gently and quizzically at me, her hands busy with cooking dinner on the stove: "Perhaps you can find the answers to your whys when you grow older."

As I stepped across the kōlam every day, I couldn't help but be reminded of the radical differences in values of food, clothing, and religion between the private, Tamil world of the home and the public, suburban street and schools that were our American world. The kōlam acted as a bridge between inner and outer worlds, between what can be controlled and what cannot be controlled, and between domestic and public space. In traditional Tamil culture, crossing the threshold was a major, self-conscious event signifying an awareness of the danger in boundaries. For our Tamil immigrant family, this cultural distinction was reinforced by the difference between American and Tamil culture, between our private and social lives. Inside the house was familiarity and security; outside the house was chaos and unpredictability—at least that is how it seemed to me. The kōlam on the threshold was literally and symbolically the border of Tamil culture in a new American world.

During the rest of my adolescence, my concerns revolved around how to balance my love and respect for Indian culture with the intoxicating assimilation that was encouraged and supported by my American teenage friends and my own internal desire for a more personal, individual sense of freedom. In this new and unfamiliar context, although our ways of life were looked on with some respect and intense curiosity, Indian culture was still perceived as strange and foreign, as if clothed in a language of bondage and restraint. I felt that we were looked upon as curious specimens that would eventually wake up from our slumbering dreams of tradition, becoming modern, "free" Westernized human beings. And we did, slowly but immeasurably.

So, gradually, I too relegated the ritual of the kōlam to the past, perceiving it as part of the fabric of Indian "tradition," "custom," and "superstition." Inevitably, the kōlam became bound to my own changing perceptions of Indian culture. The lens of modernity was telescoping our family's reality—our lived experience—into a fixed and "primitive" past, encased in the "superstitious," "unnecessary," and "backward." In the gaze of the "advanced" culture, our Indian culture was teleologically shrinking to become quaint, picturesque, and sentimentalized. I reflected this tension, simultaneously experiencing myself watching and being watched, leading to increasing combativeness on my part in relation to my parents.

From 1972 onwards, I fought constantly with my parents over many rights: to wear my hair out unbraided, to wear pants, to wear blue jeans, to talk to boys, to stay in a dorm for college, to refuse an arranged marriage. Throughout these seething battles, I could feel the fabric of the culture we had all brought with us from India fraying at the edges, with gaping holes of knowledge and shifting realities. I sensed that India, too, was changing, but was frustrated that I could not witness those changes. The kōlam, during this combative time in my life, was very much in the background, in a way a representative part of what I was fighting against—"superstition, tradition, blind faith." One day I felt the sensuousness of being a Hindu, and loved the rituals, the fasting and feasting; the next day I was an agnostic, the day after an atheist, and then, back around again, during the days following. Despite my resistance to conform to the expected patterns of a dutiful Tamil daughter's behavior, my mother would continue to draw the kōlam daily, revealing that she still wished my well-being.

As you have already seen, my relationship to the kōlam is personal as well as intellectual. Although I had grown up surrounded by it, it was only through encountering others who were interested in the kōlam that I became engaged with this tradition. So, I will begin this book with the following stories, which hint at the origins of my intellectual interest in the kōlam. Each of these stories set the stage for beginning and continuing my research.

Ivan Illich

The kōlam did not excite my intellectual curiosity until I was in my 20s and living in California, where I was far from both India and my parents in Maryland. Although the kōlam is a women's ritual, ironically, it was one man's sharpened probing interest that enabled me to begin thinking about the kōlam as more than a quaint tradition that had little to do with me, causing the kōlam to leap forth from the background to the foreground of my life.

In the fall of 1984, I attended a conference at Claremont College to be with the philosopher Ivan Illich, a Catholic priest, whom I had met previously in Berkeley, California, and who later became an informal teacher and friend of mine. He invited us to stay with him. Illich was born in Vienna, raised partly there and in Italy, and lived in Mexico. He was tall and towering, wore loose and comfortable clothing, and exuded an intensely overwhelming and powerful physical, charismatic presence. His hands gesticulated emphatically, parsing the space in front of him; his eyes leapt through his black, thick-framed glasses. He emanated a daunting intellect and knew 13 languages. He was one of the most brilliant critical and incisive commentators on Western society.

At the time, Illich was writing a book, *H_2O and the Waters of Forgetfulness: Reflections on the Historicity of "Stuff,"* a poetic history of the perception of water as sacred in the West and a concomitant history of the perception of waste. After dinner one evening, he excitedly shared his index-card section on the ritual creation of space and pointed to one of his working footnotes of Stella Kramrisch's (1983) work on the *dhūli chitra* and the *yantra,* the Sanskrit versions of the kōlam. Illich had summarized:

> . . . making [Indian floor paintings] is an exclusive privilege of women, and the skill is handed down from mother to daughter, whose training begins in the fifth or sixth year. Before she can marry at twelve, a girl must have reached full competence. These "yantras" have not changed much since pre-Hindu times and are native to old India. They are still practiced by Brahmin women. Each yantra forms a will directed to an end: within the yantra an invoked invisible presence finds its allotted place. . . . In the magical circle and sacred squares of the yantra, power is spellbound, cannot escape, and thus creates space. These yantras do not form abstract patterns; they are the shape of conceptions. . . . The moon, the sun, the stars, and earth are integrated in them, along with the things desired by the young woman. The whole cosmos is conjured up to bless and fulfill them. Although the yantras are not sanctioned by the Vedas, they are customarily considered essential to temple building. (1985: 14–15)[3]

He then asked me with intense curiosity, "Do you know anything about these yantras? Or the Tamil version of them, the kōlams?"

I am deeply embarrassed now when I recall it, but I confidently exclaimed then: "What! Kōlams? There is really nothing much to say about them. They are just what women do every morning. My mother made them every morning when I was growing up. There is nothing to know about them." I added, "But I will be happy to draw you some tomorrow morning before sunrise on the front threshold of this house and then you can ask me any questions you want and I will try and answer them." I rose early the next morning to draw the different kōlams I had promised, and then, sitting on the stoop together, he plied me with questions for hours. My answers were consistently, "Well, I never thought of them that way." Or, "I don't know. I could ask my mother and see if she knows the answer." It was to be the first of many long conversations with him over the subsequent years.

This conversation rekindled my earlier childhood desire to know more about this ritual art form. Illich's insistent questions made me realize the importance of the kōlam and how it absorbed and reflected the diverse ideas underlying Tamil women's cultures. This was the beginning of my intellectual and physical journey into understanding the kōlam. For the first time, I became intrigued by the larger implications of these blessing designs, and a series of questions arose in my mind: Why do women make it *every* day? How do women weave their desires into the kōlam? How do women perceive the ritual creation of space through it? How does a young girl learn it from her mother? Do men ever make the kōlam? What is the relationship between the yantra and the kōlam? How is the kōlam related to temple building? These questions burned like flaming seeds in the back of my mind for many years.

Festival of India

In the spring of 1985, my mother was invited by Dr. Richard Kurin, then the associate director of the Office of Folklore and Folklife at the Smithsonian Institution in Washington D.C., to draw kōlams for the Festival of India. The Festival of India was a massive undertaking by the US and Indian governments to help each country better understand the other. Because of my mother's deafness, he asked me to translate for her and to present short lectures on the kōlams. In preparing for these presentations for audiences of several hundreds, I discovered to my surprise that there was very little published material in English about the kōlam. I felt angry, knowing that millions of women were performing this important ritual and there was nothing written about it. My feminist ire was aroused.

I had to rely on interviews with my mother and other women in the Tamil-American immigrant community to better understand the practice. My mother now seemed willing to explain what she had been unwilling to when I was a child. I incorporated this knowledge into my daily lectures at the American Folklife Festival. After each presentation, I was left even more intrigued by the intensity of the audience's interest and questions. My mother and I performed together, steeped in the kōlam and the wider context of folk performers from India (Figures 1.6 and 1.7). A highlight of the festival was her appearance in the religion section of the *Washington Post.*[4] We all marveled at the photograph of our mother, sitting on the wooden platform—so serious, so proud—with her passport facial expression on, as we called it. Until that event, my mother's world had been restricted to the private family environment in which the kōlam was not an art form but just another household chore embedded in a Hindu ritual. For the first time, she was being honored and recognized for this ritual, and in a public American space. All this was reflected in the pride and joy I saw in her face.

Figure 1.6 Pichammal Nagarajan speaking about her kōlam at the Festival of India. Courtesy of Smithsonian Institution, Washington D.C., July 1985.

Figure 1.7 Vijaya Nagarajan explaining the kōlam with Pichammal Nagarajan at the Festival of India. Courtesy of Smithsonian Institution, Washington D.C., July 1985.

The event represented a change for me too. Almost for the very first time since I was a young child, I saw my mother as a fount of oral and visual knowledge, a woman who had been raised in a world of oral storytelling and ritual performance, a woman who knew much, but who had moved to a world where that knowledge was no longer organized by its ritual or cultural contexts or reflected in them. The ground had literally shifted beneath her feet; her ritual knowledge had become devalued in the move from India to being an Indian immigrant in America. The notion of "tradition" itself had become devalued and disparaged and had acquired a noxious, negative value. In terms of oral and visual knowledge, she was rich and abundant, not the shadowy, marginalized, sad reflection I had seen before in the mirrors of a postcolonial modernity where the highest levels of education and high-class cosmopolitanisms were the only things that mattered. Now, I saw her as a fuller self, rather than inadequate or scarce. I saw her struggles with me more poignantly now, as I realized what she had been up against—a daughter who was fast becoming Americanized, armed with the tools of an American educational literacy, and who therefore looked down on her, even unconsciously, for not being as educated as she was and for not knowing English as well. The kōlam made me see her and the millions of women like her around the world in an entirely new light.

I found another delightful surprise at the festival: a whole sea of scholars and activists who were shaping the study of India at the conference, *Contemporary Indian Traditions*.[5] I met Stella Kramrisch, a petite, intimidating powerhouse with the same Viennese accent as Illich. This legendary 89-year-old Austrian art historian had lived and taught for 30 years in India and had taught for decades at the University of Pennsylvania. It was her quotation that Ivan Illich had asked me about. This was thrilling: it was as if Illich had provided me with a spool of thread that, as I unwound it, brought up treasure after treasure—of persons, ideas, and wide areas of knowledge. Kramrisch taught me that the kōlam was just one of the many ritual forms of threshold designs throughout India.[6] I discovered to my amazement that hundreds of millions of Hindu women made these ritual designs during festivals or other celebrations throughout India and the world. They were drawn on floors, walls, pots, hands, and feet, and echoed on saris and other clothes. Though it was Tamil women who were making these ritual designs on a daily basis, the kōlam was far from unique. It is unclear whether these ephemeral art forms throughout India that have more recently become occasional were once daily rituals like the kōlam. However, Kramrisch admitted that she knew no more about the kōlam than what had appeared in her few paragraphs of published writing. I was disappointed, but it again revealed the huge gap between what women knew in the oral tradition and what was published in the scholarly literature.

She emphasized then and at our subsequent meetings, "It really requires fieldwork. Go to India and talk to women for a long time and then you may begin to understand this ritual." Returning to India for a substantial period of time had been a dream of mine ever since my family's emigration to the United States years ago. Now the idea of traveling there with a clear purpose—to understand this traditional ritual art form—filled me with the greatest excitement, desire, and pleasure. I cannot fully describe the complex range of feelings with which I looked forward to returning to my original home.

Non-Dualism

During these same years, in my mid-20s, as I navigated through these experiences, I met A. K. Ramanujan, a professor at the University of Chicago. He was a gifted translator of Tamil poetry and folktales, an award-winning poet, and a critical thinker on Indian studies. A soft-spoken, serious man, he was not that tall, yet he carried himself in such a way that he personified a dense kind of energy. Like my other mentor, Ivan Illich, behind his thick, black-rimmed glasses, he had some of the most alive eyes I have ever encountered. I remember one meeting vividly at his office, where we spent some time discussing the next steps for researching the kōlam in India; I wanted his advice. In the middle of our conversation, he inquired, "You are talking about the kōlam, but there is something deeply sad about you. What is it?"

I looked at him, startled. I burst out, "Well, it has been a hard time. Every single day, I am torn apart with the question: 'Am I an Indian?' or 'Am I an American?' I do not know the answer to these questions, and I feel lost. I am 25 already and I am not sure which direction to go. I cannot explain this to my parents because they insist on my being very traditional and orthodox, and I have not been able to fit into that cloth for at least 10 years. And yet I do not feel entirely comfortable with my American peers, who have their own concerns, needs, and strange customs, which I feel quite uncomfortable around. I do not know what internal cultural cloth to put on every day." I felt near tears, askance at my emotional outburst, not having imagined talking to him this way.

He was silent for a while and I thought I had ruined my meeting with him. Then he said clearly and kindly, "You can be both, Vijaya. You do not have to choose. You are both American and Indian. You can study the kōlam and go back to India and become more of yourself through this work." I felt a huge release because his words were coming from experience: he also was an Indian who had lived in America for decades. In fact, a *New York Times* obituary after his sudden, unexpected death during a routine surgery quoted him as saying he was the "hyphen in Indo-American" (Lambert 1993). At that time, there were many fewer Indians in the United States than there are today. As an Indian immigrant back then, you felt as if you were a small island in the middle of a vast ocean. This was the first time I had been able to speak with someone about the coexistence of two cultures in one self; I no longer felt alone in this struggle. I walked out of that room with my self-doubt transformed into a focus on earning, repossessing, and translating one part of my past traditions for myself. Looking back now, I see how the kōlam became a bridge to reconcile my Indian and American selves, both literally and metaphorically.

I was to return every year to India for the next seven years, 1987 to 1994, sometimes for a month or more, sometimes for a year, for a total of three years. I returned again from 1998 to 1999 for another winter. One of the highlights of these many research travels to India was meeting and befriending Chandralekha, a leading choreographer (1928–2006) who was also a deep lover of the kōlam (Figure 1.8).

Chandralekha wove the kōlam into her many choreographies and had an almost mystical relation to it. The kōlam served as an invocation and inspiration for her work combining ancient Hindu philosophy and contemporary Bharatanatyam, yoga, and martial arts. In particular, her choreography for *Navagraha, Yantra, Prana,* and *Sri* evoked the kōlam by incorporating stitching movements of dots and lines. Each of the dancing bodies on stage seemed to

Figure 1.8 Chandralekha, Dashrat Patel, and the author at the Spaces Center, Chennai. Photo by Lee Swenson.

echo a dot or a line of a moving three-dimensional kōlam. A glittering line of dancers zigzagged as if the kōlam lines were moving of their own accord.

Chandralekha, from 1987 to 2006, provided me with generous shelter not just for the body but also for the mind. Her presence permeates through this book as she was one of the most influential forces in my life. She was my host in Chennai and my best friend in India. Her bold creativity, her acute self-knowledge, her unique sensibility, and her ability to push the boundaries of our ways of seeing reminded me so much of both Ivan Illich and A. K. Ramanujan.

My research in India was deeply rooted in childhood memories and experiences, not just texts, theories, and ethnographies. To more fully illustrate the ways in which my background has fueled and informed my research, I have woven into the text some of the key memories and experiences that guided my pilgrimage toward "knowing" the kōlam.

This book represents a culmination of thought and work that gestated from 1984 to 2015, but in some ways all of my life. The contours of my inquiry have been shaped by many different voices and experiences: the individual women (and even men) I spoke with during my multiple residences in India; the writers, artists, and scientists with whom it was a privilege to work closely in my activist work; and the teachers who guided my education in graduate school. I have also been shaped by my own intuition and experience as an Indian and American student, scholar, and bicultural resident of both India and America. This work records and shares the story of a long moment of time; it is like a still photograph that captures not only an instant of life experience, but also the edges around it. You can sense that life is still moving on, trembling with new experiences, insights, and clues.

Writing: A Mongoose and Snake Fighting

While working on this book, my desire to write as a writer on the one hand and as a scholar on the other struck me as akin to the struggle between a mongoose and a snake. They are both seemingly deadly to each other, the scholarly inimical to the literary. I try with each page to code-switch between the two voices; both are mine. Sometimes the mongoose wins. Sometimes the snake wins. You will see, reader, how it goes. I hope these words bring as much pleasure to you as they have brought me.

The first three chapters set the stage for the analysis to follow. The analytic chapters are rooted in years of fieldwork. In the first chapter, *Beginnings,* I trace the way I noticed the kōlam as a child in India and rediscovered it as an adult in the United States, describing the people who guided me. Chapter 2, *Following Lines of Beauty,* covers my research journey into India and outlines the key places where I conducted my research and the key people who taught me what I know. In Chapter 3, *Rituals,* I lay out an overview of the kōlam.

Chapters 4 through 11 are like spokes in a wheel, circling around different clusters of related keywords that women used to explain the kōlam to me. They are explorations of language, narrative, and ritual knowledge. Chandralekha's concept of "reference points" in a culture deeply moved me. We can almost see them as a metaphor for the recurring analytic points of return around which larger set of arguments are drawn. For example, in Chapter 4, *Thresholds,* I analyze the ways in which space and time configure the appearance and disappearance of the kōlam through the categories of auspiciousness and ritual pollution (i.e., menstruation, death rituals, and absence). In Chapter 5 I trace the mythical origin of the kōlam to the ninth-century saint Āṇṭāḷ and discuss her poetics. Here, I explore metaphors of forgiveness. Surprisingly, her exquisite and sensual love poetry echoes the themes of women's storytelling about the kōlam. Chapter 6, *Designs,* gives a typology of the basic kōlam designs, the ways in which Tamil women divide up the multiple rivers of patterns.

An extension of this chapter is Chapter 7, *Embodied Mathematics,* where I examine closely four aspects of the underlying mathematical nature of the kōlam designs: symmetry, fractals, picture languages and array grammars, and infinity. I end with a rumination of Chandralekha and how she embodied kōlams in her contemporary choreographies. In Chapter 8, *Competitions: From Village to City,* I explore three sites of intensive kōlam competitions—a village during the Pongal harvest festival, an Āṇṭāḷ festival in Madurai, and a large sports-like arena at the Gandhi Museum in Madurai—and what these three sites reveal about the transformation of the kōlam.

In Chapter 9, *Embedded Ecologies and the Earth Goddess,* I argue that the presence of Bhūdevi, the earth goddess in the Hindu pantheon, in these kōlam narratives is a kind of "embedded ecology" and "intermittent sacrality," two concepts I introduce here. Chapter 10, *Marrying Trees and Global Warming,* extends this analysis by examining the kōlam as a ritual of generosity in the larger context of auspiciousness of plants and trees. In Chapter 11, *Feeding a Thousand Souls: A Ritual of Generosity,* I look more closely at the phrase "feeding a thousand souls" and its relation to the larger Hindu ritual discipline of giving food to strangers. In the final chapter, I include my own realizations and stories. The themes of "tradition" and "modernity" are woven throughout this book, as they are a central preoccupation of kōlam-makers.

I offer this work on the kōlam as a tribute to the countless women who gave me the gift of their precious time to teach me what they knew about the kōlam. It is their faces, their voices, and their knowledge that I hope you see bursting through my webbed words.

2

Following Lines of Beauty

Kōlam: 1. Beauty, gracefulness, handsomeness, . . . 2. Color, . . . 3. Form, shape, external or general appearance, . . . 4. Nature, . . . 6. Ornament, . . . 7. adornment, decoration, embellishment . . . 8. Ornamental figures drawn on floor, wall or sacrificial pots with rice-flour, white stone-powder, etc., . . . 10. Play, sport . . .

—*Tamil Lexicon*, University of Madras, 1982: 1195

Multiple Journeys

To explore the underlying meanings of the kōlam, I went on my first short research trip to India during the winter of 1987–1988. During this three-week journey I encountered the deeply familiar encapsulated in the unfamiliar. My family had immigrated to America in 1972 and I had returned to India only once since then, in 1981. Much of what had struck me as familiar in that earlier trip—the slower pace of life, the casual spaciousness of hospitality, and the easy intimacy of friends and relatives—still existed in the small towns and villages I traveled through that winter. But I could also see that India was now shifting slowly toward the more modern consciousness that was familiar to my American self. The kōlam, I found, mirrored these shifting senses and meanings.

I first headed for Thanjavur, a small town in central Tamil Nadu, eight hours by train south of Madras. It was the closest town to where I was born, and as my first memories of the kōlam were steeped in my grandparents' village in the early 1970s, I thought that I would be comfortable there, though I knew no one and did not know where I would stay. And I had no memories of ever having been there. As I stepped out of the Thanjavur train station, I looked critically at myself, wondering whether I would be able to pass as a local. I was wearing a purple half-sari, an indication of my unmarried state, and one I thought I would be more protected in. My hair was bound into one long plait down my back, stilled by coconut oil. Only my American backpack revealed my foreign origins. I would have to buy a locally made simple cloth bag as soon as possible to hold my field notebooks, camera, and tape recorder. But overall, I judged I would be able to pass local scrutiny and radiated a sense of confidence I did not feel. I noticed immediately that there were no single unaccompanied women in the entire train station. I pretended I knew where I was going; I found a simple and spartan state government hotel that seemed safe.

The next morning, I woke up around 4 a.m. in pitch blackness. Dressed in a simple cotton sari, I left my hotel, looking around carefully to make sure I was not followed. I walked in one direction for 10 minutes. In the glow of a kerosene lamp, I saw a young, slightly plump woman making a gigantic labyrinth kōlam in front of her hut. Just beyond the hut was a large sign for a lumberyard; I noticed wooden poles stacked against the partially fenced front yard. Her kōlam was spectacular. It was large and filled with dots that were laid out parallel to each other. A single line circled the dots without touching them. I asked her for permission to watch her make it. Surprised, she said yes. I could tell she was unmarried, as she was not wearing a *tāli* (wedding necklace) or toe rings. She was still dressed in her loose, long, cotton nightgown. It took her about an hour to finish the huge, complex kōlam and when she did, you couldn't tell where she started and where she finished. It was all of a piece, a sequence that left no trace of its actual path. It was one of the most beautiful kōlams I had ever seen. It was entirely different from the ones I had seen my mother create when I was growing up. I was intrigued.

Shyly, my voice trembling, I asked her if I could talk with her and learn about the kōlam. She looked startled and asked her father for permission to talk to me. When he agreed, she smiled at me and we sat down together on a *charpoy*, a bed of wooden posts tied together with jute yarn placed outside the house. I plied her with questions. Realizing I had more questions than she had the time to answer, she glanced anxiously at the front door where her father had just appeared. She said, all in a rush, "I have a lot of chores to do right now, but in the afternoon I will be freer. Come after lunch, say around 2 or so." I smiled at her in gratitude, asked her permission to take a few photos of the freshly made glowing kōlam, and promised to return with my tape recorder. She, too, nodded encouragingly.

Each day I would wake up around 4 a.m. and head quickly into the town while it was still pitch-black, a few scattered streetlights determined to shed a bit of light. Day after day I walked down the streets of Thanjavur looking closely at the best kōlams until midmorning and made appointments to return later in the morning or afternoon to meet with the women who had made them. The kōlams were everywhere: on the thresholds of homes, businesses, and temples (Figures 2.1a–c, 2.2a,b, 2.3). I found that women enjoyed talking about the kōlam with me in the afternoons, when men were at work and children were at school; it was their time to practice their kōlams, catch up on other chores, or take a nap. I discovered that one of my deepest challenges was taking photographs in the dark. Just as human eyes could barely see the kōlam in the darkness before dawn, so, too, the camera's lens had trouble capturing its splendor.

(a)

(b)

Figure 2.1a–c Woman bending down and scooping rice flour from a steel container and beginning the process of making the kōlam.

(c)

Figure 2.1a–c Continued

(a)

Figure 2.2a Wood merchant's daughter at the beginning of a labyrinth kōlam (also called pulli or shulli), Thanjavur.

(b)

Figure 2.2b Wood merchant's daughter at the end of a labyrinth kōlam (also calld pulli or shulli), Thanjavur.

Figure 2.3 Women making kōlam together, Thanjavur.

Everywhere I traveled throughout Tamil Nadu that winter, women warned me it was dangerous to travel alone. Many shook their heads despairingly, saying that my father and mother were negligent in letting me travel so far away from America without a man accompanying me. Women I interviewed said repeatedly, "Haven't you heard the news? Girls and young women are being picked up by middlemen, kidnapped and taken to the red-light districts of Bombay and used to serve there. The horror of it; be careful, be careful! We cannot believe that your father let you come here all by yourself and did not come here to protect you." I promised them I would be careful. I tried to look even more purposeful when I was on the street. I made sure that I didn't catch any man's glance or gaze, knowing full well that here a look was equivalent to a touch. I kept my gaze downward, but I had to keep my eyes open enough to see where I was going. I was both protected and not protected by my brown skin. There were no other young Indian women who lived alone, staying in hotels, doing research. Just because I was a young woman traveling alone I stood out, no matter how much my way of dressing and speaking fit into the local landscape.

I was scared the first few days, but most people were still asleep, even if on the sidewalks; the tea-selling *wallahs* were not even up yet. I convinced myself that I was safe, and for the most part I was. I set out in a different direction every morning: to the railway colony, or to the *agraharam*, the Brahmin street; one day to the neighborhood behind the bazaar, the next to the medieval interior made up of small narrow pathways; one day to the temple street, another day to the Chettiar merchants' streets, and so on. And back around again.

Most of the main roads eventually led to the Bṛhadīśwara Temple, or the Big Temple. This thousand-year-old temple was built during the height of the Chōla dynasty in the 11th and 12th centuries, from 1095 to 1110. The temple is still surrounded by a gigantic moat, which is fast becoming a cesspool of waste, but one can still imagine the drawbridges rising during an imagined medieval onslaught. Daily I strode through the temple *gopuram,* a gigantic sculptured trapezoidal gate-tower with rows of carved figures. This was a classic south Indian temple structure with an immense central tower, a *vihāna,* visible for miles around the town. This vihāna contained a very large *sivalinga,* set within a humongous yoni. It is often interpreted as a representation of Shiva as a pillar of fire, though other interpretations include a male and female symbol of cosmic reproduction. It was nearly 60 meters high. I was drawn to this temple again and again throughout my stay and met many people there who were integral to my research.

People Who Taught Me

Once I met a striking elderly woman named Rangachetty, sitting on the thousand-year-old stone steps surrounded by the temple's tall stone pillars. I could tell she was a widow by the light orange cotton sari wrapped over her shorn head. She stared balefully at me through her thick black eyeglasses, curious to see a young Indian woman wandering around alone in the temple. Catching my eyes and moving her hands authoritatively, she demanded I come to her side: "Who are you? What are you doing here?" When I explained what I was doing, her face lit up. She moved closer to me and told me with pride about the grand celebration that had been held a few years earlier, in 1984, to mark the thousand-year anniversary of the building of the temple. Scolding me affectionately, she insisted, "You really missed something. You should have been here."

I met with Rangachetty every day for several days and puzzled over her source of unflinching power. She commanded those around her, and it was unusual for a widow in her 60s to attract such adoration and to display such natural decisive power. Another woman explained that Rangachetty had been widowed since the age of 12, just before her first menstrual period, and as a virgin widow she evoked high respect. She had many adopted children and grandchildren. She was from the *Chettiar jāti* (a merchant caste), was a problem-solver in the community, and headed the women's section of the Tamil Sangam.[1] With her authoritative manner she was able to request (and sometimes firmly demand) that people assist me in my studies on the kōlam. She absorbed me easily into the community and helped me enter other caste communities besides my own. She invited me to ceremony after ceremony, and soon I suspected from her mischievous grin that she wanted me to marry one of her kin.

Karuppan, the *thanjāvūr ētuvār* (singer of the temple's sacred songs), was another figure I met in this medieval temple. When I asked him his caste, he smiled and said serenely, but a bit impatiently, "Look, you can see from looking at me who I am and where I am from. Just say I am one of the very important people at the temple, who wake up the gods and goddesses just before dawn. Yes, it is true, there used to be a time when my people were not allowed into the temples. But it is very different now. I am accepted and treated very well here." He beamed at me, with his round face, portly belly, and garrulous laughter. He was full of stories.

One of the ētuvār's tasks, to sing the morning songs at the temple from the medieval corpus of the *Tēvāram*, was performed at the hour before dawn, the same time that the women of the town were creating kōlams. His role was to awaken the temple's gods and goddesses and the town's inhabitants with song. I realized that he and the women simultaneously were waking up the entire town with their rituals. He offered much insight into the ritual of the kōlam, especially as to its metaphorical, ritual, and physical manifestation of "being awakened" in one's own body. Once before sunrise he took me through the small threshold doors tucked inside the giant temple gates. We had to bend over deeply to fit into the tiny space and step over the high front threshold in the darkness before sunrise. It was then that I heard his full-throated singing to the huge two-story sivalingam, waking up the temple complex and the city. He sang various saints' medieval Tamil songs with his beautiful heightened melodies while the stars pulsed out of sight just behind the arc of the horizon in that hour of blackness. At the same time, women throughout the city had already woken up and were drawing the kōlam.[2]

One afternoon, between the first and the second gopuram towers of the temple, there was a young elephant standing beside piles of hay. He would bless temple pilgrims by lightly pressing his pink snout at the end of his trunk, dripping with saliva, on top of their heads and collecting coins in return. The *mahouts*, elephant keepers, stood nearby and quickly collected the coins before the elephant sloshed his trunk gently on the next grateful pilgrim's head. I noticed complex drawings on the elephant's forehead, similar to the bindi on women's foreheads (Figures 2.4a, b). One was a gigantic "om" symbol written in Tamil against a background of three horizontal white lines, symbolizing the forehead mark of a Shaivite, a follower of the god Siva. I realized that just like the decorated temple elephant blesses pilgrims on the temple threshold, the kōlam-maker blesses passersby with her drawings on thresholds. The temple elephant's

(a)

Figure 2.4a Temple elephant bathed and decorated with giant red forehead *pottu* with Saivite marks, three horizontal lines (close-up), Thanjavur.

(b)

Figure 2.4b Temple elephant "working" at the Tanjore Brihadeeswara Temple's threshold *gopuram,* blessing worshippers and receving coins with trunk. Author interviewing head mahout and assistant mahout. Photo by Lee Swenson.

snout was akin to the women's hands on the ground, both making the previously profane, foreheads and thresholds, sacred.

The five mahouts were nervous around me at first, but I was nervous around them, too. Slowly, I befriended the head mahout, and one day he invited me to come and see the elephant being bathed and its forehead decorated in one of the sacred Kaveri River tributaries, a mile or two from the big temple on the outskirts of town. I jumped at the chance. On our way there the next morning, men and women walked out of their huts and placed their head under the slobbery juicy tip of the elephant's trunk to receive his blessings.

When we arrived at the river, the mahouts released the elephant into the deep waters, still with chains binding his legs. After he had splashed and frolicked for nearly an hour, the men called him back to the shore and he lay down, half in and half out of the water, as if he were going to take a nap. He seemed to know what would happen. Using small river stones, the five men rubbed, massaged, and cleaned the elephant's body. One climbed up and sat near his forehead, another on his back, another on his thighs, and another near his tail. They scrubbed the elephant's leathery thick skin until it shone. The elephant, utterly calm, did not move.

Finally, one of the men climbed onto the top of the elephant and, using gray-white ash powder, *vivūthi,* drew in the center of his forehead a symbol of the god Shiva, four or five parallel white lines with a big red bindi. The elephant's forehead marks intrigued me and I was curious to know if there was any connection between the kōlam and the bindi. I began seeing sacred threshold marks everywhere I looked, not just on thresholds of homes, but also on bodies, foreheads, stones and new clothes.

Outside of the temple area, I met Kāvēri, a young woman who would, over my next trips, become one of my closest friends. Unmarried, of an unclear jāti, she had trained as a physicist during her undergraduate education. She worked as a travel agent and came from a large family with limited resources. Full of energy, bright intelligence, and humor, and deeply enamored of the kōlam, she was an excellent guide to the town, its people, and the surrounding villages. She had a broad network of friendships in the community. She refused to take any money for her research assistance, asking me whether I got paid for my research beyond my expenses. I told her that I wasn't receiving a salary but was happy just to have my expenses covered. She said fiercely, "Since you cover my expenses, I will not take any income from this work with you." She refused to step out of the gift economy. She was utterly joyous in doing the work with me and gave me the gift of a beautiful companionship and friendship during my extensive travels. It was almost as much of an adventure for her as it was for me: while helping me with my research, she gained the freedom to explore the surrounding area in a way she had not been able to do before as a young single woman. (Years later, when I returned to Thanjavur, Kāvēri sent a car to get me and my family and took us out to dinner. She had become a highly successful travel entrepreneur and founded her own business, shepherding group tours to visit sacred pilgrimage places throughout the region.)

I traveled to as many village streets and neighborhoods as I could outside of Thanjavur on this and other trips. In the village of Tiruvaiyāru, I met Saroja, an elderly woman of the Brahmin Iyengar caste and a gifted storyteller. A beautiful round-faced woman, Saroja wore her sari in the *madisāṛu* style, folding it between her legs so it resembled a loose pair of pants. Her narratives had a self-assured authority and she contributed many folktales concerning the goddess Lakshmi to my study. I returned to her many times because of her generosity and because she had tremendous oral knowledge about the kōlam.

I also walked to *cheri* villages (formerly known as "untouchable," now also known as *dalit*) located outside the main streets in each village I traveled to. The kōlams in *cheri* villages were sometimes the same, sometimes different from other castes. Sometimes they had Christian themes, as some *dalits* were Christian. They proudly showed me kōlams of Christmas trees, figures of the baby Jesus, and the words, "Happy Christmas!"

In one of these villages, I met an amazing woman named Acchamma, who took charge of me as soon as I entered her village. I learned slowly her source of authority: she had grown up in Singapore and had come to this village through an arranged marriage. On the day I spent with her, soon after I had settled into her thinnai, fifty women gathered to add their commentaries on the kōlam to Acchamma's. They often interrupted her to offer their own views, and their voices commingled and were set off from each other, giving multiple perspectives. That day was one of the highlights of my research. Sensing the importance of the kōlam to so many women, listening to the varying interpretations of what the kōlam meant to them, and basking in the multitude of Tamil women's voices being spoken simultaneously and arguing playfully all made me feel enormously indebted and grateful to them. This was a Zora Neale Hurston moment for me, being washed in the sounds of vernacular Tamil. I wish I could capture on this page those crisscrossing, bubbling rivers of Tamil vernacular speech.

During one of the many harvest festivals of Pongal I attended over the years, I went to a village near Chidambaram and stayed there for nearly a week (Figure 2.5). While I was interviewing a group of elderly women, one of them burst into the middle of the conversation and asked, "So, who are you going to marry, an Indian or an American? We are all curious." Stunned, I laughed and then stayed silent, not sure what I wanted to say. Then I replied, "Well, *Pattīs* (grandmothers), what do you think?" One elderly grandmother said immediately, "Well, we see that something in you is very satisfied with traveling this way and talking to elderly women like us. Well, no Indian man will put up with this kind of traveling you love to do from village to village, moving in the world as a stranger to others, so we all think you should definitely marry an American! He will understand your nature better."

Figure 2.5 Multicolored labyrinth kōlam with hot-pink border and lotus flowers.

I laughed and thought, here in this deeply traditional world, these elderly women, many of whom had never left their village, were more open than my own parents who, though they had migrated to the United States, had no such imagination. They were limited in their sight to the same kind of person that they were expected to marry in the early 1950s; their ideas in this realm could not change even in the middle of America. I felt sad and at the same time strangely heartened that these orthodox elderly women strangers understood some parts of me better than my own parents.

Even in the last days of December 1987 and the first weeks of January 1988, I could sense that life in India was quickening around me, though I was still enjoying the kindness of strangers who lifted my baggage into the train and shared food with me. Wrinkled, unstarched cotton saris were being exchanged for easily washed polyester ones: no ironing needed, a smooth exterior. Heavy hand-pounded copper and brass pots for carrying water were being replaced by plastic buckets, which were lighter, newer, and brightly colored. But at the same time, dried cow dung patties were stored as cooking fuel alongside adobe huts thatched with straw; women walking together carried water from wells or village ponds back to their homes. And women wore saris, with teenage girls wearing half-saris, post-menstrual wear, indicating their marriageability.

The next winter (1988–1989), I returned to India, this time to the mountains in the *ādivāsi* (the "original ones," formerly known as "tribal") lands of Tamil Nadu. Stella Kramrisch had claimed in one of her essays that the kōlam and other similar ritual arts had emerged from the ādivāsis, the earliest inhabitants of India who had lived here for thousands of years. They have a large presence and influence in India, making up nearly 10 percent of the population, according to the latest census.[3] In the hill station of Ooty (Udhagamandalam), I visited the Toda people, one of the ādivāsi groups, and they shared with me their own ritual design tradition depicting the sun and the moon done on the thresholds of their temples. These designs were carved in steel with half-moon–shaped roofs and dedicated to the "spirit of nothingness."

In Kothagiri, a nearby town, I stayed for 10 days with Irular villagers, accompanied by an unmarried Irular schoolteacher named Savithri who had returned home for her vacation. She was well educated, could speak both Irular and Tamil, and took me under her wing. She had a deep sadness, as if like me she was split, facing two opposite directions within herself. We walked together for miles in the deep mountain forests and visited women from the Irula, Korumba, and Kota peoples. Their houses had simple rather than elaborate kōlams in front of them. I was amazed to find kōlams made afresh every morning in front of sacred tree shrines, marking them as pilgrimage places in the middle of the forest, every mile or two (Figure 2.6). It was the first time I had noticed the kōlam there, but I would see these kōlams at many more tree shrines throughout the

Figure 2.6 Irula tribal groups decorating sacred grove with kōlams, Nilgiri Hills.

plains. I wondered whether the kōlams had begun as a way to honor the *yakshis,* the voluptuous spirits said to reside in certain sacred trees.[4]

Six months later, I arrived in the temple city of Madurai to study advanced Tamil for nine months. During this time, I would wake up early some mornings and bicycle out in different directions from my neighborhood with my male research assistant, who was from the Thevar caste and who also became devoted to the kōlam. I would go to nearby villages or toward the temple in the center of the city. Here I discovered some kōlam-makers who had their own rich traditions distinct from Thanjavur and the mountains of the Eastern Ghats.

In Madurai, I met Meena, a 29-year-old unmarried Tamil woman from the Brahmin Iyer caste still living with her parents. Her somewhat melancholy character, attributed by her parents to her unmarried state, became animated during our discussions on the kōlam. She was considered one of the best kōlam-makers in Madurai and volunteered to do her unique handiwork at local temples, where she carpeted the floors with her delicate yet strong hand. I rarely encountered anyone with her sensitivity to the ritual and aesthetic significance of the kōlam. We talked often and at length. Though she was shy, she had been listening to people around her speaking about the kōlam for a very long time. She spoke so softly that I sometimes had to strain to hear her, what she said about the kōlam was so profound and thoughtful that she deeply influenced my views of it. Whenever I returned to Madurai, I visited her. Years later, while I was writing my Ph.D. dissertation in Berkeley, I received a joyous invitation to her wedding in Madurai and was thrilled that her desires had been fulfilled.

Next, I made an important discovery about the kōlam when I met Kamala. At first I thought she was a woman but soon realized she was an *ali.*[5] Alis are men who sometimes dress as women. (The term *ali* is not used as much now; *arivāni* is used or the north Indian term *hijra.*) They are their own caste and have their own traditional occupations such as wedding cooks and vegetable sellers. Kamala had a beautiful sari on, her eyes were ringed with kohl, her hair was in a long braid down her back, and her persona was feminine. But her hands gave her away; they were big and strong and I noticed she did not speak with them as most Tamil women did. I asked why she looked so familiar and she replied in her husky voice, "Where do you live?" When I told her, she grinned at me, "Oh, I come and sell vegetables at your doorstep every day. We have bargained many times." Looking closely at her I realized she was right, but I had never seen that she was a transgendered person; I had mistaken her for the exclusively single-gender category of woman.

When Kamala discovered that I was studying the kōlam, she invited me to her house to watch her make the kōlam every morning, as other arivānis in her neighborhood also did. I was surprised to learn that she did the kōlam some days and her partner would do it other days, depending on which one of them felt like a woman when they woke up. I learned that when an arivāni woke up in the morning and took on the identity of a Tamil woman, she would wear a sari, pick jasmine flowers and tie them together in a long string to place on her head, and then draw a kōlam on the front threshold. I became fascinated by this fluidity of gender and how the kōlam served as a marker of gender (Figure 2.7).

Savithri, a middle-aged widow from the Iyer jāti in Madurai, was also an important figure to me. She was well known for creating a gigantic kōlam with 100,000 dots on a piece of cloth which took her a year to make (Figures 2.8a,b). Savithri had devised a systematic way to teach the kōlam to others, beginning with simple designs and moving to more complex ones. She taught me the embedded repetitive patterns within the more complex kōlams. I had only recently learned of the mathematical properties of kōlams from formally trained mathematicians, and she introduced me to the ways in which a kōlam-maker might also see those mathematical properties.

Though women were very warm and welcoming to my interest in the kōlam, most men were dismissive of my interest. Once I was in the small town of Srivilliputtur, the birthplace of the saint Āṇṭāḷ, and was sitting with an elderly

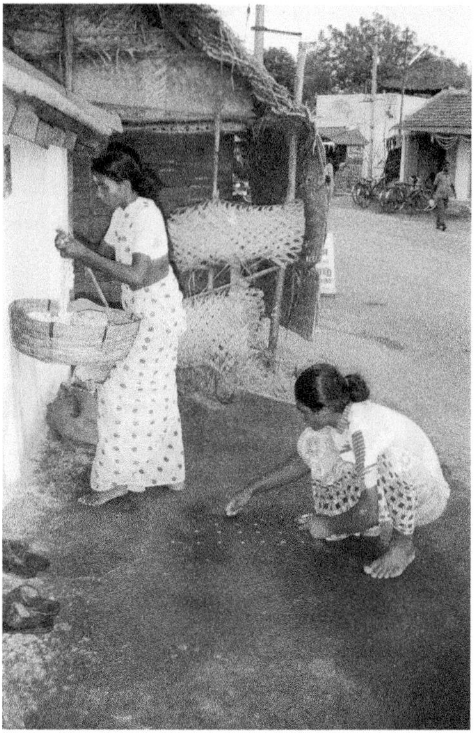

Figure 2.7 A kōlam made by an aravani, a person of India's third gender, Madurai.

(a)

Figure 2.8a V. Leela's 100,000-dot kōlam on cloth with one continuous line circling labyrinth design, Madurai.

(b)

Figure 2.8b Detail of 100,000-dot kōlam.

woman, watching her adult son, a priest, do a pūja. While I was interviewing her, her son stopped his ritual and said, "How can you possibly be doing a project on the kōlam? There's nothing to know about it! Nothing at all!" in a tone of angry puzzlement. His mother rolled her eyes sardonically, her chin jutting forward in quiet anger. Addressing the group of women we were sitting with, she said, "He doesn't know how to cook either . . . but he certainly knows how to eat!" All the women laughed, including me. Perhaps the priest reacted this way because the kōlam is deeply embedded in the oral tradition. But there were also exceptional men who were thrilled that I was working on the kōlam and were eager to share their knowledge with me.

Shivamurti, a professional storyteller, was one of these men. Hired by households and temples on ritual occasions, he had a wide repertoire of stories—especially myths—and spoke of the ways the kōlam figured in important epic traditions, such as the Rāmāyana and the Mahābhārata. Our discussion circled around the themes of wealth, poverty, laziness, and auspiciousness in narratives.

A male kōlam-maker who provided me with many clues about the future development of the kōlam was Salām Āli, a Muslim boy of fourteen. He insisted on entering kōlam competitions against the wishes of his grandparents and father.

When asked what motivated him, he replied simply, "I like them, the patterns, the challenge of trying new designs. It delights me. It makes me joyous." He competed passionately despite the fact that it is highly unusual for a boy—let alone a Muslim boy—to be involved in the creation of one. Āli spent hours each day drawing them; he was not interested in the ritual meanings, but saw the kōlam as a way to develop his talent for design, pattern, and order on paper.

Another figure I met was Aiyaswamy, a Hindu astrologer and actor in his early 70s. Energetic and cackling with good humor, his voice rang with nuanced textual and oral knowledge. He always seemed to have *pān* in his mouth, the red betel juice from the areca palm nut known to be an energy stimulant. We discussed Sanskritic aspects of the kōlam and the relationship between the kōlam and the yantra (a ritual diagram used in intensive meditation), pointing to its meditative roots. I remembered Stella Kramrisch's brief allusions to the yantra and the kōlam and hoped that Aiyaswamy would provide critical clues to their relationship—which he did.

He emphasized that while the kōlam can be obscured by aesthetic ideas, its significant ritual aspects should not be ignored. He told me again and again, "The kōlam—listen to me carefully—is *not* art, it is *ritual.* That is the most important thing you need to know. Don't believe anybody who tells you it is just an art form. They are deluded with its surface beauty. They don't know its real significance." He spoke about the intricacies of visual grammatical constructions of the yantra and the kōlam.

Utterly captivated, I discussed the kōlam with him for an entire week, all day, from nine to five. At the end of the week, I told him that I would like to give him a gift of money, as he had given me so much of his time. I felt bad that he had to give up his highly renowned astrological practice for a week to teach me what he knew about the kōlam. He refused to take any payment and was almost offended that I would offer any. Annoyed, he scolded me and said that the kōlam is a gift and, similarly, knowledge of the kōlam is also a gift, not something you pay for.

What Aiyaswami enabled me to see is how the kōlam and the knowledge of the kōlam is deeply embedded in the gift economy (which is often written about in the fields of anthropology and economics). The kōlam exists outside of the process of barter and exchange, in the realm of drawing, desiring, praying, and wishing. It was only then that I realized that you do not buy a hand-drawn kōlam or sell it; the only exceptions are the design books or stick-on design patterns you can buy in the bazaar. Lewis Hyde, the author of the profoundly moving work *The Gift: Imagination and the Erotic Life of Property,* elaborates on the meaning of the gift economy as it relates to artistic creation and production. The gift of creativity is a subtle balance between the gift that moves from one stranger to another and the gift that becomes converted to a commodity in the marketplace. In the case of the kōlam, some middle-class and many upper-class families, because of their time scarcity, may hire a household servant and *pay* her to make the kōlam. This ritual then becomes reduced to a job, part of the household task of cleaning the threshold. Do the benefits of making the kōlam go to the maker of the kōlam or the household? Probably both.

On the very last day we met, I suddenly had an inspiration about what gift I could give back to Aiyaswamy, a gift that did not match what he had given me in terms of knowledge but one that fit better into the part of Tamil society that was rooted in reciprocity. I remembered the way in which my mother and father would serve others in their home. It was called to *parimāṟṟathu* a guest, a ritual term signifying a deep level of honoring, with food or other articles, a person or deity in a ritual expression of gratitude. The act of *parimāṟṟathal* involves serving the other person food or other articles before you serve yourself, to serve the other person as if you were serving a god or goddess. That last day, I helped with the cooking and served him lunch before I ate. He seemed genuinely pleased with my simple cooking and serving, reading into it my gratitude for his gift of knowledge.

A Yogini

Throughout my travels in India, in discussions with art historians, activists, and philosophers, over and over I was told that if I was interested in the kōlam, I should talk to one woman in southern India: Chandralekha, the choreographer, Bharathanatyam dancer, and philosopher.[6] When I first met Chandralekha in Madras (later Chennai) in early 1988, our meeting was so intense that it felt as if we had already met many times before. Chandralekha was one of the most sensual people I had ever met. She appeared nearly as a vision, with her long white hair streaming around her face, and in the center of her forehead was a large red bindi made with kumkum powder. Her expressive kohl-rimmed eyes focused intensely on the person she was talking to. Often she would burst into giggling laughter. Our shared love of the kōlam infused our close friendship for nearly two decades. This led me directly into the many layers of her generosity; she shared with me her many friendships, her household compound, and her life. And I shared my world of activists, poets, and artists. The passionate intensity with which she lived her life had a deep magic to it, as if she were the very embodiment of Gabriel García Márquez and Salman Rushdie, as if she could envelop the intensities of India into herself in her own unique way, as if she were playing Indian knowledge streams like an instrument tuned to her own special tuning fork.

She lived in one of the first permanent houses nestled off to the side of a street edged by the Bay of Bengal. The design of her house was inspired by village houses. Whenever I saw her, she received me like a long-lost daughter and took me under her wing; she made me feel utterly at home, with her sparkling joyfulness of life that so often provided the bedrock of a family in India. I would often knock on her grand wooden door, after letting myself in at the outer gate, filled with the smell of jasmine flowers. I would hear the rustle of her bare footsteps coming nearer. When she pulled open the heavy door, her eyes leapt out of her open face as they caressed me with a startling happiness, showering me with love. She grabbed my hands, folded them within hers, and hugged me as if I were a long-lost friend that she had been waiting all morning to see. My body always relaxed into her friendship and embrace. She would invite me to sit on one of the two broad flat swings in her living room, big enough for three or four adults each. We would cross the freshly made kōlam outside her door.

She taught me to see the practice of the kōlam as a bodily one, filled with gestures, folded body movements, and a vocabulary that echoed the multiple gestural and bodily knowledges surrounding it—of yoga, martial arts, cooking, cleaning, waking up, stretching, the folding of the spine. She taught me to see the kōlam as embodying meaning alive to the touch. Until I met her, I had seen the kōlam as only a visual practice, for the eye to behold. But after I met her, I began slowly to see the kōlam also as an intertwined set of vocabularies of the body: physically touching the hand to the earth, using a sea of gestures, living in a world of play and courage of the spine and the body.

In the 1980s and 1990s, Madras did not yet have the cosmopolitan bustle that it would soon acquire; it was still a sleepy, laidback city with its own rhythm and playfulness. Chandralekha was a part of this tempo. Her deep knowledge of Bharatanatyam, Sanskrit, yoga, Hindu philosophy, and Indian martial arts helped her to make connections between what others saw as completely separate fields of knowledge and bodily practices. I felt like she was walking me into an ancient observatory whose dials and controls she had been playing with for eons. Most of all, she was eager to share her discoveries. The kōlam, for Chandra, was linked to many schools of traditional knowledge, such as geometry (lines, circles, triangles, and the primal dot), mathematics (the scale of the body), and aesthetics (a sense of beauty that was not modern but yet could be paradoxically very contemporary).

Chandralekha represented a critical link between my bohemian life in the San Francisco Bay area and the cosmopolitan-vernacular Indian cultural world, one where Europe and the United States were not at the center of the discourse. She straddled the multiple worlds of alternative politics, body philosophies, and playful creativities with a great sense of humor and ebullience as well as insight and seriousness. Besides meeting in Madras frequently, we traveled together to Italy, Montana, and Hawaii and met in Germany, Berkeley, and New York City. Throughout the long period of my most intensive research on the kōlam, from

1988 to 1998, Chandralekha was one of my points of reference, one of the primary dots I moved around in my research and learning.

The choreographies she created were attuned to the contemporary historical moment but also included traditional vocabularies like the geometric kōlams, which she transformed into three-dimensional dynamic and vibrant forms. She influenced the major contemporary American choreographer Mark Morris to create his own piece on the kōlam, which was performed both in New York City and in Berkeley.[7]

After her death Sadanand Menon, a journalist and art critic who worked closely with her for nearly four decades, wrote:

> The late dancer-choreographer Chandralekha left behind some 40 notebooks of kōlam patterns she had drawn. They were to inspire her later work, including the 10 major dance productions she choreographed in a burst of creative energy from the mid-1980s onwards, beginning with "Angika" in 1985, which sought to contextualize the human body, to her last composition, "Sharira" in 2001, which celebrated male/female energy. . . . She devised a pedagogical method on how the line moves through the dots.[8]

Here Menon highlighted the direct influence of the kōlam on her choreography, the ways in which she had a line of dancers moving through invisible dots on the stage. (See Chapters 6 and 7 for more about of her specific choreographies.)

Chandralekha had a mystical understanding of the kōlam and a unique way of looking at the world of "tradition." She was not fully a part of the school of "tradition" or the school of "modernity" and did not believe in picking and choosing from them to create some sort of collage. She believed the kōlam had tremendous value as a cultural construction and served as a way of holding cultural knowledge that should never be discarded. She loved the playfulness of the kōlam and how even in the context of ritual play, there were so many other meanings inside it. Chandralekha saw the kōlam as a way to resist the relentless process of modernity and its devaluing of traditional cultures. At the same time, she did not reify the kōlam as simply an emblem of a romantic version of the past; rather, she saw it both as embodying another set of values and capacious enough to be contemporary on its own terms. She used the concept of "reference points" from the traditional vocabularies of art, culture, or ritual form as point of departure for a longer journey of the self and the culture toward a larger and more dynamic understanding of the world.

This reminded me of the philosopher Raymond Williams' concept of "keywords." (Williams 1983). Williams returned to England after World War II and realized the students he had left behind in college were speaking a new modern language, a language that he had to struggle to learn. In some ways, Chandralekha's "reference points" are the mirror image of Williams' keywords; they are part of the language you leave behind when you enter the realm of modernity. And if you lose the reference points that were in your traditional vocabulary, you will become lost in the sea of modernity, unmoored and ripe for exploitation by the commercialized, commodified cultural worldview. The kōlam, too, has its own reference points, and this work is an attempt to uncover the ambiguities, evocations, and provocations within its many embedded vocabularies.

So far I have mentioned a few of the places and a few of the people I met while working on this book. I followed these lines of beauty. There were many more people and many more places, too many to recount here, but all of their voices and knowledge helped me see the kōlam better. I have identified some of them, but even when they are not named it is important to remember that their varied perspectives continually inform this book.[9]

I found kōlams in front of wayside shrines; in front of golden haystacks piled high, shining in the sunlight; on raised wet walking paths in the middle of rice fields. I found them in front of tree temples in the middle of Irula and Korumba ādivāsi forest lands in the Nilgiri Hills. I found them being drawn at a secular kōlam competition in Madurai by a Muslim boy, who loved the kōlam because he was in love with the fields of art and design. I found kōlams drawn during the festival of Pongal, in front of households, like strings of golden light sparkling in the fresh dew, blinding the eye with their brightness, drawn in the beams of a kerosene lamp. I found women competing to make the best kōlams in track team–like competitions cosponsored by the Gandhi Museum and the Colgate-Palmolive Company.

I even found kōlams being made at sunset, though this was rare. When I asked why, a woman replied, "We make the kōlam at dusk in order to say goodbye to Lakshmi and hello to Mūdevi, so we can go and rest and sleep. We also make the kōlam to feed the night creatures so animals, too, do not go hungry before sleep."

I did not find kōlams in front of menstrual huts, next to bodies, or at the door of households that had experienced death or illness, a lack of will or energy, or a lack of time. I did not find kōlams in front of spaces—of grief, of mourning, of blood. The kōlam, in contrast, signifies touchability, intimacy, generosity, and feeding a thousand souls.

I discovered for some Tamilians, I was a Brahmin, a Thanjavur Brahmin woman, who had left and then returned and who moved with the strange freedom of the Western woman. For others, I was a lover of the kōlam, returning again and again, seeking to understand something that is so common that it passed beneath everyone's notice for a long time.[10] Returning home, for me, meant recovering my Tamilness, in the language as it folded itself inside my tongue and lips and breath, in the folds of the sari laying in and about my body, in discovering the freedom of a sari as I rode a bicycle.[11] For me, these eight journeys to India represented a time of coming home. I found many friends and families who adopted me, and I adopted them; we were devoted to each other over those many years. I walked among kōlam-makers, scholars, and activists and learned from all of them. In this book I offer a bit of that complex layered journey, both inward and outward, to India and back again.

No one bothered me. I was mostly safe. Except for one time.

It was an ordinary train ride from Thanjavur junction to Tiruchi, the British name shortened from the original Tamil name of Tiruchirappalli. I saw the Tamil letters on the long rust-colored train. It was the only train that was available that hot January afternoon. The express trains were all full, so I decided to take the slow afternoon train. It was siesta time, and the entire countryside went silent; you could only hear the big black flies hopping from fruit to fruit on the stands and the mosquitoes humming from hot skin to hot skin. The dust swirled everywhere on that side of the town; there was no irrigation, so there was just dried-out, parched land.

An hour later, I had my camera equipment and field journals ready to go. I bought yogurt rice and tamarind rice from a nearby restaurant. The food was wrapped first in banana leaves, then recycled newspaper, and then finally each packet was tied swiftly and neatly using thin twine. I hoisted my heavy backpack onto my back, stepped onto the platform, and started reading a book. When the train arrived, I saw it was an old steam engine. Boy, this train looks slow, I thought; maybe this was a mistake. No, this was the only day I had to visit the Sri Ranganathaswamy Temple, and I had to see that beautiful, lying-down Vishnu in black schist marble to find out if the kōlams were any different than the ones in Thanjavur.

I got onto the train, found the women's compartment, and sat there and waited for others to join me. No one did. I thought it was a bit strange, but I wasn't worried: maybe there were no women like me traveling alone this afternoon. I fell asleep, leaning my head against the jostling train, my book on one sari-covered thigh and my open journal on the other. My pen lay nearby on the slatted boards of the train seat.

All of a sudden, I woke up, my eyes sleepy. I heard young men's loud voices, laughing too boisterously. At first I didn't think anything of it, though I sat up straight and adjusted my sari across my short blouse, making sure it was properly covered. I picked up my book and journal and started looking at them as if I had been reading and writing intently, putting on a mask of concentration I did not feel. I adjusted my wire-rimmed glasses nervously and began working. That was the impression I was determined to give.

The voices got louder as they approached my compartment and they echoed strangely. To distract myself and to ease the tension I was feeling, as if my throat was locking up somehow, I stared out the window. At that moment the long train curved in that desolate dried-up landscape. There were no glowing wet rice fields here. Instead, it was barren as far as the eyes could see. The curving train—there was something odd in that, but I couldn't place it somehow. Then it came to me in a flash: all the windows were blank. There was no one else on the train but myself and this loud and quickly approaching group of men. That was why their voices were echoing! There had not even been a conductor who had asked about my ticket. My pulse rose, and for the first time in my entire trip in India traveling alone, fear rose like bile in my stomach.

Suddenly, the six college-aged men stood there, watching me brazenly from the door, and then suddenly they were all in the compartment, scrambling around me. I looked directly at them. I couldn't think of what else to do, even though I knew I was forbidden to meet the eyes of strange men. I knew this was a provocative act in itself, but they had already provoked. So what else could I do?

"What do you want?" I asked in as authoritative of a tone of voice as I could muster.

"Oh, nothing. We just wanted to sit here," said the ringleader.

I replied sternly, "But this is a women's compartment. Men aren't allowed to be here. You need to leave now."

They ignored my words. They kept just staring at me, as if they were a group of fishermen and I was their catch. I could feel their bodily excitement building. I knew that if something happened here today, my adventures as a woman traveling alone in India would be over, and a part of me would die here. I could not allow that to happen. But what could I do? I tried to remember the one self-defense class I'd taken in college, but not one defensive move came back to me. Besides, it was six against one; I had never been taught to deal with odds like that.

The men held brown paper bags with crunched openings between their legs and I smelled alcohol. They were sitting crammed against each other, bristling with energy and vitality and excitement, as if they couldn't believe their good luck. What were they thinking? What did they want? I imagined their bodies swaying like cobras leaning in to kill the mongoose. I kept nervously glancing out the window, dry, tall, yellowed grasses sweeping by. This place was new to me, nothing like the rich green rice fields I was used to in Thanjavur. My screams would go nowhere in this vast emptiness. I could imagine my dead body lying out there, eaten by ravens or vultures, my bones rotting away.

I had another hour to go on this empty train before we would reach our destination, the famous Vishnu temple that had seemed so important to visit that morning. My mind whirred. Could I offer them my camera, tape recorder, or video camera? Would they divide them up? How much money could I give them to leave me alone? How much did I actually have on me? Would it be enough to get out of this situation? I kept my eyes on them as if they were just water passing by, a river gurgling forward, as if they were just time itself, moment to moment, my breath held in suspension, waiting for whatever came next.

They jostled each other, punching each other playfully, as if to say, no, you go first, why don't you try her first? Then one of us will get her. Their eyes grew big with longing and desire, as if they burned with fire.

I straightened up my spine; I knew I looked taller if I stretched it out. Perhaps I could intimidate them. I reached toward my heavy backpack, wide open and loose. My camera was lying outside, my notebook pages were filled with my scrawls, my black pen was waiting to keep writing whatever I had been in the middle of writing.

And suddenly my mind clicked into place. I remembered what my father had taught me years before: depending on their age, I should treat Tamil males as if they were my own kinfolk. I was 26, and these youths were about 21. So I stared playfully at them, as if they were my younger brothers, and bombarded them with questions: "What are you studying in college? Which college are you studying at?"

I tried to sound as laconic as possible, as if they could not expect anything from me, as if fear had never entered my imagination, as if my voice could escape this lonely train if it wanted to, as if I could disappear from their sight willingly, as if I had powers they could never even imagine I had but that I could surprise them with if I needed to.

The only man without a paper bag wrapper said curiously, "So, what are you, a young woman, doing here? Why are you on this slow train to Tiruchi? No one ever takes this train. Everyone takes the express train these days. Are you an outsider?"

An idea popped into my head. "Oh, I'm a magazine reporter from Bombay. I work as a staff journalist for the national magazine India Illustrated Weekly. *Have you all heard of it?"*

Immediately, the young men acted as if they had been lassoed by my words. They put away their crunched paper bags as if they wanted me to forget they ever had them.

The one who had begun his questioning asked me in a serious but increasingly nervous tone: "What is your article on? What issue are you reporting?"

I smiled calmly and said, "I am here reporting on how women are treated in Tamil Nadu, whether modern life has changed the traditional male roles, whether men treat women differently than the earlier generation of men who treated women so badly. So can I interview all of you for my magazine article?"

My words had a magical effect on the young men. Now the tables were turned; suddenly, they were the examined ones, they were the prey, and I was the huntress. I reached for my tape recorder, turned it on, and began plying them with questions. They answered as quickly and politely as they could. It was obvious they couldn't wait to get out of that women's compartment. My very presence seemed to awaken a primal fear in them.

Though they left a few minutes later, I did not relax until we reached our destination. I was as terrified as I had ever been, and I had never been so relieved to see a crowded train station. I knew I had escaped a potential calamity, and I felt grateful for my quick thinking.[12]

3

Rituals

Just before slivers of sunlight crack open the horizon each morning along the river in the ancient Tamil city of Madurai, Meera steps over the night-blackened doorway of her family's house onto a quiet street to draw a new kōlam for the day. Her shadow spills onto the thinnai. This charged liminal space between the outside and the inside of the house separates the intimacy of everyday life in the household from the more public and wider social nexus of community life. As the emerging sunlight glimmers around her, Meera begins to create the "canvas" on which the kōlam will be drawn by sweeping the front porch and beyond into the public area with a broomstick made of coconut frond. The sound of the family broomstick striking the earth is echoed by the varying rhythms of other women's movements as they clean their own front thresholds. The carefully cleaned area can be as small as a spice box or as large as three times the size of a doorway, depending on the ritual occasion, the time available, and the mood of the creator.

When Meera walks down to the river's edge, she sees the skyline of the ancient temple, with its four gopurams jutting into the sky. These temple towers are organized in concentric squares centered on the temple for the fish-eyed goddess Meenakshi. Meera's street, which is perpendicular to the Vaigai River, is full of homes built of the traditional adobe, modern concrete, and straw. The sides of the houses touch each other, sharing the edges and barriers of households.

After carefully sweeping away yesterday's dirt, Meera turns into the house, walks through several doorways lined up in a row, steps over the threshold in the back of the house, and approaches the brick-lined well. She draws water with an aluminum bucket. Bowing slightly at her waist from the weight of the water, she gathers fresh cow dung, a ritual ingredient, from the floor of the stall where the cows have slept during the night and hurries through the house, the contents sloshing in the bucket. She reaches the front door and crosses the threshold once again. After mixing the cow dung and water in the bucket with her hands so that no lumps remain in the mixture, she ritually splashes handfuls of cow dung water over the earth, forming a darkened wet "canvas." Cow dung water is antiseptic, she says; it keeps away *kirumigal,* or small insects. For her, it is one of the primary ritual ingredients in the creation of an auspicious and unpolluted canvas. Once again, she takes the coconut frond and sweeps over the wet earth, creating a brushed effect.

She then bends over, stretching far from the waist to reach the edges of the visualized framed space that will hold her rice-flour designs. With a half a coconut shell for a bowl, Meera pinches the white rice flour, laying the design flowing out of her mind through her hands down onto the earth, deftly translating it into remarkable patterns, ones that are meant to fulfill the Hindu notion that everyone, to keep their karma in balance, must feed a thousand souls every single day. Her hands move gracefully and quickly.

In these purposeful hand movements Meera may create geometric designs: concentric squares, interlocking triangles facing opposing directions, elaborately adorned circles, labyrinths of lines that circle a series of dots but never touch them; or she may create figurative designs: pairs of peacocks, a squirrel crunching a walnut, a Bharatanatyam dancer in cobalt blue and brilliant yellow, or even a schoolboy in the middle of a soccer kick (see Figures 3.1–3.9).

Meera has been painting the kōlam since she was seven or eight years old, and as she grew up her work improved. Unmarried and educated, Meera came from a family that gave her tremendous cultural freedom to pursue her interest in the kōlam, seeing it as a kind of ritual work.

Figure 3.1 Bicycle on giant labyrinth kōlam, Thanjavur.

Figure 3.2 Painted kōlams, Srivilliputtur.

Figure 3.3 A figurative mouse kōlam.

Figure 3.4 A Bharatanatyam dancer kōlam.

Figure 3.5 A Swiss girl on snowshoes kōlam.

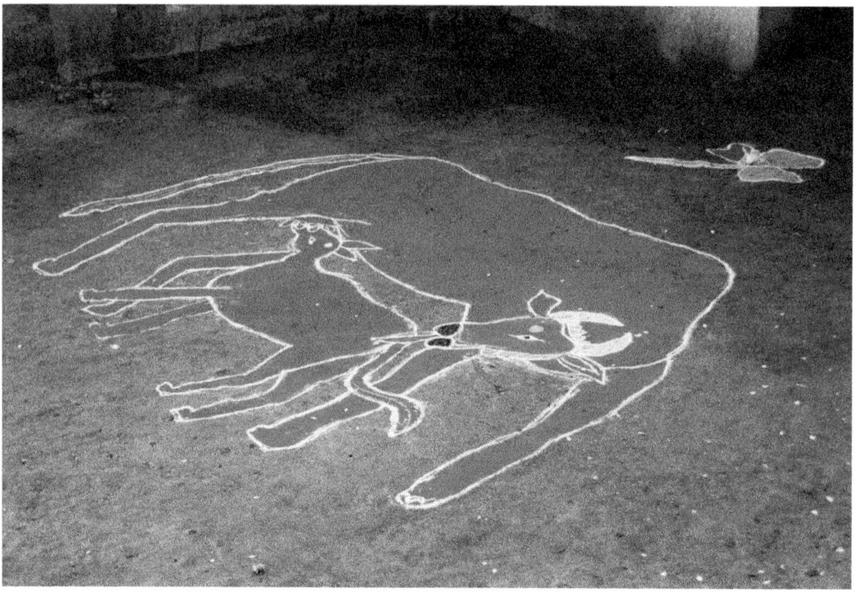

Figure 3.6 Cow with calf figurative kōlam.

Figure 3.7 A household with a mother and three daughters, four kōlams, village near Chidambaram.

Figure 3.8 Snake kōlam, Thanjavur.

Figure 3.9 Kōlams (yellow circles with red dots) to Mariyamman, the goddess of smallpox, on the walls of the house.

Her world has been centered in the town of Madurai, where her many years of discipline and concentration have made her a quiet authority on the kōlam.

I came across Meera's beautiful and magnificent kōlams before I met her. I first found them many miles from Madurai while at an ancient temple, which was surrounded by an even more ancient sacred grove, tucked in the waterfalls and rising hills. Her kōlams struck me as extraordinary. They were beautifully balanced in color, form, and symmetry; the lines were as straight as if they had been made with a ruler; the shapes were curvaceous and voluptuous, full of form and feeling. I was struck by their sense of abundance. There were so many of them, one after the other; it was as if the woman who had made the geometric designs had woven in all of her wishes and desires into their very being. They were exquisitely and carefully painted in acrylic, a semi-permanent material I had never before seen used to create kōlams. The choice of medium itself seemed bold, from my perspective, subverting what I thought was one of the core qualities of the kōlam, its ephemeral nature and effervescence. You knew that no matter how beautiful the kōlam was, it would not be around in a few hours. Yet these acrylic kōlams were traditional in their symbolic qualities, serene in their maker's sureness of hand.

I was to find out weeks later, as I searched and found her, that the kōlams were very much like Meera herself. After making numerous inquiries, I was excited to trace her to her family's home along her street by the Vaigai River. Once we met, I felt deeply connected to her; we were both unmarried at the time and we both loved the kōlam. We both sensed that there was a lot more to the kōlam than its first appearance would allow us to imagine. I went back to her again and again, circling back with more questions, year after year.

Ritual Play for Millions

Like Meera, every day throughout Tamil Nadu, millions of women rise before dawn to perform the ritual practice of the kōlam on the thresholds of their houses, on the temple grounds, at businesses, and at the feet of divine images in the main domestic shrines (Figure 3.10). The kōlam reveals a woman's state of well-being for the day, and by extension her household's state of well-being for the day: are she and it ready for hospitality? Is she overjoyed, having just had a much-desired healthy newborn and, therefore, the household is celebrating? Is a full-grown daughter or son of hers marrying today? Is she in her state of blood-time? Is she in sorrow or mourning and therefore not available for hospitality and, in fact, in need of others' help and assistance? Does she have an abundance of time and overflowing energy to give? Is she undergoing a fast for a particular god or goddess or saint today in order to obtain a particular desire or willed

Figure 3.10 Girl standing on geometric kōlam (connect-the-dots).

positive intentionality? Is she rushed for work, and therefore the kōlam has a look of being done in a brisk, harried fashion?

Kōlams are designed to invite, attract, host, and maintain close relationships with Lakshmi, the goddess of wealth, luck, and good fortune, and Bhūdevi, the goddess of soil and earth (see Figure 3.11 for Lakshmi and Figure 9.1 for Bhūdevi). Ubiquitous in ritual and cultural life, the kōlam is one of the most visible ways a sense of sacred space is created. It is said to bless those who smear it accidentally with their feet, the power of the hands of the woman kōlam-maker passing through it to the anonymous feet or bodies walking by.

When making a kōlam, the woman holds the rice flour in her right hand. Women either use their own materials, grinding the rice the night before, or use ground red earth and fancy bazaar-bought powders, mixing the colors themselves. Kōlams—ephemeral "painted prayers" (Huyler 1994)—appear and disappear in the early morning light.

The aesthetic image that emerges from a woman's hands on the threshold is the culmination of a process. Whenever they have time, women practice creating new designs diligently in their personal or family notebooks, and then compare them with each other and copy designs. They carefully guard their notes and drawings about all the kōlams they have practiced and memorized, from experiments and successes to mistakes and failures. These notebooks may be either lined or unlined, like the school notebooks children use, or larger, like the

Figure 3.11 One of the most popular iconic images of Lakshmi. (Source: Author's collection.)

ledgers of a bookkeeper. Some of the kōlam patterns in the notebooks may even be filled in with color.

While the name of a kōlam design is often recorded in the notebooks, the name of the person who designed it is usually not included. Since rituals are realized in the form of community knowledge rather than by individuals, kōlam-making is an anonymous practice. It is not considered necessary (nor is it often done) to identify the creator of a particular kōlam.[1]

Occasionally, if an unusually beautiful and visually striking kōlam appears, a neighbor may ask, "Who drew your kōlam today?" If pursued further as to why this one attracted her gaze, the person may say that it has *latshanam*, or "shining," a quality of inner beauty that not only emerges from an object but also permeates it.

A kōlam-maker's personality is sometimes judged from a design. Many women, Janaki and others, have often told me, for example, that when the potential groom's family is visiting a potential bride, the first impression she makes on the groom and his family is through her kōlam. If the design is particularly detailed and complex, she is understood as someone with "a lot of patience" and the will to create beauty around her, reflecting her "traditionalness." The kōlam, until recently, was viewed as something that a Tamil girl had to excel at before puberty, one of the many skills she would need to run a household.[2]

When beginning a kōlam, a woman imagines a small template; once she fully enters the process, however, she may add elaborations and extensions of the design. For example, she may begin with a simple lotus flower pattern of eight petals and continue with more abstract petals that lead to a denser ornamentation. When the kōlam is complete, it seems as if the hand has made one continuous line and the body one continuous movement. To the untrained eye, her body seems to move with its own choreography.

A closer look at the actual making of the designs reveals that the hand moves on the surface of the earthen "canvas" in a jagged rhythm. First, in some kōlams, a matrix of single dots laid in rows and columns may be used as reference points for the final drawing. Next, in a purposeful manner the hand lays down remarkable curvilinear lines, circling the original matrix of dots. Once one section has been worked on and nearly completed, the woman moves to another section and she faces an entirely different direction. With each swerve of the pattern, her body shifts and turns, since it would be physically difficult to execute the overall design in one continuous line if she stayed in one place.

Emerging from women's practiced hands, the kōlam may catch neighbors' glances, or it may pass almost unnoticed, as it is such a common feature of everyday life. Once the kōlam is finished—minutes later—it becomes an ephemeral rug that is worn away during the day under the feet of passersby and those who cross the threshold of the house. By 8 or 9 o'clock in the morning, the kōlam has already been worn away by the feet of pedestrians and the wheels of cars, bicycles, and scooters. All that remains is the scattered residue of ground rice to be swept and wiped clean the next morning. The households with many children always "lose" their kōlams first as the kōlams are smeared and erased by infants and children wandering on top of them. Those who wish to have children hope that one day their designs will be gone by midmorning also.

The kōlam is a practice that engages a great deal of imagination. While the woman is creating it, she exhibits a set of gestures as a visual art form—a sequence of bodily movements requiring a quality of attentiveness akin to dance or yoga. Learning to make the kōlam is like learning to play an instrument. Dexterity of movement is necessary for the practice, the audience plays a role in its performance, and periodic bursts of intense activity are crucial to its mastery.

The kōlam is located within the realm of ritual life and shares the characteristics of rituals in general: to attract the attention of particular goddesses, to communicate with the divine, and to share the emotional qualities of the household. As a ritual, it is a social obligation—that is, something that must be done. Indeed, there are many "shoulds" with the kōlam, but these are not hard-and-fast rules; rather, they are guidelines that can be broken as the need arises.

Among these "rules" is the idea that the kōlam should be created before the first rays of the sun touch the ground, before dawn, and before the last rays of the sun leave the horizon, after sunset. My mother and many other kōlam-makers of her generation (that is, women who were born in the 1920s and 1930s and grew up in the 1940s and 1950s) would say that it is inauspicious to create a kōlam in daylight. Those applied after sunrise might indicate a lazy woman who wakes up late. However, from the ways women speak about this ritual art, this obligation is far from a burden or a task to be avoided. On the contrary, they are keen to communicate to the outer world that their household is alive and well, functioning harmoniously, and that there has been no illness, suffering, or death during the night.

The kōlam is created with a sense of both enjoyment and duty among girls and women. Quiet afternoons when everyone else is taking an afternoon nap are filled with sketching and drawing simple or elaborate kōlams in rough ledger notebooks. Plans for the next day's kōlams are excitedly made and remade. The type, degree of elaboration, and colors of the kōlams that will be drawn on the thresholds the next morning are all eagerly discussed.

The kōlam is a subtle barometer of *cupam* (Sanskrit, *subha*), a state of auspiciousness or happiness. It is a way to convey information about the household to the outside world, indicating that the people in the home are in good health, that food is in reasonable abundance, and that the household is hospitable. To *sadhus* (holy men and mendicants), the kōlam is a sign that perhaps they can expect a bowl of rice that day. Its absence on a threshold indicates that some negative event has happened during the night, so the family cannot be hospitable to a stranger or friend that day. It may signify to passersby that a sorrowful event has occurred, such as a death in the family; that the woman of the household is menstruating; or that there are no women in the household. It could also indicate an extremely busy woman who labors in the fields, or in an office, from early morning to night. Absence of a kōlam serves to alert passing neighbors, who will immediately think of what they can bring to the suffering occupants, such as gifts of comfort, household help, food, and clothing.

One elderly woman, Pārvathi, looked thoughtfully at me on a lane in Madras and described the kōlam as she remembered it from her youth:

> Well, before we had a really steady postal system or TV, radio, news, or whatever, and a person would walk for days to come to a relative's house, they would first look at the kōlam to see if everything was okay. If there's no kōlam they'll go to the neighbor's house rather than going into the relative's house, and ask them if somebody died. If somebody says, "Yes, somebody has died," then they'll go through the neighbor's house to the back and enter with a state of sadness. Rather than saying,

"Oh, I'm so happy to see you!," they would try to be of help and cook, or do whatever needs to be done. The reason you put that sign out is to have the visitor or the guest match the mood of the household.

It is clear that visitors must take into account the mood and emotions of the household. Therefore, the kōlam is a visible ritual that not only creates beauty but also integrates the emotional sense of household, hospitality, and kinship between the inside world of the household and those who cross its threshold.

Creation of Sacred Space

The kōlam acts as one of the key markers of both ritual space and time in Tamil culture. It is made partly as a sign to attract the gaze of the divinities. The time between 4 and 5:30 a.m. is called *Brahma muhurta,* or "the time of Brahma," when gods and goddesses turn their faces toward humans. The kōlam marks the beginning of things: it inaugurates the day and it begins fire rituals, celebrations, and festivals. Drawn most elaborately to mark a woman's marriage and childbirth, yet significantly absent during periods of menstruation and mourning, the kōlam visually celebrates auspicious states of transition. Its large or elaborate designs announce births, coming-of-age ceremonies, and marriages, marking on the threshold that it is a special day of celebration in that household.

The purposeful cleaning, wiping, ordering, and adorning of a particular area on the threshold creates a sense of sacred space. The ground acts as the canvas, while the kōlam is an offering to that ground. The act of creating the kōlam each morning serves as a springboard that sets in motion a series of positive intentionalities and unifies the making and recreating of family and community life at the daily level. Making the kōlam is often the first ritual performed at a threshold of a house, domestic shrine, or temple. It initiates most public or private ritual events. In a sense, the kōlam is the enactment of a ritual relationship with the world as a whole; it invites and solidifies in a visible and aesthetic form the relationship of a Tamil woman to the earth she walks on.

Hospitality: Feeding a Thousand Souls

One of the most frequent answers I hear when I ask why the kōlam is created is the expression "to feed a thousand souls"—in other words, that it is a dharmic offering, a gift to small, non-human creatures. It took me a long while to figure out what that meant. The rice flour from which the kōlam is made feeds the ants, birds, and other wandering animals; thus it manifests thoughtfulness and generosity to other creatures. The day begins more auspiciously if one practices *dānam* (Sanskrit, *dāna*), or the act of giving, as the very first ritual act. Here an act of giving is for souls who are strangers rather than the more typical reciprocal gift giving to a relative, friend, or neighbor, where there may be an expectation of a parallel gift in return. The kōlam represents a "feeder to souls" with no expectation of reciprocity. (I will be delving more into this aspect of the kōlam as a symbol of generosity in Chapter 11.)

Some women also told me with a grin, "Perhaps feeding rice flour to ants and insects in the early morning fills their stomachs up so that they go on about their business and they don't bother you the rest of the day." The idea that the kōlam prevents ants and insects from entering the house speaks of a certain kind of interrelationship with other creatures. If a household is hospitable to insects via the kōlam, they may walk off with full bellies, satisfied, and not get into the rice flour in the kitchen.

Invitation to the Goddess

Rice flour is also seen as an offering to Lakshmi, the goddess of well-being, abundant wealth, good luck, and good fortune. In an agricultural economy where wealth is still largely measured in terms of one's access to rice, rice fields, and rice products, Lakshmi holds a vital place in the Tamil cultural imagination. Throughout the Tamil landscape, I discovered that wherever there were rice paddy fields there was a heightened eagerness to discuss the kōlam. This was not surprising, since rice shapes the riverine landscapes, especially in the Kāvēri and the Vaikai River deltas surrounding the large towns of Thanjavur and Madurai. Parrot-green fields of rice framed my discussions on the stoops of the many households where I spoke with women. Where there were seasonal downpours of rain, irrigation canals organizing the movement of water from one rice paddy to another, and temple towers rising up in the horizon, there seemed to be an enthusiasm for the kōlam that was infectious. Therefore, the presence of rice in the landscape seemed to evoke the cultural creation of the kōlam. This is not surprising, as the kōlam is made from wet or dry rice flour. Even the kōlam patterns that are based on a matrix of dots laid down as if in a grid resemble, according to a few Tamil women, the planting of rice seedlings in the wet paddy fields. That there is a symbolic transfer back and forth between the planting of rice and the placing of dots on the earth makes both literal and figurative sense. I noted that wherever there was a drier climate and fewer temples on the horizon, there seemed to be less interest in the kōlam.

As she is said to live in the grains of rice, one treats rice with the utmost respect.[3] Bhūdevi, the goddess of the earth, is also worshipped. The kōlam is one of the many rituals designed to attract, host, and maintain close relationships with both Lakshmi and Bhūdevi, treating them gently and with honor. By making it, a woman worships Lakshmi by inviting her into her household, and Bhūdevi by asking her forgiveness for all the harsh effects on her earthly body of greedy human deeds. And a woman worships Mūdevi, the goddess of laziness, by inviting her into her household before sunset so that she can invite rest and sleep into her body.

Most of the women I interviewed talked about the importance of creating *mangalam* (Sanskrit, *Mangala*) (auspiciousness) and the role of the kōlam not only to indicate but also to attract well-being. That is, the kōlam is associated with bringing prosperity and good health into the household. The woman of the house is referred to as "Lakshmi" as she is the one who is seen as having the power to make this happen. She and Lakshmi have a special relationship, which is solidified by the ritual of the kōlam. Like the goddess, the woman has the power to attract wealth and prosperity into the household and to prevent poverty from crossing the threshold.

By making the kōlam, the Tamil woman creates an ephemeral shelter for the goddess Lakshmi and invites her into her home. She is creating a painting, a diagram, or a place where Lakshmi can be invited, rest, and be hosted. Meera elaborates on the relationship between the kōlam and Lakshmi: "The kōlam helps the goddess come and be there. You create a seat for her. She comes and watches your household for you." Although the kōlam is an object of beauty, it also acts as a shield or guardian. While Lakshmi actively directs wealth, health, and happiness into the household, she simultaneously wards off misfortune, illness, and grief. Some of her symbols are the lotus flower, the conch shell, and the chariot.

Numerous Indian folktales and stories tell of how families came to enjoy wealth, prosperity, and good fortune because of the kōlam or similar women's ritual designs.[4] For example, in the folktale "A Golden Sparrow," a poor old woman wiping and cleaning the threshold of her house with cow dung just before making the "rangōli" design gets struck by a thorn, which after some time turns into a golden sparrow and showers her with wealth. Even the thorn, initially a painful injury, turned into a boon of wealth (Ramanujan 1997: 71–2). The rangōli-making woman displays a pious, well-meaning, and generous heart, in contrast to the avarice-filled neighbor who tried to copy her actions and ended up losing her hand to gangrene. Not just the actions by themselves, but also the positive thoughts that go with them, make the real difference in the outcome.

Another folktale in the same collection, "King and Peasant," tells of a queen who trades places for six months with a poor peasant woman who has unwashed pots and pans piling up in her washing area, floors greasy with dirt, and a chaotic and disordered household. The queen insists to the king that their poverty was more due to mismanagement of their resources than a God-given fate. As soon as the queen arrived into the peasants' house, she "swept it, washed it, drew rangōli designs on the floor, cleaned all the pots, burned incense for the gods." She told the peasant man, "You must go into town every day and work there. You must bring home whatever you earn and give it to me. You must never come home with an empty hand. If you can't get work on some days, you must still pick up something, at least a stick from the road, and bring it home." Within the six months, the queen had turned the fortunes of the peasants' household around, but the peasant wife who had continued her slothful ways at the palace had lost many jewels and treasures (Ramanujan 1997: 94–6). Many folktales use the kōlam as a metonymic device to indicate cleanliness, concentration, virtue, and piety.

In addition, the kōlam plays an important role during festival days for women and various goddesses. Orienting rituals toward particular deities, as in the case of the kōlam with the goddesses Lakshmi and Bhūdevi, is not unusual in Hinduism. As far back as the Vedas, Hindu rituals were intended to invoke particular gods and goddesses. In theology this is often referred to as "henotheism." As Christopher Chapple, a theologian, observes:

> In this system, religious ritual is initiated out of a human need for structure aimed toward the fulfillment of a particular goal, symbolized by a particular deity. For instance, the goddess Vac is invoked through sacrificial offerings to enhance one's power of speech. For the period of time during which her services are needed, she becomes the preeminent focus of one's religious devotions. At a later time, one might turn to Saraswathi, the goddess of learning, for success at studies. Indra, the warrior god, is invoked for purposes of conquest and strength. (1993: 194)

The kōlam is a way for people to turn to Lakshmi and invoke her in their everyday life. It reflects, indicates, and manifests her attributes.

Another god mentioned often is Ganesh, who is represented during the month of Margaḷi (mid-December to mid-January) with yellow pumpkin flowers stuck in a cow-dung cone that is placed in the center of the kōlam.

The availability of the many other gods and goddesses with distinct attributes is central to the preoccupations of Hinduism. In general, whatever stage you are in your life, whatever your needs are, you can pick and choose whichever god or goddess you are attracted to; that particular form is often called *ishtadēvata*. An infinite variety of divine beings have forms with very specific attributes and qualities. Depending on your particular caste or sub-caste, region or ethnicity, neighborhood or street, *sontha oor* or village of origin,[5] there are multiple affiliations and associations that you may be attached to or ritually committed to. Ultimately, it is believed that all the divinities are melded into one unknowable universal form. The kōlam participates in this network of affiliations and obligations by focusing on a single goddess, Lakshmi, one of the many manifestations of the universal form.

Warding Off the Evil Eye

The making of the kōlam is also intimately connected with the Tamil concept of the "evil eye."[6] For the kōlam-maker and all those who cross the threshold of her home, the kōlam is drawn to deflect the ill effects of the evil eye. It is bound up with the ability of the individual, the family, and the community to deal with jealousy and covetousness, both within themselves and within others. These emotions are considered to be so strong that they can wreak chaos in a community in the same way that a disease can devastate a person's health. The eye can covet an object. When the envious eye touches the desired object, the eye has the power to affect the well-being of the object. The kōlam acts as a net, a catcher of feelings, and a protective screen for the emotions emitted by those who pass by the doorway or cross the threshold.

During one of our many conversations, Meera explained, "The evil eye is carried around by ghosts, demons, and bad spirits." When I inquired where these evil spirits were located, she replied:

> The malignant spirits are not necessarily wandering around in demon form outside of our selves. Most of the time the demons are in us. They are in you and me. Whenever you are just walking down the street and find yourself envious, jealous, full of purāmai, or thinking of someone with evil intentions, your own evil eye can affect the person you are thinking of. It can directly affect that particular person's house, children, health, and everything that belongs to them. The wealth, comfort, and security in their body, home, and even family is in danger.
>
> This force of emotion can come from your unconscious or conscious. So you may not realize you are being jealous of someone. But that is why, you see, you need to protect others and protect yourself with the kōlam. If you have a house, and you think how beautiful and attractive you are, or how beautiful and attractive your house is, then you can cast the evil eye on your own self, your own body, your own family, [even on] your own house. That is why you need to protect yourself with the kōlam from within the house and from outside the house from the effects of the evil eye.

> Now you cannot get too vain about making the kōlam, either. If I get vain and boastful about the fact that I have made beautiful kōlams at local big temples and even that you have come here to talk to me, I can destroy myself with the effects of my own evil eye as well as others' evil eyes. The demons of covetousness can eat me up. So I have to be very watchful over myself to not stir up my own pride.

The emphasis here of how the kōlam prevents the harmful effects of the evil eye reveals how significant this is in Tamil culture. In general, people are very careful about praising anyone excessively because it is felt that calling attention to yourself or your family can bring bad luck. Showering too much praise on yourself or others, for the same reasons, is also frowned upon because such an act, mixed with conscious and unconscious intentions, may cause envy, which creates a destructive force in the community. Envy coming from within the community is believed to be one of the most dangerous forces in existence. It is, therefore, publicly condemned and resisted on both personal and community levels. The kōlam acts as a catcher for people's envy and other ill feelings.

Prayer to the Divine

The kōlam also represents a kind of prayer to the divine. Prayer, by definition, is a personal activity informed by an individual's desires, wishes, and relationship to the divine. For example, a prayer for continued blessings or for help, support, and aid in enduring suffering is meant to call the attention of the divine eye or gaze. Thus the kōlam, as it draws the attention of the divine and diverts malignant influences, is simultaneously an anonymous and a highly personal ritual. Women often referred to the kōlam as a protector and guardian of the household.

To understand its protective intentions it is useful to refer to cultural anthropologist Ray's discussion of the purpose of *vratas*, women's ritual vows, and especially *ālpanās*, the parallel ritual art to the kōlam in Bengal: "In the religion of brata [vratas], art is an indispensable means of communication between the devotees and the gods . . . the purpose of these ālpanās was originally to keep dwelling place, city, or village safe and prosperous, and to make the cultivated land fertile and fruitful, by magical performance" (Ray 1961: iv [quoted in Pearson 1996: 156]). Linked to Lakshmi, who epitomizes fertility and abundance, one reason for making the ālpanā and the kōlam is to bring prosperity, fertility, and fruitfulness into the household.

The desire for relief from poverty and scarcity made sense to me in a country where hundreds of millions still live below the poverty line, but the desire for fertility made less sense when I first heard it. There was hardly a shortage of people in India, and as an environmentalist, I was concerned about the long-term balance between population and sustainability of community resources. My own desire for children had not struck me yet, so I "turned off" automatically whenever I heard the desire for fertility expressed. In fact, I thought it was strange when confronted by the daily reality of the enormous fertility in India. I felt that doing the kōlam in the hopes of overcoming infertility was purely a belief with little scientific basis.

But years later, when I was forced to confront my own infertility, I realized my mistake. The kōlam is about desiring life as a force in itself, and doing it always reminds you that you are alive. Even in the midst of despair over infertility, the kōlam reminds you that you are not dead; life goes on and your desires matter, in a kind of pilgrimage toward fertility and well-being. It was a shocking epiphany for me when I realized how intimately the kōlam is tied to the specific articulation of unexpressed and expressed desires for Tamil women, and it made a kind of intimate sense to draw your innermost desires into the very kōlam you make every morning.

Laxmi Tewari proposes that making this ritual art form can also be viewed as "an act of pilgrimage": "The preparation of materials and the process of painting or sculpting symbolize the journey to the place of pilgrimage. Worshipping and offering food to the painting or sculpture are acts of *darsan* . . . by which a devotee experiences the presence and power of the deity. At the conclusion of the worship, the offerings . . . are distributed as prasād" (1991:15). Women often made a direct reference to the kōlam as an act of pilgrimage. Several woman told me, "Stepping on the kōlam is like stepping into the Ganges; you are cleansed and blessed at the same time."

This amazed me: the Ganges herself comes to your doorstep in the form of the kōlam. This confirms what Eck has recently extrapolated in her work *India: A Sacred Geography*, where the Ganges is both literally and symbolically within the many other sacred rivers throughout India.[7] Stepping on the kōlam on millions of Tamil doorsteps in Tami Nadu carries the same power as stepping into the Ganges. It is not just other sacred rivers that the Ganges is embedded within; it is also at the threshold of your own house.

In Festivals and Celebrations

For festivals from Pongal and Navarāthri to Krishnajayanthi, Kārthigai (Figure 3.12), and Deepāvali, women draw the kōlam to announce that their household is ready participate in the festivities.[8] Especially grand kōlams are drawn for these occasions, with all the appropriate signs and forms. From mid-December through mid-January during the Tamil month of Mārkali,

Figure 3.12 Pongal kōlam decorations on each threshold, each kōlam's edge bumping against the other, and overflowing Pongal pots of rice. Midmorning, village near Tirunelvēli.

kōlam-making reaches its peak.[9] At the end of this period is when the Pongal festival, celebrating the bountiful harvest, takes place. Pongal is the most prominent festival in Tamil Nadu and is celebrated by Tamils from every caste because it marks the winter solstice. The word "Pongal"—literally "boiled-over rice pot"—has two related meanings: boiling, bubbling, swelling, and leaping; and largeness, fullness, abundance, excess, profusion, bloom, and splendor. The kōlam is one of the most significant ritual acts during this festival.[10] Pongal literally brings in the harvest, so kōlam-making at this time represents the height of agricultural abundance, fertility, and prosperity in the Tamil agricultural cycle.

There are three to four days of festivities, depending on the region of Tamil Nadu, the caste, and whether it is an urban or rural setting. There may be variations as well. The first day is called Bhogi, to represent the discarding of old and broken materials, the clearing and deep cleaning of the household. The second day is the highlight of the festival and is the day that is actually called Pongal. The kōlam performed for this day is highly anticipated and is always drawn elaborately.

The peak of this festival involves cooking, in front of each household, a pot with rice, often grown from the family's own fields or newly bought at the market. A newly bought clay or brass pot is placed on top of a brand-new clay fired kiln, all of which is set on the surface of a newly drawn kōlam. Newness,

Figure 3.13 Sun worship ceremony—kōlam underneath as a base of Pongal ritual, Thirunelveli District.

freshness, and cleanliness are emphasized. The family members spend the early morning tending the fire and the pots, filled with rice, molasses, and sweet spices. At dawn, all the household members gather around to watch the rice boil over, singing, "Pongal o Pongal!" The cooked rice overflowing the pots signifies hope for abundance in the new year (Figure 3.13). Similarly, the large, exuberant kōlam, also made of rice, symbolizes the overflowing of wishes and prosperity.

The above image (Figure 3.13) shows a scene from Kumbakkenai, a village along the Thāmirabarāni River in Tirunelvēli District, typical of hundreds of hamlets and villages throughout Tamil Nadu (see also Figure 1.2a). As you can see, a small boy stands on a kōlam that extends from the threshold of one house to beyond the middle of the street. It is somewhat circular, with rust-red powders filling in the spaces between the lacelike filigreed lines. The center is filled with abundant color and the design moves outward like the petals of a flower; the petals are similarly scaled but slightly unevenly shaped, resembling the lotus flower on which Lakshmi sits on, meditating. Just beyond the outer rim of the last layer of petals, a bounded frame holds the kōlam steady to the eye. On this special day, the most important one of the Pongal festival, the kōlam is particularly expansive. Where does one begin and where does it end? It stretches out to the limit in all directions, into the household and as well as beyond the front threshold, touching the neighbor's kōlam. In a nearby household, a woman pours rice and water into a clay pot while a man sets the firewood beneath it. They are both preparing for the moment when the pots will be overflowing with the new harvest's rice.

The third day is called Māttu Pongal, or the Pongal for celebrating cattle, both milk cows and oxen, an emphasis on animals. The fourth day is Kannu Pongal, a time to worship the ancestors by cooking special foods for them. These foods are laid in a prescribed manner on banana leaves outside of the main house and crows are called down to eat the food (crows are considered to be the earthly representatives of the family's ancestors). Kōlams are drawn underneath and often near the banana leaves.

The kōlam marks the varying temporal rhythms of a family, community, caste, region, or religion. Though mostly drawn in Hindu religious contexts, the kōlam is multi-religious. Often, for example, a Christian woman who also believes in the auspiciousness of this ritual might make a substantially larger and denser kōlam on Christmas Day. Some castes may have specific family or lineage commitments to specific astrological calendars, and the density of the kōlam highlights those communities on those days. Orthodox Hindu castes and families may observe the period between mid-July and mid-August with rich colorful kōlams, while others may mark the festivals of particular saints with hand-drawn portraits. Christians and Jains often make the kōlam, but not usually Muslims (though as I mentioned previously I did find one Muslim boy who loved the kōlam and competed in the public competitions in Madurai). Secular Hindus often conceive of the kōlam as a marker of beauty rather than a ritual.

On the Threshold

A form that bridges the internal, private space and the external, public space, the kōlam falls into the category of "threshold rituals."[11] The threshold is a reference to the doorway in and out of a household or temple, pointing to a gateway (Figure 3.14a, b).[12] It is located at the edge of women's spatial world, the boundary between the home and street, between the inside and outside of the household (Ardener 1993). The threshold is considered to be an extremely dangerous edge, a portal where negative, unfriendly forces can enter, so an awareness of thresholds is encouraged in Tamil culture. The kōlam guards the borders from harm, envy, and inhospitable forces. The woman's first crossing of the threshold (she is the first one up in the morning to make the kōlam) helps protect her husband, her children, and her household from harm, illness, and injury throughout the day.

Typically, a household has many thresholds; a kōlam may mark each one. Eventually, one is led to the kōlam in the domestic shrine. In reality, the outer threshold space is "semiprivate"; it can be considered either public or private depending on standpoint and context. The kōlam has traditionally functioned to outline the separation between interior and exterior worlds. In one sense, the

(a)

Figure 3.14a Wet threshold kōlam in and around *thinnai.*

(b)

Figure 3.14b Threshold kōlam. Another view of Figure 3.14a.

"inside" and "outside" of the threshold is a visual play on a metaphorical experience of self as one crosses from the familiar and intimate space of the domestic household to the unfamiliar and public space of the street and the buzz of community life beyond.[13]

The phenomenon of thresholds has been studied and reported in many cultures.[14] Shulman (1985) sees the Tamil threshold as the focal point of a labyrinth that is "externalized" at the edge. A difficult, dangerous journey begins at the point of not knowing what is to come. Just beyond the house is the unknown and inescapable. Shulman characterizes the threshold and the kōlam eloquently:

> One cannot enter the house without passing through this man-made [woman-made] focus of auspicious forces, which sets up a protective screen before the home. Of course, one cannot see the screen itself, but only its focal point at the threshold, the point at which it emerges into form—a complex form at that, carefully planned and executed, a reflection of some inner labyrinth externalized here at the boundary, the line dividing the inner and the outer, the pure from the chaotic. The boundary is dangerous. . . . Like any vessel of divinity, they are tirthas—points of crossing. They simultaneously contain and obscure: imbued with power in their own right, they point beyond themselves to the wholeness of the divine. (3–5)

There are rituals, proverbs, and sayings that make one especially aware of thresholds, or what Shulman calls "an open-endedness in principle; the presence of permeable and self-conscious boundaries" (7). He continues his meditation on the kōlam:

> Why place a labyrinth at the gateway? . . . The inner paths of the mind are no less tortuous and no less permeable by the unknown. Space and consciousness intersect at the threshold of divinity. . . . The beyond keeps breaking in upon the present; it can never be ignored. . . . In effect, one always stands on a threshold: whichever way one turns, infinity stretches just beyond. (5–6)

Shulman's poetic rendering of the threshold attests to the implications for spatiality in the kōlam, a marker of the transition between the known and the unknown. Bachelard, a French phenomenologist, further considers the metaphorical nature of the separation created by the threshold:

> Outside and inside form a dialectic of division, the obvious geometry of which blinds us as soon as we bring it into play in metaphorical

> domains. It has the sharpness of the dialectics of yes and no, which decides everything. . . . It must be noted that the two terms "outside" and "inside" pose problems of metaphysical anthropology that are not symmetrical. To make inside concrete and outside vast is the first task, the first problem, it would seem, of an anthropology of the imagination. (1964: 211–15)

Bachelard's eloquent testimonial to the asymmetrical, lopsided bifurcation of the threshold matches the Tamil awareness of the importance of thresholds.

It is, therefore, no accident that the kōlam ritual is done on thresholds. In the Tamil world, awareness pervades of the thresholds of places: houses, villages, and towns. There is also an awareness of the boundaries of persons: their gender, age, life stage, caste, or class. For example, Aiyanār guards the *ellai* or the border of a village. This deity's spirit soldiers ride horses in the middle of the night to protect the village from malignant spirits and robbers. Ephemeral rice-flour lines mark, create, and maintain boundaries in the cultural web of Tamil everyday life. The kōlam exemplifies the ritual importance of the threshold; it parts the inside from the outside, the protected and "safe" world of the home from the more dangerous, vulnerable, and unguardable world of the outside.

While thresholds are the most common sites where kōlams are made, they are not the only places where they appear regularly. For example, a kōlam is often drawn as the first ritual act on the ground just before making the brick platform in a Vedic fire ritual. The Vedic fire ritual is one of the most male Hindu rituals, yet it is initiated by a female ritual art. The kōlam is also drawn on walls to initiate and mark a woman's vows for health, fertility, and long life. Unlike those drawn on the ground, this kōlam is kept on the wall for months to signify the active presence of spiritual power and women's vigorous participation in a lively, animated spiritual life. It is also used in the *villakku pūja*, a lamp ceremony organized by groups of women to assuage suffering or illness (Figure 3.15). In this context the kōlam serves to actively acknowledge the participants' desires to themselves and to others—whether it is to gain a husband, a child, or a sense of inner calmness.

Kōlam Knowledge in the Commons

How is knowledge of the kōlam passed on? Early one morning in Madras, I was walking on a street and watching women emerge from their doorways to make the kōlam. I asked an older woman, obviously the grandmother of one household, "How did you learn the kōlam?" With a look of surprise followed by a gentle and compassionate smile, she replied softly, "You don't learn to do the

Figure 3.15 Kōlams underneath women's lamp ceremony, Madurai.

kōlam. It is not to be learned in that way. You practice and it comes to you gradually." Like most Hindu folk practices, kōlam-making is not taught through a training center, a school, or a formal educational structure. The knowledge lies in the daily practice of the ritual, not in the accumulation of institutional knowledge.

It is the women themselves who fashion the historical roots and explanatory functions—the "whys"—of the kōlam. Every family usually has someone—a sister, a mother, an aunt, or a grandmother—who is known for her exceptional kōlam-making and abundant knowledge about the kōlam. In every village, neighborhood, or street where the kōlam is made there are one or two women who are considered to be exceptionally adept. However, there are no explicit "experts" as there are in other visual arts like dance, music, painting, or theater. Knowledge is scattered far and wide as millions of Tamil women practice the kōlam ritual; thus, the transmission of this knowledge is equally decentered.

At its core, the kōlam has an ephemeral, abundant, and communal nature. Let's look at some of these traits as they relate to the world of economics and value. To begin with, the kōlam cannot be bought and sold on the market (with few exceptions). It is created on a surface that cannot be stored or transported—the ground itself. For the most part, it resists individualization; it is a part of the common intellectual and artistic knowledge, akin to common property resources in the environment.

I have come to see it as a part of the commons: the commons of common knowledge, the commons of shared beauty, the commons that lies on the threshold between the private, domestic space of the household and the larger, more inclusive public space. These terms are more complicated in the Indian landscape, where "private" and "public" do not have the same meanings or implications. The Tamil words *pothu* and *poromboke* parallel what we generally understand as the "commons" in English.

The kōlam lies deep in the heart of the gift economy, giving and receiving without keeping a strict accounting between those who receive and those who give. It is not property, in the strictest sense of the word; it is not governed by rules of ownership and copyright. Yet, interestingly, women do keep their kōlam practice notebooks private and share them only with those who are genuinely interested in the ritual form. That aspect is not public or an aspect of the commons, although the kōlam itself is offered as a gift to the world for its beauty.

Since the number of kōlams is infinite, it may be considered an abundant rather than a scarce form of knowledge. The knowledge of the kōlam is not expensive or limited to the privileged few. In other words, it is a visual gift from the woman of the household to the whole community. Knowledge is most often passed from mother to daughter, or grandmother to granddaughter. Learning to do it requires little more than a basic interest on the part of the student, coupled with a teacher's willingness to pass on her knowledge by example.

The kōlam reflects the preoccupations of women in Tamil culture. It touches upon many levels of their daily lives, from the practical to the mythological. In a context where suffering, death, illness, and poverty are everyday realities, a woman's positive intentionalities are believed to actually make a difference in people's lives. The power of her hands is fluid, and the female personification of energy, or *sakti*, moves from the women's active, creative hands to the kōlam, to be picked up by the feet and transported throughout the day. The kōlam appears on the streets day after day—the visual signs of women's blessings in the vicinity, "fluid signs."[15] In this world, women's blessings are believed to have an effect. I often wonder: Are women's blessings themselves a kind of commons?

All Around India and All Around the World

While my focus in this book is on Tamil Nadu, Tamil women elsewhere make the kōlam as well. As I mentioned in Chapter 1, I have seen the kōlam in Tamil diasporic communities throughout India—in New Delhi, Bombay, Kerala,

Bangalore, and Calcutta. In these contexts, added meanings included a strong reference to Tamil identity. Wherever there are Tamils, there are usually one or two women who are known as excellent kōlam-makers and who are called upon to help draw the kōlam for weddings, births, vows, and other special occasions.

Beyond India, many emigrant Tamil women practice the kōlam avidly. For instance, in December 1993 I was surprised to come across a kōlam—huge, bright, and lustrous—at a roadside restaurant outside of Colombo, Sri Lanka. It seemed so incongruous in the surroundings of the violence-ridden countryside that the Tamils and Sinhalese were battling over. Further, with the Tamilian diaspora the kōlam has traveled well beyond South Asia, all the way to New York City, Washington D.C. (see Chapter 1 for an autobiographical example), and Fremont, California (see Chapter 12).[16] The boom in Hindu temple-building throughout the United States, England, and even France has enhanced the visibility of the kōlam as well. Kōlams can be found in Paris, London, Malaysia, Durban, and wherever Tamils have settled throughout the world.

Although the Tamil word kōlam refers explicitly to women's ritual and threshold drawings among Tamil peoples, this type of women's ritual practice is far from unique to Tamil people (as I mentioned in Chapter 1). Numerous kōlam-like rituals are performed by women and men throughout India and, in fact, throughout the world. For example, the parallel ritual form in Andhra Pradesh is called *muggu* (Das 2011; Kilambi 1986). In Uttar Pradesh, Maharashtra, and Gujarat, rangōli is one of the women's many expressive traditions. In much of northern India, it is known as rangōli or rangāvalli (see Nagarajan 2013 and Government of India 1996). In Rajasthan, women paint walls and floors in the ritual called *māndana* (Saskena 1985 [1952]; Saksena 1979). In Bengal it is called *alpanā* (Chatterji, Das, and Tagore 1948; Das Gupta 1960).[17] Within Sanskrit traditions there are *dhuli chitrā* (Kramrisch 1983 [1968]), yantras, and mandalas; these are related but not equivalent forms.[18] In many women's ritual traditions throughout India, kōlam-like ritual diagrams serve as one of the foundations of women's *vrat* (vow) practices. Pearson observes:

> One element that appears to be distinctive of women's vrat traditions is the making of decorative and symbolic designs out of such ephemeral substances as powdered rice, wheat flour, rust colored chalk and turmeric. Maithili women (from eastern Bihar) are well known for the quality of the designs they create on their walls and floors for such occasions as weddings. (1996: 155–7)

She contextualizes these designs as an integral aspect of women's practicing of ritual vows. They are sometimes drawn to signify that which is wished or desired, or to increase the efficacy of the vow itself. In *The Earthen Drum: An*

Introduction to the Ritual Arts of Rural India, Pupul Jayakar presents a range of folk ritual arts from Indus Valley sites (about 2200–1800 BCE), including clay images, metal icons, and paintings. Some of these are ephemeral, daily practices like the kōlam, and others are more permanent forms that have lasted thousands of years. Jayakar elaborates on a range of geometric forms within these rituals that represent goddesses:

> The goddess of renowned form assumes, in time of protection, the form of a straight line. In time of dissolution, she takes the form of a circle. Similarly, for creation she takes the brilliant appearance of a triangle. . . . The symbol of sakti and Kāma-Kāla, the goddess as erotic love, is described in a Tantric text: Two circles are the two breast nipples, one circle is the face, below them are three cave-like triangles. (1980: 15)

Although she does not focus on the kōlam itself, Jayakar uses yantras and "magical drawings" to trace the presence of ritual arts among the larger categories of "The Mandalas and Magical Drawings" and "The Vrata Mandalas." She also considers the larger context of painted kathās and ephemeral images of worship within which the kōlam is embedded.

Beyond the Indian context, in Angola in Africa, there is a tradition of drawing figures in the sand called the *lusona* (Gerdes 1991) that resemble the geometric dot kōlams with lines circling in and around them. Gerdes has worked extensively in reconstructing the mathematical understandings implicit in them. (I expand on this in Chapter 7, where I delve into some of the mathematical structures underlying the kōlam.)

John Layard, an early anthropologist and folklorist in England, analyzed kōlam designs and compared them with Melanesian tattoo designs (1937).[19] Layard claimed that the kōlam originated in the ritual of the labyrinth. He connects the drawing of labyrinths in the Melanesian island of Malekula to an imagination of life after death. He refers to a book on rangāvalli (or rangoli) by Panditin Godavaribai that was published in 1867 in Mumbai. Though I was not able to track this 1867 reference, we can assume that if he had actually seen this text, which he probably did, then this is possible evidence that these kinds of chapbooks were being printed in India as early as 1867. He analyzes the kōlam ritual as an early conception of the labyrinth as an important accessory to the attainment of future life and consequently of success in this world and to prevent inauspicious and unlucky influences from entering.

Even more curiously, in the 1930s, around the same time as Layard, M. M. Banks (1935), another folklorist, published in the notes and queries section of the *Journal of Folklore* a photograph originally taken in 1908 of a kōlam-like design made on the threshold of a home in the English countryside (Figure 3.16)

Figure 3.16 Caum design on threshold in English countryside. (Source: Banks 1935.)

(also see Banks 1937). I still remember the amazement I felt when I discovered this photograph in the main library when I was a graduate student at University of California, Berkeley. I was stunned, as it had never crossed my mind that the West could have a parallel tradition to the kōlam that resembled it in eerily familiar ways. In this context, it appeared that the Western tradition of the bride leaving the threshold of her natal home and crossing over the threshold into her new married home might very well have included a kōlam-like design drawn by women.

Eurwyn Wiliam (2014), an archeologist and folklorist in England, writes brilliantly and extensively on this phenomenon. He substantiates this folk practice with extensive documentation and examples from the past 200 years. Wiliam states:

> British farmhouses and working-class homes were adorned with more ephemeral decorations as well. It was common practice in the late nineteenth and early twentieth centuries for wives, daughters and servants in such homes to decorate earth, stone and tile floors, particularly around the hearth and threshold, with patterns using a variety of materials including hearthstone, rubbing stone and the sap of green leaves. (153)

According to Wiliam, in Wales the custom was known as stoning in English, stono or (more rarely) fflowro ("to flower") in Welsh. He quotes from others who had observed the practice closely in 1850: "The blue stone floor, always clean, shines resplendent with many arabesques worked in chalk by stout, red armed Peggy, our servant girl. Peggy is quite proud of her work, and surveys its artistic effect with much satisfaction." Another report of a memory cited in 1899: "Years ago . . . considerable preparation was made for receiving a baby into the family, and for the custom associated with this, namely the coming of the neighbors to 'see.' The walls would be papered and the lime-mortared floor 'flowered' with foxglove leaves." Another witness claimed that:

> it is still the custom . . . to ornament the floor . . . in chalk or soft white stone. I have many times seen the lady of the house take a bunch of green sappy herbs and ornament her lime-mortar floor with the most quaint devices and that in a surprisingly short time. When done and dried the floor looked as if it had been covered with a green carpet and really looked well, and the pattern lasted for weeks. (153)

Another recording of this custom was in the formal inventory of historical monuments of Wales in 1914: "It is the universal custom to decorate the stone forming the threshold with a crude geometrical pattern traced with pumice stone." In 1929, a scholar reports the custom as "decorative charms." What he describes next is startlingly parallel to the Tamil custom of kōlam-making:

> Indeed, in many villages and isolated country cottages . . . the doorstep, often an undressed, fairly level slab of stone, is washed every morning and whilst wet it is chalked and left to dry. Sometimes the chalking is a kind of chain-linked pattern along the edge of the stone, the circles or links being fairly large, with another chain traced over it, the circles in this case passing through the middle of the others. Less frequently I have seen a pattern of rows, and occasionally simply a band along the edge of the stone enclosing another band. In some cottages, the same kind of pattern would be chalked indoors on the floor, along the walls. (155)

Wiliam analyzes the function of the threshold in Wales:

> As the access point to the house, the threshold was held to be "sacred" and although normal everyday entry into the house was easy, informal, and unrestricted, at certain times of the year it was governed by rules that transformed the whole question of access into a ritual and poetic

> battle of wits between the inhabitant and those wishing to gain entry. The step marked the boundary between public and private areas." (155)

Wiliam explains the various flooring types and the relationship to the kinds of decorations that were made. The reasons for making these threshold designs varied, but one of the consistent ones given was to "keep evil spirits out of the house. The patterns run around the slated steps, and elaborate as they often are, the essential thing is that there should be no gap in them, because the evil spirits could enter into the house through the gaps" (155). This explanation, indeed, connects us to one of the popular reasons Tamil women say they make the kōlam: to prevent the debilitating effects of the evil eye.

Further examples of kōlam-like ritual arts around the world include Native Californian acorn-flour threshold designs (Margolin 1981: 25) and Haiti's vodun ritual (Brown 1991). In most cases throughout the world, many of these kōlam-like rituals are performed only during special occasions. What sets the Tamil kōlam apart in the world is its everyday quality. It's not created to mark extraordinary circumstances; indeed, for the most part it indicates a state of ordinariness—that everyday life is continuing to function smoothly. Only the larger, more elaborate kōlams are made to signify a special celebration or festival of some kind.

The kōlam is a symbolic container of social and metaphorical traffic. It acts as a gathering place for aesthetics and ritual, tradition and modernity, metaphor and symbol, as well as the worlds of women and men in Tamil daily life. Braided into Tamil culture, the kōlam binds together conceptions of hospitality, prayer, celebration, the goddesses of wealth and earth, the evil eye, and the sanctity of the threshold. Like a mirror that helps us see who we are and what we look like to others, the kōlam reflects Tamil women's culture both to the insider and the outsider. A sign of the social circulation of women's energies, the kōlam is an identity marker of gender, bearing the traces of women's presence in the vicinity. Through the kōlam, women act out their roles as protectors and caretakers of the family and household. It is an integral slice of the Tamil woman's daily life, providing a glimpse of the world in which the "she" is powerful and active and communicates directly with the powers of the divine. These fluid, ephemeral designs mark the conversations between the woman of the household and the divine.

4

Thresholds

We make the kōlam to indicate auspiciousness
and to prevent ritual pollution.

—Janaki, Tirunagar village

The Kōlam on the Front Stoop and the Red Dot on the Forehead

As we have discovered, kōlams are used to mark space: the thresholds of shrines, houses, and temples and the edges of streets, trees, and stones. They also mark time: dawn and dusk, the month of the winter solstice, the rice harvest festival of Pongal. The absence of a kōlam marks time in a different way. It could mean the onset of menstruation, illness, or death. It could express laziness, poverty, or a lack of interest. It could signify that the household is not Hindu (perhaps Christian, Muslim, Sikh, Buddhist, or Jain, though sometimes some of these communities also perform the ritual). Or it could signify that the woman is a very modern Hindu woman who has a busy, cosmopolitan worldview and does not believe in the efficacy of performing such rituals.

In the village of Thirulaiyaru, I spoke with a Brahmin grandmother in her home, who told me that the *pottu* is to the body what the kōlam is to the house. The pottu (or bindi as it is called in Hindi or Sanskrit) abounds in everyday life; it is a red dot that is centered in the middle of a woman's forehead. Traditionally, the design, which can be either one or two dots, has been a filled circle of red or shades of burnt sienna—a reflection of its mercury oxide nature. Today the colors can be parrot green, magenta, bright yellow, or any range of colors that match the woman's sari or outfit. In other words, the pottu is no longer limited to the more traditional shades of dark red.[1] Many women, including myself, often use stick-on forehead dots for their convenience because of the need to move rapidly in modern society. The traditional powdered version is something you have to put on frequently throughout the day, and the turmeric intermixed with the mercury oxide can leave a stain on your clothes.

It took me many years to realize that these two kinds of ritual designs--the kōlam and the pottu—are more intimately connected than I first imagined; they form a kind of kinship with each other, mirroring and echoing each other. They are parallel ritual expressions of complicated and nuanced concepts such as auspiciousness and inauspiciousness, purity and pollution. These keywords (Williams 1983) are central to understanding the inherent ambivalence of expressive ritual power in Tamil women.[2]

Many scholars have addressed this question in anthropological literature on India. The key anthropologist who has explored the ambivalence of female ritual power is Frederique Apffell-Marglin, who focuses on the *dēvadāsi* (temple dancer) tradition in Orissa. Her two books, *Wives of the God-King: The Rituals of the Dēvadāsis in Puri* (Apffell-Margalin 1985) and *Purity and Auspiciousness* (Carman and Apffel-Margalin 1985)[3] carefully and sensitively tease apart the various ways in which auspiciousness, inauspiciousness, purity, and pollution intersect, overlap, and contradict each other. These two texts were critical for my understanding of the dual notions of auspiciousness and ritual pollution. Isabelle Nabokov (2000) discusses the ways in which certain rituals toward the dead shape the "self," creating a larger sense of identity but at other times fragmenting the identity; in doing so she thoughtfully and provocatively pushes the Tamil conception of the edge of the self.[4]

The visual presence of the pottu, kōlam, and other forms of ritual traces of worship indicate that a space has been initiated for ritual purposes. A comparison of the kōlam with the pottu deepens our understanding of the way visual signs function metaphorically and spatially.

As Mangalapatti from the village of Rengalachetty once said to me, "The kōlam is the pottu of the house; the pottu is the kōlam of the house. Do you understand how that is so?" Lakoff and Johnson, leading scholars of metaphor theory, have observed; "The essence of metaphor is understanding and experiencing one kind of thing in terms of another" (1980: 5). So, too, it is with the kōlam and the pottu.

This chapter explores how ritual marks on the thresholds of houses and on bodies mean what they mean. In my many conversations with Tamil women over the years, I found that one of the most common leitmotifs of the kōlam on the front stoop is that it indicates "auspiciousness and prevents ritual pollution." They are binary in that both their presence and their absence carry meaning. What is confusing to the outsider standing on the threshold is that the presence or absence of the kōlam can mean a number of things. You can't be sure what is going on in the household without pulling together a multitude of clues and signs.

The pottu on the forehead, similarly, reflects a state of being. When present, it signifies auspiciousness. When absent, it could reflect a state of ritual pollution. Ritual pollution is a concept that, though not unique to India, is prevalent throughout Indian cultural forms. It could be associated with either a body or a household that is filled with death, or something that is associated with death, or anything that is considered "unclean." Unclean often means the presence of blood such as from menstruation, the slaughtering of animals, childbirth, and so on. Yet it can also mean tears from grief, suffering, or illness. In contrast, a state of auspiciousness is signified by life-enhancing and life-giving qualities. While the two states are both accepted as part of the wholeness of life, they are nevertheless often kept separate from each other.

Auspiciousness: What does this word mean to us now? The denotation of the English word implies a good omen, a bringing forth of success, or giving promise of a favorable future possibility. An old-fashioned word, it could be attached to a person or a thing and generally means something favorable, propitious, kind, having good fortune, happiness, or promising prospects. Shakespeare spoke of "promising auspicious gales" in *The Tempest* (*Oxford English Dictionary*, 1987). The word *auspiciousness* is rarely used in contemporary English, but the roughly equivalent Tamil and Sanskrit word *mangalam* is popular and present in everyday life among many castes, classes, and regions.

Technically, according to the *Tamil Lexicon*, mangalam means luckiness, auspiciousness, propitiousness, achievement, means of accomplishment, splendor, good deeds, goodness, virtue, excellence, prayer, and blessing. I think of mangalam as an essential goodness, or an orientation of goodness toward yourself, your family, your community, and your world. It is also a consequence of acting from a place of goodness or positive intentionality. By doing so you create an echo of goodness back toward yourself, and all that you love flows over you, your family, your community, and your world.

Mangalam also refers to auspicious objects, such as the marriage necklace, which in Hinduism serves a similar ritual function to the wedding ring in Christianity (*Tamil Lexicon* 1982). A variety of words are joined with mangalam to evoke auspiciousness; for example:

Mangala-chol refers to an auspicious word, or language of benediction or blessing.

Mangala-chūthiram is the twisted thread in which the tāli, or pendant, is strung.

Mangala-thirunal are the holy days of a festival.

Mangala-nathi refers to a sacred river.

Mangala-perathai means turmeric, bards, or letter of marriage invitation.

Mangala-purushan refers to a man who is always happy.

Mangala-pathinaru refers to the 16 auspicious objects, including sword, umbrella, fan, conch, seat, head ornament, royal discus, pots containing fragrant drops, and so on.

Mangala-mukūrtham refers to the auspicious hour.

Mangala-snaanam is the bath at the beginning of an auspicious ceremony.

Mangala-devi refers to a goddess; Lakshmi, Parvathi, and Durga are considered to be the most mangala goddesses.

Mangali or mangalai is a married woman.

Mangala-pichhai is when a wife prays to save the life of her husband when he is in danger, the begging of auspiciousness like the ancient Hindu myth of Savithri.

There are many pages in the *Tamil Lexicon* of variations of this kind of mangalam, which implies sacredness, goodness, holiness, and a state of blessedness. Mangala also suggests an underlying sense of completed tasks, finished work—a sense of unbrokenness and completeness. The complex worldview that the word or concept mangala reveals is located, thus, in layer after layer of cultural folds of meanings.

Amangala or *mangu-thal* is the opposite of mangalam. It means to grow less; to diminish; to become dim, as when light dims at sunset or when the eyesight goes; to grow pale; to lose luster; to be obscured in splendor and glory; to fade, as in beauty; to decline in prosperity; to be reduced in circumstances, power, or authority; to be deprived of freshness (as in the countenance); to be in decay, to be ruined, to die, and to perish. It connotes a time of dearth or adversity, unpropitiousness, cloudiness, dullness, doubtfulness, confusion of mind, or gloominess.

Thus, the desire for mangalam, and not the lessening of it, is very much in people's minds when they embark for the day. They have a sense that anything untoward or unplanned can happen. Making your wishes for the positive known to yourself, to the goddesses and gods, and to the outside world is thought to be an integral part of the concept of mangalam.

What we see here is a desire for that moment of fullness before the fading. We may wish for good luck and prosperity and no harm to our loved ones and good health, but in the back of our minds we know that mangalam never lasts forever. Sooner or later, we all encounter calamity. The Japanese express this idea using the term *waki-saki*, or noticing the ephemerality of beauty or the inevitability of suffering.

I see these ritual marks of auspiciousness as a form of communication, a way of letting what is or is not happening inside the house or the body to be visible to the outside world. They represent a silent but visible announcement of levels of auspiciousness and bind together a multitude of strands of local vernacular thought.[5] The question I am interested in figuring out is: How do the kōlam and the pottu define and articulate these concepts of auspiciousness and ritual pollution?

The kōlam functions as a key semiotic indicator on the Tamil cultural landscape, mapping the individual's passage from degrees of ritual purity and auspiciousness to those of ritual pollution. It also, I think, speaks out of a cosmology or worldview that is soaked through with the ritual imagination of time and space. When a "traditional" Tamil woman looks out of her stoop, she witnesses her world as contoured, shaped, and punctuated by these kinds of nonlinear ritual marks that reveal this embodied worldview.[6]

The kōlam is linked to auspicious and ritual pollution in three important ways: (1) its presence or absence prescribes social relationships, determining the boundaries of appropriate interaction between auspicious and inauspicious people, places, and objects; (2) its location marks several types of thresholds, both spatial and temporal, indicating the boundaries between auspicious and inauspicious worlds; and (3) conversations surrounding the kōlam connect the notions of mangala (auspiciousness), amangala (inauspiciousness), mati (ritual purity), turam (particular menstrual pollution of ritual distance), or teetu (generalized ritual pollution). Here I will focus on the folk notions of auspiciousness and ritual pollution, which are active, fluid, and porous in the sense that they aren't fixed as they shape and constrain the domestic interactions of Tamil women.

Presence and Absence of Kōlam on the Front Stoop

The presence or absence of the kōlam on the front stoop is equivalent to announcing that a household is open or closed to the world. When I see a kōlam, I know that the woman is functioning at a high level of openness and the household is open to being approached by outsiders. If I were a wandering sadhu, an ochre-dressed holy man or woman, a minstrel or a beggar, I would see the house as a possible site of hospitality where I might receive a meal or some rice in my begging-bowl. The presence of a kōlam would indicate that this household is healthy, so it may have a surplus to give to the community. However, if there is no kōlam, people who come to visit may use the back entrance, thinking that there could have been a calamity during the night.

Telegraphing receptivity and hospitality, the presence of the kōlam indicates the continuity of active domestic life for yet another day—the ability of the household to serve as a welcoming host to visitors. As one Tamil Brahmin woman, Lakshmi, from the village of Aiyappur said, "Listen, Vijaya, in the time before phones and telegraphs, the kōlam was the way we found out what happened in the house during the night. If there was a huge vishesham (special event) kōlam, and we knew that there was no wedding planned that day, then we may guess that a baby has been born or the girl in the house has come of age." She mentioned this last part because a girl's first menstruation is announced with a huge kōlam, celebrated and acknowledged publicly as auspicious, even though menstruation in general is considered polluting. The first blood of a growing girl spells the loss of her childhood and the loss of blood indicates a potential death-like state. Here, then, is the paradoxical category of the auspicious but ritual polluting status. The birth of a child, likewise, is both auspicious and ritually polluting, and a giant kōlam will appear as a birth announcement. Until recently, the experience of childbirth was akin to a near-death experience.

In the words of Padma, an 83-year-old Tamil Brahmin Iyengar woman in Srivilliputtur (a traditional small town where the famous saint Āṇṭāḷ is thought to have been born in the ninth century): "If someone dies, then one should not put the kōlam for one year. Otherwise, if someone has not died, you have to put the kōlam every day. If you do not put the kōlam, it is *akkiyanam* (spiritual ignorance). That means someone will die in your house. You should not *not* put the kōlam. You have to put the kōlam." Therefore, if the presence of the kōlam is a generous invitation for the outside world to come in, its absence might indicate its opposite—a closed household, a site of suffering, death, and other ritually polluted or polluting states of being. I say "might" because there can also be other reasons for its absence: if a woman is experiencing menstruation or childbirth, if she is ill, or when there has been a death in the family she is not expected to make the kōlam. She is considered to be in an incapacitated state and not in a position to be giving.

The continued absence of the kōlam signifies the gradual ebbing of suffering in the family, and its reappearance visually marks the end of the period of suffering and ritual pollution. Suffering is accepted as an inevitable part of everyday life, and the kōlam makes this state comprehensible by recognizing it, accepting it, and announcing it to the community as a whole. As one Kerala Tamil woman put it, "The kōlam is done to prevent future suffering, to be able to manage our current suffering, so we know when it is happening around us, to reduce tension, a kind of meditation." Suffering is to be known and publicly acknowledged in hopes of being prevented. Veena Das beautifully explains what externally oriented suffering is:

> [The external orientation] holds suffering to be accidental . . . holds existence to be blameworthy but points to the capriciousness of the gods, the inexplicability of the world, and the contingency of life as

> the reasons for suffering. It does not make the sufferer internalize her suffering, nor does it posit a meaningful world or a just god or a comprehensive scientific discourse within which suffering can be made comprehensible. Dare one say that it gives irresponsibility a positive sense (1995: 139–40)

Thus, the Hindu concepts of auspiciousness and ritual pollution make possible both the recognition and the celebration of joy as well as the interpretation and support of suffering. It might be said that the visual sign of the kōlam affirms life with its presence and affirms suffering with its absence. The kōlam enjoins all who enter the house to mingle in the emotional state of the household, whether it is joyful because of a happy event or people are suffering because of a terrible calamity. As Clifford Geertz, one of the leading anthropologists of the last century, once said: "The problem of suffering is, paradoxically, not *how* to avoid suffering, but how to suffer, how to make of physical pain, personal loss, physical defeat, or the helpless contemplation of others' agony something bearable, supportable—something, as we say sufferable" (1973: 104; italics are mine).

Therefore, we can say that the kōlam is a sign of a community's visibility of suffering, as well as over chaos and pollution (Hart 1973, 1979). By providing an orientation to the emotional state of the household for the community, the kōlam imposes a pattern on the landscape that reveals the existence of satisfaction, happiness, and suffering in each individual household.

The presence or absence of a kōlam on the threshold visually cues outsiders on what to expect and therefore how to behave with the family. For example, the absence of the kōlam may prompt neighbors and friends to look in on the household and bring gifts of food and clothing or to offer comfort. An absent kōlam prescribes a supportive response from the viewer to the suffering of the householders. It also engenders a sense of responsibility to enter the household in an empathetic emotional state. In this way, the kōlam affirms suffering by structuring the community's response in situations of grief, pain, and loss.

The Pottu, or Dot on the Forehead

If the kōlam marks a boundary to a building, the pottu marks a boundary to the body. Commonly consisting of one or two red dots and occasionally a black line, the pottu or bindi can have a multitude of forms and meanings, telegraphing relevant cultural information to informed viewers. The pottu varies in frequency, style, and color, according to the woman's caste, religion, class, and marital status. As with the kōlam, through the presence or absence of the pottu, a woman is visually communicating her state of mind. For example, it reveals whether she is available for marriage or unavailable, among other things. This guides people's behavior toward to her, letting them know whether they can joke with her as a sister or must bow down with respect as to a married or older woman.

The absence of a dot is akin to the absence of the kōlam. A black line generally indicates a prepubescent girl, who is still considered a child. This status implies that she is "teasable" in the way that a younger sister is, and that she is able to receive gifts from a broader range of people in the community with no special meaning attached. If a mature Hindu woman is not wearing a pottu, it is likely that she is a widow. However, if other signs do not corroborate this (e.g., wearing a beige or white sari and no jewelry), then the absence of a pottu could indicate she is menstruating or in a mourning state, or that she is just too busy working to put on a pottu—or she may be a modern woman who wants to show that she is not traditional. Some women believe that placing the pottu on their forehead can bring about a long life for their husband, either the one she has at present or the one she might have in the future. It is believed, then, that a Hindu woman may have the ability to keep her husband alive. The other side of this belief comes to the fore for widows, who are believed to have a conscious or unconscious desire for their husbands *not* to have a long life, and it is this perversity that has sometimes led to the maltreatment of widows in India. Non-Hindu women who wear the pottu, such as Christians or Muslims (which is rare), may be making more of a fashion statement than the repertoire of signs that the pottu means for a Hindu woman.

When the dot on the forehead is present, it signifies that a girl is past her first menstruation and therefore eligible for betrothal and eventually marriage. The red color of the pottu has both a literal and metaphorical significance. In Tamil culture, red is usually worn after a girl has passed the stage of "blood magic," or puberty (Buckley 1988). Red is one of the key colors of the sari worn during the wedding ceremony and also symbolizes the potential and actual power of fertility and, just as important, potential sexuality. Among certain sub-castes, if a woman is wearing two red pottus, one in the center of her forehead and the other at her hairline, this signifies that she is married. In West Bengal, the red powder is pressed onto the center-parted hairline and continued onward partway along the hairline.

Kramrisch has observed the significance of the color red in the kōlam: "Sometimes the threshold is dressed in red dots, similar to the red dot commonly seen on an Indian woman's forehead. The dot is a symbol of the seed, the source of life" (1985: 252; 1983: 105–7). She also says that the threshold zone is "protected by the design traced on the floor in an unbroken line forming loops and enclosures, each marked by a dot in its center" (1985: 245–54).

The woman of the household is well aware that her power stems from being able to create mangala (auspiciousness), and she wears indicators such as the pottu, bindi, tāli (wedding necklace), toe rings, or henna on her hands and feet to acknowledge this fact. Each morning, after her "purification" bath and before she puts the new pottu on her forehead, she offers a prayer for the longevity of her present or future husband, her family, both near and far, and the larger, wider community. The belief is that she has the ability to keep her husband alive, and therein lies some of her power as bearer and container of auspiciousness. At this time she is also considered to be in a non-polluting state, capable of personal and household generosity to the community.

The red powdered dot is also placed on new clothes as they are offered to the deities of the household shrine before being worn for the first time, offered to household guests on their departure, and made as a sign of a recent visit to a household or temple shrine (both males and females). However, these signifiers have less importance today. In recent years, the markings have shifted from being a religious ritual to being a beauty enhancer, like just another kind of makeup. Consequently, the way the pottu is used (or not used) transcends caste, class, and religious affiliation and may be more of a fashion statement.

There is even a political connotation here. Many modern women in India, including feminists and postcolonialists, refuse to wear the pottu. They see it as a leftover symbol of patriarchy and the age-old oppression of women. Chandralekha, the dancer-philosopher, saw the bindi as a way of rediscovering traditional forms of women's ritual power and reinfusing them with contemporary significance and meaning. She once told me with great passion and intensity, "We cannot let the Hindu right usurp our rich Hindu symbols. We must not give them away as if they were worthless and unimportant; they are our riches, too. We, on the left, cannot and must not give them up; we must reinvigorate them, as if they mattered in our present times." So the pottu, too, is a richly layered, contested symbol of Hinduism, of womanliness and auspiciousness.

Bringing the Kōlam and Pottu Together

As we noted earlier, metaphorically, the pottu is to the body as the kōlam is to the house. Just as the kōlam marks the threshold between the interior of the household and the community outside, the pottu on the forehead marks the threshold between the internal body/soul and the external world. The same visual metaphor can be observed in the red henna that is applied to the hands and feet as a ritual marker of ceremonial time and space, as in marriage ceremonies or during festivals. The significance of the literal and metaphorical edges of the body is elaborated in folktales, proverbs, notions of hospitality, and there are many stories about the inauspicious consequences that follow if a woman does not put a kōlam on her threshold or a pottu on her forehead (see the section on folktales in Chapter 3).

As we have seen, the kōlam is a way of bringing about the fulfillment of a woman's wishes. A woman's power to create a sphere of "positive intentionalities" moves in two directions: outward to the world beyond the threshold, and inward to the household. The "auspicious" power travels from the woman's hands through the kōlam and upward into the feet and bodies of those passing through its energy field. The pottu is also a way of projecting a woman's power to bless her body and those of her family.

Marking Thresholds of Space and Time

Another way the kōlam expresses concepts of auspiciousness and ritual pollution, in addition to its presence and absence, is through its location in space and time. In other words, it is created at particular places at particular times, indicating the boundaries between the auspicious and inauspicious worlds.

The spatial threshold is a powerful metaphor in Indian secular and ceremonial life, a charged location between two spaces, one of which is ritually pure or impure and one of which is auspicious or inauspicious. The kōlam is created on three types of spatial thresholds: (1) the household shrine in the kitchen (where holy shrine meets practical kitchen), (2) the entrance to the main house, and (3) the entryway to the local temple. As we have seen, the most common site for a kōlam is the front entrance to the house, distinguishing inside from outside, household from commons, and private from public. Kōlams on household shrines and interior thresholds mark the movement of family members from the inner sanctum into all the interior doorways all the way to the front door—the place where the house meets the street. Kōlams in doorways of temples announce the arrival from secular to sacred space.

First, the kōlam on the household shrine in the kitchen marks the woman's domain, creating a threshold between the secular kitchen activities and the separate and sacred space of the divinities inhabiting the shrine. The gods face the worshipper from the east (the most highly valued sacred direction), and the worshipper prays toward the glancing gods. In relation to the rest of the house, the kitchen is considered to be the abode of the gods and goddesses in the secular world of the householder because it is the place where the food is prepared. The preparation of food is considered a sacred activity, turning matter into energy. It is the center where all the family's ritual activities are started, maintained, and completed. In fact, the entire cooking area is the literal and metaphorical hearth—the spiritual and psychological core of the household—and the most valued site for generating auspiciousness. Architecturally, the kitchen is also the most protected part of the household. One of the few fully walled and bounded rooms, it is the most distant from the outside world (Blier 1995).

The second type of kōlam is created on and beyond the threshold of the main body of the house, facing the village path and dividing inside and outside, known and unknown, safe and unsafe worlds. Proceeding down the village street, you can observe that each household marked with a kōlam is in an auspicious state of being. Between sacred and profane, auspicious and inauspicious, controllable and uncontrollable, the threshold guards the house from the chaos of the outside world. This design on the front of the house demarcates the ritually polluted commons from the private, auspicious domesticated household space. David Shulman, one of the leading scholars of Hinduism, has eloquently referred to the kōlam as a protective, invisible three-dimensional form in front of the house. Although it is seen through its visible two-dimensional form, in an imaginary sense, it not only lies on the street in two dimensions, but it projects upward to protect the entire space in front of the house like an invisible wall or barrier. Shulman points to the threshold area as the "point at which it [the kōlam] emerges into form—a complex form at that, carefully planned and executed, a reflection of some inner labyrinth externalized here at the boundary, the line dividing the inner and the outer, the pure from the chaotic" (1985: 3). This type of kōlam may also be seen as a visual metaphor for the division of the commons, the shared public civil space, from the controlled and contained space of the home, and therefore, metonymically, the woman of the house.

The significance of the threshold in Tamil culture is reiterated by A. K. Ramanujan's work in Tamil poetics. He describes the classical Sangam poetic division of the "interior" (*aham*) and the "exterior" (*puram*).[7] In his translation of the poet Dēvara Dāsimayya we can see the importance of the front yard or first threshold of the household. Dāsimayya says:

> To the utterly at-one with Śiva
> there's no dawn,
> no new moon,
> no noonday,
> nor equinoxes,
> nor sunsets,
> nor full moons;
> his front yard
> is the true Benares,
> —O Rāmanātha (Ramanujan 1985 [1973]: 105)

Dāsimayya's reference to his front yard being the true Benares was echoed in many women's description of the kōlam on the threshold of the house being like the river Ganges. The Ganges flows through Benares and is a part of what makes Benares so sacred (Eck 1982a).

The third type of kōlam is made at the village temple. Typically, temples have a series of entryways leading to the center where the divine image is located. The kōlam delineates each temple threshold from the preceding one. In a South Indian temple, a kōlam marks each threshold for the advancing worshipper, from the outer entrance to the innermost "womb-chamber" of the divinities. This sequence of kōlams in a temple marks the passage of worshippers as they travel to the interior shrine to visit the gods and goddesses and receive *darshan*, or blessing (Eck 1985). At the edge of a village, a temple may be conceptualized as a giant, three-dimensional kōlam marking the threshold where the village ends and the rest of the world begins. Here again, the kōlam maps the journey from the street, which is a ritually polluted space, to the sacred temple, which is a ritually pure space. The three types of thresholds can be seen as an ever-widening circle proceeding from the deep innermost part of the structure, to its edge, to the public buildings of the temples.

The designs of the kōlams drawn in the kitchens, doorways, and temples reflect symbolic *tirthas* (Sanskrit, "crossings")—that is, spaces to be crossed with a consciousness of the sacred (Eck 1981). When a space has been sacralized, people within it have a more generous orientation simply because they have announced that they are a functioning and abundant household.

Kōlams at the front entrance to the house are made as an offering and a blessing; they are stepped on and erased slowly under passing feet. Because the kōlam is considered sacred, stepping on it transfers some of that sacredness to the person, just as the blessed waters of the Ganges pass on sacredness to the bather. In the words of one Tamil woman, "Stepping on the kōlam is like stepping into the Ganges River." Another woman agreed: "Stepping on the kōlam is akin to taking a bath in the sacred Ganges River, an act that purifies body and spirit."

The door to the house has the most contact with the outside world and therefore is considered the least sacred space. Therefore, the kōlam in front of the house, depending on the design's degree of sacrality, is meant to be trampled on. In contrast, the kōlam at a household shrine should not be stepped on because it marks the center of the sacred space. The temple's kōlam should also not be trampled on because it is believed to be highly charged with divine energy. Kōlams made at household shrines function as porous boundaries between earthly and divine realms, while those made within temples are part of a continuum of sacredness.

Thresholds in Time

The temporal demarcation that the kōlam marks is the threshold between night and day and between day and night. That's why it must be created before the sun rises every day, at that point when darkness is transformed into light, when the world is in a state of "betwixt and between." (As I noted before, the kōlam used to be performed at sunset as well.) In Hinduism, a great deal of ritual life occurs at dawn. As I mentioned in Chapter 3, the time between 4 and 5:30 a.m. is called *Brahma muhurta*, or "the time of God's face," when the deities turn their faces toward humans. The kōlam is a visual, aesthetic signal designed to attract the gaze of the divinities.

The kōlam could be considered a parallel to the male yogic positions of the *surya asana*, "the worship of the sun," in the sense that both of these rituals honor the sun god, Surya, and are to be done before dawn in order to become aware of the penetration of the sun's rays into the body and to consciously welcome the sun into one's everyday life. I say "could" because historically yogic postures were primarily done by men as a way of paying homage to the sun; the kōlam can be seen as a kind of female yoga. What is interesting is that women make the kōlam as a way of welcoming the sun into the household at exactly the same time of the day. The whole practice of addressing the sun is so significant that the ritual practice of drawing a symbol on the ground is mentioned in the Rig Veda, which is over 3,000 years old. According to Stella Kramrisch:

> The most ancient Sanskrit treatise on Indian painting prescribes the worship of the sun god through an eight-petaled lotus flower drawn on the ground. Several other Purānas speak of the art of drawing the sun on the ground and that the sun was worshipped in a circle in early days. However, this practice was not sanctioned by the Vedas; it belonged to those outside the Vedic pale. The drawing of a magic diagram on the floor, however, became essential in building a Hindu temple. (1983: 105–7)

Kramrisch here sets the stage for understanding the magic that was embedded in the worship of the sun by drawing an "eight-petaled lotus flower" on the ground—which happens to be the most common motif in the kōlam, and highly auspicious in and of itself. This may be the earliest specific design motif reference in eons of Indian literature.

What is also worth exploring is the broader relationship between auspiciousness and time. Madan points out one of the congruencies between the two:

> There are many auspicious and inauspicious moments in one's life, just as there are in a day. The most auspicious moment of the day is the rising of the sun. It fills the earth, the sky, and the heavens with light and brings with it the promise of good works and wisdom for men . . . sunrise manifests the glory of God, enlivens our intelligence, and purifies the whole earth. (1987: 48)

In addition to demarcating the boundary between night and day, the kōlam serves another important temporal function. The month during which the winter solstice occurs, mid-December to mid-January (which is called Margali in the Tamil lunar calendar), is the time of year when the sun is at its lowest point in the sky. During this period, kōlam-making marks the sun's nadir, which is the zenith of the Tamil agricultural cycle. Margali is considered to be the month that spans the beginning of one day in the life of a divinity. In other words, if one year in human experience is equivalent to one day in the community of gods and goddesses, then Margali is the beginning of a new divine day.

At the end of Margali and the beginning of the next month, Thai, is a threshold period that is celebrated with the Pongal festival, the most popular festival across all castes and classes throughout Tamil Nadu. This is a highly auspicious time for the community, signifying the abundance of the fields during the harvest. In the village Krishnagudi, Chellamma, a young, lively woman from a dalit caste, who lived in a lovely house with beautiful squash plants gracing its side and roof, expressed joyful anticipation at this time of year:

> The ammans [goddesses] are coming . . . We feel this is when everything good is coming. The happiness . . . is coming. Food is coming. Children are coming. Wealth is coming. Beauty is where the divine comes from. Rice is turned in. The fields are brimming over with the harvests. It is when we are at the wealthiest time of our year and most hopeful of financial security.

The kōlam is the site where the woman of the household hosts the divinities of rice, wealth, and the earth itself.

Kōlam-making reaches its annual peak during Margali and its monthly peak during the Pongal festival, when the best and most elaborate kōlams are created. Draping the kōlam on every surface imaginable becomes the event of the day. This is an auspicious time for honoring the divinities but an inauspicious time for human celebrations. As Geetha, a young woman, put it:

> The reason we create such elaborate kōlams during the month of Margali is because the threshold, the doorway between heaven and earth, is the most open during this time. It is the time to communicate with the gods and goddesses. That is why we go on pilgrimage during that time. It is also a great time to die, because you automatically go to heaven. It is a bit like dying on the banks of the Ganga.

On the other hand, Margali is considered a highly inappropriate time for marriage because one's energies should be devoted to spiritual rather than material matters.

The temporal appearance and disappearance of the kōlam spans multiple castes, families, lineages, and religions. As mentioned in Chapter 3, Christians might make substantially larger and denser kōlams on Christmas Day. Hindu orthodox castes mark the period between mid-July and mid-August with dense kōlams, and other families or castes may mark the festivals of individual saints that are particularly related to them.

When the Kōlam and the Red Dot are Absent

Paradoxically, as I have mentioned before, while some activities and experiences such as childbirth and menstruation are considered to be ritually polluting, they are also valued as auspicious and life-affirming. My interest in the concept of ritual pollution stems from a lifelong awareness of its multifaceted nature within Indian culture. To an outsider, the isolation during the state of menstrual ritual pollution may seem like an inconvenience or insult to women, which I mostly agree with, but I suggest that it can also be a period of welcome rest and conviviality. The positive—or at the very least ambivalent—aspects of ritual pollution are rarely reflected in fieldwork accounts of childbirth, menstruation, or death. I will share two personal stories that hint at these underlying emotional paradoxes.

One of my earliest encounters with the idea of ritual pollution took place during that long visit in our ancestral village, Rettakudi, when I was nine years old (mentioned in Chapter 1). Our family had just returned to India from America, and I was encountering many aspects of Indian culture that I had forgotten about or not known. A few weeks after we arrived, my mother simply disappeared from view and I couldn't find her anywhere. Whenever I asked my father or grandparents where she was, they looked away as though I had asked a very embarrassing question. Curious and sad, I thought my elders were hiding something ominous from me. I concluded that my Amma must have either run away or died. My elders seemed oblivious to my grief.

Not one to give up easily, the next day I followed my grandmother all around the house, at a discreet distance. I felt like Pippi Longstocking. After we had eaten lunch and everyone was moving to their respective corners for napping, I suddenly noticed my grandmother putting together a simple meal of rice and vegetables and wrapping it carefully in banana leaves. But why? The whole family had already eaten. She walked out the back of the house, through the cowshed that circled it, and on toward the front. I followed her, wondering who she could possibly be on the way to feed so surreptitiously. Standing behind the door of the cowshed, I watched her walk across the dusty wayside path and place the small bundle before the threshold of a little hut that I had never noticed before. Her gestures were distant, as if she were making an offering to a goddess or to someone who was untouchable.

To my surprise, she called out my mother's name and announced, "The food is here! Is everything going well?" My mother's voice, restful and contemplative, answered softly with a faint ring, as if from a distance, "I'm fine, Amma, thanks. How is everything out there?" I was deliriously happy to hear my mother's voice at last. *She is alive after all!* I thought. *I hear her voice, and now I must see her. Or maybe she's just a ghost from the dead.* My grandmother, meanwhile, replied in an amused tone, "Your older daughter, Vijaya, is giving us lots of trouble. She keeps thinking you have disappeared. She doesn't at all understand what is going on. Don't you teach her anything useful in America?"

As soon as my grandmother returned to the main house, I saw my mother's bangled hand reach across the threshold to pick up her food. The shadow of her form appeared and disappeared so quickly that I wondered if I had only imagined it. Leaping across the threshold of the little hut, I felt as if I were on a dangerous mission to rescue my mother and return her to the main house. I pushed open the heavy wooden door and cried out with joy. The room was very dark, and I could barely see my mother's form lying in a shadow-laden, dusty corner. I thought again with great relief, *She's still alive!*

I dashed inside, but then stopped abruptly, puzzled by what I saw. My mother was frowning and seemed angry with me, and I noticed that she had no pottu (red dot) on her forehead. She also looked different in that her hair was in disarray, unbound, and relaxed, away from the prying eyes of a dense household community.

Upon seeing me, she said sharply, "Shoo! Get out, you silly monkey child! You shouldn't be here."

"But, Amma, I thought you had died!" I blurted out, jumping happily into her lap and blithely ignoring her instructions. "Why are you here? Is this where you have been all this time? Nobody would tell me where you were. I am so happy you are still alive! Can I take you back to the main house now?"

She replied:

> No, don't touch me. I hope no one saw you. I am turam [distant]; no one can touch me now. Listen, don't tell your grandmother you came here. She would be very upset if she knew. But it is probably all right; you're still a child so it shouldn't affect you because you didn't realize the effects of your actions. But don't tell anyone you have seen me. I am turam . . . later I will tell you what that means. I promise to be back tomorrow. Just think that your mother didn't have to work for three days, and she's having some quiet resting time and reading her magazines. So, run off, my foolish little monkey—and be sure to wash your hands and body wherever parts of your body touched mine. But don't go in through the front door of the house. Enter the backyard through the

> cowshed at the side of the house, and wash at the water pump or the well. Look around and make sure no one sees what you are doing. Then wait a while before you touch your grandmother. She is madi [pure], you know.

Puzzled and disturbed by her behavior and her stern tone of voice, surprising in my mother's usual indulgent self, I rose out of her lap, left the little hut, and washed as she had instructed. Then, contrary to all I had been told, I ran into the main house and immediately demanded of my grandmother, "What is my Amma doing in that house? Why have you put her there?" She replied with the mysterious word *turam* again. She added, "For three days your Amma will be in the other house, and then she will come out and join us on the fourth day, after she's washed her hair. Then she can eat with us again."

From that day onward, I began to notice the sudden disappearance and reappearance of other women to and from the small huts scattered throughout the village, set apart from the main houses, paralleling the sudden disappearance and reappearance of the kōlams. The neighboring women would bring food to these huts for each other, and a few days later all the mothers, wives, and daughters would return with glistening freshly washed wet hair, once again considered "touchable."

I had mixed feelings then as a child, and I still do now as an adult, with the practice of isolating orthodox women during menstruation in a village. It is important, however, to place this experience in context. Even back then, this was done only in villages, not in towns and cities. In cities these rules had already been relaxed even as far back as the 1970s. In single-family households, which were becoming more common in cities, there was no one to take care of a woman's duties while she took three days off for ritual reasons, so there was no way these rules could be followed. They can only be practiced more easily in an extended-family household.

Menstrual Distance in Suburban Maryland

As a teenager, whenever American friends crossed the threshold to our home in suburban Maryland, their first comments were invariably about the-rice flour paintings that my mother created on the threshold each morning. "What is that? Can I step on it?" they would always ask. Of the pottu I wore most days on my forehead, my friends would ask whether it was blood. "Is it going to spill out of your forehead? Why are you wearing a red dot? Do you have to put it on every single day? What would happen to you if you didn't wear it?"

If one of the women in our house was *veetil illai*, or "not in the house" (menstruating), or if all four of us (my mother, myself, and my two younger sisters) were "not in the house," my astonished and puzzled friends would witness my father running back and forth between the kitchen and the living room serving tea, sweets, and the cooked food he had prepared. He would discreetly set the food down at a suitable distance from himself; we would wait until he moved away, and only then would we eat. We had become turam, or "distant." I never told my American girlfriends what was going on, as I was afraid that there would be too much misunderstanding between us. My friends' eyes would enlarge in surprise, but they never asked me a question and I never offered an explanation. I felt as if the two worlds I moved through were coming into contact, and I wasn't sure how to translate one world into the next.

Whenever I think of menstrual time, an amusing image comes to mind: my father backing fearfully away from us as we playfully stretched our hands to him over the threshold of our ritually polluted spaces and encroached upon his ritually pure space. He would retreat, fast, beseeching us to stop, saying with panic and annoyance, "Don't touch me, don't come closer!" as if even the intersection of the ritually pure and impure would cause him enormous pain or destroy him in some way. The look of terror in his eyes and the cold stiffness in his face were not ones we saw often. As a teenager, it made me feel powerful to think that I could make my father fear me because I was a woman who had become turam.

Since menstruating women were not allowed near spaces where gods and goddesses were housed (in temples and kitchens), my sisters and I could not touch anything in the kitchen and consequently could not do any housework at that "time of month." I remember the times spent "not in the house" as restful, unruly, indulgent, and playful—periods when we were permitted to be completely lazy. All three of us young women were treated particularly well; we were served with tea, food, and sweets and our wishes were fulfilled, with no effort on our part except asking for them.

When the fourth day arrived, we would take our head baths and become ritually pure again, losing our special space of quiet and rest. Reflecting on this experience, it is not difficult to see that this kind of bodily experience of ritual pollution had its own mix of positive and negative valences in terms of women's sacredness and ritual power. The emotional and cultural ambiguity of ritual pollution illustrates the living paradox of women's ritual domestic power.

Mapping Auspiciousness and Ritual Pollution

While the degree of ritual pollution can be inversely related to the degree of auspiciousness, the demarcations between ritually polluted and auspicious states are in fact more complex than that. As mentioned before, menstruation and childbirth are auspicious conditions, even though they are situated in a ritually polluted state of being. Death is usually considered to be both inauspicious and ritually polluting—although even this state is ambiguous because it is linked to the continuity of the family lineage, since the dead person joins the ancestral clan. For example, days of worship that commemorate the dates of ancestors' deaths are considered to be ritually polluted and auspicious at the same time, since these occasions focus on both the loss of family members and the continuation of blood kinship ties. In one sense, the kōlam reflects the conjoining of states of being that are auspicious and "pure" (i.e., ritually nonpolluting). That is why the kōlam is not made when women are menstruating or the family has experienced a death, to show that it is a household that is currently not hospitable.

There are two exceptions, however. When a girl attains her first menstruation, a huge feast is made, a giant kōlam is created, and food is served to a larger community beyond the immediate family, similar in intensity to a small wedding. It means she is crossing a significant threshold in her life; she is now capable of reproduction. When a child is born, a huge kōlam is also made, though in this case food is brought in by neighbors because childbirth is considered to be a state of incapacity and closed hospitality.[8]

The Role of Domesticity and the Ideology of the Householder in Hindu Everyday Life

One of the best ways to understand the role that ritual pollution plays in the society is to understand the role and ideology of the male householder in Hindu traditional life. I sense often that female householders see themselves as holding equivalent ritual importance.

The state of the household, the pragmatics of everyday life, and the concern for material existence are all part of the significance of the kōlam, pottu, and other ephemeral rituals that signify the life of the householder. The importance of the householder has been long eclipsed by the ascetic in scholarly treatises. In the West, there has long been a fascination with the sadhu, the wandering monk who renounces the world in search of pure truth and understanding. By contrast, the householder, a worldly character, is a much more realistic and popular expression of Hindu personal conduct and moral life. According to Madan:

> The figure in the centre of the stage is a rather homely character, namely, the householder (grhastha). If not exactly cast in a heroic mold, he is not the "phantom-like" man either that Dumont (1970: 48) considers him to be. It is the ideal of his life to "live in the world" but to do so

> in the light of the renouncer's philosophy (see Dumont, 1970: 12, 41 et passim). Translated into the householder's idiom, renunciation becomes the twin ideals of self-possession and detachment in the midst of worldly involvements, which are not considered by him evil in of themselves. What he seeks to resist is being enslaved by such involvements. He hopes to mediate between total indulgence and total renunciation. It is, indeed, all a matter of relations. (1987: 2–3)

In the idiom of the non-renunciated realm of the householder, the kōlam ritual can be seen as an "affirmation of a disciplined this-worldly life as the good life" (3). It expresses everyday concerns, hopes, and desires, such as good health and prosperity within the family. Many women in Tamil Nadu express the view that the kōlam not only brings auspiciousness and goodness but also creates an orientation toward disciplining earthly desires. The householder must always be aware of binding her desires, constantly incorporating ascetic values into daily life. This relates to Madan's interpretation of the religious ideology of the householder as one that "acknowledges the sovereignty of good: the desired must be brought under the regime of, and encompassed by, the preferred" (3). The continuity of domestic life is at the heart of the notion of auspiciousness.

Within the domain of the kōlam, domesticity reigns in the model of the married woman householder as the source of the flow of auspiciousness throughout the community. Creating the kōlam is an active way for Tamil women on a daily basis to articulate their desires. It is a form of prayer in which the women of the household directly communicate their intentions to the goddess Lakshmi. Madan discusses the nature of this type of intentionality:

> The distinction between the state of auspiciousness and the creative agent . . . is most important as is the relation between the two. . . . The point to note about these usages and similar others is that it is not the person himself or herself who is auspicious but rather his or her intentions, actions, or even merely the presence (and witnessing the same), which are so and are, therefore, expected to have happy consequences. The ultimate source of auspiciousness is, of course, the divinity. (53–54)

Therefore, auspiciousness is itself bound with positive intentions, actions that are themselves expected to be overflowing with goodness and are likely to spread all around (Nagarajan 2000: 565–6). The most popular representation of the binding of auspiciousness, positive intentions, and goodness is in the form of Lakshmi.

The Moral and Good Life

Lakshmi is the goddess of auspiciousness, good luck, wealth, wakefulness and alertness, quickness, and abundance, as mentioned earlier. When Lakshmi is invited in by the woman of the household, a portion of the divine auspiciousness is transferred to the earthbound realm of the woman householder. Indeed, the woman is often referred to as the Lakshmi of the house. Like the goddess, she has the power to attract wealth and prosperity into the house and to prevent poverty from crossing the threshold. Since the female householder is seen as the creator of mangala, when domestic life is interrupted, the flow of auspiciousness also comes to a halt. On the other hand, the opposite can occur: there can be a lack of transference of auspiciousness, which is generally attributed to the goddess Mūdevi, or Jyestha, as she is often called. Mūdevi, who as we know is Lakshmi's sister, is the goddess of sleep, restfulness, laziness, ill luck, poverty and scarcity (see Leslie 1992; Nagarajan 1993).

During one of my winter trips, I decided to go on a search for the temple of Mūdevi and I asked where to go. Many women said things like, "It is definitely in the next village over, not here in ours. Go there and ask them about it." Yet when I would go there, the women in that village would feel insulted and say, "Who sent you here? We certainly don't have an image of Mūdevi. Who would want to worship her? She is the goddess of ugliness, depression, nightfall, dirt, laziness, and so on. No one in this village worships her!" And then, someone there would say with a smile, "No, no, no, I have heard of the image somewhere in some village. But I don't know exactly where. Wait. I think it is near this temple in that village." And when I would go there, there would be no image there, either. Finally, I was told, she was the god Shani's wife and I should go to his temple to find her. When I finally did discover his temple, alas she was not there either. So the search went on, fruitless. I finally concluded that I was not meant to find her after all. No one, it seemed, wanted Mūdevi to live among them. They would much rather have an image of her sister, Lakshmi, for obvious reasons. Here is a common story of Lakshmi and Mūdevi.

In the winter of 1988, as I walked at dawn in the narrow medieval walkways of the town of Thanjavur, I met with a very knowledgeable elderly woman, whom I respectfully called pāttī (grandmother). During one of our many conversations she told me, "You know, Vijaya, the real reason we do the kōlam is to banish the goddess Mūdevi from our bodies and house, from all those near and dear to us, just.... Do you know the story of Mūdevi and Lakshmi?" When I answered, "No, but tell me the story," she began:

> Lakshmi and Mūdevi were sisters. Mūdevi was the older sister, and they had a fight one day over who was more beautiful. They argued and

> argued over this until they finally decided to pick an arbiter to end their quarrel. They went to all the three gods, Brahma, Vishnu, and Shiva, and all agreed to sit and hear the case on this issue. When the three gods conferred, they came to a compromise that satisfied both sisters. They said, "When Lakshmi walks towards you, she is more beautiful. Her front half is lovely. When Mūdevi walks away from you, she is more beautiful. Her back is lovely." You know who Mūdevi is! She is the goddess of sleep, restfulness, laziness, and even poverty and scarcity. So she does look more beautiful when she walks away from you. Lakshmi is the goddess of wakefulness, abundance, and wealth. So when you wake up in the morning, what the kōlam does is to banish Mūdevi and invite Lakshmi in. This story is not meant to insult Mūdevi, because you need Mūdevi, too. In the evening, when you are trying to go to sleep, when Mūdevi doesn't come to you, it is very painful and difficult for the body if it cannot rest. It is just to say that there are appropriate times to rest and to wake up.

The elderly woman ended with a gleeful smile. While she was telling this story, we sat on her front threshold and watched women coming from all directions to collect water from the pump across the street. At first light, the women's voices filled the air, exchanging news of the night and hoisting brass pots on their hips. Since news travels fast in semi-urban India, I wasn't surprised when another woman walked by us. She was just beginning her job for the day, sweeping the city. She said in a loud voice for all to hear:

> Hey, I hear you are asking everyone the question why we do the kōlam? You haven't asked me, but let me tell you the real reason we do the kōlam. It is to show that we are household women, not dēvatācis [dancing girls, courtesans, or prostitutes]. Why would a dēvatāci need a kōlam? So, the kōlam shows you are not a dēvatāci. You are a woman of a house. It shows you spent the night there. I dare you to write that down in your notebook. Will you, I wonder?

She grinned. Women sitting with me on the porch across the street and the women across the street at the water pump roared uncomfortably with laughter. I turned quickly to catch the sweeper woman's gaze, to have an extended conversation with her, but she disappeared beyond a cloud of street dust. When I tried to track her down later, to thank her, I couldn't find her. She makes a very interesting distinction between householder and dēvatāci in terms of what the kōlam represents along the continuum of domesticated sexuality versus non-domesticated sexuality.

The kōlam then, is a sign that proclaims her moral status, separating the woman of the house from women who have chosen not to take the householder path.[9] It gives us a clue to the puzzle of why a Hindu woman does not need to do any purifying rituals before she makes the kōlam, as she would in most other rituals. It is perhaps more about rising directly from the marital bed and from the body having been in a potential or actualized sexual state and announcing that directly through the kōlam. It is the direct emergence from auspiciousness or sexual satisfaction of the marital relations that the kōlam in part signifies, not the mapping of ritual purity.[10] The fact that the woman does not need to purify herself before making the auspicious kōlam makes sense, for it is not purity that the kōlam represents, but rather auspiciousness and sexual satisfaction within moral and cultural social bounds.[11]

Let's look more closely at the relationship between Lakshmi and Mūdevi. When a woman wakes up, she brushes her teeth and then does the kōlam. It is the very first ritual action she does. When women start making the kōlam, they are slightly drowsy, but as time passes, their body and eyes become more and more alert as the design is completed. So making the kōlam is the way women wake up to the day. Lakshmi is the ultimate embodiment of auspiciousness; she is what women desire more of, to have economic security in the family.[12] Most household shrines honor this goddess, and it was she who was mentioned most frequently in women's stories about the kōlam.

Furthermore, the ritual principle of auspiciousness is further embedded in cultural notions of morality, value, and the meaning of life. In his landmark study of non-renunciation, Madan observes, "For the common Pandit, the life of the man-in-the-world—epitomized in the role of the householder—though arduous, is the moral and good life. It is a life worth living" (1987: 47). Tamil female householders equally substantiate their desires for a "moral and good life" through the daily practices of banishing laziness and attracting status, wealth, material possessions, health, children, good fortune, and other forms of auspiciousness. The kōlam, according to many Tamil women I spoke with, is a visual statement that "We are living in this world and experiencing life fully; we want to be free from poverty and ritual pollution and have a life worth living." The underlying assumption is that weaving ephemeral designs by hand while thinking desired thoughts and prayers has the power to shape the reality of that day, orienting that individual toward "goodness" and virtue and helping to create the possible good luck to come. Here we can see that both auspiciousness and inauspiciousness are considered equally vital aspects of life; one cannot exist without the other.

5

Āṇṭāḷ

It is true that the life stories of some of the saints
do carry the message that a devotee's
purity of intent is far more important
to god than technical correctness in ritual forms.[1]

—Norman Cutler, 1987

Āṇṭāḷ is a renowned ninth-century Tamil medieval saint and is one of the key leitmotifs in women's stories on the origins of the kōlam. Women speak of Āṇṭāḷ as the creative force behind the kōlam, saying that she was the very first Tamil woman with the idea of making this ritual form in the name of the divine.[2] Thus the legendary origin of the kōlam comes to us in part from Āṇṭāḷ.

In February 1993, I went to Srivilliputtur, Āṇṭāḷ's legendary birthplace, to search for clearer links between Āṇṭāḷ and the kōlam. While there, I spoke with Saraswathi, an 83-year-old Vaishnavite Brahmin, who had been widowed from the age of 45. She scolded me for asking such an "obvious" question, and answered impatiently:

> Of course Āṇṭāḷ was the first woman to make the kōlam for Krishna. Ever since Āṇṭāḷ thought of the idea, we have been making the kōlam. Of course, the kōlam could have existed before, but it was Āṇṭāḷ who offered it to Nārayanan [a form of Vishnu] and he was the first to accept her offering of the kōlam. Ever since then, we have been making the kōlam for him, for the divine. The kōlam is from the parampāra [ancient tradition]; we do not know where or when it began, but we know the first Tamil woman whose kōlam was accepted by Krishna as a sweet offering, and that woman was Āṇṭāḷ. And ever since Āṇṭāḷ, we have been making the kōlam for Krishna.

The idea that the kōlam comes from parampāra and is handed down orally is prevalent among Tamil women. However, there is no accurate way to trace its origins because of two factors: the oral transmission of knowledge about the practice and the few existing written sources on the ritual art form. These rare references are what makes Āṇṭāḷ's reference to a related ritual art form in Sanskrit, the mandala, so profound. It speaks of the presence of this ritual art as far back as the ninth century in Tamil Nadu.

Here I will be using the words *Vishnu, Krishna,* and *Narayanan* interchangeably because they all refer to the same entity. Vishnu is part of the sacred triumvirate of Brahma, Shiva, and Vishnu, three primary gods of Hinduism. It is interesting that Āṇṭāḷ orients the kōlam to Krishna and not the other more familiar Lakshmi, Mūdevi, and Bhūdevi.

Norman Cutler (1987) discusses "the place that history, audience participation, and reception play in the absorption and recirculation of a hagiographical figure" (27) such as Āṇṭāḷ:

> This author, the saint-poet, is a persona who stands somewhere at the boundary between the "real-life" author, in the Western critic's sense of the word, and an "implied author" who exists solely in the words of his composition. For a Tamil Vaishnava or Shaiva audience, the saint-poet is a composite of a voice heard in poetry, a legendary figure whose life story is recorded in hagiography, and a sacred personality who is enshrined in temples. Tamil audiences have never distinguished the saint, whose identity is fashioned from poetry, legend, and ritual, from a historical author. (28)

Cutler's description of the saint-poet echoes my own observations on the cultural context of the legendary figure of Āṇṭāḷ.

Āṇṭāḷ is also named as the originator of the kōlam in the stories that women of diverse backgrounds tell about the saint. It was clear that the story of Āṇṭāḷ's relationship to the kōlam was important for women of Vaishnavite and Shaivite backgrounds, as well as those from many other castes. From the cosmopolitan city of Madras, to the bustling sacred city of Madurai, to the small town of Thanjavur, Tamil women consistently advised me that if I wanted to know more about the kōlam, I should visit Srīvilliputtūr, the birthplace of Āṇṭāḷ: "There you will talk to the older women, and they will tell you how it is that Āṇṭāḷ began the kōlam." One middle-aged woman living in Tiruvaiyāru said, "You must go to her temple there to understand her better and to understand where the kōlam came from."

When I was in Srīvilliputtūr, an 85-year-old woman told me, "Just look in her songs. It is clear that she offers the kōlam to Vishnu." From her words I expected to see an explicit reference in Āṇṭāḷ's work (her songs) to the kōlam, but we shall see that this is not so obvious.

Oral Literary Criticism

The links between Āṇṭāḷ and the kōlam represent a fragmented landscape of oral and written narrative, folk wisdom, and ideology. Within this landscape, I will trace the literal as well as the metaphorical correspondences between Āṇṭāḷ's story and the kōlam. I will not attempt to present a detailed examination of Tamil women's narratives about Āṇṭāḷ, a translation of her poems, or an in-depth analysis of her presence in temple worship in Tamil Nadu.[3] My aim, rather, is to convey the ways in which Āṇṭāḷ retains a lively presence in the kōlam tradition as it is practiced today. By interweaving women's accounts of Āṇṭāḷ's connection to the kōlam, I will attempt to shed light on the underlying analytic parallels between her story and the kōlam narratives.

Folklorist A. K. Ramanujan devoted many years of his life to describing the interlacing of oral and written worlds in India, emphasizing the continuities between the classical and folk worlds in both realms. Blackburn and Ramanujan (1986: 26) reveals a serious gap in the study of nonverbal folklore in the field of Indian studies. As he observes, all too often Indian studies emphasize either oral folk traditions or written texts; rarely are they brought together to serve as counterpoints to each other. Along the same lines, Alan Dundes (2005, 1966), advocates a more serious look at what he calls "oral literary criticism." Expanding on Dundes's call, Kirin Narayan (1995b) defines oral literary criticism as "the meanings attributed to folklore texts by the people who use them" (243). Inspired by the need for more studies that link nonverbal traditions and domestic folklore, I wish to explore the narrative reference points of the kōlam within the classical and literary traditions of Tamil Nadu, which continue to be mapped out today. This chapter traces the multifaceted relationship of the kōlam to Āṇṭāḷ, one of the 12 Vaishnavite Alvars.[4] What is the relationship between the historical Āṇṭāḷ in the textual traditions of the Bhakti movement and the contemporary Āṇṭāḷ located within Tamil oral narratives about the kōlam?[5]

In examining the story of Āṇṭāḷ and her role in the creation of the kōlam, I apply Caroline Walker Bynum's (1991) concept of "comprehensible and self-contained" fragments of history. As Bynum observes, "Historians can never present more than a part of the story of history and that [sic] these parts are true fragments, not microcosms of the whole; but such a conception of the historian's task does not, after all, preclude making each fragment as comprehensible and self-contained as possible" (9). Bynum's call to make "each fragment as comprehensible as possible" has served as a guidepost for this chapter. Here I set out to compile these fragments and interpret what they could mean in the larger story of the kōlam.

A Saintly Figure

Āṇṭāḷ is one of the most popular saints in Tamil Nadu. She was born between the eighth and tenth centuries, probably in the ninth century, in the small town of Srivilliputtur.[6] Srivilliputtur is tucked in the shadows of the Eastern Ghats, nearly a four-hour journey by bus from Madurai. As you approach the town, you first see the beautiful gōpurams (towers), one white and one black, which pierce the sky and dominate the landscape of partially surrounding mountainsides and the flat alluvial rice fields that stretch for many miles into the distance. Manifold images of Āṇṭāḷ cast in stone or bronze, featured on poster prints, are displayed by households, temples, and religious associations. Āṇṭāḷ is commonly known as *cūtikkoṭuttavaḷ* ("she who had given what she had worn"), and the word Āṇṭāḷ means "she who rules." She is also seen as an embodiment of the goddess Bhūdevi.

Āṇṭāḷ is celebrated and honored as the only woman saint of 12 Vaishnavite saints.[7] As a woman and a Vaishnavite devotee, she commands a wide following within diverse circles of believers. She is strikingly beautiful, and her popular image, with its gold-covered, rounded, and fanned-out hairstyle, sets her apart from other female saints. Her wide hips give her a fullness of figure and she is laden with gold and jewels, resembling those of goddesses—especially Lakshmi, the consort of Vishnu. Like Lakshmi, she stands on a lotus flower. Her face bears a slight smile; her ears are pierced with gold *jimikkihal* (thickly decorated hanging earrings). Her most striking iconographic characteristic is the thick garland of flowers, half as large as her body, bordering her. This dense foliage surrounding her enables her to be immediately identified as Āṇṭāḷ, "the one who rules."[8] One of her hands is bent to hold up a parrot sitting on a lotus flower, while her other hand is placed casually near her hip atop the thick garland. On closer observation, we can see that she is surrounded by at least two layers of thinner garlands that twirl around her neck and descend close to her body. She wears a *nāmam*, the line of red down the middle of her forehead that signifies a Vaishnavite believer (Figure 5.1).

The following is a version of the story of Āṇṭāḷ that I heard often from women.[9]

Āṇṭāḷ's father, Periyāḻvār, was one of the Bhakti aḻvar saints of the Vaishnava canon, a composer of sacred hymns and a worshipper in his own right. According to hagiographical accounts, one day he heard a baby's cries near a sacred *tulasi*

Figure 5.1 The most popular iconic image of Āṇṭāḷ. (Source: Author's collection.)

(Indian basil) bush in the temple garden. Investigating their source, he found a girl child and named her Kōtai, an earlier name for Āṇṭāḷ; he proceeded to adopt and raise her.[10]

As Āṇṭāḷ grew older, she became more and more enamored with Vishnu. At the temple in Srīvilliputtūr, her daily duty was to gather tulasi plants (the plants themselves were considered a consort of Vishnu) and flowers to weave a mixed garland of them for Vishnu. She then waited for the appointed time of the offering ceremony (*pūja*). Usually, those participating in the ceremony, whether it involved food or flowers, must not ever sample the delights of the offering; they must not taste the food or even smell the flowers before they are presented to the deity. Doing so would diminish the purity of the offering. Children, of course, often have a hard time restraining themselves. After she wove the garland, Āṇṭāḷ would mischievously place it around her neck and admire herself in the mirror, while smelling the flowers and imagining herself to be Vishnu's bride. She would then bring the sacred garland to her father, who was to make the offering during his worship ceremony. He was unaware that his daughter had already worn the flowers herself in her play-acting. This went on for some time.[11]

One day Periyāḷvār happened to see Āṇṭāḷ as she was acting out the part of Vishnu's bride. He was very upset at his daughter's apparent lack of patience and scolded her for breaking the code of religious worship. He reminded her that

Figure 5.2 Āṇṭāḷ with huge garland.

now he would not be able to offer the ritually polluted flowers to the god that day. Periyāḷvār apologized to Vishnu for having no flowers to offer him, since they had been used and were now spoiled by his daughter. He promised to bring pure flowers the following day. But that night Vishnu appeared to Periyāḷvār in a dream and asked, "Why didn't you offer me the tulasi flowers today?" Periyāḷvār replied, "My daughter foolishly wore them before I could offer them, so they became spoiled and I could not then give them to you." To his utter amazement, Vishnu replied, "That is the garland I want you to offer me; I prefer the flowers used by Āṇṭāḷ."

Stunned by Vishnu's reply, the next day Periyāḷvār watched his daughter carefully during her play-acting. Slowly he began to realize that the god had chosen Āṇṭāḷ (and that she had chosen him and not a human man), and that his daughter must therefore be an incarnation of Vishnu's wife. He began to think of how he could arrange for Āṇṭāḷ's marriage to Vishnu, her chosen bridegroom (Figure 5.2).

As we will see later, the story of Āṇṭāḷ echoes the origin of the kōlam, but for now we must visit certain retellings of the story. Many Tamil women told me this same tale with a few variations. Let's examine the narratives in more detail to note the parallel moments of dynamic tension that are invoked.

Vidya Dehejia (1990), the scholar and art historian, retold the classical version, and it clearly echoes the oral hagiographic retellings I heard in Tamil Nadu:

> The Tamil hagiography commences the life of Āṇṭāḷ by comparing Śrīvilliputtūr with the sacrificial ground where Sītā was found by Jānaka. This informs us that Bhū Devī manifested herself as an infant girl at the spot where Viśnucitta [another name for Periyāḷvār] was hoeing the ground for his sacred basil. Naming the child Kōtai of the fragrant tresses, Viśnucitta raised her as if she were the goddess Śrī. As a very young girl, she would, in her father's absence, adorn herself in bridal garb and wrap around her glossy tresses the long garland that had been prepared and set aside for the evening pūjai of Viśnu. Thus adorned, she would gaze into a mirror to see if she looked a bride fit for the lord. She would then return the garland to its place, and Viśnucitta, unaware of the "desecration," would offer the garland to Viśnu. Many days passed in this manner until the Alvar discovered Kōtai's secret. Deeply perturbed by the flagrant disregard of *sastric* rules, Viśnucitta performed the evening pūja without making an offering of the garland. That night, Viśnu appeared to him in a dream and told him that the garland worn by Āṇṭāḷ was especially dear to him and had an added fragrance. Viśnucitta realized that Āṇṭāḷ was no ordinary child but had in her a touch of the divine.[12] (7–8)

The key elements that surface in the retellings of Āṇṭāḷ's story are (1) her imagining herself as a bride; (2) the woman "who had given what she had worn"; and (3) the preference of the divine for Āṇṭāḷ's "used" garland. What does this last point signify in this story? How did the "used" garland escape the traditional dualistic categories of ritual purity and ritual pollution? And what does the worn garland signify to the Tamil worshipper of today?

Beginning with the contradictions of offering objects that are both ritually pure and polluted in the context of a pūja, I argue that the garland that Āṇṭāḷ offers to Vishnu represents the entire metaphorical field of "forgiveness." The circulation of objects within Hindu ritual is strictly encoded for purity and pollution, and only in exceptional circumstances is a polluted object offered to the divine. What Hindu children often learn is that you rarely offer something that has been touched, consumed, or smelled to the divine; the offering needs to be fresh and unused. So one would think that when Āṇṭāḷ presented the used garland, she would have been chastised for it and told to go back and make a fresh garland and then offer it again. Without going through all this, a ritual error of this type could normally not be forgiven. But in this story, Vishnu not only forgives her, he embraces her. By allowing her to offer a garland she had worn, he made her equivalent to him. Even a human husband would not allow this transgression; a pious wife would, for instance, rarely eat off her husband's plate and then give it back to him.

In Āṇṭāḷ's story, the "used" or ritually polluted garland desired by the divine also represents the sweat passed between bodies, the exchange of bodily fluids, and the mingling of shared desires between lovers. I suggest that Āṇṭāḷ's "used" garland is a symbol of Vishnu's forgiveness of Āṇṭāḷ's ritually mistaken acts and, by extension, our own.

I must have first heard this story of Āṇṭāḷ when I was just eight or nine years old. I was immediately intrigued. Vishnu's forgiveness of Āṇṭāḷ breaking a ritual taboo was extremely gratifying to me. I felt a deep relief under the burden of my own ritual errors that such unintended mistakes could be forgiven. Each time I unintentionally broke a ritual taboo, my mind would immediately leap back to the story of Āṇṭāḷ and the fear of an impending punishment would fade away. If Āṇṭāḷ could get away with a ritual error, then maybe I could too.

Raised as a bicultural child, back and forth between India and America, I always felt as if I was making ritual errors, and Āṇṭāḷ's story often gave me courage. It made me think that even if I made ritual errors, as long as my intentions were good I would not be severely punished. This was echoed by my mother's easy forgiveness of any ritual errors. Her attitude seemed to be that as long as you meant well, it would turn out fine in the end. This made an enormous difference in my experience of Hindu rituals in everyday life. It made the ritual labor of following the extremely demanding instructions for festival worship much more bearable and enjoyable.

When I was eight years old, an Indonesian friend at her birthday party offered me a beautiful bowl of multicolored chips that resembled thick potato chips. I still remember their unusual glow. These chips were lime green, purple, pink, and yellow. I had never seen chips like that before and was fascinated and enthralled. Every time I could, I would look at them out of the corner of my eyes, wondering when I could eat them. When that magical moment finally came, I asked my Indonesian friend if they were vegetarian chips and she said they were, in an unusually somber tone of voice. I first ate one, then another. I couldn't stop eating them; they were delicious.

My friend stared at me as if something magical was going to happen. But realizing that nothing untoward was going to happen, she scolded me, disappointed: "You are lying. You said you could not *eat meat. You* can *eat meat. Nothing ever happened to you. What you ate was fish, but you did not turn any color. Your mouth and body did not reject the fish chips. You ate it just as I would."*

I looked at her horrified and felt utterly miserable. I had been raised as a strict vegetarian, not allowed to consume meat, fish, or eggs. The entire birthday party took on an eerie glow. I imagined the fish bits inside of me protesting that they wanted to be alive again. I rushed out of there, crying and upset. The fish chips had a taste I had never tasted before, and I scolded myself that I should have known better and should not have eaten those magically colored chips! Back in our apartment, sobbing, I told my mother what happened. She hugged and reassured me that as I did not know that they were actually fish and hadn't been told the truth, I would be forgiven. Intention was more important than the actual deed. Relieved, I brushed my tears away and went back to the birthday party, much calmer.

It must have been then that my mother told me the Āṇṭāḷ story, and throughout my childhood I would keep myself alert for similar stories. The story of Meera Bai, a female saint from Rajasthan in northern India, had a similar impact on me. Although she desired to join the divine, this was not acceptable in her society. She persisted in her own path anyway because her love for the divine was so strong.

In Āṇṭāḷ's story, it is notable that her *prasād* (ritual offering) is accepted and even preferred by the divine. Āṇṭāḷ enjoys the flowers herself and then offers what is essentially her "waste" to the divine. Thus she subverts the paradigmatic ritual offering protocol through the sincerity and intensity of her love and desire for Vishnu. Such a reversal in the flow of prasād is highly unusual.[13] Āṇṭāḷ is a woman and Vishnu is a man, so the flow is altered in two ways: from woman to man (rather than man to woman) and from human to divine (rather than divine to human).

This symbolic act of pollution and forgiveness continues to be embodied in Srīvilliputtūr, where Vishnu's preference for Āṇṭāḷ's "used" garland is reenacted regularly at the Āṇṭāḷ shrine. Dehejia (1990) describes how the temple ritual highlights the climactic moment in Āṇṭāḷ's narrative:

> At the appropriate moment in the morning pūja of Viśnu, Āṇṭāḷ's discarded garland is placed ceremonially around his neck. At noon, this same garland travels to the shrine of Āṇṭāḷ's father Periyāḷvār, and is offered to him. Honored visitors to the temple of Śrīvilliputtūr may be blessed by having Āṇṭāḷ's discarded garland placed momentarily upon them, and they may be given one of its wilted flowers as prasātam. This unique ritual, in which the wilted garland worn by Āṇṭāḷ the previous evening is placed upon the image of the mighty Lord Viśnu, is a daily reenactment of a crucial point in the legendary story of Āṇṭāḷ's bhakti, her total rejection of human love, her longing for union with the lord, and the lord's ultimate acceptance of her as a special devotee and as his bride. (6)

In the frequent reenactment of this climactic scene, this ritual moment of sacralizing Āṇṭāḷ's used garland serves as a linked community memory for the inhabitants of Srīvilliputtūr. It is as if humanity itself is forgiven, too, for its unintentional errors. This daily reenactment provides us with a clue to the intense importance of this aspect of Āṇṭāḷ's narrative. What is intriguing is the power of bhakti or love overcoming the usual stark dichotomy between purity and pollution: the used garland retains its sacredness despite its polluted nature—in fact, *because* of its polluted nature. The god himself converts the "waste" to a desired gift because of the giver's intense love and devotion. Here, the intention of an act of love supersedes the actual reality of the "used" garland.

Āṇṭāḷ's Song-Poems

According to legend, Āṇṭāḷ composed two song-poems, the *Tiruppāvai* and the *Nācciyār Tirumoḷi*. The *Tiruppāvai* is a sacred vow song popular throughout Tamil Nadu today and is especially prominent during the month of Margaḷi. It has 30 stanzas, one for each day of the month, of Krishna and the gōpis in Brindāvan. When Āṇṭāḷ was a young girl, the elders told her that if her desire for Krishna was so strong, she must enact in her own village scenes of play between Krishna and the gōpis, female cowherders, because only then would her lord descend and be with her. So Āṇṭāḷ imagines the place of Krishna's play, or *līlā*, in the setting of Srīvilliputtūr. The song goes on to describe Krishna's beautiful appearance:

> . . . we sing the praises of the supreme one who
> slumbers along the milky ocean . . .
> your form is dark as the hue
> of the primordial lord . . .
> O lord of illusion
> who dwells on the banks
> of the sacred brimming Yamunā . . .
> O golden creeper
> of the clan of cowherds, . . .
> O peacock of the woods,
> with stomachs smooth and curved
> like the snake's dancing hood, . . .
> Lord reclining
> upon your ivory-legged couch
> soft with cotton and silk and down,
> lit by the glimmer of tall lamps,
> your head upon the breasts of Nappiṉṉāi

whose hair is braided
with clusters of flowers,
O lord of broad-chested splendor, . . .

—Dehejia 1990: 43–58

These beautiful descriptions of Vishnu lead up to the *pāvai* vow, the vow of bathing in the river in the early morning.

The second poem, the *Nācciyār Tirumoḷi,* is an erotic poem full of moving and suggestive images about Āṇṭāḷ's intense love and desire for Nārayanan (Vishnu). It is rarely sung in popular settings, only occasionally at weddings. The imagery is highly sensual and erotic, describing the changing body of a young girl becoming a young woman, who aches for union with Nārayanan. She scolds Nārayanan for abandoning her, and for transforming her body into that of a woman without being her lover. Her breasts are budding, Āṇṭāḷ says, and of what use are they if he doesn't come to use them?

. . . I dedicated my swelling breasts
to the lord who holds
the conch and flaming discus.
If there is even a whisper
of giving me to a mortal,
I shall not live.
O Maṉmatha,
would you permit a roving jackal
to sniff and eat
the sacrificial food
that brahmins offer
to celestial gods? . . .
To keep my vow
I eat but once a day,
body neglected, unadorned,
tangled hair in disarray,
lips pale and dry . . .

—Dehejia 1990: 76–77

In the *Nācciyār Tirumoḷi* we find the earliest historical Tamil reference to patterns ritually created on the thresholds of households, but here it seems they are made of sand. For example, in the very first stanza of the very first song of the *Nācciyār Tirumoḷi,* Āṇṭāḷ sings:

Through the month of Tai
I swept the ground before my house,
made *sacred mandalas* of fine sand.
The month of Māci has begun,
I have adorned the street,
offered worship to your brother and you.
How can I live
without the lord of Vènkatā?
O formless god,
unite me with the
one who holds the fire-tipped discus.
At the silvery break of dawn
I bathed in the stream,
Lit a sacred fire of tender twigs.
With fine white sand
I decked the street
and kept my vow to you.
Make an arrow of honey-laden flowers,
Write on it the name
Of the lord dark as the ocean.
Aim me at my target,
The lord who rent open
The beak of the bird.
Kāmadeva, unite me with my chosen one.

—Dehejia 1990: 75; my italics

Here is a more recent translation of the same two first stanzas (Venketesan 2010: 147):

In the month of Tai
I swept the ground and drew *sacred manḍalas.*
In the beginning of Māci
I *decorated the street with fine sand.*
After all this adornment for beauty's sake, O Anaṅga
I asked you and your brother:
"Is it still possible to live?"
Unite me
With the lord of Vēnkaṭam
The one who holds in his hand

The discus tipped with fire.
I adorned the street with fine white sand.
I bathed at the crack of dawn.
I fed the fire with tender thornless twigs.
I have completed my vow to you, O Kāmadeva.

—Venketesan 2010: 147; my italics

In the second song, Āṇṭāḷ beseeches Lord Vishnu not to keep destroying the sandcastles that she and the other children are making at the edge of the ocean:

. . . The month of Paṅkuṉi is here
we have adorned the street for Kāmadēva,
O naughty Śrīdhara,
do not break
our sandcastles.
With aching backs
we spent the day
building sandcastles.
We had not time
to sit and gaze at them. . . .
You who slumber
upon the surging ocean,
do not break our sandcastles. . . .
With soft white sand
we built castles of our fancy.
Along the street we drew
auspicious diagrams—
Keśava, O wicked Mādhava,
have you no eyes to see?
If you erase them
still our hearts will melt
with love for you,
we shall bear you no grudge. . . .

—Dehejia 1990: 79–80; my italics

And here is a more recent translation of the same stanzas by Archana Venketesan:

. . . The time of Paṅkuṉi is here
And we have adorned the streets for Kāmadeva.
Do not be wicked now, O Śrīdhara!

Do not break our sandcastles!
Our backs are aching, we toiled
Over these sandcastles all day.
Allow us to enjoy our efforts;
Let us gaze upon them fully. . . .
O fierce lion slumbering upon the boundless ocean!
You who delivered that wild elephant
From his anguish.
Merely seeing you makes our heart ache.
We have toiled so hard,
Sifting fine sands with our wrists
Thick with bangles.
You who recline upon the brimming ocean
Do not break our sandcastles! . . .
We built these lovely sandcastles with fine white sand,
to decorate every threshold.
Even when you destroy them
Even when our hearts break
Even when we melt
We cannot be angry with you. . . .

—Venketesan 2010, 151–2; my italics

Note these important allusions to the kōlam: in the first stanza, "I swept the ground before my house, made sacred mandalas of fine sand"; and in the second stanza, "Along the street we drew auspicious diagrams." In neither one does Āṇṭāḷ use the word *kōlam*. In the first, she uses the Sanskrit word *mandala* (a Sanskrit term that refers to circular threshold designs resembling the kōlam), which is also a drawing with fine sand, but in this case it is based on a circular design. The second reference, "auspicious diagrams," is clearly a description of a mandala. This suggests that Āṇṭāḷ's offering of mandalas precedes the kōlam tradition. Or, it is possible that the preexisting kōlams could have intertwined with the mandalas that accompanied the migration of the Sanskrit-based Brahmins southward through peninsular India. Brahmins may have brought their yantras and mandalas from northern to southern India in the early part of the first millennium AD. It also seems possible that before this migration, the kōlam arose independently of the northern mandala tradition, and that when the mandala arrived in southern India, it probably commingled with an already fully existing tradition of the kōlam. Another interpretation is that using the word *mandala* may have been a way to make the poem seem "more Sanskritic," which is associated with an elite culture (see Chapter 6 for another formulation of this conjecture).

The use of the word *mandala* in the first stanza can be seen as problematic. One commentator, Virāgavācaryarkan (1956), interprets the word *mandala* along with the verb *ittu* (to write down). This verb is often associated with the kōlam. This interpretation seems to go along with the understanding that it refers to the threshold designs. But simultaneously he offers another definition for mandala, one that refers to a measure of time of 40 to 45 days. This further complicates the interpretation. Both Dehejia and Venketesan's translations, though, disagree with this interpretation, and I would agree with them.

The second reference is actually the word *kōlam*, but here I would argue that it is much more ambiguous. Looking into this more deeply, I discovered, to my surprise, that this path was not at all clearly laid out. The translation depended on how you placed the modifier to the noun of the sandcastles. Some commentators and interpreters both then and now have crossed this particular bridge in different ways. Some have interpreted it as the kōlam that is the subject of this book (Dehejia 1988)[14] and others have interpreted it as the kōlam that means either form or decoration (Venketesan 2010: 151–2). Dehejia translates it as "auspicious diagrams" and Venketesan translates it using a broader brush as "form" or "decoration" of the ephemeral sandcastles. It clearly depends on how you translate this. If the word *kōlam* is an adjective that modifies the sandcastle, then it clearly refers to the sense of form or decoration. But if we translate it as its own independent noun, then it more likely refers to the threshold designs of the kōlam. And even if we translate the word *kōlam* here as decoration, it could still refer to the threshold designs rather than the sandcastles—or it could even refer to both (Madvathasan 1962). In this commentary the word *kōlam* is interpreted as simply "decoration," but here too it is ambiguous. It could be referring to the decoration as the sandcastles made of white soft sand or it could be referring to simply another kind of decoration (i.e., threshold designs made of soft sand flour), which also could refer to the kōlam.

The sandcastles (*chittral*) on the threshold are made with "fine white sand," the same material used to make the mandalas or kōlams from the earlier stanza. According to this text, stanza 518, coming in the middle of the second section of this long poem, refers to "that form that you erase" (13) (Āṇḍāḷ 1966). Here, it seems the word is used as "form," yet I would argue that it is ambiguous: "form" could be referring to the threshold art form of the kōlam, as it is being used in the context of creating decorations on the threshold with white soft sandcastles. Dehejia and Venketesan differ in their translations and the commentaries themselves differ in each of their interpretations, about erasing the form or the drawings. It is not clear, and I remain open to these multiple interpretations.

A more recent commentator stated that it is, indeed, the kōlam, "kōlangal pōttōm" or "we made the kōlams" (Shankaranarayanan 2002: 25). This gives added weight that it could be the very kōlam we are looking for.

Another question arises: Why would Āṇṭāḷ refer to the same kind of ritual designs using two different words, *mandala* and *kōlam*, only a few stanzas apart? Was she thinking in poetic terms, to have a diversity of words as she talks so much about the ephemeral sandcastles? We don't know, so we must leave it at that level of uncertainty. It is certainly intriguing to think that this could be the very first reference to the word *kōlam* as in the threshold designs. We can reasonably state that at least one of the references, the mandala one, clearly refers to kōlam-like threshold drawings and that the second one is likely to refer to them.

At a broader level of interpretation, it is curious that in that first stanza in the *Nācciyār Tirumoḷi* Āṇṭāḷ orients herself to Kāma, the god of desire, rather than to Vishnu. Venketesan argues that "Āṇṭāḷ does provide a fair amount of detail on the elements of her ritual vow to Kāma—she talks of drawing sacred diagrams on the earth, making paintings on the wall, and she mentions all of Kāma's symbolic accouterments, including his sugar cane bow and flower arrows" (191–2). Venketesan characterizes the *Tiruppāvai* as "an enactment of a ritual prayer (the pāvai nōṉpu) undertaken by young married girls for the attainment of a virtuous husband. In the *Nācciyār Tirumoḷi*, the desire is unaltered, and the virtuous husband remains Viśṇu" (192). According to Venketesan, the commentator Piḷḷai states that "she draws beautiful magical diagrams (maṇḍala) only with soft, white sand, because it is bright as the sattva guṇa (the virtue of luminosity) that Viśṇu embodies" (192).

Parallels Between Āntāl and the Kōlam

Why do Tamil women still feel compelled to connect the origins of the kōlam with the historical figure of Āṇṭāḷ? In the Tamil cultural imagination, the character of Āṇṭāḷ strikes a particular chord in the hagiographic context. First, there are few women saints in the Tamil canon. For another, what is unique about Āṇṭāḷ is that it was her very transgressions that brought her closer to the divine. The metaphors embedded in both her story and in the songs have parallels in the ones embedded in the kōlam. If you compare the two song-poems of Āṇṭāḷ with the kōlam narratives, four striking parallels emerge: sacred time, "waking up," forgiveness, and generosity. In addition, parallel sets of divinities are the common focus (Table 5.1). Here we will go through these four parallel metaphors and correspondences.

Table 5.1 Parallels between the kōlam and Āṇṭāḷ's story.

	Kōlam	Āṇṭāḷ's Story
	Disappearance ("used up") symbolizes women householders' generosity, love, blessings, and desires traveling into the community	*"Used" garland symbolizes Āṇṭāḷ's pure love and desire for Viṣnu*
Divinity	Āṇṭāḷ Bhūdevi Lakṣhmi Viṣnu/Krishna/ Nārayanan	Āṇṭāḷ Bhūdevi Lakṣhmi Viṣnu/Krishna/Nārayanan
Sacred Time	Early morning *(brahmamūrthi nerum)* Month of Mārkali	Early morning *(brahmamūrthi nerum)* Month of Mārkali
Waking Up	To bless the community To awaken the community To host the divine	To reenact scene of Krishna and *gōpi* To awaken girlfriends To awaken Viṣnu
Forgiveness	Asks forgiveness of earth goddess for using and burdening her throughout the day	Receives forgiveness from Viṣnu for ritually polluted offering
Generosity	Auspicious powers are activated as rice-flour designs are worn away by passersby	Auspicious powers are activated after garland is worn by Āṇṭāḷ
	Women's blessings travel into community	Āṇṭāḷ's love is offered to Viṣnu
	Kōlam becomes *prasād* for Bhūdevi	Garland becomes *prasād* for Viṣnu
	Women show off their kōlam designs, offering their best efforts to the divine	Āṇṭāḷ shows off garland in the mirror, offering herself to Viṣnu

Sacred Time

The notion of sacred time operates identically in the narratives of Āṇṭāḷ and the kōlam. The *Brahma muhurta* (early morning) and the month of Margaḷi (from mid-December to mid-January) are respectively the most auspicious daily and yearly times for both Āṇṭāḷ and the kōlam. The period from 4:30 to 6:00 a.m. one and a half hours before sunrise, is considered to be the most auspicious time of the day (see Chapter 3 for more details). This is also the time referred to in the *Tiruppāvai* for waking up the lord. Āṇṭāḷ sings, "Bathing at dawn, . . . We bathe in the clear waters at the break of dawn." She prays for a time of rain and abundance in the fields, "Let plenty come to all as we joyously dip in the Mārgaḷi waters." Here, the references to dawn and the month of Mārgaḷi are clear.

Moreover, the month of Mārgaḷi is the most auspicious time of year for the celebrations of Āṇṭāḷ and the kōlam. For Tamil women, this is when the ritual practice of the kōlam and the singing of Āṇṭāḷ's songs are at their peak.[15] Women consider it especially important to complete the kōlam before sunrise during the month of Mārgaḷi because it is believed that all the gods and goddesses are circling just before dawn. After the sun comes up, they disappear. As they stroll just above the ground, they notice this house and that house because of the beautiful kōlams out front. This is why the Tamil woman wants to have the best kōlam—to attract the deity's beneficent gaze toward her house, with all the blessings that the grace of that glance entails.

Women frequently quoted Krishna's words from the *Bhagavad Gita*, "I will reside in the month of Mārgaḷi. You will always find me there." This illustrates the importance of this time period. Even Krishna refers to himself as "the Mārgaḷi of the year" in the *Bhagavad Gita.*

Waking Up

Both the kōlam and Āṇṭāḷ narratives involve the act of "waking up." The kōlam is drawn to awaken the community by blessing and hosting the divine, and by welcoming the sun. Women often say that they begin making the kōlam when they are still tired and lazy from sleep, but by the time they are finished they feel refreshed and alert. Thus, as a woman creates the kōlam, she herself is slowly waking up, emerging from the obscurity of dreams and sleep to the concreteness of her body and her daily activities. In both a literal and metaphorical sense, the kōlam is a daily call to wake up the body and mind and to face the divine.

Similarly, Āṇṭāḷ uses the metaphor of "waking up." In the *Tiruppāvai*, the theme of waking up is both a concrete act and a metaphorical call for the human and the divine to come out of the stupor of an unlived life. In reenacting the scene of Krishna and the gōpis in Brindāvan, Āṇṭāḷ calls her girlfriends to awaken and walk in the chill of predawn to take a bath in the *kulam* (manmade pond). Central to the notion of the poem is the idea of "waking up." Āṇṭāḷ makes her way through the streets of Srīvilliputtūr, trying to rouse up her girlfriends to sing the praises to the lord—"leave your sleep," "sleep no more," and "arise from your sleep." The Venketesan translation follows:

Listen: even the birds are chirping.
Can you not hear
the vibrant sound of the white conch
from the temple of Garuḍa's lord?
Wake up, child! . . .
  That primordial lord
    who rests on his serpent
    upon the ocean of milk. . . .
Can you not hear
  the pervasive
  screech and chatter of the
  āṉaiccāttaṉ?
Witless ghost of a girl
do you not hear
  the clink of long necklaces
  and the jangle of ornaments,
  as the women of Āyarpāṭi
  whose hair is fragrant,
  swish and turn their churning rods
  in the curd?
O you who are our leader
how can you just lie there. . . .
O beautiful maiden
come now—open your door.

(2010: 56–7)

In celebrating the *pāvai* vow—the centerpiece of the *Tiruppāvai*—young, unmarried women commit to waking up early, going to the temple before dawn, and singing to Krishna. Gradually the poetic voice shifts the focus from urging the young maidens to arise to calling to Vishnu himself to wake up, urging him to hear the women callers. In Venketesan's translation, Āṇṭāḷ calls out:

Guardian of the mansions
of our master, Nadagopa
You who guard his gates
where banners and flags fly high
Unlock these jeweled doors . . .
so we are here,
pure and unsullied
to awaken him
with our singing. . . .
Please open these doors. . . .
Arise!
God of gods,
you sliced apart the sky
and spanned the worlds
Do not sleep
but wake up now! . . .
You laze upon this bed. . . .
Please answer us. . . .
Abandon your sleep. . . .
You were born among simple folk
whose livelihood was tending cows
So you cannot refuse our small services.
We are only yours.
We serve only you. . . .
and those who flawlessly recite these verses
will instantly earn the reward
of the grace of our beloved Tirumāl
whose eyes and face are radiant
whose four shoulders are like four dark mountains
and having received all this
they will be joyful forever.

(2010: 66–80)

As we can see, Āṇṭāḷ's song-poem and the kōlam serve a similar purpose, to initiate a dialogue with the divine as the first act of the day. By its aesthetic nature, the kōlam calls out to passersby to wake up and be aware of the grace flowing from the divine presence. Similarly, Āṇṭāḷ's poems call to the divine to awaken and bestow grace on the seekers. The three parallels are (1) the seeker awakens; (2) the deity awakes; (3) the divine shares its presence with the community.

Thus the creation of the kōlam reminds Tamil women of Āṇṭāḷ's call to the divine, and these parallel metaphors function to reinforce the divine other's presence in everyday life.

Forgiveness

One of the main reasons for making the kōlam is to ask in advance for the forgiveness of the earth goddess, Bhūdevi, for using and burdening her throughout the day. As Tamil women state, "We make the kōlam to show Bhūdevi that we are thinking of her as the first act of the day, that we recognize her suffering when we ask her to bear our weight." In this way, the kōlam acts as a field of forgiveness between Bhūdevi and the woman of the household. Similarly, in Āṇṭāḷ's story, Vishnu's act of receiving the used garland creates a field of forgiveness between him and Āṇṭāḷ. Thus, the metaphor of forgiveness is echoed in both ritual acts of devotion.

Significantly, the earth goddess Bhūdevi is often merged with the saintly figure of Āṇṭāḷ in the kōlam narratives. The parallel representations of Bhūdevi and of Āṇṭāḷ is not merely coincidental. The idea that Āṇṭāḷ originated the practice of the kōlam to show women how to worship Bhūdevi could be a result of the collapsing of these two figures, one human and one divine. I suggest that the worship of Bhūdevi through the kōlam is an orientation toward Āṇṭāḷ, who in turn becomes the conduit or pathway to Vishnu through the kōlam. In other words, the threshold where the kōlam is drawn could be considered a place where women ask forgiveness of Bhūdevi, of Āṇṭāḷ, and ultimately of Vishnu, through the intermediary of Āṇṭāḷ.

Generosity

As I examined the hagiography of Āṇṭāḷ and the elements outlined in the ritual practice of the kōlam, I observed another significant correspondence: the metaphor of generosity, a theme that is repeated throughout this book. A parallel narrative function occurs between the offerings of the polluted garland and the kōlam. The climax of Āṇṭāḷ's story occurs when Āṇṭāḷ willfully gives Vishnu the flowers she has worn; likewise, the climax of the kōlam narratives occurs when the rice-flour designs disappear or are "consumed." Vishnu prefers the garland that has already been used to Āṇṭāḷ's satisfaction. Similarly, when the kōlam is carried off by the feet of passersby through its being used (or dispersed), its auspicious power spreads throughout the community. As the kōlam is slowly depleted, it becomes a "gift of waste" representing generosity and love to the divinity as well as the community.

This led me to draw an analogy between Āṇṭāḷ with the garland and the Tamil woman with the kōlam. I suggest that the woman of the household, who creates the kōlam to be smudged out by passersby, is daily reenacting the narrative moment in which Āṇṭāḷ's lovingly worn garland is offered to Vishnu. In the Āṇṭāḷ narrative, the garland symbolizes Āṇṭāḷ's pure heart and her innocent desire for Vishnu. The traces of rice flour as the kōlam is worn away, depleted, eaten, or consumed by "a thousand souls" symbolizes the woman householder's love for the divine, her household, and her community. Just like Āṇṭāḷ admired the garland on her body before giving it to her divine love, women "show off" the kōlam for each other in the early morning and feel satisfaction at offering their best efforts to the divine.

In yet another parallel, just like Bhūdevi receives the offering of the depleted kōlam from the woman of the household, Vishnu receives the offering of the wilted garland from Āṇṭāḷ. The auspicious powers of both the garland and the kōlam actually become activated by being used and the resulting state of depletion. The function of the kōlam is to enable women's blessings to travel throughout the community, while the function of the garland is to be worn or "used" by the daughter before it is offered to the divine as a sign of love and affection. Through the woman householder, the kōlam becomes the *prasād* (the taking back of "leftovers" after they've been offered to gods and goddesses) for Bhūdevi, just as through Āṇṭāḷ the wilted garland becomes the prasād for Vishnu.

In conclusion, the use of Āṇṭāḷ as inspiration for the kōlam is not accidental. In fact, the parallels between the story of Āṇṭāḷ and the practice of the kōlam are striking. The daily creation of the kōlam reenacts Āṇṭāḷ's offering of the used garland and reminds the Tamil woman of Āṇṭāḷ's call to the divine. The story of Āṇṭāḷ echoes the underlying meaning of the kōlam: that ritual acts of love create fields of forgiveness.

Historical Appearance of the Word *Kōlam*

Let's examine the use of the word *kōlam* in other Tamil literary texts before and after Āṇṭāḷ's two poems. I found multiple references to the word *kōlam* in ancient Tamil Sangam poetry, from the third century BCE to the third century CE, which preceded Āṇṭāḷ's poems by many centuries. According to the *Index to Sangam Literature*, there were many references to the word *kōlam* in ancient Tamil texts. However, I found that not a single one of those kōlam references referred to threshold designs.[16] Rather, all the them referred to the other meanings of the word: disguise, form, and decoration. V. Saroja, the leading scholar on the kōlam in the Tamil language, also found no explicit references to the kōlam in ancient Tamil literature (see Saroja 1992; Saraswathi and Vijayalakshmi 1993).

A few references occur after Āṇṭāḷ mentioned the kōlam in her poems. In the 13th century, a few hundred years after Āṇṭāḷ's references, the word *kōlam* occurs in a medieval temple inscription listing the duties to be conducted by temple women (Orr 2000: 118–20). Leslie Orr records an important reference to the kōlam in her intriguing and compelling work *Donors, Devotees, and Daughters of God: Temple Women in Medieval Tamilnadu*:

> In the thirteenth-century inscription already discussed . . . ten temple women were assigned to various duties, including applying kappu (protective substances or adornments) to the deities—a task that I classified as an attendance function—as well as making decorations (kōlams) in the great hall (mahamandapa) of the temple and cleaning and applying kappu in the first and second prakams (surrounding courtyards). This is the only Chola period inscription that specifies that women performed the service of cleaning temple floors . . . Both Tamil and Sanskrit bhakti literature exhorts devotees to serve the Lord by cleaning the floors of his shrine, but this is the only inscription that suggests—through its careful assignment of duties to specific women—that cleaning the floors of the temple was considered an honored task in the Chola period. It is also the only inscription that indicates that making auspicious designs (kōlams) had a place in the Chola period temple or that this was a distinctively feminine task, as it is in contemporary South India. (Orr 2000: 119)

What Orr has described here is extraordinary for its historical value in determining that making the kōlams was part of the domestic routine of Tamil women associated with temples in the 13th century. That it was "considered an honored task" also reveals the value of this kind of decoration in the grand ritual context of large medieval temples.

Women making the kōlam also became a symbol of a flourishing kingdom and a virtuous king. Shulman, for example, refers to the excellent king Vallāḷamakārājan, whose kingdom thrived and "the tiger and the cow drank from the same watering place, . . . women decorated the street with kōlams, rain fell on schedule, and the hungry were fed" (Shulman 1985: 332).[17] V. Saroja points to the 17th-century song "Meenakshiammai kura," which contains the phrase "cleaning the threshold and writing the kōlam on it" (1988: 7).

The next reference I found was in an 18th-century household manual of women's duties and responsibilities written by the Sanskrit pundit Tryambaka in Thanjavur. Julia Leslie, in her illuminating book *The Perfect Wife*, describes the kōlam in an 18th-century context of worshipping the threshold:

> The goddess, deity of all, always resides on the threshold. . . . "Anyone who touches that threshold with his foot or crosses over it without worshipping it first will find no happiness . . ." "If a woman walks over ground that has been smeared (i.e., with cow-dung) but not marked with the auspicious sign of the *svastika*, she will lose three things: her wealth (*vittam*), long life and her good reputation." . . . Tryambaka concludes that "the goddess Lakshmi, complete with all her attributes, always dwells in the house that always shines as a result of smearing (with cow-dung) and auspicious powder designs (raṇgavalya)." (64)

Here, worshipping the threshold by decorating it with auspicious signs is emphasized as a way to attract Lakshmi to occupy the threshold. This idea has come up repeatedly in women's oral narratives on the kōlam.

Given Āṇṭāḷ's references to the kōlam (or mandala) in the ninth century, a 12th-century Tamil inscription, and a 17th-century reference to the kōlam, it is clear that the kōlam is not a recent phenomenon. It has been around in some form or other for over a thousand years.

6

Designs

I was nine years old when I learned to make my first kōlam design in my grandparents' village, Rettakudi. One day my mother's hands would guide mine, filled with rice flour; the next day it would be my grandmother's hands. Do it this way, not this way, they would say. I mastered the relatively simple ones after a few days. It was easy to draw, though not entirely obvious at first. My first one was two triangles opposing each other, in balance (Figure 6.1). It ended up looking like a star, though you didn't draw it as if it were one: you drew one triangle on top of the other, but facing opposite directions. At the time I didn't know what it actually meant; later on I learned that the triangles represented the male and female genders. They were facing each other, opposing, in tense symmetry.

Its most common colors, red for female and white for male, can also symbolize the threshold merging with male and female energies. The kōlam could be seen as also being linked to a representation of sexual pleasure, since women literally get out of the marital bed before sunrise and make the kōlam even before bathing. The transition from sleep and the marital bed into making the kōlam can therefore be considered a post-sexual act. In fact, the first design I learned when I was nine is that specific one. These designs operate on at least two levels. The first level has an explicit design quality, and the second is more implicit and known to only a few. It is a more secretive tantric knowledge that has more explicit references that would not be divulged unless necessary in a particular ritual context (Apfell-Marglin 1985).

After I learned those first designs, we returned back home to New Delhi and I saw my mother and other Tamil women draw them. Ironically, I didn't pay much attention to these designs until we migrated to America a few years later. Here in the suburbs, my mother would draw either the opposing triangle design or other simple designs. On special feast days she would draw square-based designs that looked like the one in Figure 6.2.

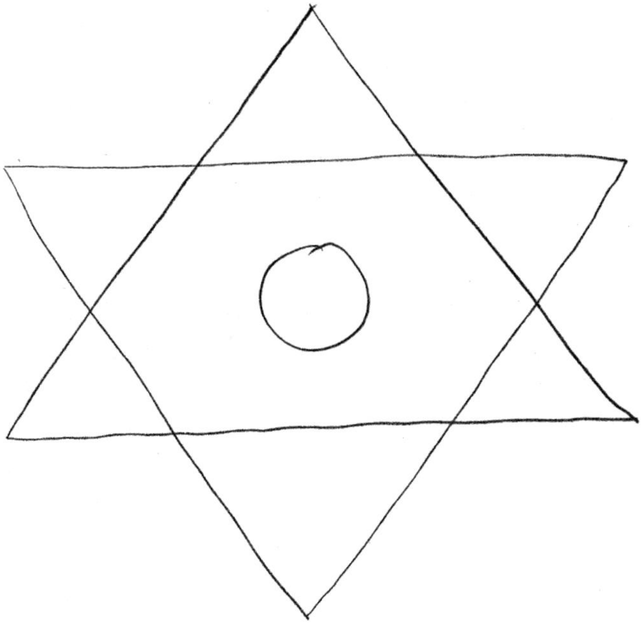

Figure 6.1 My first kōlam.

It was only years later, when I began looking more closely at the designs, that I realized how tremendously complex they were. I began seeing rivers and rivers of patterns, sometimes intertwining with each other. What follows is a description of the range of designs I discovered.

Basic Design Categories

Tamil women often divide kōlams into two major categories: the everyday ones and the highly ritualized, rarely performed ones. Among the everyday kōlams are the *pulli* (dot) and the *katta* (square) (Figures 6.3a–e). Both types reflect the aesthetic value of structural balance and symmetry. Among the ritualized ones are the *navagraha* (nine heavenly bodies), days of the week, and *yantra* (mystical geometric design) kōlams (Figures 6.4a–d). Most of these are geometric and involve drawing dots, curved lines, squares, and triangles in either elementary or advanced ways. Some women also divide the designs into either the traditional (*itheegam*) or modern (*nagareegam*) categories. As we go through each of these

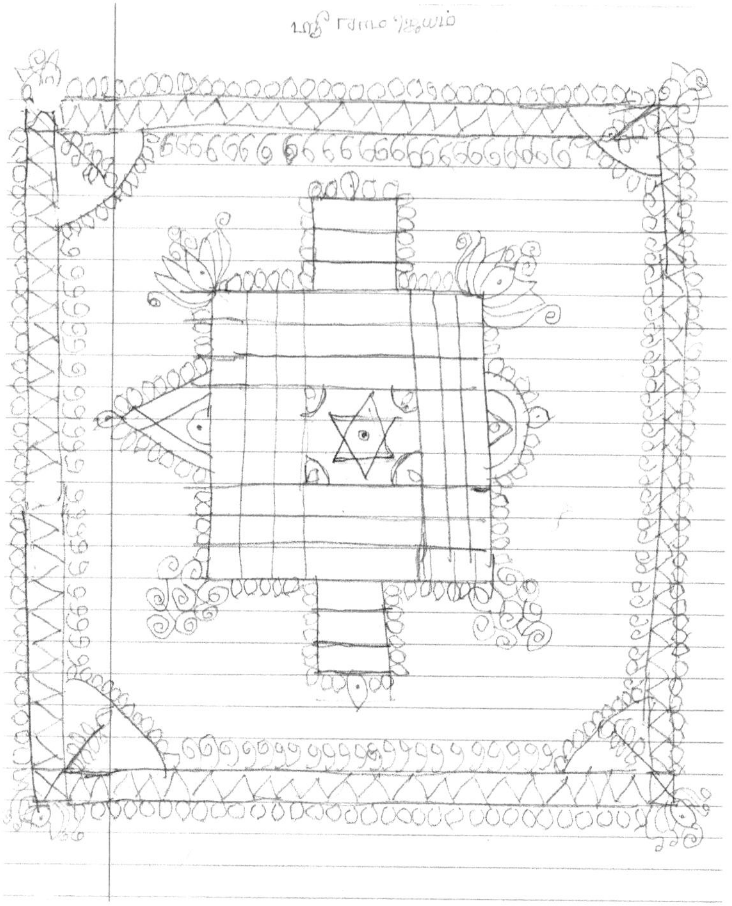

Figure 6.2 Square-based kōlam. Drawn by Pichammal Nagarajan.

basic design categories, we will see how these divisions intersect and overlap with each other.

Pulli (Dot) Kōlams

The most popular design is the pulli (dot) kōlam. Women lay down a grid of dots that frame the final finished drawing, like a scaffold for a building. The most challenging kōlams look like they are twirling on the ground as women lay the dots down and then draw curved lines around them in systematic geometric ways. Making these takes years of practice. They contain many mathematical principles, of which the maker may be either conscious or unconscious. (These mathematical principles will be discussed in Chapter 7.)

(a)

Figure 6.3a Woman making giant labyrinth kōlam, village near Thanjavur.

(b)

Figure 6.3b Progress on the giant labyrinth kōlam.

(c)

Figure 6.3c Nearly finishing the giant labyrinth kōlam.

(d)

Figure 6.3d,e Square-based kōlams, Madurai.

(e)

Figure 6.3d,e Continued

(a)

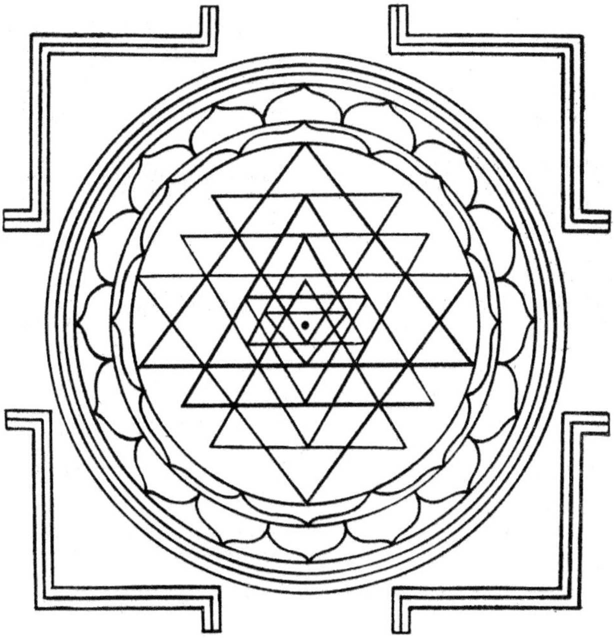

ŚRĪ-CAKRA

Figure 6.4a Sri Chakra. (Source: Inset diagram from Sastri and Ayyangar 2000 [1937].)

(b)

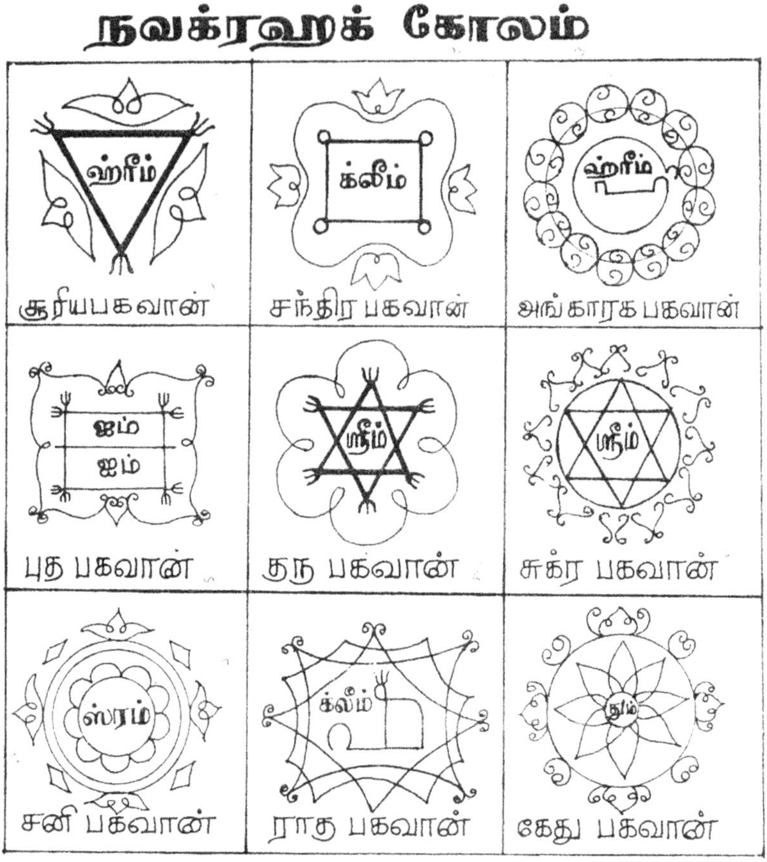

Figure 6.4b Navagraha (nine heavenly bodies) kōlams. (Source: Author's collection.)

The easiest kōlams are the connect-the-dots variety. Women lay down a series of dots and make a line from one dot to the next one. The figures may be geometric or figurative (Figures 6.5a–c). Pulli kōlams contain both traditional and modern elements.

In some of the most difficult kōlams, the lines don't touch the dots. These pulli kōlams are sometimes called *shulli* (curving) kōlams or *sikku* (knot) kōlams because they involve overlapping stringed lines, almost as if they were overlapping knots. As before, the kōlam maker lays down a series of horizontal and vertical dots that serve as a grid for the underlying pattern. But in the next step, the maker does not connect the dots and instead uses them as reference points. The lines curve *around* the dots, forming various geometric shapes that are circuitous and mysterious. This type of pulli kōlam often includes the most

(c)

Figure 6.4c Highly ritualized three-dimensional yantra kōlam. (Source: Author's collection.)

fascinating and mathematically complex designs. The common motif in which endless lines cross and recross around a number of dots forms a kind of labyrinth (see Figures 6.3a–c), which is why they are called labyrinth kōlams. One way to create this form is for the woman to place anywhere from three to 50 dots inside a selected area. The average large kōlam is based around a central line structure of 25 dots. There are a number of rows of dots, with each one placed under the other; every row has one less dot until we come to the very last row, which consists of only a single dot. This forms an inverted triangle. This triangle can be mirrored to form a diamond shape. Finally, a continuous line with no beginning or end is drawn that encloses all the dots without ever touching them.[1] Other geometric forms can also be derived from the labyrinth design, such as elaborate circular figures that sometimes resemble mandalas, or sacred circle designs.

(d)

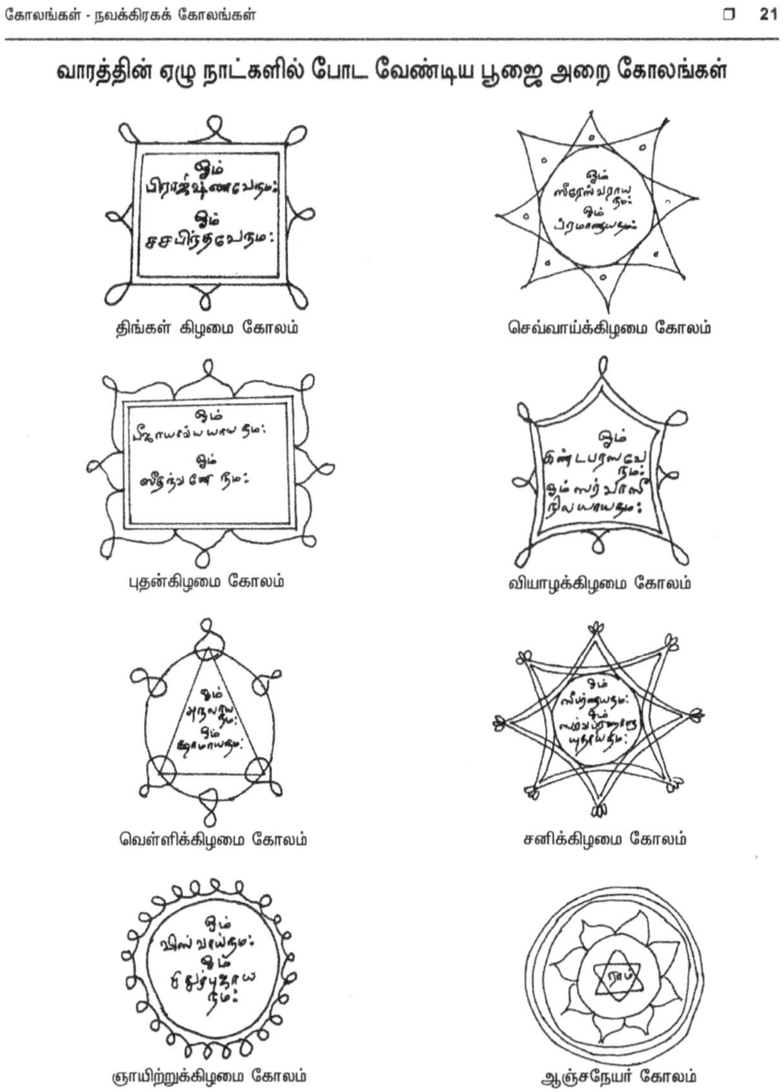

Figure 6.4d Days of the week kōlams plus a Hanuman kōlam. (Source: Balu 21).

Katta (Square) Kōlams

The next category is the katta, or square, kōlam, which begins with laying a grid of parallel and perpendicular lines. Often both Brahmins and non-Brahmins refer to these as Brahmin kōlams. They resemble a top-down view of a temple, with four tall towers (*gopurams*) and sacred tanks (local manmade reservoirs, or *kulams*); four sets of lines indicate the steps leading down to the center of a reservoir (see

(a)

Figure 6.5a Women in the middle of making a connect-the-dots type kōlam, lotus flower design, Thanjavur.

(b)

Figure 6.5b Connect-the-dots kōlam, Thanjavur. Photo by Lee Swenson.

Figure 6.2). These kulams are made by the community and are most often created within the temple grounds. Pilgrims use the tanks to bathe or at least wash their feet to purify themselves before entering the temple proper. The tanks can be as small as a large pond all the way up to 23 acres. Both the temple and the tank are

(c)

Figure 6.5c Connect-the-dots kōlam (close-up), Thanjavur. Photo by Lee Swenson.

usually rectangular, with trapezoidal towers rising into the sky on all four sides of the temple compound, and this is reflected in the kōlam design. As Brahmins were often linked with temples as priests and administrators, it makes sense that temple-like designs would be associated with them.

Katta kōlams have no dots. They are created with a series of parallel lines that are perpendicular to each other and are often connected into concentric squares. The woman starts at the center with a square and then works her way outward, drawing different shapes and linking them to other geometric shapes such as trapezoids, rectangles, or triangles. She might bind the whole design together with a circle or square at the outside so that it resembles a mandala.

Katta kōlams can also be made with extended outer layers of lotus and other plant motifs that increase the density of the design for especially charged auspicious occasions (Figures 6.6a,b). These are at the borderline between geometric and figurative designs. These katta kōlams do not appear in the bazaar-bought kōlam design books, perhaps because they are done primarily by Brahmin women. Also, some of these katta kōlams are remarkably similar to highly ritualized yantras (see Figures 6.6a,b).

Highly Ritualized and Rarely Drawn Kōlams

Next we move to two overlapping minor categories: the navagraha (nine heavenly forces) kōlams and the yantra kōlams. Both are highly charged with ritual

(a)

Figure 6.6a Katta kōlam with four trapezoids accompanied by small labyrinth figures, Thanjavur.

(b)

Figure 6.6b Katta kōlam with expanding abstract flower motif, Thanjavur.

power and presence and thus are never drawn on front thresholds where they could be stepped on. Rather, they are drawn under tightly circumscribed ritual conditions, in front of domestic ritual altars, and only after lengthy rites of purification. They are drawn with a deeply respectful attitude because they are considered extraordinarily powerful and distant. These kōlams are not intimate or casual. They are considered to be some of the most powerful kōlams, due to the forces they represent, and must never be drawn frivolously. They accompany highly specific ritual vows and observances; even my mother, a devout kōlam-maker, rarely drew them.

Navagrahas (Nine Heavenly Forces)

One of the most widely known and yet rarely practiced kōlam designs is the navagraha. The reason they are rarely drawn is because they are highly ritualized. The word *navagraha* refers to nine heavenly bodies or forces: Surya (sun), Chandra (moon), Budha (Mercury), Shukra (Venus), Mangal (Mars), Guru (Jupiter), Shani (Saturn), Ketu (Dragon's Tail), and Rahu (Dragon's Head). Ketu and Rahu are not actually bodies; rather, they are the elliptical nodes of the intersections of the orbits of the sun and the moon. Each of these navagrahas is represented by its very own kōlam, too (see Figure 6.4b).

These kōlam designs are often found in women's ritual texts in small chapbooks available at local bazaars. There are many variations of the kōlams for each of the navagrahas and they are not consistent across different chapbooks. Each one is also often accompanied by chants in Sanskrit or Tamil. A visit to many large south Indian temple complexes is incomplete unless you circle its section of navagraha divinities, making an appropriate number of circumambulations (three, nine, or 18). In addition to each having its own kōlam, there is an entire typology associated with each one. Each is associated with a day of the week (some of the days are shared among the celestial forces), a color, a grain, a flower, a metal, a gem, an animal, a pilgrimage site, and a particular benefit that comes from worshipping. For example, the sun is linked with Sunday, red, wheat, red lotus, copper, ruby, a seven-horse chariot, and increased knowledge. Saturn is linked with Saturday, black, Gingelly (sesame seed oil), black kuvalli flower, iron, sapphire, a crow, and reducing illness and debts.

The Nagapattinam district (earlier called Thanjavur district), the Thiruvarur district, and the new smaller Thanjavur district have the rare good fortune of having all nine temples associated with each of the navagrahas in one distinct area. These are the particular temples where these heavenly forces are housed and adored. These sacred places are Suryanarkoil (Surya [sun]), Thingalur (Chandran [moon]), Vaitheeswaran Koil (Angaraka [Mars]), Thirvenkadu (Bhudan [Mercury]), Alangudi (Guru [Jupiter]), Kanchanur (Shukran [Venus]), Thirunallar (Shani [Saturn]), Thirunageswaram (Rahu [elliptical node]), and Keezha Perumpallam (Kethu [elliptical node]). During the winter of 1998–99, I set myself the task of visiting each of these temples to take a closer look at the relationship between the kōlam design and the heavenly body and force it represents. I discovered that people came to these temples for a specific purpose: to cure a disease; to heal from an injury (either physical or mental); or to stop a string of bad luck (e.g., infertility, nonmarriageability, job losses). Even though they were in out-of-the-way places, these temples were still immensely popular (although not as much as Madurai's Meenakshi temple or Thanjavur's Bṛhadīśvara temple).

The most striking temple was the one dedicated to the god Shani, or Saturn, in Thirunnallar near the Bay of Bengal. The planet Saturn represents a specific kind of ill force called *shani dōsham*; if it was present in your life, it was considered to be extremely bad luck. Shani was married, I discovered, to Lakshmi's sister, Mūdevi, the goddess of bad luck, sleepiness, dullness, and laziness. I thought it seemed like a perfect arranged marriage: they were matched in their qualities of bad luck and were made for each other. Although I had heard rumors of Mūdevi's existence in a temple, I was never able to find her and was obviously discouraged from doing so. But her husband Saturn was often found in every large temple complex as part of the "nine heavenly bodies" area.

Whenever I experienced a string of painful or sorrowful events, my mother would say with an air of certainty, "Oh, you are being ruled by the forces of shani dōsham; it will last seven years." It served as a way for her to understand my suffering. Perhaps the notion of this kind of force comforted her, knowing that it might be temporary, lasting only a few months, or at most seven years. She believed that after this time the negative force would be exhausted and release me from its grip. My mother would often recommend during these times that I worship Shani to plead with him to extricate me from his firm clutches.[2]

Navagraha kōlams need to be drawn in front of a lamp lit in the household pūja area, using five different kinds of oils with hand-shaped cotton wicks (Raghavan and Narayan 2005). They need to be accompanied by intensive prayers, chanting songs, and flower offerings. Then it is believed that the obstacles blocking whatever is desired may be removed. If, for instance, a married couple has irreconcilable conflicts, then these conflicts will disappear and a new sense of harmony will be achieved. The belief is that husbands will change their negative qualities into more positive ones. Children will begin behaving and developing better habits; the economics of the household will thrive; illnesses will be healed. By drawing these navagraha kōlams, it is believed that your previously unsolvable problems will be resolved.

These kōlams have an air of intrigue and mystery around them. They resemble another set of mysterious kōlams called the yantras, which we will now discuss.

Yantras

Besides the navagraha kōlams, yantras, another geometric design category, have a unique place. *Yantra* in Sanskrit literally means a machine, instrument, or mystical diagram (Khanna 1979). A yantra is drawn not on the thresholds of a home, business, or temple, but in an area where no one will step on it, such as the pūja (household shrines) and temple shrine areas—and only at highly auspicious times. Although they have different design elements, these often overlap with those of the ordinary kōlams, yet they are always taken very seriously (see Figure 6.4a c). These diagrams resemble the katta kōlams in that they are often square-based with four entrances, or lotus flowers that seem to keep expanding into multiple layers.[3]

These particular yantras are ancient, powerful mystical designs done on copper plates or drawn by hand. They are created to generate ritual power under highly specified conditions. These rituals are not often performed because they are considered to be too dangerous to be done on an everyday basis. Throughout the entire time the women are creating them, they are in an intensive state of meditation and may also chant. They undergo intensive rituals of cleansing before creating them, so they are in a highly purified state. Girls do not make the yantras; they are considered too powerful for ones so young and inexperienced.

In general, these traditional designs are the most complex in terms of both drawing and symbolism. Like the navagraha kōlams, yantras are not made on ordinary days of the week. Not many women I spoke with mentioned them, although male priests and other male religious professionals did. Unlike most other kōlams, which are made by women, these yantras are often made by specialized professional religious men, either at the temple, for highly specific ritual activities such as building a temple, or on other ritual occasions. So there is somewhat of a gender divide, although it is not strictly held to, where yantras are done mostly by men, kōlams mostly by women (Khanna 1979).

One subcategory of yantras are the ones drawn by Adi Shankara (788–821 CE), who founded a prominent school of Hinduism called Advaita (non-dualism). In his well-known medieval text *Soundarya Lahari* ("Ocean of Beauty") he brought together chants and the visual geometric embodiment of the energy of the goddess in the universe through the yantra ritual diagrams (see also Śaṅkarācārya 1965; White 1996). The chants are done while drawing a particular yantric ritual diagram, but only by trained specialists, whether men or women. These drawings have some interesting overlaps with the everyday traditional kōlams drawn by women, and we will discuss these as we go cover some of their qualities.

The *Soundarya Lahari* describes the beauty of the primal goddess Shakti from head to toe and praises her as the powerful one, the central force of the universe, without which Siva, her spouse, the male god, is listless, empty, impotent. There are 103 designs and chants in Sanskrit that parallel each other. These are considered to be some of the highest homages to the goddess Devi. The *Soundarya Lahari* hints at the fullness of the meditative power inherent in the kōlam; in other words, the ways in which the goddess is acknowledged, honored, and worshipped. Her feet, body, and face all are described as lotuses, and lotuses also are the most popular motifs in the kōlam. The kōlam, too, is a visually drawn praise to the goddess.

One of the basic forms of the yantra and the kōlam is, as I mentioned at the beginning of the chapter, two intersecting triangles that stand opposed to each other. These are seen as the union of the male and female energies of the universe. One triangle represents the yoni, or female creative power, and the opposing one represents the male creative power. They intersect and combine to create beauty, regeneration, and fertility. Underlying the meaning of this diagram is a profound valuation of the strength and power of Shakti in her primal geometric form. Without these connections to her, Siva is considered to be inert and without creative energy, rhythm, and mobility. In fact, he is incapable of acting independently; reproducing; being heroic, potent, or luminous; or even being seen unless he is united with Shakti. Although girls begin learning the kōlam as I did by making a set of two opposing intersecting triangles, it turns out that this is the actually most elemental form embedded in the heart of the Sri Chakra design and other yantras in the *Soundarya Lahari* text. So even though young girls are not allowed to learn to create the full Sri Chakra yantra, they do learn and practice the elemental structures.

The Sri Chakra yantra is the ultimate embodiment of the primal goddess (see Figure 6.4a). It is probably one of the most complex yantras and is one of the most ancient devotional aids to worshipping her. In fact, this design is considered equivalent to the goddess herself and is connected to hidden mystical powers. While constructing it, the worshipper is saying *mantras* (sacred chants). This design is also thought to contain extraordinary magical healing powers—for example, to cure blindness, mental illness, and so on.

At the center of the Sri Chakra design, deep within its geometric (and figurative) layers, lies the bindu, a dot. The dot represents the infinite, expanding power of the universe. As we recall, the labyrinth kōlams are essentially matrices of dots laid down with lines circling around them.

According to George Joseph, an ethnomathematician:

> The Sri Yantra consists of nine interwoven isosceles triangles: four point upwards, representing Sakti, the primordial female essence of dynamic energy, and five point downwards, representing Siva, the primordial male essence of static wisdom. The triangles are arranged in such a way that they produce 43 subsidiary triangles, at the center of the smallest of which there is a big dot (known as the bindu). (George 1991: 20)

Another interpretation is for the core of the diagram to consist of five triangles with their apexes pointing down, representing the female goddess in her primal form of Shakti, and four triangles pointing up, representing her consort, Siva. "Without their conjunction, the Sri Chakra, which may be taken to signify the origin of the world, cannot be formed. In other words, the universe will cease to be, when there will be the mahā-pralaya, the final dissolution" (George 1991: 20). The leitmotif of this text is that Shakti, the goddess personified in her three aspects of will, wisdom, and activity, "is essential for Siva, to accomplish anything" (George 1991: 237–240; see also Kuliachev 1984).

Yantras are found not only in the *Soundarya Lahari* but in many other texts. However, the *Soundarya Lahari* is one of the most common places you can find them. As mentioned earlier, this text has a collection of 103 mantras, each with its own yantra (Śaṅkarācārya [1937] 2000). Each of the 103 yantra designs has its own permutation and combination of triangles, dots, squares, and curved lines and a specific ritual prescription of actions. This prescription can be performed on a daily basis over a period of four to 365 days. The range can be from 108 to 30,000 repetitions. Food offerings are also made to the goddess in the form of the yantra, and they can be made from sugarcane, black pepper, sweet cakes, honey, fruit, yogurt, rice, sweet rice, and coconut (Śaṅkarācārya [1937] 2000).

The benefits of worshipping the goddess through the diagrammatic yantras are said to be many: acquiring learning; curing a terminal disease; winning over an enemy; gaining success, wealth, or progeny; healing an eye disease; promoting sleep; increasing the flow of milk in women for their infants; warding off evil spirits; and increasing physical strength and virility (Śaṅkarācārya [1937] 2000). There are specific yantras for removing the evil eye (*drishti*), increasing wealth (*kubera*), and conquering space (*vasthu*). There are also *mahasakthi* yantras, copper plates kept in the pūja area and worshiped using stringent purity rituals. The yantra and the navagraha kōlams can lead us directly to decipher the ways in which geometric forms are imbued with multiple cultural understandings and interpretations.

Modernity and the Kōlam

We have just discussed the traditional kōlams, pulli, katta, navagraha, and yantras. Now we will look at the modern ones.

The modern kōlams, the figurative and landscape designs, are very popular. Sometimes women start to make them by laying down a traditional grid of dots, so they could be mistaken for the beginnings of a traditional kōlam. But unlike the complex patterns in which twirling lines circle the dots without ever touching them, these dots are simply joined in a connect-the-dots fashion, using straight or curved lines (see Figures 6.5a–c). The lines may form any sort of geometric shape—rectangles, squares, triangles—with each shape contiguous to or in contact with the next.

Connect-the-dots lines also create figures of highly auspicious natural elements such as plants and animals: lotus flowers, tulips, sunflowers, seashells, cows, butterflies, snakes, peacocks, rabbits, cats, fish, ducks, mice, swans, and elephants. Often the cows and elephants are decorated, just as they are in real life (Figures 6.7a,b and 6.8). More auspicious material objects include open

(a)

Figure 6.7a Peacocks, Thanjavur.

(b)

Figure 6.7b Grand figurative kōlam of Pongal pot and sugarcane stalks, Mayiladuthurai. Photo by Lee Swenson.

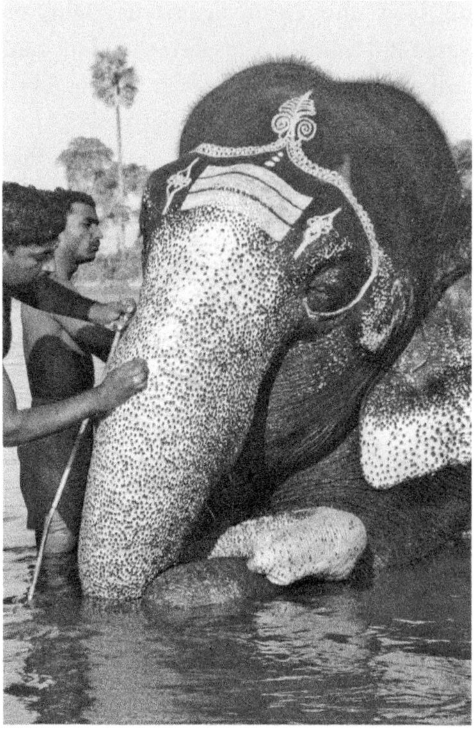

Figure 6.8 Close-up of mahouts drawing Shaivite forehead symbols, Bhrihadhisvara Temple, Thanjavur.

umbrellas, Ferris wheels, lit mud lamps, mud pots overflowing with neatly stacked round sweet *laddu* balls, dolls, Hindu temples, Islamic mosques, Christmas trees, temple chariots, folk dancers, and cooking bowls. Sometimes the designs include words like "welcome" or geometric shapes and patterns. They can contain political messages of interreligious harmony or saving the environment (Figure 6.9). They serve the same function as banners, pamphlets, or leaflets (see Chapter 8 on kōlam competitions for further details). Some have color poured into them for special feast days so they resemble the northern Indian rangōlis, or "colored designs." Many are symmetrical as well.

Modern kōlams are more direct in their meanings, not allusive and implied like the traditional ones. They can include iconographic and playful designs of Lakshmi; the god who removes obstacles, Ganesh; a snake; or the god Krishna. Some of the figures are auspicious ritual objects, but just as often they reflect modern life. I have seen designs featuring big pots and pans, a child kicking a soccer ball, lotus flowers, brass prayer lamps, flower pots, and a wide range of musical instruments. Some of these signify desires of success, auspiciousness, or achievement. These are all vividly colored, cartoon-like figures (see

Figure 6.9 One of the winning entries in the kōlam competition that included a mosque, a church, and a temple as part of its figurative design, Madurai.

Figures 3.3–3.6). Some may be Disney cartoon figures (such as a playful Mickey Mouse or Donald Duck), peacocks, a sinking *Titanic*, or a squirrel chomping on a huge nut. Many figurative kōlams are practiced and copied directly from line drawings in schoolbooks and the kōlam chapbooks found in bazaars (see the section coming up on kōlam chapbooks).

Landscape kōlams are a relatively recent innovation. These pictorial and postcard-like images convey contemporary messages of interreligious harmony, landscape scenes, and environmental credos (Figure 6.10). They appear more in kōlam competitions than in everyday life on household thresholds.

Changing Materials

The tools for making the kōlam have been changing. As women's work takes them outside the home and time becomes more precious, various types of stenciled patterns, which allow the woman to create a kōlam in only a fraction of the time, have swept the market since the 1970s. The rolling stenciled cylinder is a tool that resembles a rolling pin. It is filled with rice flour, and when the woman rolls it on the ground, the flour seeps out through holes to form a repeating pattern. The holes in the cylinder are punched by itinerant toolmakers. Clustered in family groups, these toolmakers wander throughout India, arriving

Figure 6.10 Map of India, inter-religious conflict poster-like kōlam.

in towns before major festivals when either the kōlam or similar ritual arts are practiced on a large scale. With these stenciled patterns, women can create elaborate kōlams much more quickly (Figures 6.11a–f).

Throughout the years, the materials used to make these "rolling pins" have changed. In my grandmother's generation, in the 1930s and 1940s, there were copper and brass cylinders. In my mother's time, in the 1950s and 1960s, they were made of aluminum and stainless steel. More recently, in the 1990s and onwards, they are made of PVC pipe.

Women also use flat copper or aluminum templates that have been pierced with holes. The recycled metal came from Santol or Pond's talcum powder cans. These pieces of metal are flattened out, reshaped, and then pierced with a hammer and nail to create different designs. They have raised edges on the four sides. The woman places one on the ground and sprinkles flour over it. When the template is removed, the flour design remains.

Over the past 20 years, plastic stick-on kōlams or decals (similar to the ones that are placed on cars) have become available. They are often used in apartment complexes and condominiums where there is no real access to the street, so the kōlam has to be made on the marble hallway just outside each door.

(a)

Figure 6.11a Itinerant kōlam toolmakers selling on roadside, Thanjavur.

(b)

Figure 6.11b Daughter of an itinerant kōlam toolmaker showing how to make an "instant" kōlam.

(c)

Figure 6.11c Daughter of an itinerant kōlam toolmaker showing how to make an "instant" kōlam (close-up of Figure 6.11b).

(d)

Figure 6.11d–f Kōlam made with rolling stencil and hand, Thanjavur. Photos by Vijaya Nagarajan and Lee Swenson.

(e)

(f)

Figure 6.11d–f Continued

Just as the traditional *kudams* (clay and brass water pots) have been widely replaced by plastic buckets, so too have the hand-drawn and stenciled kōlams been replaced by plastic stick-on decals. They come in a full range of geometric and figurative designs: dot kōlams, yantra, square kōlams, flowers, nine planet kōlams, and so forth. They are often white against a dark red or maroon background, imitating the dark brown earth they would normally be drawn on. They are also often placed or stuck on in the pūja, or the domestic altar area, as it is a sacred place where people do not step on the kōlam. Despite these time-saving tools, the kōlam is still functional and elaborate at symbolic and mythic levels.

However, there is a major problem with this new method. One of the goals of the practice is to make a new kōlam each day, but the plastic stick-on kōlams are hard to remove. This can be frustrating since, as a ritual requirement, the kōlam must remain ephemeral during highly auspicious occasions such as marriages and festivals. Here, making a new kōlam every day is essential.

Another new twist to the traditional kōlam practice is to make them using acrylic paint on temple floors (Figure 6.12). Instead of disappearing in one day as it would if made out of dry rice flour, or lasting a few weeks if made with the wet rice flour mixture, the acrylic kōlam lasts for months. As mentioned in Chapter 2, Meena, who in the Madurai area has been specializing in acrylic kōlams, has become known for them in the surrounding temples. As a traditional ritual practitioner, she is at the cusp of the shift from traditional to modern materials, from temporary to a more permanent nature. Since the 1980s, women have also been switching from local plant dyes to commercially bought, chemically colored powders. The significance of the kōlam in everyday Tamil life will surely change with these shifts in materials.

One of the trends that is disturbing to many women is that as rice flour becomes more expensive, more people are turning to ground stone powder. They often comment that one of the original reasons for making the kōlam was

Figure 6.12 Painting with acrylic paint on temple floors, Meenakshi Temple, Madurai.

to feed ants, insects, and small animals. How can an animal be fed on stone flour? One woman said sadly, "It shows you how much we have lost the reasons for doing the kōlam, how much we are forgetting why we do this." This is another sign that the kōlam practice is leaning toward an appreciation of its artistic skill rather than its original ritual purpose.

Notebooks and Chapbooks

As we have seen, kōlam designs are carefully thought out and practiced before they are created for public viewing. The repertoire of designs is characterized by a repetition of key elements, and over time the patterns become familiar and intimate to the practitioner. A core design or key image structures the initial pattern. Yet, because of the maker's years of training and practice, the patterns still appear unplanned, as if they emerged spontaneously from the woman's hands. At the same time, there is a degree of freedom within the structure, and aesthetic innovations are occurring constantly. Enhancements such as lotuses, abstract leaves, curling stems, and theater-like curtains may also act as a frame around the borders of a key image.

Nearly every woman who makes a kōlam keeps a notebook to record a variety of designs. This is usually a simple ledger book commonly found in markets; it could also be a small schoolbook with plain pages or a large ledger filled with blank pages. Here you can see the rough drafts, with scratch-outs, mistakes, cross-outs, and repeated practicing. These are done mostly in pencil, but they can also be done with a pen or markers, so they can resemble the increasingly popular color-filled kōlams.

Besides the threshold, the most common place to find the kōlams is the market. Local bazaars feature stacks of kōlam pamphlets, including hundreds of designs that women share enthusiastically (See Figure 6.13a).

This could not have happened prior to the invention of the printing press. I could not find any kōlam designs in palm leaf manuscripts. At the Thanjavur Sarasvathi Mahal Library, I asked the librarians about this and found no evidence of explicit kōlam patterns prior to mass printing, though there were literary references to the kōlam prior to that time (as mentioned in Chapter 5). Printed booklets go back at least as far as 1884 and increased in volume throughout the 20th century. A postcard with a kōlam in it, dating to 1905, came into my hands (Figure 6.13b),[4] and it actually resembles a more contemporary kōlam (see Figure 8.2). A kōlam chapbook published in 1928 has designs surprisingly similar to those found in contemporary chapbooks.[5] Layard and a recent doctoral dissertation on ephemeral floor designs throughout India referred to chapbooks having been published in the 1860s (Tadvalkar 2012).

(a)

Figure 6.13a Cover of "Kolaputthakam" (Kolam book), 1884 (Courtesy of Roja Mutthiah).

(b)

Figure 6.13b Postcard of woman doing kōlam, "Chalking the Doorstep, Madras." Higginbotham & Co., Madras and Bangalore, ca. 1905 (Courtesy of Omar Khan).

I have collected over a hundred of these chapbooks from bazaars and roadside stands in the many Tamil towns and cities I traveled to: Chennai, Madurai, Thanjavur, Chidambaram, Tiruchirappalli, Srivilliputtur, Thirunveli, Ooty, Salem, Coimbatore, and many more. Whenever I would go to a market, I would look for a bookshop or kitchen utensil shop that would carry a few of these. Here I will describe four representative chapbooks.

The chapbook covers tend to be brightly colored, often turquoise blue, pumpkin orange, or rose pink. One cover features Ganesh on an expanding, multicolored lotus; the lotus lies on a heaven of flaming blue, echoing the color of Ganesh's pendant. Inside, the kōlams are identified by the number of dots laid across horizontally and the number of dots arranged vertically—for example, 3 times 3, or 5 times 5, or 11 times 11. Labyrinth kōlams are placed alongside duck figures, candles, and Christmas trees in conjunction with abstract circles and mazes.

On another chapbook cover, Donald Duck is taking a picture of Minnie Mouse making a beautiful kōlam, with her gloves on, in front of a grand golden-colored Midwestern-style barn. In the upper left corner, a luminous sun sleeps with eyes closed. So we have a blend of modern and traditional: a 20th-century American cartoon character is making the kōlam before the sun rises, following the age-old ritual prescription.

In another chapbook, *Changing Superstar Kōlams,* Rajinikanth, one of the most popular movie stars in Tamil Nadu, is watching a woman making the kōlam. Perhaps this indicates that making a very traditional kōlam will attract the gaze of young, modern Tamil men, even a movie star!

The fourth book features a traditional labyrinth on the cover and is entitled *Vasan's Rangōli,* referring both to the name of the store, Vasan, and the parallel northern Indian women's ritual painting tradition of rangōli.

These modern kōlam chapbooks with their attractive covers fascinated me. I can easily imagine my mother feeling pleased to see this male movie star gazing at the kōlam-maker, marking the threshold as a place of courtship. I am sure it helped to sell this chapbook, enabling millions of contemporary kōlam-makers to actively connect the kōlam to the increasing Westernization and modernity around them.

Despite the wide proliferation of these kōlam design chapbooks, there are still an enormous variety of kōlam designs, distinguished by their motifs, regional variations, and caste, gender, and class variations. However, designs have become more uniform and prefabricated than in the past. Regional variations are recognized and regularly discussed among women. For instance, a particular type of curved square design characterizes the kōlams created in and around the town of Srīvilliputtūr in southern Tamil Nadu. On special occasions a red border is created. This type of kōlam design even predominates among immigrants from Srīvilliputtūr living in Madras, and is identified with the Iyengar Brahmin caste. Although Tamil women referred to a diversity of regionally identifiable kōlams, in actuality I found far less regional diversity than these conversations had led me to expect.

V. Saroja is a leading Tamil scholar on the kōlam from Madurai. In her analysis of caste distinctions of kōlams (1988), the *padikōlam* or step kōlam, done mostly for festivals, is drawn by Iyer Brahmins to indicate a pilgrimage to the home of Shiva in Kailash, the mountains in the Himalayas. She states that these kōlams tend to predominate among Brahmins, though other castes also perform them ritually. Even in these there are variations between different subsects of Brahmins, such as Iyers and Aiyangars. Iyer Brahmins often chant the *slokas* that go along with the kōlams. Aiyangar kōlam-makers tend to perform daily kōlams that go along with the *Vishnuahasranāmam*, an ode to Vishnu.

The oldest kōlam chapbook I discovered was through the help of an amazing elderly gentleman, Roja Muthiah, who was an incessant collector in a village outside the town of Karaikkudi. I went there for the first time with David Shulman and Narayana Rao in December 1987; they kindly took me, a first-year graduate student, along with them. Literally every room in his home was stacked high with papers, women's magazines, old books, and newspapers. At the time it seemed to me that this man who held onto the past of Tamil culture so assiduously would fade away with all his materials sometime in the future, as if his focused accumulation of high-rise piles of old papers and books would vanish after his life was over. Its value, I was then sure, would never be recognized in his lifetime. His two daughters helped procure some of the materials. He knew the location of obscure materials and could track them down within minutes.

When I asked him if he had any old kōlam books or materials, at first he said, "No, I don't think so." But he agreed to look through his materials. Without looking at me, he grumbled, "Come back next year." I did so, and he grinned at me with great flourish and pride, saying, "Look what I found. A kōlam chapbook that was published in 1884! I was hoping you would return back."

I held the original chapbook with astonishment and delight. It was browned with age and had bug-eaten edges. The decrepit brown-paper cover featured the old printing of a Tamil letterpress. He photocopied it for me (Figure 6.14). I bowed down to him with a deep and heartfelt thank you. Soon after, I said in a rushed way, "I have to leave very soon." He laughed heartily and pointedly replied, "All of you from over *there* come on winged feet!" I laughed uncomfortably in recognition.

It came as a deep surprise to me to learn that, years later, with the wide support of scholars throughout the world who had been helped by this elderly gentleman, he and his materials were immortalized into the Roja Muthiah Research Library in Chennai.

Dance and the Kōlam—Chandralekha

The kōlam captivated the choreographer Chandralekha, and she played with the kōlam often in her compositions. She had long white hair, which she wore

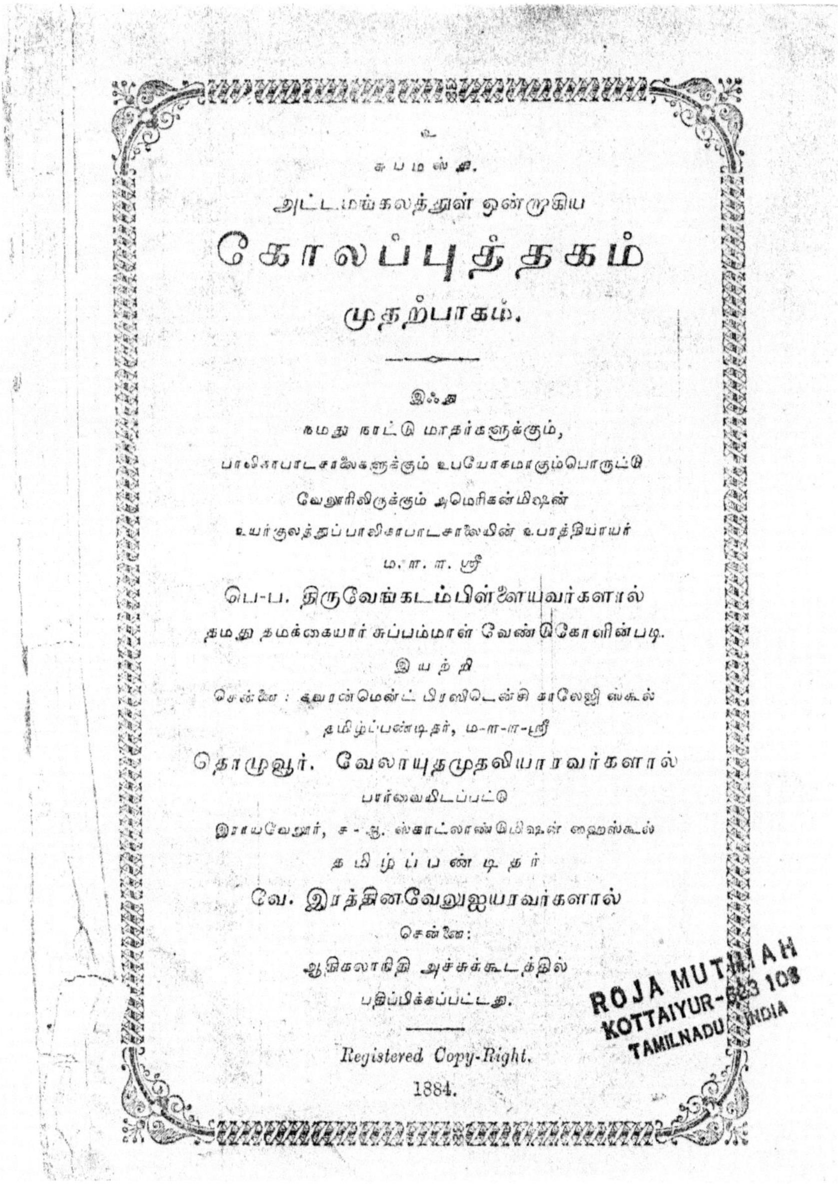

Figure 6.14 Kolaputhakam (kōlam book), 1884. (Source: Author's collection.)

unbound and free. When you saw her, it seemed as if you were seeing a vision of a dream. She laughed often, as if she were a girl expressing surprise and delight at what she saw or heard. Chandralekha spoke to me again and again of the place the kōlam had in her creative work on Bharatanatyam, a classical Indian dance. Often she said passionately: "The kōlam is at the *center* of many of my dance

(a)

(b)

Figure 6.15a,b Chandralekha's troupe dancing on roof against the backdrop of the sky. Photo by Dashrat Patel. (Source: Author's collection.)

choreographies and it is a foundational critical reference point in Tamil culture and Indian culture, in general"[6] (Figures 6.15a, b).

Her work circled around and through the philosophical understanding of many of the critical Indian body traditions: Bharatanatyam, yoga, martial arts, and the kōlam. Bharucha, in his marvelously insightful work on Chandralekha, writes that she focused on "explaining the graphic formations of the kōlam" and mentions her "numerous experiments with dots on a sixteen point square grid" (1995, 82).

In 1985, in one of her first radical choreographies, *Angika: Traditions of Dance and Body Language in India,* she explored the multiple ways in which the body's energies are renewed. She thought of the kōlam as not just a women's ritual art form but also a bodily expression that fused the experience of the woman's body with the rising sunlight glimmering around her, a way to renew herself and the world she inhabited. She spoke of the vital place of the spine in the body, and she emphasized repeatedly to me that the kōlam being made by bending the spine in the body was critical to its creation. She states:

> The tradition of physical expression in India is long and unbroken and it needs a mere cursory look to discover the obvious and integral relationship between the physical principles involved in work, eating and healing practices, ritual, martial arts, yoga, dance. When placed together side by side they reveal the tight unity of their dynamic structures and their common origins—as evident in the principles of "mandala," of squaring or circularising the body for holding the earth. (Chandralekha et al. 1985)

She used kōlam designs as evocative metaphysical fluid structures embodying a rich range of metaphors and creativities. In 1990, she incorporated the navagraha kōlam designs in her piece, *Prānā: Traditions of Aātyā and Asanā.* In 1995, she created an entire dance around Shankara's *Soundarya Lahiri* called *Yantra.* In *Yantra,* you could see the kōlams as dancing points on the surface of the floor as you normally would see them; then, you would see them as three-dimensional, floating, almost like waves of streaming light of dots, held in her dancers' bodies as if they were the dots themselves. The dancers embodied dots of condensed and expanding energy, quivering dots of containment and exhilaration.

She saw each dancer as a dot that swirled into space as lines, circles, triangles, mandalas, yonis (female regenerative spaces), and yantras. Her play with the geometric shapes of the kōlams brought together kōlams in motion; dancing three-dimensional dots, squares, triangles, and yantra kōlams dominated her choreographic space. Bharucha expands on this idea:

> *Yantra* is . . . a startlingly modernist version of traditional principles of energy in the body. Drawing on what Chandra describes as a "vocabulary of inwardness," the production draws us into an elusive journey of the body as it moves through . . . [the] five breathtaking elaborations of yantra (diagrams of the body) into the still point of the bindu around which the dancers find their centres in solitude. At one level,

> the exploration is a deepening and maturation of the quest which was visible in *Prana*, where the *grahas* (planets) were abstracted through yantras—geometric forms shaped through yogic movement. But the significant difference in *Yantra* is the insertion of erotica, inflection of sexual energy animating the intimate spaces within and between bodies. Inspired by the visionary poetry, *Soundarya Lahari* . . . Chandra has crystallized her choreography around the central image of the *trikona* or triangle . . . Through superimpositions and rotations of the body, caresses of movement and ceaseless flow, the form of the triangle is mesmerizingly dynamised by the dancers. . . . For Chandra, this is not merely the perception of "beauty" or "aesthetics" but the capacity to retrieve vital energies coiled within our bodies, which can enable us to "cope with and confront," in her words, "the daily assaults on our senses, the unprecedented degradation of our bodies." (1995, 338–339)

Many of these dances were performed all over the world. She not only used the kōlam designs in her own choreographies but also influenced other world-class choreographers to do so outside of India. For example, in 2001, Mark Morris, the well-known American choreographer, became influenced by the kōlam after spending time with Chandralekha in Chennai. He gave the name *Kōlam* to a choreographic piece that was commissioned by the famed cellist Yo-Yo Ma and his Silk Road Project in 2002. It premiered in Berkeley, California, on April 19, 2002, and in Brooklyn, New York, on March 25, 2003. Critics mentioned the word *kōlam* in their reviews. As Joan Acocella wrote in *The New Yorker* (2003):

> . . . the most ambitious new work that Morris presented this season: "Kolam," for ten dancers, to a complicated score by Ethan Iverson, an American jazz composer, and Zakir Hussain, an Indian drum virtuoso. "Kolam" is the Tamil word for the ornate colored-powder drawings with which Indians adorn the walls of their houses and temples—"They're blessings," Morris says, "visual prayers"—and this dance is more decorative, visually, than anything else Morris has ever made. It has circles and crosses and cascades, twirling and handstands and splits. It has Indianesque costumes (by Katherine McDowell), plus ankle bells. Unlike most of Morris's work, it even has a set: a backdrop of heroically scaled red and yellow smears by the English painter Howard Hodgkin.

Here, the reviewer explains what *kōlams* are, and Morris's articulation of their significance as "blessings" and "visual prayers" has now been introduced to certain layers of American audiences through his relationship with Chandralekha.

In his review on CultureVulture.net, Arthur Lazere notices that the dancers "bend to the side from the waist with impressive elasticity." The "Kolam in movement" is what sets it apart in dance vis-à-vis the kōlam in everyday life, which is two-dimensional and still:

> Called Kolam, for the Indian folk art form in which powders are used to draw intricate geometric designs according to strict rules, both the music and the dance are characterized by repeated patterns and variations. . . . A spotlight creates a large circle center stage. Together with changing pairs of dancers who stand at the perimeter of the circle and bend to the side from the waist with impressive elasticity, an area is defined in which the other dancers create a variety of intricate patterns—it is a Kolam in movement. A slow section of the music is danced with suggestions of birds flying and a reaching upward for the sun.

The "reaching upwards for the sun" could refer to the time of day that kōlams are often performed.

Another reviewer, Rajika Puri (2003), suggests that Morris brings his usual whimsical air to the piece.

In this dance, Morris displays his virtuoso skills in interlacing yoga postures and classical south Indian Bharatanatyam dance movements against the background of a growing colorful kōlam on the floor. What strikes me is how the geometric kōlams, though deeply rooted in Tamil cultural forms, could adapt to the needs of a contemporary American choreographer. [7]

In addition to these choreographies, the geometric kōlams have been featured in Tamil movies and advertisements. They even appear on a logo for the Institute for South Asia Studies at the University of California, Berkeley. These kōlam designs have become representative of an evolving traditional ritual art form that combines beauty with the metaphor of hospitality and welcome.

Beauty

Beyond their ritual and celebratory nature, the kōlam designs themselves are of intense interest to women, and many aesthetic considerations inform the making of them. Versatility and innovative ideas are valued. New ideas are praised in the critiquing process and then incorporated into newer versions.

Kōlams are generally drawn using white ground rice or stone flour. However, bright, multicolored, and circle-based kōlams are also popular, serving as vehicles for stunning color combinations in attractive powders. The kōlam's bounded paradigmatic set of parameters is coming under increasing scrutiny and is being overtaken by more contemporary considerations such as the purposeful intent of the kōlam-maker, intense variety and bursts of color, design, and playfulness. But each wave of so-called modern kōlams is then displaced by even newer ones. Modern ones (e.g., those with movie themes such as "Titanic") have become increasingly popular, much to the distress of women who have been carriers of the "traditional" designs.

Which set of criteria is used when judges evaluate the aesthetics of the kōlams in public competitions or in neighborhoods? In other words, when is a kōlam considered "beautiful"? A beautiful kōlam design displays a uniform line width that indicates painstaking care, much like fine, evenly spaced stitching in an Amish quilt, or the inside skin of an ancient Mimbres pot centered around delightfully balanced, hand-wrought lines. It is important that the line appear to be continuous, so that the actual starts and stops are never visible in the final form. This is harder than it sounds, and one of many aspects of doing the kōlam that requires real expertise. This is why it takes about six years, generally from age six to twelve, to gain mastery.

Excellence is also expressed by how much a certain kind of lustrous beauty (*latshanam*) shines from the inside out. This word is also used to describe a type of beauty that resides in faces and houses, implying that they have a lustrous glow coming through them. It could be related to the Tamil word *ilaṅgu*, which refers to that which shines, emits rays, gleams. One other criterion for beauty is called *Lakshmi kadaksham*, which means "similar to the goddess Lakshmi." It implies a charisma that draws the eye into the kōlam. The design feels inviting, generous, and hospitable, all qualities of the goddess.

The beauty here is not just abstract or isolated. It is very much connected to creating an ethical relationship to the world. The qualities that make a kōlam beautiful are not purely image-based. Rather, they are inextricably linked to notions of ethical qualities of goodness. A beautiful kōlam is not just two-dimensional; it actually has an aura of beneficence and goodwill that emanates from it, like a three-dimensional visual prayer. This is why women often say that the ethical purpose behind this ritual art form is to "feed a thousand souls." It is as if beauty is linked with the generous attitude of wanting to feed and satisfy the hungry. They are hungry, but they don't know where to go. The ones who are in need have to be able to find you, and the kōlam practitioner has to attract their gaze through the sheer beauty of the designs. This is what makes the kōlam more meaningful—that beauty is conjoined with ethics. The kōlam is, indeed, a visible ritual of generosity (see Chapters 10 and 11 for elaboration).

In conclusion, in the kōlam, beauty is interlaced with ethics. Within a variety of forms (pulli, katta, yantras, and navagraha), auspicious motifs and shapes swirl around each other to create an infinite array of kōlam designs. These beckon the wandering stranger to a hospitable place.

Now we move to a specific aspect of the kōlam design: mathematics.

7

Embodied Mathematics

At dawn, Parvathi steps out of her suburban home at the outskirts of Madurai and, after cleaning the threshold, begins drawing a series of dots on the ground, her sense of symmetry embodied in her hands and the way she moves her body. Thinking to herself, "31 dots," she lays them down carefully and methodically, each one spaced out evenly as if she had drawn them with a ruler and a pencil. Careful not to swipe the dots she has already drawn, she moves diagonally, this way and that, unconsciously lifting the bottom of her sari halfway up and tucking it into her waist, her purple underskirt peeking out (Figures 7.1a–c).[1]

Folding her body at her waist, her face bent forward as if she is doing a yoga pose, she puts down these 31 dots, each dot a triangular point from the line of dots she has just laid down. She continues with a line of 29 dots, then 27, until she reaches just a single dot. Then, walking carefully to the other side of the original series of 31 dots, she begins laying down dots in a parallel series, a mirror reflection of the side she had just finished creating.

Her hands are remarkably sure in their execution and her thoughtful face looks concentrated, poised with intensity. She begins drawing a line curving around the dots, the line not crossing around the dots more than once. At first it looks as if one end of the line will never touch the beginning, as if a snake cannot touch its head to its tail. But slowly her fingers and her body dance purposefully forward, and after many flourishes of curving lines, the lines meet so that you can no longer tell the beginning or the end; she has created seemingly infinite, symmetrical loops.

Other kōlams show us the same fineness of hand (Figures 7.1d,e).

I was first forced to focus on the idea that mathematics were embedded in certain types of kōlam designs in 1993 in the small fishing village of Injambakkam, outside Madras (now Chennai) along the Bay of Bengal coastline.[2] At his home, my teacher and friend Dr. C. V. Seshadiri excitedly presented me with a foot-tall stack of books and articles on mathematics and the kōlam. At his insistence, I spent most of my time at his worktable trying to read and absorb these

(a)

Figure 7.1a Young woman sweeping front threshold area in preparation for making a kōlam, Mayiladuthurai. Photo by Lee Swenson.

(b)

Figure 7.1b Young woman laying down the dots for a labyrinth kōlam. Photo by Lee Swenson.

(c)

Figure 7.1c Young woman making a labyrinth kōlam. Photo by Lee Swenson.

(d)

Figure 7.1d Labyrinth kōlam.

(e)

Figure 7.1e Giant labyrinth kōlam, Madurai.

materials.[3] One after the other, these articles explained the fascinating relationship between the kōlam and the field of mathematics. But frankly, I was stunned, overwhelmed, and confounded. I didn't think I could ever plow through these articles on advanced mathematics: I hadn't touched any form of mathematical thinking for over a dozen years, ever since I had been a second-year undergraduate engineering student, after which I had switched to economics. Nevertheless, Dr. Seshadiri insisted that I promise him that any book I wrote on the kōlam must include this mathematical knowledge.

Over the years I was pulled again and again toward this material to fulfill my promise to him, each time filled with unease and uncertainty. What I've learned and understood so far is outlined in this chapter. I'm not a mathematician. I'm a folklorist-anthropologist who is intrigued that these women's ritual diagrams contain within them complex mathematical properties that have intrigued mathematicians and computer scientists for decades.

The study of the kōlam and the exploration of its mathematical properties is a part of the field of ethnomathematics (Ascher 2002a, 56). Ethnomathematics is the relationship between culture and mathematics and reflects the idea that mathematical principles, properties, theories, and concepts can be steeped within cultural, ritual, and artistic forms. We are surrounded by ethnomathematics in the patterns of everyday life, such as houses, woven baskets, mosaics, tiles, and quilts. Most of the time, we're unaware of these layers of mathematical complexities. According to Marcia Ascher, at least 6,000 different cultures have existed during the past 700 years, and many of these have traditions that involve mathematical principles. She explains:

> Seeking mathematical ideas that were part of oral traditions most often involves re-examining, with a mathematical perspective, the work and materials of anthropologists, archaeologists, linguists, and cultural historians. . . . In essence, concepts of time and space and order placed upon the natural, supernatural, and social worlds all may involve mathematical ideas. . . . What sets the kōlam tradition apart from other cases I have studied is that it has contributed directly to an academic endeavor: The intricate figures have entered the realm of computer science. The figures have provided material for illustrating known approaches to the analysis and description of pictures and also have stimulated new approaches. This makes the kolam tradition a rare and especially interesting case.[4]

Ascher explains the relevance of this field to the study of the kōlam. She points to the kōlam as a unique example of a ritual art design form that not only reveals mathematical principles but also has contributed to furthering theories in the field of computer science—specifically in the areas of array grammars and picture languages. (We will look more closely at this later in this chapter.)

In this chapter I will focus on four aspects of mathematical understandings within the design structure of the kōlam that strike me as critically important: symmetry, fractals, array grammars and picture languages, and infinity.[5] I will also explore briefly the concept of embodied mathematics as it emerges from the study of mathematical metaphors of infinity. I will end with some reflections on how Chandralekha's choreography expressed the three-dimensional nature of the kōlam.

Symmetry

Many kōlams are symmetrical: they are balanced, weighted equally between one side and another. Symmetry is a concept that seems intuitive and clear to most of us, yet on closer examination it is much more complex than it initially appears. Kōlams have intrigued formal mathematicians who specialize in "symmetry" (Hargittai 1989). The mathematical concept of symmetry is in the subfield of geometry. According to the *Oxford English Dictionary* (1987), symmetry "is attributed to a figure or a shape whose parts are equably distributed about a dividing line, plane or point. It is also seen as capable of being divided into two or more exactly similar or equal parts that mirror each other." In his essay "What Is Symmetry?" Alan Mackay (1986) presents the roots of the word *symmetry* in classical Greek as " 'the same measure,' due proportion."

Geometric kōlams embody symmetry. As we saw in Chapter 6, the geometric kōlams are the dot (pulli or shullis) and square (katta) kōlams. Whether it is a pulli kōlam or a katta kōlam, they tend to be shaped by a symmetrical balance along a vertical or horizontal axis, or along both axes. Some designs are symmetrical around a central vertical line; other kōlams have a bilateral symmetry, meaning their parts mirror each other across a central dividing line (Figures 7.2 and 7.3). Some exhibit a 45-degree rotational symmetry around a central point. Rotational symmetry is when you rotate a design a certain number of degrees and get essentially the same form—though at first glance, it may appear quite different or distinct. That is, in a design with 45-degree rotational symmetry, if you turn the form around 45 degrees, you get a certain parallel form. Others have 90- or 180-degrees rotational symmetry. When the pulli kōlams are made, they express a kind of movement in time and space that creates a rotational symmetry, where a set of dots is laid down and circled around in a certain way. The first four figures show 90 degrees around a rotational point. They are symmetrical and yet turned around in different ways, depending on the degree of rotation (Figure 7.4).

Structural elements also echo throughout the patterning. Such characteristics create a sense of balance in the viewer's gaze. Frequently a vortex of depth is created around which the structure rotates, forcing the eye to move to the center of the diagram (Figure 7.5).

Paul Gerdes (1989), a mathematics educator based in Mozambique, has explored the "lost" symmetries of the kōlam. Using Layard's analysis of kōlams (1937), he argues that kōlams were probably transformed from original, single, continuous-lined kōlams to ones with multiple superimposed closed paths. These later kōlams were considered "degraded" versions of the originals. I found no oral evidence of such a perceived degraded value from my extensive conversations with Tamil women, though I did not ask directly about this hierarchy of values.[6]

As we've seen, many of the geometric kōlams have an intrinsic symmetry about them. The figurative and the landscape kōlams are more like pictures and embody in their forms the qualities of balance and harmony. Mackay states: "The Chinese word [for symmetry], also embedded deeply in Chinese culture, indicates reciprocity." (See Chapter 11 for more on this concept as it applies to the kōlam.) Does this give us a clue as to what symmetry may imply for the underlying

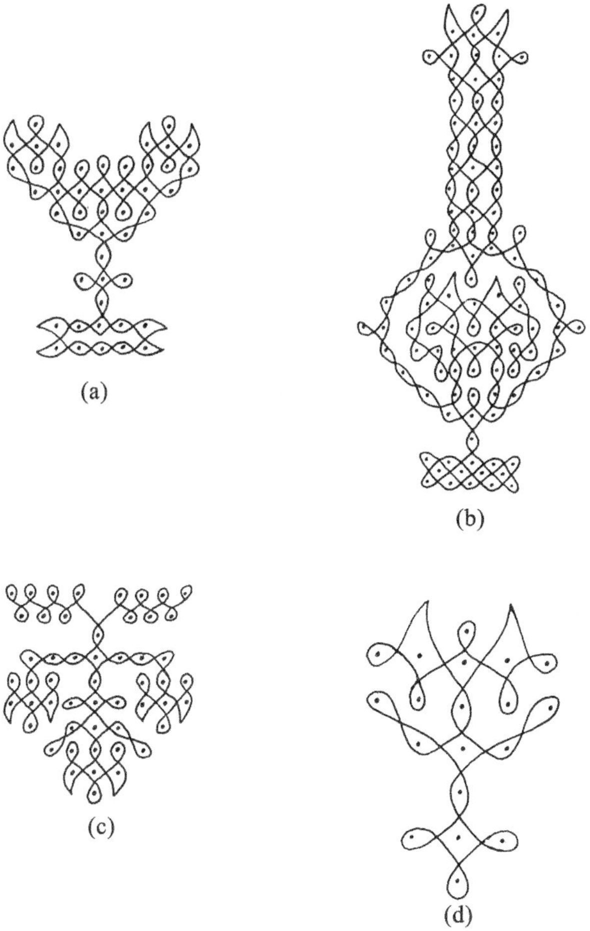

Figure 7.2 Some kōlams: (a) Sandal Cup; (b) Rosewater Sprinkler; (c) Hanging Lamp; (d) Nose Jewel. (Source: Ascher 2002b: 165, Figure 6.1.)

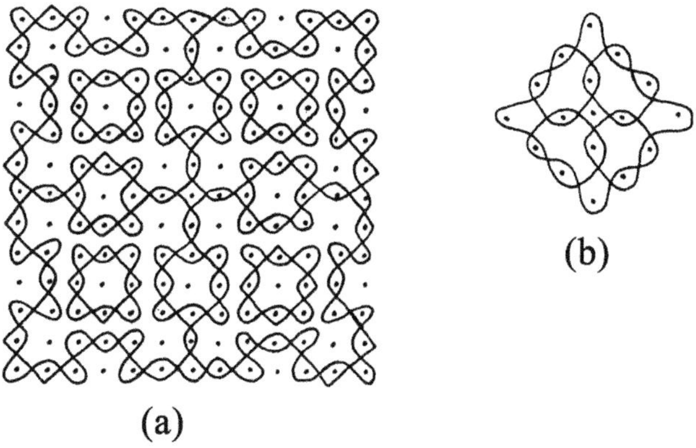

Figure 7.3 Some kōlams: (a) Vine Creeper; (b) The Ring. (Source: Ascher 2002b: 166, adapted from Figure 6.2.)

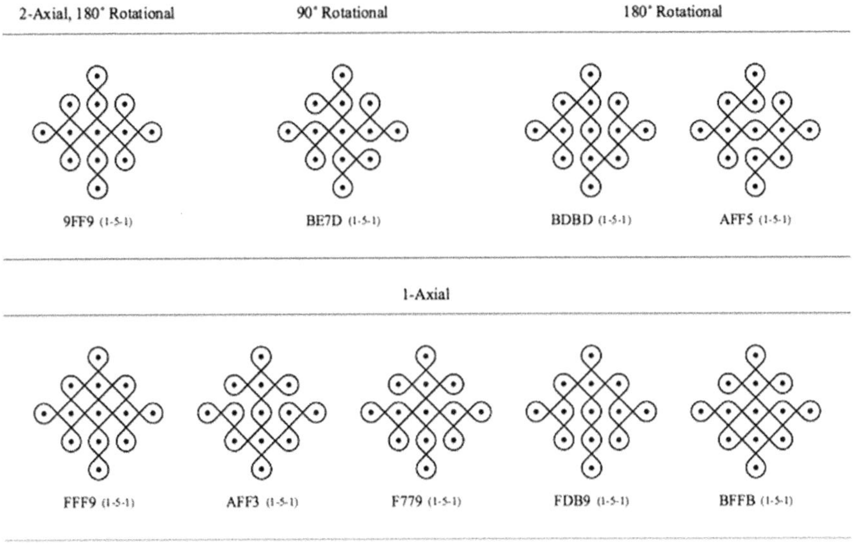

Figure 7.4 90 degrees around a rotation point. (Source: Yanagisawa and Nagata 2007.)

philosophical sense of the kōlam? Mackay suggests that "once having identified as 'symmetrical,' we can divide it into motif and rule of repetition. That is, we can see on two levels at once; the level of physical structure and the level of informational or organizational structure" (1986, 190). That the informational or organizational structure is in fact us seeing that symmetrical form from outside of it, is especially intriguing. Mackay extends this to Gödel's paradox: "In looking at an apparently closed symmetrical system we see that is not, after all, closed." The implication is that as the outside perceiver, we are seeing the closed system, but in fact it is not, as we are also part of another quite larger system, though this one is harder for us to perceive. In other words, if we can identify an object as symmetrical, or as proportional, then, by definition, we have the perception of an outsider who can see that symmetry from outside that very symmetry, implying a higher order of hierarchy behind the perception of symmetry.

According to Hargittai, a mathematician who specializes in symmetry, "Beyond geometrical definitions, though, here is another, broader meaning to symmetry—one that relates to harmony and proportion, and ultimately to beauty" (Hargittai and Hargittai 1994: xv). Darvas expands this line of thinking farther: "According to ancient thought, harmony pervades nature and its laws, at once expressing artistic harmony, proportion, and beauty. Translations from two thousand years later referred to this as symmetry" (Darvas 2007, 44).[7]

The ideas of the women I spoke with sometimes overlapped with those of the mathematicians, but other times they had their own distinctive take

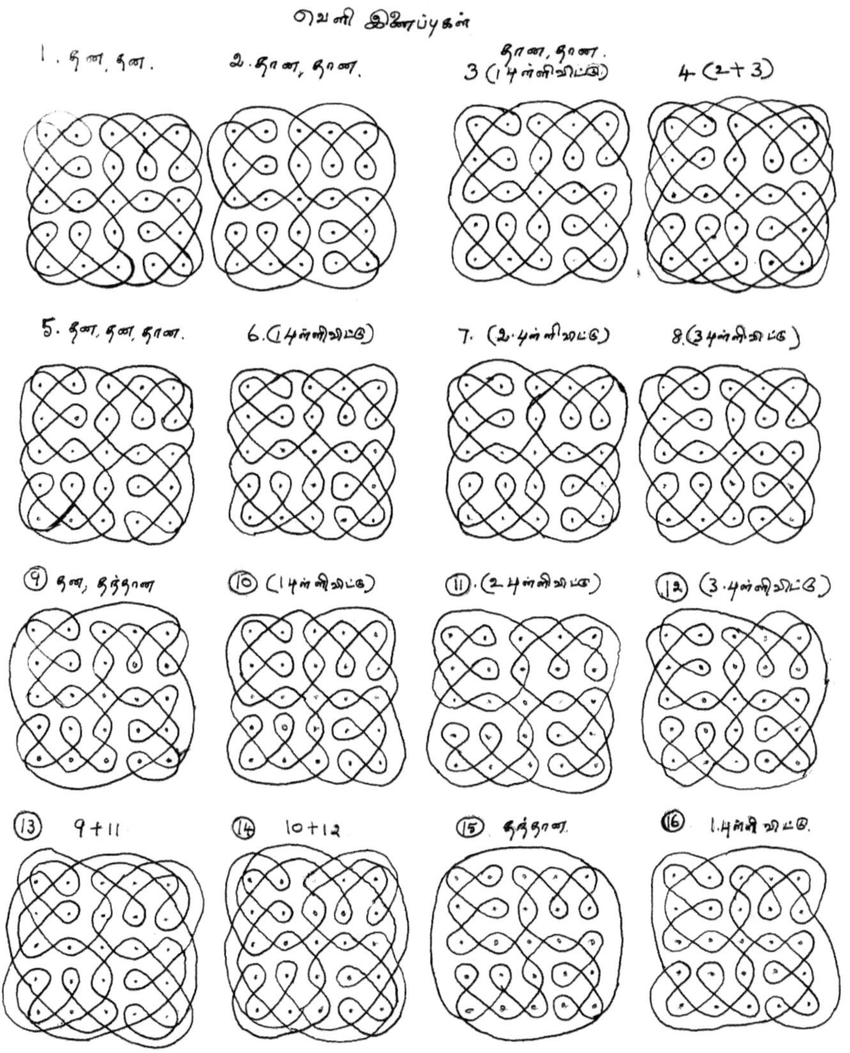

Figure 7.5 Examples of 5 × 5 kōlams, Madurai. (Source: Author's collection, from Leela Venkataraman.)

on these qualities. Tamil women spoke of *a<u>ll</u>aku* (beauty) and of *latshanam* (brightness), and these often implied symmetry. The women saw the kōlam as symmetrical in the sense of bringing about a sense of harmony, reflecting a sense of reciprocity, and literally bridging the inner and the outer worlds, between giving and receiving. As kōlam-makers would slowly reveal to me, the symmetry of the kōlam became a visual meditation on proportionality, balance, and harmony.

Fractals

A second critical contribution that the kōlam has made is to the subject of fractals. The *Oxford English Dictionary* (1987) defines a fractal as "A mathematically conceived curve such that any small part of it, enlarged, has the same statistical character of the original." Some kōlams exhibit a fractal nature.[8] For example, in the kōlam in Figure 7.6, the larger design motif echoes the smaller versions tucked into its very structure.

Ascher (2002b: 156) provides an insight that applies to the broader context of kōlam designs that include fractals:

> Some kōlam figures constitute families; that is, there are groups of figures that share common characteristics. In some cases, the larger figures in a family are made up of several joined copies of smaller figures; in other cases, the family members are derived from each other in more subtle ways. The conception and organization of families of kōlam figures seem particularly expressive of mathematical ideas.

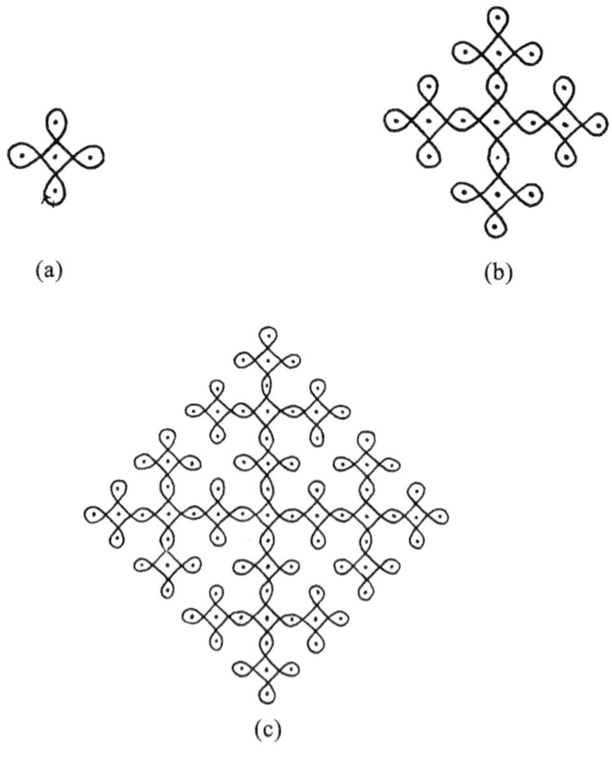

Figure 7.6 Fractal example of kōlam: Anklets of Krishna. (Source: Ascher 2002b: 174, Figure 6.6.)

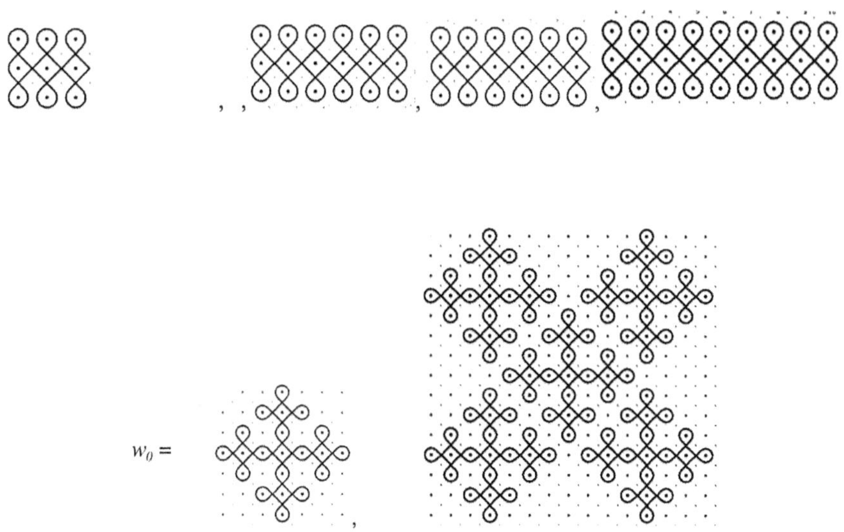

Figure 7.7 Sequence of border kōlam patterns; subunits add together to make a larger unit. (Source: Robinson 2007: 59, Figures 5 and 6.)

The conceptions and organizations of certain families of kōlams express fractals (Figure 7.7). The kōlam is created by transforming and superimposing basic subunits. Families of kōlams are made from each other through various patterns (Ascher 2002c; Katz 2002; Layard 1937; see also Robinson and Ascher 1991).

Fractals have two different scales: they have recurring patterns on a smaller scale that are reproduced on a larger scale in the same design. This happens often in the kōlam design patterns. In one example of this kind of fractal, exponential growth, similar configurations are arranged as families of subunits that are repeated and enlarged. These repetitions and enlargements can be expressed as various arithmetic, geometric, and exponential progressions. This pattern is similar to Sierpinski's triangle, where each side of the triangle is replaced by another triangle (Figures 7.8 and 7.9) (Ascher 2002b: 178, Figures 6.9 and 173, Figure 6.5).[9] As Ascher says, Siromoney and his Madras Group "make us more aware that the kōlams are careful constructions with definable growth patterns" (165).

Women use recursive geometric patterns that start out simple but, after many repetitions of the same pattern, end up looking very complex. "Recursive" refers to that which is put back into the design to repeat at smaller and smaller levels. The whole is repeated in part, again and again. Biological mathematicians study how nature uses the same kind of recursive patterns; for example, the patterns of a leaf are remarkably similar to the tributaries of river systems, which can be seen from satellite photos of the earth. Similarly, the kōlam patterns are echoed at smaller and larger scales, and imagined into infinity.

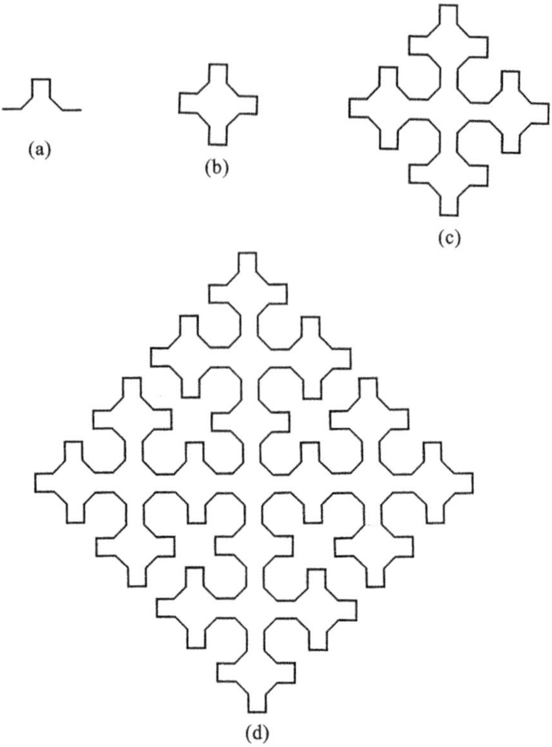

Figure 7.8 The Snake: numerous replications that reveal fractal nature of this kōlam. (Source: Ascher 2002b: 178, Figure 6.9.)

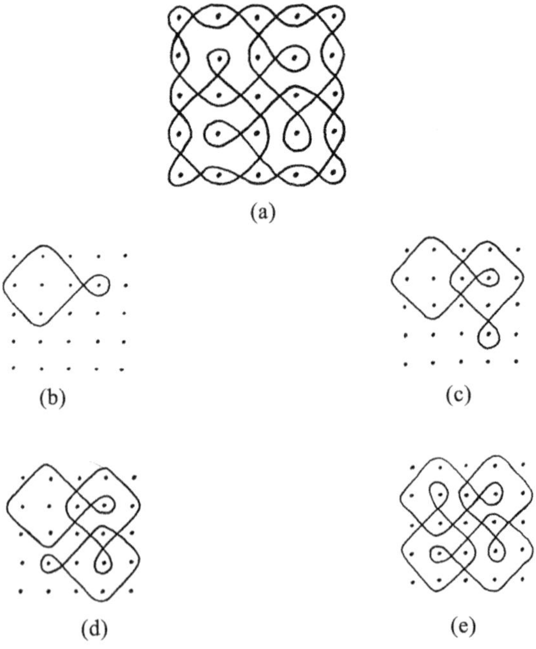

Figure 7.9 Typical kōlam. (Source: Ascher 2002b: 173, Figure 6.5.)

Picture Languages and Array Grammars

Within the last four decades, there has been an extraordinary flowering of Western-trained mathematicians who have been inspired by the intrinsic design properties of the kōlam.[10] Dot kōlams in particular have attracted the attention of mathematicians, especially computer scientists. The kōlams have revealed significant theoretical insights.

Some types of kōlams have repeated motifs in larger and larger iterations, with the larger unit composed of an arrangement of the smaller units. This is similar to the concept of fractals (Figure 7.10). These kōlam figures that have relatable patterns generated from one to the other are of most interest to theoretical computer scientists. As Ascher states:

> The complex and intricate figures are intriguing in and of themselves, but, what is more, in many cases, their creation involves the transformation and superimposition of basic subunits, and there are families of kōlams whose members can be derived from each other in patterned ways. Replicating the richness of these figures and their growth patterns became a challenge to computer scientists who were creating picture languages and were studying formal language theory." (Ascher 2002b: 161–2)

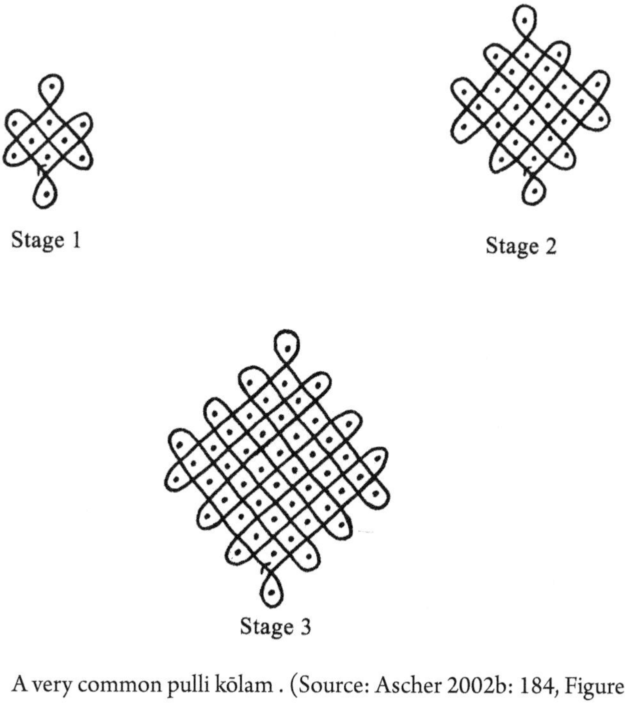

Figure 7.10 A very common pulli kōlam . (Source: Ascher 2002b: 184, Figure 6.12.)

Computer scientists, in their attempt to teach the computer how to do certain operations, have found in the kōlam how this can be done through language-created pictures. Picture languages use sets of basic units combined with formal rules to make larger and larger patterns. Computer scientists have used this formal language theory for programming computer languages. In Madras, Dr. Gift Siromoney and Dr. Rani Siromoney, a husband-and-wife team of mathematicians, along with their Madras Group, began to use pulli kōlam designs to study picture languages (1974) (see Ascher 2002b; Subramanian et al. 2006). These computer scientists and mathematicians used the kōlams as a way to describe picture languages and used them to create new languages.

They contributed rich insights into the structure of picture languages. According to Ascher (2002b: 168), picture languages are:

> the formal analysis and description of pictures. Akin to natural languages and computer languages, picture languages are made up of restricted sets of basic units and specific, formal rules for putting the units together. The kōlam design provided a rich supply of figures that could be used as examples of some languages. . . . The languages are, essentially, concise statements of algorithms, or formulas, for generating kōlams.

The picture languages are therefore formulas for creating the kōlam figures, as if they were visually displayed grammatical elements, a kind of symbolic grammar.

When computer scientists looked at the ways in which Tamil women were drawing the kōlam, they were stunned to find that the women were actually expressing certain mathematical formulas. The scientists then tried to reproduce the kōlams on the computer. Having to break down the instructions needed to recreate the kōlams into a logical order taught them something about the inner nature of these kinds of picture languages. How do we get a computer to create a picture such as the kōlam?

Siromoney (1974) has also explored the theoretical models for generating two-dimensional arrays, or matrices. As he states, "Each kind of kōlam pattern can be treated as a two-dimensional language and a grammar can be constructed to generate it. The number of designs that can be constructed from each kind of kōlam pattern is infinite" (Ascher 2002c: 63).[11]

Array grammars, by definition, have to do with algorithms, or formulas. These formulas create two-dimensional graphic displays and varying qualities of information. Computer scientists have focused on the study of algorithms, which is defined by a set of rules that the kōlams are built on. A systematic procedure and technique is used to create the patterns of kōlams. Ascher explains: "As computer scientists have tried to capture kōlam figures with picture languages, they have highlighted the richness of the kōlam structures and their algorithmic nature—in other words, the orderly, step-by-step way they are built" (Ascher 2002a: 5). It is important to remember, though, that "The languages do not necessarily replicate how the women of Tamil Nadu conceive of and draw the kōlam figures. Nevertheless, they underscore the fact that the kōlam, and particularly the families of the kōlam, are more than just a collection of individual pictures; systematic procedures and techniques unify them" (Ascher 2002: 5). What the languages revealed was that these picture languages can account for some of the kōlam design families. Women creating kōlams on the ground begin with dot arrays, a two-dimensional laying down of dots. These dots prefigure the final scales of design figures.[12] In fact, some kōlam-makers say that laying down the initial dots in a careful, systematic way is essential to creating that final, polished look. Any kōlam-maker is aware of the inherent dangers of an initial sloppy two-dimensional grid.

This systematization of the kōlam designs and the attempts to reproduce them through formulas have contributed to our deeper understanding of such graphic displays of information, the creation of singular or multiple closed curves, the relationship between the laying down of the dots and the final produced figure, and ultimately the foundational systematic language underlying the creation of pictures.[13]

Infinity

Infinity is the fourth mathematical concept that I discovered was embedded within the kōlam. In the field of geometry, the notion of the "infinite" conveys the sense that there is no determined limit and indefinite length, magnitude, or distance, or it may refer to that portion of space that is infinitely distant from us (*Oxford English Dictionary* 1987). This concept of infinity inplies a sense of unimaginable distance from the present moment through space.

The concept of infinity is related to the kōlam in at least two ways: (1) Might the kōlams be pictorial representations of infinity compressed onto the ground? Do kōlam designs have embedded within them a sense of infinity? and (2) Can an infinite or seemingly infinite number of kōlams be drawn through the expansion of any particular basic template?

For the first aspect, it is interesting to look at the design form itself. In the category of pulli kōlams, the form goes in and around the laid-down dots, appearing to have no beginning or ending. Often the continuous closed line is drawn with the ending connecting to the beginning of the looped line so that it looks like a seamless whole. These are "associated with the never-ending cycle of birth, fertility and death, and with concepts of continuity, totality and eternity" (Ascher

2002c: 58). It can also imply a complex labyrinth, a dense form that keeps the outside chaos at bay (Shulman 1985: 3).

Leela Venkataraman, a master kōlam-maker in Madurai, was one of the most passionate women I met along my path and helped me understand both senses of infinity in the kōlam. What made this elderly widow unique was her ease in seeing the kōlam in a systematic, mathematical way. She had taken math workshops on the kōlam with S.V. Thambirasu, an elementary-school math teacher near Coimbatore who had slowly discovered the foundational mathematical structures embedded in the kōlam. Soon after, she became a devoted teacher herself and taught many women in workshops about the mathematics of the kōlam. She was intrigued with determining how many variations there could be in each kind of kōlam. For example, how many different kōlams can be made from a 5 × 5 pattern of dots? She would answer this by drawing out the many permutations and combinations (Figure 7.11).

Her creativity and innovation with the kōlam in a broader way also made her unique. She learned how to make figurative and geometric kōlams on still water, using colored powders. Amazingly, the patterns stayed put. She also experimented with making kōlams using colored lentils—red, yellow, orange, green, white, and black. She also introduced me to musicians who had worked with the rhythm of musical movements and making the kōlam. Her imagination of the kōlam was unusually wide.

One year, wondering how large she can draw a kōlam, she decided to make a kōlam with as many dots as she possibly could, "just to see what it would look like." Because of the length of this endeavor and in order to keep track of the pattern, she decided (wisely) that she wanted to have a permanent record. She drew the kōlam with 100,000 dots on a 10 × 10-foot piece of cloth with a blue pen. It took her more than a year to place the dots and circle the labyrinth kōlams carefully without making any errors. She proudly showed me the finished design. I was struck by her dedication to satisfying her curiosity and her desire to make a permanent record of her 100,000-dots kōlam. I didn't count them, but it certainly was the largest hand-drawn kōlam I had ever seen (see Figures 2.8a–c). She helped me see that the smaller pulli kōlams were the subunits of an expansive pulli kōlam that stretched out infinitely, at least at the level of imagination. This was the first time I had pictured the kōlam stretching out into infinite space.

In a parallel fashion in the larger public sphere, both within India and outside among Tamil communities, there is increasingly a collective desire to make larger and larger kōlams, as if to aspire toward a pictorial representation of infinity, as if the kōlam itself represented a compressed sense of infinity. In 2009, in Kumbakonam, a college student drew a kōlam with 150,000 dots in

Figure 7.11 5 × 5 dots (pullis), different variations.

an attempt to make the *Guinness Book of World Records* ("College organises a special painting exhibition" 2009). In 2010 near Thanjavur, in honor of the sacred month of Margali, 23 male and female college students and some of their teachers drew a giant dot kōlam of a temple cart with 65,000 dots, creating a 416-foot-long image ("Kōlam draws huge crowd" 2010).[14]

In Malaysia, college students have been competing to make the largest kōlam. In 2010, 150 students made a gigantic figurative kōlam using 1,000 kg of rice and grated coconut, setting a record for the largest kōlam drawn (Fernandez 2010). Groups and individuals in Malaysia and Singapore have been trying to achieve recognition for creating the largest kōlams. The kōlam is a very public representation of Tamil cultural forms in these countries, and the creation of the "largest kōlam" illustrates the way that Tamil culture has been integrated into these national cultures. All of these kōlam-makers, including Leela Venkataraman in Madurai, are expanding the kōlam to make it as large as possible in a concrete way, as opposed to imagining infinity in an abstract way. Another way of looking at this act of extending the kōlam is the imagined potential of stretching the kōlam so that the dots continue toward infinity. This connects the physical possibilities of drawing the kōlam with as many dots as one can with the abstract notion of infinity.

The other way that infinity can be expressed in the kōlam, besides imagining extending the kōlam infinitely, relates to the number of kōlams that can be drawn. Tamil women often talked about how they worked through one of the most mysterious questions: How many kōlam patterns could they create given a specific grid of dots?

It turns out that mathematicians have also been interested in this question. Ishimoto (2009) asks: How many infinite kōlams can be drawn based on a given grid pattern of dots? If the grid pattern is 1-3-1 (i.e., one dot on the first line, three dots on the second line, and one dot on the third line), there is only one "infinite" kōlam. Here the word "infinite" implies the continuous single line circling around the dots without a seeming beginning or ending. But what if the kōlam is a 3 × 3 or a 10 × 10 grid of dots?

Answering this question turns out to be a complicated mathematic problem. Ishimoto argues that the best way to find out is to use knot theory. He does this by analyzing one type of kōlam, the diamond kōlam. If we write down the number of dots in each row, one after the other, the patterns can be represented by a sequence of numbers from the top row to the bottom (so 1-3-5-3-1, then 1-3-5-7-5-3-1, and so on). Tamil women represent this kind of diamond pattern using that very code (1-3-1 or 1-3-5-3-1, and so on). They will say or write in their notebooks "1-3-1," for example, as a shorthand code description of these types of kōlams.

Ishimoto (2009) calculates that there is only one solution for the 1-3-1 pattern, 240 solutions for the 1-3-5-3-1 pattern, and 11,661,312 solutions for the 1-3-5-7-5-3-1 pattern. Although Tamil women were not aware of the exact number of possible variations, they knew what it was very large, or close to infinity (Mimica 1998). The women's observations matched the mathematician's calculations. Although not often mentioned explicitly, women's framing of their knowledge of the kōlam involved its vital mathematical properties.

Embodied Mathematics

Over the years I have often wondered how the body intuits mathematical concepts such as infinity and thought of the concept of embodied or embedded mathematics, paralleling my thinking on embedded ecologies (Nagarajan 1998, 2000). George Lakoff, a cognitive scientist and linguist, and Rafael E. Nunez, a psychologist, offer a thick description and analysis of embodied mathematics in their groundbreaking book *Where Mathematics Comes From: How the Embodied Mind Brings Mathematics into Being* (2000). They argue convincingly that our sense of mathematics comes out of our bodily orientations and bodily experiences. They insist that mathematical notions of infinity come out of our sense as embodied beings and, therefore, are in essence metaphorical (2000: 150–80).[15] In other words, they claim that the field of mathematics is intertwined with the perceptions of the human body and the mind that resides within the human body, not independent of them. Astonishingly, they assert: "For human beings—or any other embodied beings—mathematics is embodied mathematics. The only mathematics we can know is the mathematics that our bodies and brains allow us to know" (2000: 346). They contend that:

> One of the great findings of cognitive science is that our ideas are shaped by bodily experiences—not in any simpleminded one-to-one way, but indirectly, through the grounding of our entire conceptual system in everyday life. The cognitive perspective forces us to ask, is the system of mathematical ideas also grounded indirectly in bodily experiences? And if so, exactly how?" (2000: xiv)[16]

They argue that there is no objective mathematical reality; rather, all mathematical inferences and deductions come out of our bodily experience. For example, in the case of infinity, they lay out a theory of embodied mathematics that sees infinity itself as a metaphor. The kōlam has been participating in this visualization of a mathematical metaphor; it has intimated and suggested the concept of infinity to Tamil women's imaginations.

Chandralekha and Embodied Kōlams

Some kōlams are embodied expressions of the concept of mandala or a geometric expression of the cosmological universe in Hinduism (see Chapter 5 for Āntāl's reference to the kōlam as a mandala). For the choreographer Chandralekha (1928–2006), the mandala is a "principle in which the body is realized as the very center of the cosmos itself" (Bharucha 1995: 59). The body of the kōlam-maker is the bindu, the point or the center of the world. As we go about our daily activities, the center of the world should not be perceived in a self-centered way, but as an activator of our own inner subtle energy. This energy is something that we can be aware of, mobilize, and impart to ourselves and others around us.

The physical body makes the kōlam. As Chandralekha explains: "learning 'how to stand', and thereby affirming the power of the spine" is her answer to the question, "Why dance?" (Bharucha 1995: 33). Correspondingly, "Why make the kōlam?" may also have as much to do with that stretching of the spine, standing and bending over, as dance does. Making the kōlam literally wakes up the body at sunrise, serving as an energizing force on the body. As Chandralekha says in one of her many conversations with Bharucha: "This process is valuable not just for oneself, but for the people and the space around us, which can be energized through concentration" (Bharucha 1995: 33). Chandralekha's idea is remarkably similar to what many Tamil women told me about why they do the kōlam. The conception of mangalam or auspiciousness is a way of understanding the creation of the space around us. So the kōlam is not just a way to represent auspiciousness, but it actually serves to create auspiciousness or well-being in and through women's bodies.

Now this takes us to an example of how we can imagine the mathematical grounding of the infinite kōlam in the body. First, according to the Tantric Hindu tradition, the dot or bindu represents the beginning of things. The dots in the kōlam are in line with this understanding of the bindu. And the lines surrounding the dots represent infinite continuity or infinity itself. These lines are often made of a single continuous closed curve or several continuous closed curves and act as continuous loops of infinity. Shulman interprets these loops of infinity in the kōlam as linked with "the continuous, never-ending cosmic cycles of birth–fertility–death, and with the concepts of totality, perfection, and eternity" (Shulman 1985: 164). This reminds us how the dots and the curved lines around the dots relate to philosophical concepts of infinite time.

Chandralekha's choreography echoes the two-dimensional kōlam patterns in three-dimensional space: "This inward/outward dynamic of the mandala,—one spatial movement curving inward and another flowing outward, radiating into expanding circles while intensely held by the bindu—is its basic strength" (Bharucha 1995: 59). This radiating into expanding circles is exactly what the kōlam-maker is always aware of: she knows that she can keep on going, that she can keep on expanding each kōlam into infinity, even though it is just being suggested and cannot be actually drawn. Chandralekha clarifies her vision of what the mandala signifies:

> In terms of the body, mandala is a holistic concept integrating the human body with itself, with the community and with the environment.

> It generates a centered, tensile, and complex visual form. It is a principle of power, of stability, of balance, of holding the earth . . . of squaring or circularizing the body and of breaking the tension and rigidity of the vertical line by a curve. (59)

Chandralekha applied these principles extensively in her rich, layered choreography. She insightfully wove the kōlam, mandalas, mathematics, and geometry into her choreographies, which were startling and provocative and had not been done before. Her lines of moving dancers crisscrossed each other on the stage as if she were drawing the lines of the kōlam with their bodies. She charged her dancers with tremendous vitality and energy, as if they were the pulsating dots of the foundation of the pulli kōlams.

Her most significant choreography in relation to the kōlam was *Yantra* in 1994. In *Yantra* the kōlams were three-dimensional, as if the kōlams had lifted off from the two-dimensional plane of the ground and were now dancers who were dots, triangles, squares, circles, and lines. The dancers wove in and out of formation as if her hands were moving them this way and that, drawing a gigantic kōlam on stage. Her stage-sized kōlams revealed the darkness beyond the lit bodies of the dancers as an active space. The spaces between the kōlam dots were dancing, too. The negative space and the positive space, the invisible and the visible, were both pulsing: the mandala, the circle, the movement of dance within and without; legs bent, knees stuck out in the front and butts stuck out in the back; feet facing each other in a straight line; faces impassive; a deeply moving stillness of multiple beings.

I remember clearly the moment when Chandralekha described her understanding of the kōlam and infinity in her own body, a clear example of embodied mathematics. She looked at me intensely and explained, "One time I made kōlams non-stop for a few days. I kept on making variations and new designs. After some time of playing around with this kind of geometric thinking and feeling, everything around me became points, dancing points in space, stretching out towards infinity."[17] She saw herself as a very vibrant, pulsating, activated point in space, similar to each of the dots in the kōlam. Perhaps, as Chandralekha eloquently and movingly points out, the kōlam is indeed a small way to glimpse infinity. It is as though in a very subtle, unassuming way the kōlam, when drawn in pulli patterns, could be seen as a small piece of cloth pulled down closer to the ground, as if it were puckered down onto the ground from an infinite series of dots that imaginatively stretch in all directions.

When a woman draws the dots of the kōlam, she could also be seeing herself literally as a pulsating dot representing eternity and continuity, the beginning and ending of things, life and death. In terms of metaphorical understandings of infinity and the kōlam, that would make a certain kind of sense. Women's relationships to the kōlam, therefore, include an understanding of pulling for a few minutes at that metaphorical cloth of infinite time and space. Every time a woman pinches rice flour between her fingers and begins to create a ritual design on the ground, she is unwittingly expressing tenets of mathematics that have been around for many years.

At the same time, the kōlams are at the forefront of mathematical discoveries and reflect complex mathematical ideas such as symmetry, array grammars, fractals, and infinity, among many more. Studying the kōlam has helped mathematicians to develop the theories of embodied mathematics, as Lakoff and Nunez have explained in their work. This very powerful idea of embodied mathematics was, indeed, the missing piece I had been searching for. When I discovered that idea, it helped me better understand the intertwining threads of mathematics and the kōlam designs.

8

Competitions: From Village to City

Pōtti: To Compete, To Play

My mother once described to me the excitement and inspiration of seeing other girls' and women's kōlams when she was a child growing up in her Kunnam village:

> After we each had made our kōlam, throughout the day when we were wandering up and down the village streets we would look at each other's to see if anyone did something different, interesting, or unusual. We would stand around a while, memorize them in our heads, and try the newness on ours the next day. We would all try to make a beautiful kōlam. But some days you were inspired and other days you were not.[1]

From village streets to city neighborhoods, the subtle notion of *pōtti* (play, competing) has long been embedded in the kōlam practice. But the translation of the Tamil word *pōtti* as "competition, rivalry, and emulation" does not adequately convey the playful aspects of the competition as perceived by the participants. Tamil women use the word *kōlappōtti* to mean "We are joining in the contest." There is a feeling of participation and camaraderie usually found in a ritual procession.

Janaki, an elderly woman from a village along the banks of the Kāvēri River in Thanjavur District, expressed it this way: "We had a lot of happiness in walking along and looking at each kōlam. Each morning that was what we talked about. Who had done the best kōlam for that day?" Throughout Tamil Nadu, older women spoke with fondness of that time. Many older women who had spent the early part of their lives in villages recalled the excitement of this convivial competition in their childhood. In the morning, while walking in groups through the village street on their way to bathe, wash clothes in the local river, or swim in the *kulam* (a manmade pond), they would carefully examine and critique each of the kōlams drawn on the thresholds of the houses.

Today the opportunities to gather and do errands together are few and far between. Modern life has brought indoor plumbing and has changed the household rhythms. I still remember the sad face of the middle-aged woman in Srīvilliputtūr, who told me:

> Now it is much more difficult to wander down the streets with your friends. Before, we had a purpose, all these reasons to get out and about. We *had* to get out. Now we have to find other excuses to get together, and sometimes we cannot find any. Sometimes we even forget to see each other. We end up not seeing each other for days and days. It is as if we have trapped ourselves in our own homes; all the household work is *inside* the home, whereas before we had a lot of household chores to do outside of the home. The younger women find it hard to find time to socialize and to get to know their neighbors. Of course, it was hard, hard work, to carry all that water for the entire household, for drinking, bathing, cooking. But it was also a lot of fun to do it together. It was a time when we did everyday chores together much more, and caught up on each other's news, gossip, and problems. We solved our problems together. We would realize we had similar ones. Now, everything is so each house, *each, each* house. Each household has its very own water. Each household has its very own WC [toilet]. Listen, until recently we used to have to go to find the best grounds to go shit together, too. We could talk all the time about what was happening in this house and that house, this woman and that woman . . . Now we do not even know what is happening in the house next door. We are much lonelier now, even though we still live in villages.

She looked forlornly at me when she said this and tears came to both of our eyes. I held her hands in front of me and felt her loneliness seep into me. I was moved by her analysis of how women's increased access to water supply and sanitation served at times to limit their mobility and social access outside of the home. It was not just seeing each other's kōlam that was transformed; an entire way of being convivial had been lost, too.

In urban contexts, women were often more separate from each other, but for different reasons. They were busier because they worked outside the house, and they lived in two-generation households rather than three-generation households, which cut down on the leisure time they had to socialize since grandmothers and aunts weren't there to feed the baby or cook the meals.

It never occurred to me that indoor plumbing, which most of us think of as a tremendous asset, would have such an unexpected consequence. Yes, it reduced women's work, but it also forced out a purposeful inhabitation of public space for women. Today women have so many duties and responsibilities inside the house that they don't have time to go out and see their neighbors' kōlams, so they can't decide who has done the best kōlam that day. Only in the month of Margali, from mid-December to mid-January, do many women allow themselves the leisure of being preoccupied with the kōlam—and then that preoccupation is intense. The very rhythm of Indian life used to offer a platform for informal competition among kōlam-makers, but with the advent of modern conveniences this opportunity was diminished. What took its place was a more formal type of competition that, we will see, has in some ways energized parts of the tradition.

Contemporary Kōlam Competitions

Over time the sense of pōtti that was part of traditional village life has transformed the kōlam competition. It has moved from the private realm of the threshold of houses to the public realm of the sports arena. Ironically, the pōtti serves to maintain and increase the visibility of the kōlam at a historical juncture when one might expect it to become just another one of the dying traditional folk arts. In the face of modernity, "postmodernity," and "postcoloniality," the kōlam ritual constantly reinvents itself. This reimagining is fueled by the complex interactions between diverse communities and shifting concepts of beauty.

The kōlappōtti—the kōlam competition—is gradually moving this ritual from traditional ritual spaces like thresholds and domestic altars to public cultural spaces such as museums, temples, women's associations, and large festivals. For example, the kōlam competition is being integrated into annual 10-day events celebrating particular deities at various temples. In some of these competitions, contestants have to make a kōlam of a certain size within a certain amount of time. Judges determine the best kōlam, using traditional criteria such as qualities of luster and the geometric complexity of the design. This movement is actively supported and guided by the women who participate to increase their presence in the public cultural arena of contemporary Tamil Nadu.

The movement into the wider social arena via these kōlappōtti raises important questions. One, how are the changing distinctions between "public" and "private" cultural spaces reflected in kōlam competitions? Two, how do the kōlam competitions reflect women's changing presence in the public sphere?

Three Kōlam Competitions

I discovered the kōlam competitions near the end of my research time and began attending them as often as I could.[2] Observing them over a period of two months in early 1994, I witnessed many changes in the traditional ritual and the nature of women's presence in Tamil Nadu as a whole. Not surprisingly, the sense of pōtti shifts in meaning and content among kōlams created in a range of social contexts. A paradoxical phenomenon seems to be occurring: on the one hand, the kōlam is declining in traditional contexts, but on the other, it is becoming increasingly popular in other wider, more social contexts. This paradox is observable in the increasing number of kōlam competitions held throughout Tamil Nadu over the past 20 years.

I will describe three very different competition sites in order to include a range of sponsors, participants, and atmospheres. The first one was sponsored by a village community in an informal setting in the heart of Tirunelvèli District. The second one, sponsored by a woman's religious association in the city of Madurai, combined both informal and formal characteristics. The third, also in Madurai, was cosponsored by the Gandhi Museum and the Colgate Palmolive Company, a multinational corporation, and was highly formalized. The first two sites represent the traditional context, while the third is modern in focus and intent.

A Village Competition

This first kōlam competition was located in the village of Ramapuram, nestled in a crook of the Tambarani River in the heart of Tirunelvèli District. The occasion was the rice harvest festival, Pongal (for a broader description of this festival, see Chapter 2). Here I found the same happy scene that Janaki painted of her village pōtti many years before, with women walking around and joyfully examining each other's kōlams, then judging them openly for their quality and luster.

Walking around the village streets for five days throughout the festivities, I could see that the making of the kōlam generated an intense wave of excitement among the women. The feeling of being in a pōtti for the title of best kōlam-maker in the village brought smiles, laughter, and heightened energy to all the participants.

How did these women compete in a village-style kōlam competition? They began the day thinking quietly and discussing with the other women in their households what kind of design they would draw that year to best showcase their skills. Then they prepared their materials of crushed powders and cleared the space in front of their houses. By 9 or 10 p.m., after the work of dinner was finished, the women went outside and began drawing for the entire night. After first contemplating the threshold space, they began in the dark to draw their kōlams with startling ease and quickness. For three to four hours their concentration was unabated, as the kōlams took shape.

There was no electricity in this village (I had searched hard to find a village that was still unelectrified, as I thought that I might find some insights about the kōlam in that context). Hundreds of the village women were making these kōlams in practically no light, with nothing but the faint glow of kerosene lanterns punctuating the darkness between houses. It was almost as if the eyes were incidental, that it was the body that was moving, circling, and almost dancing through space, a kind of yoga of fluid movements. The whole body seemed to be instinctively moving in the same pattern that the hand was moving, the hands pouring rice flour over the fingers and then expertly creating the design. Complex geometric loops and folds were left on the ground, visibly connecting the community together. It made me aware that the kōlam was more than a visual art form and that it had as much to do with the body as with the eyes.

The women created beautiful kōlams, outlining the very square edges of the front of their thresholds. In the competition for space, the goal was to run the designs as close as possible to the neighbor's house without invading her territory (see Figure 3.13). As I stood there looking at it one day, I had an epiphany. This edging of the kōlam was a marker between the household and the commons, the wider social and environmental space that the entire village inhabits and shares. With the whole process, the women are playfully pushing themselves farther and farther into the public space, and simultaneously the household is brimming over onto the street. Perhaps the kōlam is itself an indicator of the physical commons, the edge between the private and the public.[3]

All night I stayed and watched. When dawn arrived and the sunlight slowly streamed in, an incredible sight stretched from one end of the village to the other. Every street was covered with wet and dry kōlams. The wet ones were climbing the walls of the houses to a level of about three feet, then traveling into and through the houses as if an ephemeral carpet had been laid down, stitching the village together with white, red, and other colors. The effect was like a delicate layer of lace, intricate in shape and design—a dazzling white, fluid, lined image of the earthen soils decorated and overflowing with rice. The white lines seemed to move and dance as I gazed at them. This wondrous sight will be forever tucked in my mind. It was in this unelectrified village that I finally got a real sense of the power of this ritual art form. Until then, I had no idea that industrial light would make such a difference in how your body does a ritual. It seems obvious now, but then it didn't.

This resplendent image of kōlams covering the entire village lasted for only a few hours in the early morning light. As the sun rose higher, they slowly disappeared under the footsteps of passersby, as the sheath of intricate white patterns was transformed into rice flour on the bottoms of feet. But because the designs were so elaborate and large, it took the entire day for them to disappear completely. Before they did, the women were able to walk around in clusters talking with each other, critiquing and judging. It was highly informal; everyone was a competitor and everyone was a judge. Every sub-caste had its own street, and the judging of the best kōlam was done within each area. You could wander into any street and see this same scene over and over.

While I can describe for you the visual effect of the kōlams, I can hardly do justice to the atmosphere of fun that surrounded this event. Listening carefully to how they critiqued and decided which one was the best, I observed the women's various impressions and ruminations. For example, one woman had maintained the symmetry over a large surface, while another had made elaborate color fillings. The kōlams were judged for their balance, clarity of expression, colors, motifs, and other characteristics.

By 4 p.m., there had emerged from the informal discussions a consensus on whose kōlam was the best and why. Every street had its "better" and "best" kōlam-makers, whose work was noted in communal memory and further commented on (see Figure 1.2). The four or five women selected as the best kōlam-makers of that street would also be considered, by consensus, the best for that year. I would hear these kinds of comments: "Did you see the way she did those curved lines, without a break in the flow?" "That was a stunning use of color in balance. I have never seen it done that way." "Look at the way she fills those spaces. They're so dense and yet each element is distinctive." There were responses also: "No, I thought that other one was much better and took more skill to do," or "But I think the geometric ones are more challenging."

This kind of discussion would go along most of the day, in and out of other everyday conversations. The slow talking through persuasion seemed to work. Everyone had done her best, a few were specially recognized, and no one's efforts were discouraged. Accomplished subtly and elegantly, street by street, village by village, without appointed judges or public pronouncements, this kind of informal competition was the prevalent form of kōlappōttis until recent times (see Figures 8.1 and 8.2). It is difficult for me to document this process of village engagement, but it emerged from long, informal discussions on the aesthetics of the kōlam itself and how much it echoed the themes of the harvest festival of Pongal.

Figure 8.1 Woman filling in space with lotus flowers in the middle of the street, the night before Pongal festivities begin. Village, Thirunelveli District.

Figure 8.2 Older woman finishing a giant square kōlam in the dark. Village, Thirunelveli District.

An Āṇṭāḷ Festival Competition

Now we move to the second kōlappōtti, and we shift from a village to the city of Madurai, from the street to a more structured semiformal setting as part of the festival of the ninth-century female saint Āṇṭāḷ. I found that this type of setting was becoming increasingly common as a place for kōlam competitions: large festivals that involved other events, such as *pattimanrams* (debating contests), drama festivals, or, as here, the Āṇṭāḷ Festival.[4] The kōlam contest was added to attract more visitors.

In 1993, I attended most of the ten-day Āṇṭāḷ Festival and participated in the procession around the city of Madurai at dawn (see Chapter 5 on Āṇṭāḷ). The festival honoring her takes place on the Madurai Meenakshi temple grounds, in the Tiruppāvai office, and in the streets. Nearly a hundred women and children walk the four sacred streets bounding Madurai, carrying aloft the image of Āṇṭāḷ in a small chariot and stopping to receive gifts along the way. For these women, mostly housewives, the celebration of Āṇṭāḷ is a way of getting out of the house and spending time with their friends. Āṇṭāḷ, too, is considered to be out and about, visiting the city of Madurai. During this ten-day period, life revolves around the festivities of this saint. There are kōlam competitions, ceremonies and dramas, and daily rounds of chanting sessions on her song-poems, the *Tiruppāvai* and the *Tiruvempāvai.*

The kōlam competition held during the Āṇṭāḷ Festival was organized by a community leader, Visālakshi, who was committed to circulating Āṇṭāḷ's songs. This celebration is alive and well thanks to her devoted efforts from the early 1950s to honor and propagate the Āṇṭāḷ experience. When she was a teenager, she was chosen to train and apprentice under an older woman, who had also been carrying out this work for most of her life. Neither Visālakshi nor her teacher ever married; each devoted her life to the public and semipublic recitation of Āṇṭāḷ's songs.

Visālakshi is a big woman with a raspy voice that projects well in large audience settings. While at different times she is a cheerleader, scolder, teacher, and organizer, she has single-handedly attended to the maintenance of the public cultural space dedicated to the memory of Āṇṭāḷ.[5] She works tirelessly throughout the year, especially during the month of Mārgaḷi, when Āṇṭāḷ's presence is highlighted. She runs weekly classes on the *Tiruppāvai,* which are well advertised in the daily newspapers, and travels to the villages around Madurai to teach. She believes that following the path of Āṇṭāḷ can reorder one's life priorities and helps to cope with the loss of belief that comes with modernity. I had heard much about her over the years, and I was eager to see what I could learn from her about the relationship between Āṇṭāḷ and the kōlam.

Each year Visālakshi organizes the Āṇṭāḷ Festival on her own. To attract more women to the saint, she decided this year to include a kōlam competition, which is very popular, as part of the celebration. This communal event begins and ends with the singing of the *Tiruppāvai*. In the context of the Āṇṭāḷ Festival, the kōlam competition is recast as a gift, an offering for Krishna through the women's adoration of Āṇṭāḷ. "The kōlam is very popular," she explained. "Everyone knows the kōlam. Not everyone knows Āṇṭāḷ. And I am hoping that the kōlam competition will bring in new women. Everyone loves a kōlam competition. People will come to a kōlam competition who may not think of coming for Āṇṭāḷ." To reflect Āṇṭāḷ's importance to growing numbers of women, Visālakshi emphasized the need to include women from all castes.

At 4 o'clock on a sunny December afternoon, walking toward a handsome house on one of the narrow byways of the old city of Madurai, I heard the shouts of children running in and out on the edge of the porch-like thinnai. The house had the large, open, veranda-like feeling of older homes. The location of this public kōlam competition had all the characteristics of a semiprivate affair, as if the interior of the household had simply expanded to the community outside. However, adult men were discouraged actively from entering the house, since it was intended to be primarily a woman's space.

A boy who was nearly 12 years old was posted at the front door as the unofficial greeter and clearly was in command of the entire area. He politely asked everyone who entered—both young girls and mature women—"Are you coming for the kōlam competition?" Recognizing us from an earlier meeting, he ushered us inside with a mature air of graciousness and a big smile. He had a disarming way of trying to do something that could not be done: contain the energy of excited young girls about to begin a contest. As soon as we crossed the threshold, we slipped off our sandals and placed them on top of the growing pile. We heard the pattering feet and melodic voices of approaching girls, who were racing around the house, chasing each other down and playfully pulling on each other's arms. "I am going to win!" a girl of about 12 said to me, her face glowing with excitement. "No, I will win!" another girl piped up, and they rushed off in a wave of giggles. Looking a bit disconcerted and disoriented by all the commotion, a few smaller children took their places.

The house, in one of the old Brahmin neighborhoods, had been temporarily transformed into a playground, with no mirrors to crash into, no chairs to spoil, and plenty of open space to run around. Āṇṭāḷ portraits, paintings, and mounted bazaar prints covered the walls. The women appeared to feel at home in this Brahminical environment, even though they came from many different castes. Clearly there had been a lot of preparation and practice for the competition all week. Flocks of middle-aged Tamil women had organized the veranda on the second floor into a vast competitive space of chalked-out 4 × 4-foot squares. The girls, ages five to 14, were given one section and the women were given a separate space.[6] A *pandal* (a broad roof topped with coconut palm fronds, held up by bamboo poles) had been erected, the judges had been chosen, and the materials had been organized. Everyone gathered in the front room, where the sunlight was streaming through a central rectangular opening in the roof (Figures 8.3 and 8.4).

The women talked exuberantly among themselves about the kōlams they were going to create. They exchanged design ideas in their notebooks and chapbooks, and generously shared their rice flour and other materials with those who did not have enough. After 30 minutes or so, each person lined up behind the numbered square assigned to her at registration. Then there was silence, and a quiet voice said, "We can begin now." For the next two hours, the concentration was intense as each contestant tried to draw her best kōlam.

The entire competition lasted from five in the afternoon until ten in the evening. It is important to note that contestants stand for the entire time. They bend and tiptoe around the elegant design, careful not to disturb the labyrinthine pattern. They have to be sure to tuck their feet between the lines with each step so that they do not smear the lines.

I had unexpectedly been invited to be one of the three women judges when the third judge didn't show up. From this perspective, I was able to closely

Figure 8.3 Teenage girls and women in arena at Āṇṭāḷ festival kōlam competition, Madurai.

Figure 8.4 Young teenage girls nearing the end of their three-hour time limit to make the kōlam in Āṇṭāḷ competition, Madurai.

observe the other two judges' tastes and expectations. I was surprised to see that the two disagreed on a significant point—the importance of modern versus traditional designs. One judge felt that the very traditional, highly geometric labyrinth kōlams were the most challenging and therefore the most beautiful and should be rewarded with a first prize (Figure 8.5). The other judge loved the modern kōlams with their huge swaths of color-filled figurative designs. She was articulate, powerful, and persuasive.

I ended up being the tiebreaker and felt awkward doing so. In the end, I was swayed by the surrounding community pressure to lean toward valuing the innovation, variety, difference, and notions of modernity that prevailed in this competition, though simultaneously I held close to me the value of the sheer beauty of the traditional kōlams. The older kōlams were, in terms of color variation, simpler than the modern ones (they were just red and white), but they had a higher degree of geometric complexity. The aesthetic qualities rewarded were (1) the degree of *latcanam* (shining, brilliance, luster); (2) density—whether the surface was constructed from layers of powdered colors, flowers, and even lentils; and (3) *putumai* (newness). Here, modernity was represented through

Figure 8.5 Women's division in Āṇṭāḷ competition and one of the winning entries. At the end of making a labyrinth kōlam, Madurai.

more cartoon-like figures and complex pictorial scenes. The third criterion, in particular, slanted the decisions in the direction of a more modern design.

Once the three winners were picked, all the participants eagerly walked around the site to examine everyone else's kōlam and make their own rankings. Because such drawings were regarded as icons of divinity temporarily invested with sacred power, the women would touch the kōlams briefly with their hands and then place their hands on their closed eyes as a sign of prayer and respect. They wanted to see what kinds of innovations had been made. How had color been used differently? How had the image been drawn, and how realistic was it? The comments made most frequently were related to the notion of *vēra māthiri irrukku*, or "It is looking different."

I saw a distinct correlation between the kinds of kōlams the women made and their age. The older women tended to create the more traditional labyrinth kōlams; they did not win this contest, because it favored modern designs. Younger women who were in their 20s, many of whom incorporated newer elements into the kōlam such as pictorial representations and portraits, were the winners. The criterion of newness was clearly valued over the level of difficulty in execution.

The older women (those over 50) complained about the selection of winners based on the category of "newness," which was unfamiliar to them. They felt that the level of difficulty and the symmetry of the frame with the design inside should be far more important factors. I agreed with them, and now wished I had gone with my own natural inclinations for love of intensity of geometric form. But the moment when I could have made a difference had passed. I was sad at my own lack of ability to see the power of the dense geometric forms, and I thought a lot more about the inability of "tradition" to compete as a category in the thrusting, insistent face of "modernity." It was always very difficult, awkward, and uneasy for "tradition," which often had a quiet, more subdued kind of energy, to defend itself against the loud arguments of "newness for newness' sake." I saw the sadness in the older women's faces; their shoulders sagged as they saw their values and perceptions being devalued.

Eventually the children became restless, and all the women left together, some disappointed, some delighted with their prizes of pots and pans or trips to Kodaikannal, a nearby resort town. There was a sadness in the lack of unanimity between the younger and the older participants.

The message was that geometry was not as important as figurative fineness. An entire way of seeing the world as geometric was giving way to seeing the world as figurative. Decoration itself was being reimagined, its signs, symbols, and metaphors. Did it matter? Or were kōlam competitions and the way they were judged a mere harbinger of things to come in India as a whole? Would modernity and its way of seeing bowl over the arguments of "tradition"? Is this why "tradition" has had to fight back so aggressively, with such maliciousness, in some recent right-wing movements—because it has felt so swept over, so ignored, so maligned by the bright, shining mirrors of modernity?

When created in the traditional way, the more old-fashioned kōlams were done primarily in white, occasionally spruced up with red borders. On special occasions, dyes in other colors, made from natural materials, were also used. The northern version of the kōlam, called rangōli, is commonly made from a rainbow of colors, making the ritual drawings distinctly different than the Tamil ones.

The modern use of a wide variety of colors, however, is not universally embraced. One mature woman who had made a large and elaborate white labyrinthine kōlam complained that the whole idea of the kōlam was changing to include color. She wondered aloud at the degree of skill involved in drawing a simple figure and filling it with beautiful colors as one would a coloring book. This launched a serious debate as to whether "if you call it a kōlam competition, should you even allow the entry of color, this North Indian influence?" The influence she was referring to was the entry of bizarre colors such as hot pink, parrot green, and DayGlo purple.

Another older woman commented mournfully:

> Soon these old ones will not even be drawn anymore. How can we compete with color? If they wanted color kōlams, they should have called it a rangōli [color] competition![7] What is happening to the kōlam? You cannot even recognize it anymore. These kōlams do not have any balam [strength] or satu [power]. They are indeed pretty, but is that what a kōlam really is?

However, another participant pointed out, "If you do not allow color, no one will come for the competition."

One woman said sharply, "We are becoming Punjabis [North Indians]. Just like in our clothes, our children are shifting from our Tamil dāvani [half-sari] to salwār-kameez [loose pants with a knee-length long shirt]; so, too, the kōlam is becoming the rangōli. We are not even fighting for our Tamil culture. We are just wanting to be North Indian without even thinking about it." However, her concerns and others similar to hers went unheeded by the judges.

With regard to this last woman's comments, in India, there are some key cultural distinctions between the northern and southern parts. And, beyond this distinction, Tamils have their own pride in their distinctive and unique language, Tamil, which is one of two classical Indian languages (the other is Sanskrit). Twenty years before, many Tamils had begun to feel pressured by the linguistic, cultural, and religious styles of northern India, in addition to the Western influences of style, dress, and food.[8] Now, unfortunately, the transition is nearly complete, and people notice the takeover of the Tamil culture by northern Indian styles. Many more women are wearing long tunics with pants instead of traditional saris. More Tamils study Hindi, a more popular language, rather than Tamil, which is regarded as regional and more parochial. They have switched from a rice-based diet to one that includes whole-wheat flat breads like chappatis, which are common in northern India. This transformation of the Tamil culture has brought a more modern and cosmopolitan outlook even to villages.

A Gandhi Museum/Colgate Palmolive Competition

The third competition was strikingly different from the earlier two, partly because it was cosponsored by the Gandhi Museum, a venerated institution, and the Colgate Palmolive Company, a customer-hungry multinational corporation looking to put down roots in this new culture. *Strange allies*, I thought to myself.

In January 1994, a huge and popular kōlam competition was held at the Gandhi Museum in Madurai. The setting, at the heart of a large public museum complex, featured huge open fields that were divided with chalk into 150 spaces for the kōlam-makers. This competition had been advertised with a registration deadline in the daily newspapers. It was so popular that hundreds of applicants were turned down because of space constraints, and finally a limited number of participants had to be selected by lottery.

Colgate had posted banners advertising its toothpaste and powders throughout the site. Some 10 to 15 managers and supervisors from Colgate were there, supporting and documenting the event with their own film crew. The extensive planning and coordination necessary to create such a presence indicated that Colgate was well aware of the significance of these competitions and the potential to further their economic goals. Their involvement was well timed, since India had only recently opened economically to foreign competition.

At 10 a.m., the bright sun shimmered over the broiling asphalt. In an open space behind the museum, nearly 140 women and their assistants were lined up behind 6 × 6-foot chalked squares; together they formed a rectangle the size of an athletic field. Hundreds of observers, mainly family and friends, had come to cheer them on. The area had been emptied of idle bystanders and cordoned off with a heavy rope. The audience was not allowed to come too close to the competitors (although members of the press were allowed to take photographs). The organizers wanted to avoid breaking the competitors' concentration. I felt as if I were at a track-and-field competition, waiting for the gun to go off to signal the beginning of the race.

In another field off to the side, a small area had been set up for nearly 20 male competitors. For the very first time, males had been allowed to enter a kōlam competition. Because the men's section was such a novelty, it attracted a great deal of attention and press. Everyone was curious about what the male kōlam-makers were going to do and how they would place in the competition. From the outset they were considered to have a handicap because they were not women, and it was understood that the rules would have to be bent for them. They were allowed additional help from their mothers, sisters, wives, and daughters, and some had one or two male assistants.

The excitement was palpable as the starting time approached. Each woman and her assistant had smoothed the surface of her generous square of red earth by clearing it of twigs, leaves, and pebbles. In addition, the women had carefully unpacked all their materials from small tin cans or plastic bags held together by rubber bands. Sketchbooks had been brought out, along with rough drawings and plans on small ledger pages to serve as occasional guides. As the women waited expectantly with their sets of colored powders in front of them, they contemplated the square of space on the ground and imagined how they were going to fill it.

When the gun finally went off, the kōlam-makers sprang forward to their squares on the red earth and began drawing with intensity and purpose. The kōlappōtti had begun, and the competitors had only three hours to show off their skills. In the heat of the noonday sun, women and a few men, Hindus, along with a few Muslims and Christians, all competed to draw their notion of the best kōlam. Their imaginations and aesthetic sensibilities would be reviewed by the judges, who would descend on their final creations to determine the first, second, and third prizes. The winner of the citywide competition would receive an all-expense-paid trip to Ooty, a hilltown resort in the Eastern Ghats. There were smaller prizes such as sets of pots and pans for the second- and third-place winners.

Many of the kōlams in this competition took the form of portraits or landscapes that resembled posters or photographs, with words written inside the kōlam and phrases tucked into the landscape motifs such as "Secular Harmony for All." Such writings expressed political sentiments in memory of the recent communal riots in Ayodhya, Bombay, and many cities in northern India. Some echoed specific symbols of religious institutions—a cross and cathedral spire, an ōm-saktī sign and a gōpuram (Hindu temple tower), the word *Allah* and a mosque tower.

One man, a professional photographer in his early 30s, had entered the competition with a male journalist. Together they had created a landscape kōlam depicting the recent Pongal festival, in which men had engaged in a bullfight. The highly dramatic painting in black, white, and splashes of red blood featured a matador taunting a bull with his bright red cloth. The three women judges discussed this creation and firmly concurred, "That is not a kōlam. That is a Western-style painting. That does not qualify. We are not gathered here to judge Western-style paintings; we are here to judge the kōlam."

This judgment showed that they were hoping to keep these masculine values of blood and bullfighting away from the kōlam, as they go against the inherent values of auspiciousness, health, and well-being. The judges felt responsible for guiding the future of this ritual art, whether located in citywide competitions sponsored by museums and corporations and advertised in newspapers, or in ordinary neighborhoods, or in village competitions attended only by locals. They knew that what happened here would influence so much more. Even the local village kōlams had already been swayed by these public and more secular competitions that featured poster-like messages. The judges felt that male participation itself was not undesirable, but depicting traditional aggressive male preoccupations was.

The women judges, all considered experts, debated what constituted a kōlam. One judge, who had done a good deal of her own research, held the strong opinion that in a "real" competition no color should be used other than the traditional red and white. Male participation was not the only issue that was controversial; the judges also sought to hold onto the ritual form of the kōlam, rather than undue influences from other regional forms like the rangōli.

Another judge, considered a great kōlam-maker in her own right, felt sad at witnessing the disappearance of labyrinth kōlams. They were abstract in nature but used a very different set of design principles, which were far more mathematical and difficult to do (see Chapter 7). The labyrinths are created by laying down a series of dots and circling them with complicated, snake-like lines to achieve symmetrical shapes resembling a netting or maze. Such precision requires the ability to imagine the lines around the dots very carefully. If even one line should go astray, like a weaving that has a wrong maneuver in it, the mistake will be obvious to everyone. These kōlams are more difficult to create than the landscape kōlams but are less colorful than the modern kōlams. The judge expressed her regret that this entire genre was no longer represented in competitions because they were not considered interesting enough.

The third judge was a professor of music at a local college who had done seminal work on relating kōlams to particular ragas in the South Indian musical system. The key criterion for her evaluation was creativity: Did the kōlam-maker stretch the genre in a significant way? (Figures 8.6 and 8.7).

Figure 8.6 A pattern with a graphic grid of musical instruments, Madurai.

Figure 8.7 A winning entry, a scene of two doves, Madurai.

All three judges were concerned about the changing nature of the kōlam as a whole. Some important questions raised in this competition were (1) What is the kōlam? (2) In what ways can the form incorporate changes without losing its essential nature? and (3) What types of changes should be encouraged or discouraged? For example, they did not approve of the trend toward secularization or the use of the kōlam as a medium for poster-like messages. No matter how spectacular, the elaborate painting-like kōlams, the picture-postcard designs, and the imitations of Disney cartoons were immediately rejected and excluded from the definition of the kōlam. In the final analysis, the winning entries were those that most closely met the judges' definition of a great kōlam: symmetry and balance, geometric complexity, and innovation.

Competition and a Secular Modern Identity

Today the kōlam has come into its own in thoroughly modern public spaces, enabling women to carve out a new presence in contemporary Tamil Nadu. This transformation can be observed by their active participation in hundreds of kōlam competitions sponsored by informal village associations, women's groups, women's magazines, festivals, textile mills, museums, and even multinational corporations. The women who participate tend to be those who have the leisure time and desire to win prizes or make a name for themselves. Thus the kōlam competitions provide multiple sites for observing the ways in which women are constructing a secular modern identity.

Yet the context in which women attempt to build a more public presence is layered, complex, and contested. It is important to distinguish the notion of "public culture" in the large-scale, institutionally sponsored kōlam competition at the Gandhi Museum from the "public culture" of the rituals conducted by women in villages or city streets (Breckenridge 1995). The experience of being selected as an excellent kōlam-maker in a huge contest with hundreds of spectators is quite different from the semiprivate, semipublic context of the village. In the latter, creations are judged by a few women in a setting limited to one's neighborhood or village, while in the former, aesthetic criteria are evaluated before large audiences in high-profile, citywide events. Moreover, these events are covered by the media and thereby enter into the cultural space of a much larger community.

Traditionally, the kōlam occupies the threshold space, which straddles and links public and private worlds, a liminal space where women outline the boundaries of their sense of place. The kōlams of individual households communicate to the outer community what is going on inside the house. But today the threshold, which is either not big enough or not available to the public, is increasingly becoming a guarded place—boarded, locked, and even screened—as the popular thinnai, or porch-like space, becomes enfolded into the security of the interior space. The threshold of the physical house is shrinking to the point where the street meets the doorway and locked gateways greet passersby. As the outer edge of the house moves farther into the street, the threshold that the kōlam can occupy is gradually disappearing.

This loss of the flow of people provided by the porous thinnai is also a loss for community life. There are still people in the street, of course, but there is no longer a place to stop, rest, and catch up. A woman either is confined totally inside the house or must thrust herself wholly into the public sphere. With the loss of the threshold, the woman can no longer engage easily with the community without having to go "out." Yet with the progressive disappearance of the threshold, ironically, women's appearance in the public sphere has increased.

One striking result of the increase in kōlappōttis is the greater recognition of individual women and their accomplishments in the broader social context. A woman's sense of individuality as it pertains to her public self is expanded significantly when her reputation, achievements, connections, and influences are cast in a larger civic context. I suggest that women's sense of "contexualization" is extending from their own neighborhood to the more anonymous civic space. Mattison Mines's (1994) concept of a Tamil as a "contextualized individual" (a person who can only be understood by knowing the context in which she was born and raised) clarifies this point:

> Tamil individuality is a spatially defined individuality; its dimension depends on the size and locality of the constituencies that form a person's social contexts. The individuality of important persons will be more widely known and their constituencies more widespread than will those of ordinary persons; but, more widely recognized, identity will also be more widely contested. And generally, the spatial dimension of a woman's individuality will be smaller and less contested than that of a man. Each person's identity is limited spatially to those among whom he or she is known. . . . Eminence, civic individuality, reputation, social trust, the organization of groups, individual responsibility, goals, control, agency—all are features of the contextual individual, and all indicate that there remains much to explore regarding Indian notions and ways of valuing individuality. (22–3)

In other words, a kōlam-maker who moves into the larger public space is expanding the number of people who know her and whom she knows. She is increasing her presence to the public. The movement of these women into public competitions mirrors the outward movement of women in Indian society as a whole. Throughout Tamil Nadu, more women are visible in public life, are working outside the home, are represented in the media as newscasters, and so on. Even in smaller cities such as Madurai, it is increasingly common to see young and middle-aged mothers riding on scooters in their saris to drop off schoolchildren at the bus stop. In the past, one would rarely see women function independently in the public sphere, although they would travel together in groups.

Moreover, such participation in the public sphere has consequences in the private and domestic sphere. Those who win prizes in the public arena bring honor and prestige to their families and increase their status in the public eye. Thus the nature of women's identity in terms of personal achievement is being transformed through their increased participation in kōlappōttis.

The kōlappōtti phenomenon reveals changing contemporary values that are linked to the prevalence of modernity in public cultural spaces. Yet kōlam competitions cannot be viewed simply as a movement of the kōlam from an interior or private setting to an external or public setting, but must be viewed in a far more nuanced way. In citywide competitions, space can no longer be differentiated by the qualities of "inside" and "outside." The traditional role of the threshold, which is to communicate what the state of the household is, is irrelevant in this distinctly nonsacred arena. Perhaps, though, we can regard this scenario as the threshold being reduced to the size of a rope, the ones in the sports arena that divide competitors from spectators. Indeed, the transformation of the kōlam from the ritual space of the threshold to the large sports arena is actively supported and guided by the women kōlam-makers themselves as a way of increasing their participation in the public culture.

Colgate and the Kōlam

I interviewed several Colgate officials who had attended the kōlam competition I discussed earlier. They had traveled from Calcutta, more than a thousand miles away, and from other metropolitan cities throughout India. They were all male. Of what possible interest could the kōlam be to the Colgate corporation? Why would they invest a significant amount of resources to host this ritual event in a secular context?

At first, I was puzzled that Colgate would be interested in such a traditional ritual art form at all. In the climate of increasing globalization of multinational corporations, it became clear that Colgate, like Coca-Cola and other global corporations, was trying to make inroads into the strong consumer base of nearly 200 million middle-class people in India. Traditionally, in India "toothpaste" consisted of tooth powders, which were placed on the right forefinger and then placed on the teeth directly and rubbed hard back and forth to clean them. As late as the early 1970s, when I lived in New Delhi with my parents as a child, I remember how we used a traditional black powder that was made from herbal ingredients and locally produced.

Another traditional option for dental hygiene was rubbing your teeth with a *neem* stick. Neem comes from a local and indigenously abundant plant and is available all over India. At dawn throughout the Indian subcontinent, especially if you were rushing by on a train, you would often see men and women rubbing their teeth with neem sticks. Traditionally believed to be cleansing for the teeth, neem is a product that is used daily and is associated with traditional notions of "cleanliness" and "purity." It is outside the global market and does not make much of a profit.

Colgate's objective is to replace these traditional low-cost products with a higher-cost modern version, which suddenly seems indispensable. This is the general trend of global commercialization. Through its sponsorship, the Colgate corporation employed the competition as a mechanism of globalization. And why would Colgate, with its Indian male middle managers, choose the kōlam as a point of intervention in the public sphere? Because the Indian representatives know two things: first, women purchase household goods, especially cleaning supplies, and second, women perform the kōlam early in the morning, just after they brush their teeth. Colgate, for the local Tamil women, epitomizes the entry into the "modern" and "global" economy and thereby conveys a "modern" sense of cleanliness, purity of result, and a set of "white and glistening" teeth. The kōlam, too, in the traditional context represents a cleansing of sorts, a sign of ordering of the traditional cosmos, a creation of purity and auspiciousness on the threshold, however temporary it may be.

The explicit reasons given by the Colgate corporate officials for their sponsorship were "The corporation need to get closer to their consumers," "to express interest in women's arts," "to get to know their consumer base," and, in general, "to improve public relations." Their implicit reasons must also be examined. I found metaphorical correlations linking Colgate with the kōlam. We can see that the company's marketing agenda ties together with the kōlam in ways that at first are not so obvious. The anthropologist Arjun Appadurai's theory of the cultural imagination readily applies:

> The image, the imagined, the imaginary—these are all terms which direct us to something critical and new in global cultural processes: the imagination as a social practice . . . the imagination has become an organized field of social practices, a form of work (both in the sense of labor and culturally organized practice) and a form of negotiation between sites of agency ("individuals") and globally defined fields of possibility. . . . The imagination is now central to all forms of agency, is itself a social fact, and is the key component of the new global order. (1994: 327)

In other words, Colgate is trying to tap into the cultural imagination of Tamil women as it is expressed by the kōlam and use it for their own purposes. This is how globalization works. Put simply, Colgate is using the kōlam to sell toothpaste. Their sponsorship of the contest exists simply to increase profit. But as a side effect of assimilating this women's ritual into their marketing strategy, they are not only incorporating women but also expanding women's own sense of agency and individual power in an anonymous civic space.

This chapter has traced the physical, cultural, and metaphorical aspects of kōlam competitions in three very different settings in contemporary Tamil Nadu. Out of the millions of women who make the kōlam, only a few thousand participate in the citywide and publicly organized kōlappōttis. Yet all the kōlappōttis, from village to urban contexts, can be viewed as "exhibitions" in which ritual has become an aesthetic value. The ritual purpose is disappearing and being replaced by an intense focus on artistic creativity. The women's pride lies in displaying themselves and their skills in the public context. "We come to show off," many women say to each other, laughing.[9]

As we have seen, competition among the women, whether in a village, town, or city, is intense and focused. The qualities of exhibition, critical examination, and aesthetic evaluation are consistent within the ritual context of the village competition, the Āṇṭāḷ Festival competition, and the Gandhi Museum competition. Such adaptability is possible because the notion of exhibition itself is not alien to the traditional ritual practice of the kōlam.

Many historians and anthropologists have studied the presentation of "traditional" rituals in public cultural spaces throughout South Asia. For example, Sandra Freitag has examined "the realm in which community has been expressed and redefined through collective activities in public spaces" (1989: 6). According to Freitag, this context is "a coherent, consistent one of symbolic behavior—a realm of 'public arenas'" (6). Such a realm impinged simultaneously on two worlds: that encompassing activity by locally constituted groups, and that structured by state institutions. Originally just the realm in which collective activities were staged, it became an alternative world to that structured by the imperial regime, providing legitimacy and recognition to a range of actors and values denied place in the imperial order.

Although Freitag focuses on colonial India, her description of "public arenas," in which symbolic behavior serves to recognize and legitimize a range of local groups and values, is useful in understanding the concept of "public culture." In the Gandhi Museum/Colgate contest, in contrast to the other more traditional kōlam competitions I witnessed, there was a widespread inclusion and acceptance of all participants, not just Hindu women. The range of "actors," or competitors, was expanded to include Hindu men, a few Muslims, and Christians. Participants say that the reason a person of any faith can join the competition is precisely because "The kōlam is not a Hindu ritual; it is really a Tamil cultural activity. Any Tamil can participate, male or female, Hindu, Muslim, or Christian, or from any other religion."

In the days following the most publicly displayed kōlam competition, I visited some of the Muslim and Christian houses to interview the teenage male competitors, their mothers, and even their grandmothers. The Muslim grandmothers, as one might expect, were not happy about their Muslim teenage grandsons participating in what used to be thought of as a Hindu ritual art form—a female art form to boot—and I was discouraged from speaking to them about it. The mother-in-law was often not told, and neither were the fathers, because it was known that it would be forbidden. The mothers, however, encouraged the new trend, saying, "It is a talent that should be supported and nurtured. The boys are developing their sense of art." They saw it as a useful, pragmatic, transferable skill.

This process of the secularization of a traditional ritual art form parallels James Clifford's understanding of the creation of the "cultural" or "aesthetic." He argues that:

> . . . the categories of art and culture . . . are strongly secular. "Religious" objects can be valued as great art (an altarpiece by Giotto), as folk art (the decorations on a Latin American popular saint's shrine), or as cultural artifact (an Indian rattle) . . . What "value," however, is stripped from an altarpiece when it is moved out of a functioning church . . .? Its specific power or sacredness is relocated to a general aesthetic realm. (1993: 226)

Whatever its explicit reasons may be, Colgate is employing only the cultural aspect of this ritual identity, and attempting to increase the presence of its own corporate identity in the process. The public relations goal of sponsoring these competitions is to introduce Colgate to potential customers and to have them associate the brand with the kōlam. Some kōlam-makers even wrote within their enclosed space, "Thanks, Colgate." One can wonder whether the "whiteness" and "cleanliness" promised by Colgate ads are being deliberately reified in the public imagination through these sponsorships.

Yet there is another way of looking at this. The Tamil women who eagerly participate in these contests do not see themselves as being drawn into or coopted by Colgate's global strategy. They have a certain kind of agency and control of their own, expressing and acting out a desire to become part of the public sphere through the transformation of a "domestic" ritual art tradition. Furthermore, the use of the kōlam as a way to express political sentiments of religious harmony and river clean-up appeared to create an entirely new arena of public voicing of women's concerns, even in a globalized context, perhaps especially so. They said so themselves.

I suggest that the sense of exhibition in the kōlam competition at the Gandhi Museum engenders a "ritual of belonging." Even in the motifs of the kōlams, the articulation of a plurality of identities reveals a commitment to accommodating the presence of the "other" (e.g., other religions, other races) in women's public culture in Tamil Nadu. The widening of a competitive arena that had previously been open only to women reveals a confidence and verve for the new directions in which the kōlam is moving. Yet I wonder if this ritual of belonging is an entry point with a global identity, rather than a Tamil cultural identity.

When I returned in the winter of 1998–99 and was in Thanjavur, I went to a kōlam competition and realized that the kōlam was transforming dramatically. The winning entries included a "kōlam" of a ballroom scene from the recent popular film "Titanic." The judges were primarily male; they were mostly art professors from local colleges. Women were still engaged in making the kōlam but were being judged by male art teachers, at least in the town of Thanjavur; in other places, there may be different trajectories.

In the public spaces of the kōlam competitions, the artistic form has become the primary focus, secularizing its religious beginnings. Colors are no longer just red and white but include vivid purple and green; the geometry ranges from the traditional labyrinth to the elaborate figure, portraits, and landscape drawings. As we have seen, some are poster-like representations carrying messages for mass readership. Penetration of corporate sponsorship into kōlam competitions is increasingly visible, even influencing the drawings themselves. For example, words such as "clean," "white," and "fresh" are increasingly found within the kōlam, and some have a bright, advertisement-like quality.

At times it can seem as if modernization and development are slowly turning the kōlam into an aesthetic object, stripped of many of its ritual and resonant meanings. Yet, paradoxically, while it is widely considered a symbol of "tradition" and culture, the kōlam can accommodate remarkable changes in form, substance, and style depending on the context. Meanwhile, women are attempting to discourage the changing kōlams from becoming a purely aesthetic object, akin to Western-style paintings, by refusing to award them prizes. Glassie observes that "cultures and traditions are created, invented, willfully compiled by knowledgeable individuals . . . out of experience" (1995: 398). Thus kōlam competitions can be analyzed as sites of significant cultural activity that reflect complex, shifting values and preferences within the broader Tamil society.

9

Embedded Ecologies and the Earth Goddess

What we separate as art, economics, and religion
appear intermeshed as aspects of the same performance.
The aesthetics, ethos, and worldview of a person
are shaped in childhood and throughout early life,
and reinforced later, by these verbal
and nonverbal environments.

—Ramanujan 1993: iv

The Earth Goddess and Embedded Ecologies

I sat with Jaya Mami in the cool and open rectangular inner courtyard (*muṟṟam*) in the center of her house, the sun streaming in through the red-tiled roof under a cloudless sky.[1] Even in December in Tamil Nadu, it was hot in the noonday sun, hot enough so that people needed umbrellas to shield themselves against the searing heat and light. She explained to me the kōlam's link to Bhūdevi, the earth goddess: "We draw the kōlam as our first ritual act in the morning to remember Bhūdevi. We walk on her. We spit on her, we poke her; we burden her. We expect her to bear us and put up with all the activities we do on her with endless patience." Many Tamil women echoed these words, saying they become aware of Bhūdevi, as they create the kōlam.

In this chapter I will discuss how Tamil women's honoring of Bhūdevi in the kōlam ritual can help us answer two questions: (1) What is the relationship between Bhūdevi and the kōlam? and (2) How does Hinduism in general treat the sacredness of the natural world? In thinking about these questions, I came up with two concepts: "embedded ecologies" and "intermittent sacrality." The presence of Bhūdevi in the kōlam conversations is a rich example of these two concepts. They can help us resolve some of the paradoxes in the relationships between the mythologization of the natural world and the conservation ethics that may or may not lead from this very deification.

Embedded ecology is the concept that many of our ideas about the natural world are embedded and steeped in cultural, ritual, and artistic forms. A botanist perceives a rose at one level. At other levels, a rose conjures up other mental pictures, which may be religious, aesthetic, romantic, or something else entirely. We can't see a rose without envisioning a lover bringing it to the beloved; romance is implicit in the rose in a way that it isn't in a violet or a hyacinth. Similarly, in India, Hindus see the earth not merely as a geological formation, or a vast multi-billion-year movement of tectonic plates, but also as an earth goddess (Eck 2012). Hindus see a river not just as a waterway, but also as the embodiment of a goddess who brings to it her own mythologies and experiences and lives in it and protects it (Alley 2002; Haberman 2006).

Looking at this concept of embedded ecologies in Hinduism, I ask the questions: What are the complex layers of subtle relationships between Bhūdevi and the ritual act of the kōlam? How has the notion of sacred landscapes been understood to be "ecological," especially by Indian environmentalists such as Vandana Shiva? How has Hinduism then been understood and interpreted as "ecological"? How can we be more precise in illuminating the contradictions between an imagined ideal of behavior and what actually happens in everyday life? I introduce here the concept of "intermittent sacrality" to resolve, at least in part, apparent tensions within environmental understandings in folk Hinduism. I came up with this term to express the ways in which people's imagination of sacrality impinge intermittently on the ways in which they relate and connect to parts of nature. In other words, I am referring to the cultural tendency to hold the earth as sacred during specific rituals, and then later on to drop the deferential attitude and practice in the midst of practical demands of daily life.[2]

Though both of these new terms may seem abstruse now, they will become clearer as the chapter unfolds. These concepts were difficult for me to figure out, so bear with me as I pose these questions and concepts and figure my ways around them. Now, we turn back to Bhūdevi.

First, who is Bhūdevi? She is one of the four goddesses constantly mentioned in women's kōlam conversations. The other three are Lakshmi, Mūdevi, and Tulasi Devi. Tulasi Devi is like Lakshmi a wife of Vishnu. She brings good fortune and protection from evil. She is represented by the sacred basil plant and is ceremoniously honored by planting in a pot (Narayan 1995, 1997; Pintchman 2005).

In Hindu mythology, Bhūdevi is the mythic, iconic, and metonymic personification of the earth.[3] The name Bhūdevi is used interchangeably with the earth. She is also a wife of Vishnu, flanking him along with Lakshmi in iconographic representations. She plays a critical role in Vishnu mythologies because what often initiates Vishnu's incarnations is Bhūdevi's call for help. For example, in the boar avatar story, Bhūdevi is carried off by *asuras* (demons) and submerged in the ocean. When she cries to Vishnu to come and help her, he comes in the form of Varāha, the boar, and rescues her. One of the most common iconographic representations of Bhūdevi shows Varāha carrying her aloft on his tusks. Bhūdevi is pictured as small, fragile, and feminine, in contrast to Varāha, who is portrayed as large, virile, and masculine (Figures 9.1 and 9.2). In this image, it is generally understood that an underlying concern for the earth as vulnerable is expressed. The effect of her weakening is perceived as disastrous. The earth, the soil, is fragile, just as the earth goddess is fragile. Both need protection. This linking of the soil and Bhūdevi is common in women's everyday language.[4]

Figure 9.1 Bhūdevi with Varāha (Google Images).

Figure 9.2 Bhūdevi as globe on Varāha's tusks (Google Images).

In the village of Enangudi near Thanjavur, a middle-aged woman, Sarada, told me:

> Bhūmidevi [another name for Bhūdevi] puts in a complaint (*muṟaiyiṭu*) to Vishnu, "I cannot stand all this meanness, the wickedness (*aṭṭūḷiyam*) of humans to the earth. You must do something, find some way to alleviate my pain." She is upset and keeps complaining of the weight (*pāram*) on her, the weight of human actions on her. That is why the *avatārs* come down to earth, because of Bhūmidevi's complaints and pleas for help.

An explicit language of protection and vulnerability runs alongside the mythologization of the earth as a goddess. The myth of Bhūdevi is implicitly related to women's ritual practices, such as the kōlam, and to Tamil women's perception of the natural world.

"Embedded ecologies" is what I am calling these implicit and embodied ways of seeing and relating to the natural world. The invocation of Bhūdevi, the stories and common understandings, is one of common themes that circulate around the making of the kōlam within women's everyday lives. Bhūdevi acts as a reminder of the fragility of the soil and the earth; she is a mnemonic device shaping the way that Hindus view the natural world. The making of the kōlam is clearly a way of culturally remembering and recognizing the natural world.

One of the reasons for doing the kōlam first thing in the morning is as a reminder of the debt we owe to the earth goddess, who will bear all human and non-human actions on her surface throughout the coming day. In their conversations with me, Tamil women referred to Bhūdevi (or Bhūmadevi) both as the physical earth, a large living being with a soul, similar to the Greek goddess Gaia, and as the particular soil at a woman's feet in a her particular village, town, or city. Bhūdevi is simultaneously both cosmic and local.

I believe that many women consciously think of Bhūdevi as they make the kōlam before dawn. As Chittra from the town of Thanjavur commented, "Bhūdevi must be one of our first thoughts in the morning." Banumami, a grandmother in her 50s from the village of Thilaikkudi, which lies along the Kāvēri River in Thanjāvīr District, explained Bhūdevi in this way:

> Bhūmadevi is our mother. She is everyone's source of existence. Nothing would exist without her. The entire world depends on her for sustenance and life. So, we draw the kōlam first to remind ourselves of her. All day we walk on Bhūdevi. All night we sleep on her. We spit on her. We poke her. We burden her. We do *everything* on her. We expect her to bear us and all the activities we do on her with endless patience. That is *why* we do the kōlam. [italics mine]

These words echo almost exactly those of Jaya Mami and many others. The earth goddess's plight and the daily offering of the kōlam are ways of paying attention to the ground that we walk on daily. They remind us that we are embedded in and dependent on the earth.

What are the ecological implications of this "poking" and "spitting"? This ritual, like other rituals to Bhūdevi, appears to be largely a symbolic gesture; that is, the reverence expressed in the ritual does not necessarily translate into environmental consciousness throughout the day. Acknowledging her enormous value through a ritual does not imply that our actions during the rest of the day must incorporate the notion of the earth's divinity. The notion that the earth needs to be "conserved" and that it should be used in a sustainable manner, in the way the word ecology is understood in the environmental movement, should neither be assumed nor expected in the everyday life of South India. The kōlam may belong to a class of *compensatory* rituals that do not imply a change of behavior outside of the ritual's time and space.[5] The making of the kōlam is a set of gestures with a function that is directly compensatory; we ask Bhūdevi to have patience with us, to forgive us, and to thank her "for bearing us."[6] A compensatory gesture that is comparable would be the ritual prayer a Bharatanatyam dancer makes before she begins her performance. She asks Bhūdevi to forgive her for stamping on her—but the dance then proceeds.

Trashing Bhūdevi

I puzzled over this paradox for a long time, the contradiction between Tamil women's reverence for Bhūdevi while making the kōlam and their seeming disrespect to her throughout the rest of the day: I frequently saw them throw trash and garbage on the earth. However, throwing of garbage on Bhūdevi and using plastic stick-on decals to make the kōlam instead of natural materials were rarely if ever mentioned as hostile to Bhūdevi. Was it then my own "ecological" hope that a mythological link to the earth would lead to a greater reverence and "caring" for the soil in everyday life?

One might think that Tamil women, who believe the earth to be sacred, would see the contradiction involved in abuse the earth to fill their needs. Although the soil, water, and forests are becoming polluted with toxic chemicals, this growing problem doesn't seem very prominent to them. This society must hunt, farm, and manufacture just as everyone else in the world does. For village women, of course, the amount of waste that is dumped into public areas is relatively small and harmless compared to that of a large Indian or American corporation or government entity, and in the past local village or neighborhood waste was even more harmless because it consisted of organic materials. The forces of capitalism see the earth not as a goddess, but as a mine to be plundered of its riches and a vast garbage sink in which to dump its waste. Compared to international companies, these women do not pose a serious threat to the environment. Whatever they throw into the street does not last very long. A cow will soon amble along and eat it, a crow will fly down and scoop it up, or it will naturally disintegrate.

At least, it used to be this way. Now, the waste of villagers is not quite so harmless because it is not always organic. They use non-biodegradable plastics, rubber, and other modern materials. People know that plastics and other household products do not disintegrate the way that bamboo and other natural materials do, but the practice continues. This change from biodegradable to non-biodegradable has even affected the practice of the kōlam. Today ground stone powder and plastic stick-on decals are often substituted for ground rice flour. Not only is this practice toxic to the earth, but it violates the central principle of this ritual to "feed a thousand souls." The conundrum is not invisible to the kōlam-makers. The older women I spoke to often asked: "Can ants and birds eat the plastic stick-on kōlam? Can animals eat plastic? Can ants eat stone?"

Humans everywhere tend to treat community areas, or the commons, with much less respect and care than we treat the interiors of our houses. The commons could be the street in front of our house, the river that flows by our village, or the creek that winds through an urban neighborhood.

One day in 1981, at my maternal grandparents' house in Kunnam village, I asked where I should throw away my used menstrual pads. I was told quietly and nonchalantly to throw them into the space between our house and the neighbor's, anywhere as long as it wasn't in our own backyard. I was horrified—yet I slowly realized that there was no other place for the appropriate disposal of such waste. The village did not have a garbage pickup and there was no community dump. I threw it over the fence with a horrible sinking feeling that I was committing an immoral act.

Yet, when I was back in America after that summer in India, I realized that in the whole "civilized" industrial world we were doing exactly the same thing. We, too, were disposing of our waste some other place where we were hoping none of us would see it again. We were dumping our waste in public spaces; the only difference was that those places were not the neighbor next door but a neighboring state, a neighboring country, or someplace overseas, seemingly far away and invisible. I couldn't help wondering what cumulative effect this irresponsible waste disposal pattern had on the commons area of a village, an urban neighborhood, or a cosmopolitan city in the West. Something about this paradox seemed oddly familiar. I was reminded of an experience that had happened some years earlier.

River Goddesses

One early morning just before first light, I sat on the shore of the Kāvēri River's Grand Anicut Canal, which skirts the medieval moat in the town of Thanjavur in central Tamil Nadu. I was watching one of my favorite sights—a temple elephant frolicking in the widest part of the channeled river. You could feel the pleasure of the young elephant bathing in the gently flowing waters of the Kāvēri, an embodiment of a river goddess similar to the goddess Ganga in northern India. This morning, three friends from the United States were with me. I turned to my companions to see if they were feeling the same pleasure watching the elephant's watery joy. To my surprise, a distinct awkwardness had arisen in their bodies and a look of horror had spread on all three faces. I was puzzled as to what was disturbing them. It was light now and people were lined up along the ghats, the stone steps on the river's edge. Women in underskirts were taking their baths, laughing together. Just a few yards away, an old man standing knee-deep in the water was brushing his teeth with a neem stick.

All of a sudden, I saw what my American friends saw. The elephant had paused momentarily and three or four of his huge droppings floated downstream, only a few yards from the old man brushing his teeth. I recoiled from the sight. I realized with a shock that this scene must have happened with some regularity during my earlier visits, but I had come alone then and could not see it the way someone from Berkeley, California would. It was only after viewing the scene through my friends' eyes that I could read the consequences of a few fresh elephant droppings floating by a man brushing his teeth in that water.

Educated mostly in America, I was well versed in basic environmental concerns and public hygiene, yet I also felt at home in India, where notions of hygiene were different. I could slip out of my Western state of mind and all its norms with the ease of slipping into a sari. However, this particular experience threw me straight back into my American identity. I realized suddenly that Indian society had a different perception of waste. The people bathing didn't see the elephant droppings as dangerous or polluting. They were simply organic matter, like leftover lettuce. What was the harm in it? Why would a man mind brushing his teeth in the same water as elephant dung? (See Figures 2.4 a,b.)

Seeing elephant dung in the Kāvēri River led me to a general notion of how Hindus see the Ganges River. Reflecting on both rivers, on elephant's dung in one and garbage in the other, another memory came back to me.

When I worked in 1985–86 as an environmental researcher for the Swatcha Ganga Campaign–Friends of the Ganges, a community activist group based in Banaras, the group found that one of the key obstacles to its campaign to clean the Ganges was the concept that the river was the embodiment of the powerful goddess Ganga.[7] This prevented people from seeing the river as a vulnerable natural form that might actually need to be protected.

Hindus who live along and bathe in this world-renowned river view it as sacred and they worship it. Yet at the same time, it was abundantly clear that they didn't care for it or protect it in the way that Western environmentalists in the 1970s and 1980s nursed intensively polluted rivers back to health. Hindus using the Ganges and other sacred rivers tended to trust its sanctity and to dismiss any thought that their actions represented pollution or caused any significant ill effects. The argument went that the goddess was so pure, clean, and sacred that she could eliminate both sin and pollutants. The way Hindus saw it, gods and goddesses protected humans, not the other way around. Humans could not protect river goddesses. since the river goddesses were the ones with sacred ritual cleansing, auspicious powers (see Alley 2002; Haberman 2006). It was not the duty of the Hindus who used the river to "clean up" a river goddess.

Garbage on Bhūdevi, the soil goddess; elephant dung in the Kāvēri River, a river goddess; human and industrial pollutants in the Ganges, another river goddess: the paradox of considering something to be sacred yet not taking care of it was becoming familiar. What are the patterns of meaning latent in these concepts? What beliefs underlie all three examples?

I believe the common theme is that it's not within the realms of human capacity and willpower to harm divine capacity in a way that would show itself in human landscapes. I slowly realized that waste, sin, and pollution are absorbed by both Bhūdevi and Ganga only because the goddesses are so large and indeterminate. In the Hindu imagination, if the natural world is a divine being, then she is capable of cleaning us and her forms of being—indefinitely. The very nature of the goddess means that she can cleanse the river of its pollution, no matter how much of it we humans deposit. The very divineness of nature makes these natural phenomena seem ever renewable. A goddess will always be able to transform dirt, pollution, and sin into pure, clean, and fresh natural substances.[8] Human scale, in fact, is seen as so small in the cosmological map that the effect of human actions on the natural landscape must be negligible. The waste of humanity is just a speck in the vast expanse of sky, earth, and water. Humans appear as insignificant when compared to the divinity of the natural world, and obviously so the deities do not need us for their maintenance. In fact, it would be considered arrogance and folly to assert that human effort could impinge upon the infinite divine, much less hurt her. From a Hindu perspective, if anything, it would be the other way around.

Complex, dense layers of meaning flow between a religious culture and its notion of landscape. Now we will delve deeper into the conceptual structures of two important ideas I mentioned earlier—embedded ecologies and intermittent sacralities. Then, we will return to the question of Hinduism and sacred landscapes and ethical actions toward them.

Embedded Ecology

Ecological knowledge is often tucked into other forms of knowledge like religion or art. For instance, many images of animals that are held to be sacred are used in Hindu religious rituals. One of the more popular is Ganesh, an elephant, who is considered to be "the remover of obstacles." In the classical dance form called Bharatanatyam, the performers often act out myths of gods and goddesses like Krishna and Pārvathi. Nature manifests through art and religion in these cases.

We know that cultural, aesthetic, and religious concepts orient people's perceptions of the natural world; these perceptions are actually embedded *within* these three areas of human life (Anderson 2005; Perlin 2005 [1989]).[9] My concept of "embedded ecologies" partly comes from Karl Polanyi (whom we will discuss later) and partly it is my own coinage.[10] It is important to be clear about the words "ecology," "ecological," and "ecologies."

The words *ecology, conservation,* and *preservation* are modern and have been used historically in different guises in the United States and Western Europe (Chapple 2001; Deval and Sessions 1985). The word *ecology* has several definitions. "The branch of biology that deals with the relation between living organisms and their environment. The complex of relations between a specific organization and its environment" represents a scientific orientation. "The study of the relationship of adjustment of human groups to their geographical environment" represents a sociological orientation (Guralnik 1980). I use the term *ecology* in both senses throughout this chapter.

The narrow scientific sense expressed in the first definition is no longer satisfying to me. I think it is important to take into account the second definition, with its sociological orientation. The "relationships of adjustment" of human groups to their geographical environment are shaped by culture, religion, and politics. Therefore, there are many different "adjustments." I think it is useful to extend the word *ecology* to the plural *ecologies* to include these culturally distinct ways of seeing and relating to the natural world.

When we say that a person is being "ecological," it could mean that she composts her vegetables and recycles her cans and bottles. It could mean that she is having a positive effect on the environment and leaving a small "carbon footprint." Today, "ecological" implies a conservationist attitude. When we say that the practice of recycling is "ecological," we mean that we reuse materials because we recognize that there are inherent limits on our use of the environment beyond its capacity to renew itself. Eco-thinkers, myself included, have tended to assume that seeing a religious (or mythological) link between the natural and cultural worlds leads to a more conservation-oriented practice, but this is not necessarily true. For example, the presence of Bhūdevi, an ecological image, does not necessarily lead to a conservationist attitude. The notion of "ecological" might mean one thing in one country and another thing in a different country, so it must be deconstructed historically and culturally. Cultural variations of "ecological" beliefs and practices must be explored within their own frames of reference. *Ecological,* here, refers to a relationship that ultimately may be neutral, positive, or negative. I will use the word *ecological* to denote a positive relationship between a living organism and its environment (with the understanding that "positive" is culturally constituted and can have a neutral meaning in different cultures). I will use the word *ecology* to denote the "sociological relationship of adjustment of human groups to their environment." In other words, ecology simply refers to the way that living beings have to adjust to the world around them. For instance, if the weather gets cold, they must eat more protein and wear heavier clothes. If the temperature heats up, they must build their houses to allow for a flow of air.

In speaking of "embedded ecologies," I want to open up a theoretical and ethnographic space for reflection on the cultural construction of nature in India. In other words, I will explain India's particular way of viewing nature and how it came into view for me while I was doing my fieldwork. Karl Polanyi, the economic anthropologist, was extremely useful in helping me understand this subject. His theory of "embedded economy" was critical when I was developing my theory of embedded ecology. In his attempts to understand non-Western economies, Polanyi formulated the notion of "embeddedness," which at the time was relatively new.[11]

According to Polanyi, "The prime reason for the absence of any concept of the economy [in more traditional cultures and as recent as a hundred years ago in India] is the difficulty of identifying the economic process under conditions where it is embedded in noneconomic institutions" (1957: 71)—for instance, in family, friendship, or community. In other words, you couldn't find, until even about a hundred years ago, what we would traditionally call "the economy" as we frame it in everyday Indian village life. My mother remembers her father telling her that when he was seven or eight years old, around 1916, he recalls when money first came into their village, Kunnam, to buy commodities such as sugar and coffee. He told her these commodities made serious changes in their daily life, as before then their need for money was low and most things were obtained through gift exchange or barter and trade. However, you would still find *traces* of the economy wherever value is exchanged for value, even if no money changes hands and nobody uses the word *economy*. There is a local regional economy, but it is not formalized; rather, it is embedded in ritual practices and organizational strategies at the kinship and clan level. It orients the cultural production and consumption of resources. Instead of Wall Street determining the value of everyday commodities, their economy centered around use-value, the value of a commodity based on its actual usefulness, not its value on the market. The notion of "economic" was subsumed under other cultural categories. Polanyi also contends that separating the category of economy from the rest of life could be an artificial construct.

I propose to extend Polanyi's understanding of embedded economies to that of "embedded ecologies." In a parallel of Polanyi's statement, I would say of India that the prime reason for the absence of any concept of *ecology* (i.e., the environment) is the difficulty in identifying *ecological* processes under conditions where they are embedded in *non-ecological* institutions. For example, a soil sample might be considered to have not only biological properties but also religious ones (i.e., it is seen as a goddess). Therefore, ecological notions, beliefs, and practices are embedded in cultural forms, particularly in religious and aesthetic practices as well as institutions. I would argue that ecological practices and beliefs are situated in a matrix of larger cultural ideas and practices, and therefore require a much more nuanced interpretation and deconstruction than has been previously attempted. The difficulty in identifying ecological processes when they are bound together within non-ecological institutions and understandings has been emphasized for the West by the cultural historian Simon Schama in his book *Landscape and Memory*. He writes, "Instead of assuming the *mutually exclusive* character of Western culture and nature, I want to suggest the *strength of the links* that have bound them together" (1995: 13–14). Here, I intend to do this for the Indian context.[12]

My theory of "embedded ecologies" does not refer to an idealized or romanticized notion of the past in India, where the relationship between humans and nature was "balanced" because religion dictated a conservation-oriented attitude. We do not know whether people lived in a relatively benign and balanced relationship with the natural world, nor whether everything was harmonious. The notion of embedded ecology should not be removed from its historical context and oversimplified. In fact, I propose that it is just the opposite—contested, historicized, and culturally specific. Within the Hindu tradition, too, there are contesting, coexisting, and multiple points of view. Depending on caste, class, religion, community, and bioregion, different people rank natural items (e.g., fire, soil, water, and cow dung) based on their values. For example, the importance of a cow would be very different for a cobbler and a priest. For a cobbler, the cow and its skin would represent the material of his trade, leather. For a priest, it would represent his trade too, only in this case it is the cow's *sacred* substances such as ghee, milk, cow dung, and so forth that he transforms into a sacred value.

Embedded ecology also refers to sacred geography, a key area for future exploration. Particular rivers, soils, groves, and mountains are imbued with sacredness; religion itself is embedded in the geographical landscape.[13] Unfortunately, in recent times the use of sacred landscapes as a political tool has undermined the public debates in India.

The term *embedded ecologies* does not refer to a world that is automatically enrolled in a project of ecology or environmentalism as would be understood in the Euro-American conservation discourse. This belief might be the prime reason for why we tend to read contemporary ecological notions about conservation into religious and gendered ideological frameworks. In other words, a subtext underlying our discourse on religion and environment is the proposition that sacrality, when attached to a natural object, makes that object revered and therefore automatically more protected. The sacrality of a natural object is thought to inspire people to be more careful and "ecologically" sensitive to the consequences of using that natural resource. A belief or practice that is labeled or believed to be ecological has to be scrutinized much more carefully to see if it actually fits a conservation-based framework.

The kōlam is made to honor the presence of Bhūdevi; elephant dung floats in the Kāvēri River; it is difficult to clean up the river goddess Ganga: these three examples are all helpful in understanding exactly how this happens. What these three examples next led me to was my own concept of intermittent sacralities. I believe that this concept and Ramanujan's idea of context sensitivity play a critical role in helping us understand the tragedy of the commons in a place like India.

Intermittent Sacrality

Hinduism is interrelated with other religious traditions in highly complex ways influenced by region, language, caste, and class. As it is the most prominent religion in India, with 83 percent of the population practicing Hinduism in some form or another, the religious tradition is bound closely not only with other religious traditions, but also with the natural world itself.

When looking at embedded ecologies in Hinduism, I have to ask two questions: (1) How has Hinduism been understood and interpreted by scholars and activists as "ecological" or "entirely in balance with nature"? and (2) How does it embody the notion that the entire earthly landscape is sacred, with the consequent assumption that the practitioners carry out this attitude throughout their everyday life? In other words, this attitude permeates life outside of the ritual practice that celebrates nature. This is especially noted by Indian environmentalists such as Vandana Shiva.

I see a contradiction between this imagined ideal behavior and what actually happens in everyday life. Consequently, I introduce the concept *intermittent sacrality* to resolve, at least in part, apparent tensions between what the tenets of Hinduism express and what the people actually do in practice. I was shocked to see that there was actually a huge gap between the fact that women did the kōlam in the morning to honor the earth as Bhūdevi, yet their subsequent actions through the day appeared to dishonor her. By looking at this concept of intermittent sacralities and how it appears in the kōlam, we can begin to understand this contradiction. To be clear, when I use the phrase *intermittent sacrality*, I am referring to the tendency to hold the earth as sacred during specific rituals, and then to drop that deferential attitude and practice in the midst of the practical demands of daily life.

For a long time I puzzled over the contradictions between religious ideology and daily practice. If the perception of natural objects were steeped in sacrality, why did that not lead naturally to a consummate sense of care and protection of those natural objects? In conversations, when I pointed out what seemed to me to be a contradiction between belief and action, both women and men would laugh at me and repeatedly insist,

> Oh, what we believe does not have to rule at all times and at all places. Just because one place is made sacred at one particular time doesn't necessarily mean that it remains special throughout the day. You have completely misunderstood us. How could we live on this earth, otherwise? We couldn't do anything, now, could we? There are so many rules and rituals that we have to follow. We are human and we need to live too. So, there is no expectation that we need to care for everything that is sacred *all* the time. We couldn't do it. We couldn't live. We have human needs and we must fulfill them.[14]

In short, natural objects are shot through with sticky notions of sacrality embedded within and through them. From the point of view of women I spoke with, sacrality is both a force and a substance. It moves around; it has volition; it is characterized by the ritual hospitality of inviting the goddess in. Sometimes the object, whether natural or human, previously not acknowledged as sacred, becomes actively sacred during a specific time period. After that, it is commonly understood that sacrality lapses and falls away from everyday consciousness so that humans can live and carry out their regular activities.

Intermittent sacrality occurs as a particular divinity is invited at a specific moment to come and be in a particular place, site, or substance, and then is asked courteously to leave. Many rituals host and dehost the divine as a guest, and the departure of the divine is as essential to the structure of the ritual as its arrival. In other words, hospitality is not expected to last forever, no more for the divine than it is for a human being. However, despite the existence of this intermittent sacrality, some objects and places—such as temples, mountains, rivers—are considered permanently sacred, the home of the gods. Also included are things of the human mode, such as temples and household shrines (which are semipermanent); these are small in scale and therefore can be kept pure. Even though the sacrality of these natural objects does not expire, the active human relationship that acknowledges the sacrality is temporary. That relationship, therefore, is intermittent.[15] This intermittent relationship with the divine has a very real impact on everyday attitudes and practices toward natural places.[16]

The kōlam is a perfect example of intermittent sacrality. A "painted prayer" for women to acknowledge the goddess Bhūdevi, it participates in this hosting and dehosting of the divine (Huyler 1994; Nagarajan 1993). As a result, the sacrality that is attached to the kōlam is also temporary. There seems to be no apparent contradiction, at least in the minds of the villagers with whom I spoke, between the sacrality, whether ritually created or not, that is attached to a particular site at one moment in time and the act of casting waste on that same site. The kōlam is a call to Bhūdevi to forgive mankind's intransigent neglect of her well-being. The expression most often used by women is *manippu kekarathu*, to "ask for forgiveness." This expression implies a care of a particular space for a period of time, but it does not imply subsequent conservation and protection. For example, soon after the kōlam is made—that is, soon after Bhūdevi is recognized, decorated, and hosted into being—she is dehosted from that space by the gradual dispersal of the rice-flour patterns via the footsteps of the passersby. The idea of *intermittent sacrality* illustrates the seeming contradiction between a belief and the way people act in everyday life, a notion that is explored in a theory called "context-sensitive thinking." A. K. Ramanujan writes about context-sensitive thinking in his now-classic essay:

> I think cultures [may be said to] have overall tendencies [for whatever complex reasons]—tendencies to *idealize*, and think in terms of, either the context-free or the context-sensitive kind of rules. Actual behavior may be more complex, though the rules . . . are a crucial factor in guiding the behavior. In cultures like India's, the context-sensitive kind of rule is the preferred formulation. (1997: 47)

Context-sensitive thinking is another way of understanding the seeming contradiction between the beliefs that people hold and the way their behavior appears to be the opposite of it. The context determines the regime of a belief, a rule, or a ritual. Context-sensitive thinking is an important element of the embedded ecologies that I am describing for Hinduism in India. Even the intermittent, recurring manifestation of the divine has an effect on everyday attitudes toward natural places.

It should not surprise us, then, that Hindu beliefs about the sacrality of the natural environment that are evoked in rituals do not always lead to a more conservation-oriented practice in the rest of everyday life, the non-ritual time and space. A ritual such as the kōlam may require asking for forgiveness for stomping on the earth; in non-ritual time and space, though, the human needs of the moment take over, like removing garbage to an unseen place, whether used menstrual pads or elephant dung moving "downstream" to another unseen place.[17]

Sacred Landscape as Ecological

Over the past few years, there has been an increased desire to understand the ecological beliefs of non-Westerners, especially more recently with the increase of environmental pollution and the breakdown of a moral order and restraint throughout the world (Hornborg 2008; Nelson 1983; Sachs 1993; Shiva 1989; Zimmerman 1987, 2011).[18] Attention has focused on religious concepts of nature in relation to landscapes, rivers, mountains, forests, and even the earth itself. An excellent example of this is the work of the environmental and feminist activist Vandana Shiva, who was trained as a physicist in the 1970s in Canada and subsequently returned to India. Shiva's effectiveness in generating environmental thought and action in India and abroad is highly laudable. Her remarkable work on understanding the Chipko women's movement and her current work on recovering native seed varieties in India is a courageous effort of resistance to the "monoculturalization" in modern life. Her most popular book, *Staying Alive: Women, Ecology and Development,* has been translated into several languages and has widely influenced Western perceptions of the Indian sacred landscape.

Much of her text is devoted to arguing against the ideology of Western development and its concomitant grid of dams, mechanized agriculture, pesticides, and misguided commercial forestry schemes. Yet the subtle assumption that Hindu women have been, and continue to be, naturally "culturally" ecological—that they are natural conservationists—pervades the text. One example she uses is the ritual worship of the *tulasi* (or *tulsi*) plant—the sacred basil—that is regarded as a goddess. She argues:

> Tulsi is a little herb planted in every home, and worshipped daily. . . . The tulsi is sacred not merely as a plant with beneficial properties but as Brindāvan, the symbol of the cosmos. In their daily watering and worship women renew the relationship of the home with the cosmos and with the world process. . . . Ontologically there is no divide between man and nature. (1989, 39–40)

She goes on to contrast the Cartesian mechanistic view of the universe, characteristic of the post-Enlightenment period in the West, and the lack of division between humanity and nature in India. In Hinduism, she argues, everything is pervaded by the sacred. She interprets the Hindu perception of the sacred in nature as meaning that it is intrinsically conducive to ecological protection.

While her assertions are elegantly made, they are not necessarily true at all times and places. Her ideas represent a false leap or elision (slurring) that because Hindus have imbued a place with sacrality, this makes them ecological.

I had made the same assumption myself for many years until I examined it more closely through my research on the kōlam. Shiva assumes, like I did and many others still do, that Hindus must be naturally conservation-oriented because they have labeled so many places, landscapes, and objects as sacred.

Shiva assumes that if a natural object is labeled as sacred, then it will call forth a cultural lifestyle that conserves the environment, creating less waste and pollution; therefore, it is ecological. She uses the image of the traditional Hindu woman performing the tulasi rites in her household to epitomize a vision of conservation and environmental ethics. However, her image *seems* to derive as much from Western notions of ecology and environment as it does from Hinduism.[19] In fact, the ritual of growing the tulasi plant protects that one plant and nothing of the greater environment; the tulasi plant may be the *only* one that is conserved in the vicinity of the household. This could be thought of as similar to protecting animals in a zoo, while the wild animals outside that zoo decline, or keeping plants in a neat garden without much relationship to the wilderness outside of it. The practice of worshipping the tulasi plant does not necessarily reflect the household's views on the conservation of the natural world outside the home, except in a metaphorical way. Therefore, the assumption by Shiva and others (including myself) that worshipping the tulasi plant leads to a concomitant and parallel preservation of the rest of the natural world is not always true.

The correspondence that she asserts may perhaps be accurate in some instances; I am simply saying that it is not necessarily true in all instances. The assumption that the attribution of sacrality to nature leads to an automatic, unreflexive, and "ecological" behavior is highly problematic. The perception of the natural world as sacred does not *necessarily* lead to more "environmental" or ecological attitudes or behavior toward nature. Having a religious attitude towards a plant such as tulasi may indeed be a kind of "embedded ecology"—an attitude toward nature as seen through the eyes of religion—but it does not necessarily imply concerns similar to those of Western conservation movements. Therefore, cultures with embedded ecologies are not intrinsically conservation-oriented.

Similar to growing the tulasi plant is the ritual involved in creating the kōlam—the cleaning, decorating, and honoring of the threshold. Yet again, the ritual does not carry over into the surrounding area, expressing the desire to protect nature. The desire is simply to make auspicious that one small space in front of the person's house, and even then only for a short period of time. I believe the mistake that we all make is to take the ideas that are expressed during ritualistic time and space and automatically assume that they transfer to the rest of life.

Although non-Western religions may show reverence toward landscapes, and therefore may contain innumerable embedded ecologies (such as ritual practices, nature tales, or natural symbols in art), these beliefs do not necessarily lead to ecological practices that resemble conservationism in the sense that the West has come to know it. It may be true, to a certain extent, that infusing the natural world with notions of sacrality does improve people's behavior, but I have misgivings about any implications that Indian religious culture has intrinsic checks and balances to restrain the rapaciousness of human greed.[20] Thus, I am uneasy with Shiva's subtext claiming that a general "ecological virtue" follows the daily watering of tulasi plants. Referring to the tulasi plant and its care as the symbolic renewal of the cosmos may indeed be true, but whether or not "the cosmic tulasi" will support the idea that a "conservation-oriented" Hinduism exists remains to be seen. Although Shiva roots her argument in Hindu mythology and Hindu notions of sacrality, her judgment of the effect of these rituals, myths, and notions is too broad and generalized. Shiva implies that women intuitively and articulately understand the limits of the natural world's capacity to provide an endless supply of resources. I am now unconvinced that a Hindu woman who waters her tulasi plant or creates a kōlam in worship of Bhūdevi as part of her daily religious practice is automatically enrolled in a general ecological project of protecting natural resources.

In the case of the tulasi plant—along with Bhūdevi, Kāvēri, and Ganga—nature is coded as divine and feminine and is personified as a goddess. Through ritual, these goddesses are expected to transform natural pollution into purity, cleanliness, and auspiciousness (Douglas 1966). At the community, village, and neighborhood scales, this transformation of pollution into ecological purity may indeed have occurred and continues to do so. The physical shift can occur on a small scale for these two reasons. One, the soil and the river ecosystem, with a smaller population and a more limited range of pollution, can transform the pollution by decomposition; therefore, an ecosystemic equilibrium can be achieved.[21] Two, the effect of the rituals on the daily use of sacred natural places is within the realm of community, village, and neighborhood responsibility. There have always been customary rules of behavior toward these places, and perhaps this does stem some of the behavior that causes excessive pollution.

The notion of sacrality might act as a brake to individual desires, ambitions, and greed in these smaller, face-to-face communities, but once the scale of everyday life changes to a mass-oriented scale, the customary limits can no longer be enforced. In the modern world and the mass-market economy it has created, it is far more challenging to submit the idea that religious beliefs, which are now vying for influence with all the other marketplace forces, have the power to mitigate human behavior and its effects. On the other hand, there is a growing viable movement combining religion and ecology that is espousing restraints on a mass level of energy and resource consumption, especially considering the looming specter of climate change.

One additional point that must be made is that the beliefs themselves are not necessarily limits; they can just as well act as a license to pollute. Let's look at how this may be so.

License to Pollute

According to the worldview of the Tamil women I spoke with, the tulasi plant *is* connected to the larger cosmological self (or Brahman in Hindu philosophy). As with Bhūdevi, the tulasi plant intrinsically holds boundless powers of purification.[22] The earth goddess Bhūdevi and river goddesses Ganga or Kāvēri have the power to absorb, purify, and cleanse pollutants, regardless of the scale. Their powers are seen not just as symbolic, but as actual and real. They are connected to the vast, broader powers of "purification" that are coded as feminine. Traditionally, in Hindu culture, many of the natural forces in the universe are seen as feminine. Energy itself, or "shakti" at a fundamental level, is seen as feminine.

Unfortunately, it is this quality of "sacrality" that may make people believe they cannot destroy the soil or the waters. The very belief in their sacredness might prevent traditional Hindus from seeing that Tulasi, Ganga, or Bhūdevi needs protection from human beings. In other words, we must ask whether the very act of sacralization obscures the necessity of conservation in the Western sense, and in fact, whether it acts as a license to pollute and whether it might lead to increasingly rampant pollution. Of course, one of the primary reasons for this ecological chaos is the lack of resources in much of India at the state and community level; they cannot respond quickly to large and small ecological crises.

The more I observed this trend, the more disturbed I became. It was the very fact of sacralization, combined with the context-sensitive thinking (that A. K. Ramanujan spoke about) that led me to the concepts of embedded ecology and intermittent sacrality. Scholars and activists who study Hindu ecological beliefs and practices will need some understanding of how ecology has come to be formed as a concept and practice in the modern West, and they will need a certain self-reflexive attitude toward that understanding.[23] The discipline of ecology has emerged in the historical context of modern science, which is one of the many traditions I was trained in. Yet I realized that it would be misleading to take that intellectual development as normative when interpreting Hindu traditions because these beliefs did not develop along the same lines. Hindu ecological traditions *are* deeply embedded in a particular cultural matrix, as Vandana Shiva rightly points out, but these traditions do not necessarily have the same effect on natural resources as the Western discipline of ecology and conservation.

Western notions of ecology are equally embedded (see Schama 1995). For instance, the Grimm fairytales from Germany, which depict "the forest" as a deep, dark place in which children get lost and are chased by wolves or eaten by witches, has irrevocably framed the Western imagination of the forest (Harrison 1992). In both cases, institutional forces frame ecological beliefs and the forces are themselves embedded with a complex of assumptions, histories, and conflicts. Implicit in the use of a term like *ecology* is the understanding that each culture and each community within a culture will have its own myths, memories, associations, and, to use Schama's word, cultural "obsessions" about the natural world.[24]

It is upsetting to me to think equally of how Western frames of beliefs also fail miserably in being able to see the ways in which humans are destroying the natural world. Kimberly Patton argues convincingly in *The Sea Can Wash Away All Evils* (2007) that our disproportional acts of pollution, whether trash, CO2 emissions, or radioactive waste, are rooted in the ancient Greek sacral imagination of matter. Poseidon, in charge of the ocean, enables the ocean to have an infinite capacity to absorb our sins. So whether Western or Hindu, our conceptual categories disable us from perceiving the huge proportional effect we have on nature. We are still locked within the limits of our collective human imaginations, whether Hindu or Western, in a misunderstanding of our proportional relationship to the natural world, as if we were still small bands of hunter gatherers set in an expansive landscape.

To understand the complexity of "ecological" readings in texts, and in aesthetic and religious beliefs, I have articulated a theory of "embedded ecologies"—that is to say, culturally or religiously framed ecological concepts. I call for a reexamination of religious beliefs in order to understand *embedded ecological knowledge* more carefully. How do we begin? Not only by listening to people's words, which can be misleading, but by watching what they actually do.[25] We need to re-understand, reinvent, and reimagine the specific ways in which cultural notions of "conservation," "preservation," and "ecological" are constituted and framed within everyday discourse. The tragedy of the commons (commonly shared land and resources such as water, air, and oceans) that we witness every day in the Indian or Western landscapes are not necessarily mitigated by the landscape's sacrality. Once we recognize that the sacrality of natural spaces is not traditionally connected with environmental protection or conservation, we can begin to see the need for a more honest awareness of some difficult and profound questions: What *does* motivate people to protect, preserve, and care for their natural environments in a sustainable way? How can embedded ecological knowledge or perceptions such as the kōlam actively contribute to bring awareness to the vulnerability of particular places, and to whole ecosystems, beyond those that are marked as sacred?[26]

Here we have seen that the appearance of Bhūdevi in the cultural practice of the kōlam is an example of an embedded ecology and that the practice of the kōlam contributes toward an attitude of intermittent sacrality. Similarly, cultural practices such as basket-weaving and making pottery and textiles in Hinduism and other religious traditions evoke certain attitudes toward the natural world.[27] Whether sacredness is imputed to earth, basil, or water, I have argued here that Hindu religious belief is not sufficient to create an environmental attitude or awareness in the contemporary Western sense of the word.

I hope I have contributed here to the complexity inherent in the discussion of this question. The next chapter explores another aspect of embedded ecologies in the Indian context of the kōlam: the relationship between culture and nature through the principle of reciprocal generosity.

10

Marrying Trees and Global Warming

> Tānam, . . . dāna: 1. Gift in charity, donation, grant, as a meritorious deed; 2. (Buddh.) Liberality, munificence, bounty; 3. Gifts, as a political expedient; 5. House-holder's life.
>
> —*Tamil Lexicon*, 1982: 1859–1860

> Tōsam, . . . dōsa. 1. Fault; 2. Sin, offence, transgression, heinous, crime, guilt; 3. Defect, blemish, deficiency, lack; 4. Disorder of the Humours of the body, defect in the functions of the bile, phlegm, or wind; 5. Convulsion, often fatal and always dangerous; 8. Illness believed to be due to the evil eye, etc.
>
> —*Tamil Lexicon*, 1982: 2119–2120

Dense Fog

In the village of Ammangudi along the Kāvēri River, Saroja, an elderly Tamil woman, shared with me her concerns and insights about the natural world.[1] I realized later that she was pointing to the ways that rituals work to bind social relationships between natural and cultural worlds. When she first used the word *mūṭipani* ("dense fog"), I was puzzled: "mūṭi" means "closed" and "pani" usually refers to fog or snow. What did she mean? Saroja explained:

> It is about the mūṭipani, isn't it? The kōlam, too, is disappearing. Do you see the connection? We are losing the ability to give to God. We are forgetting that we need to practice giving constantly. I understand why the mūṭipani is disappearing—we have forgotten to be generous. We used to give, our people. We used to give to each other. We used to give to the gods and goddesses. The kōlam is about giving, do you know? I keep hearing that the mūṭipani is disappearing above us in the sky. I have the solution to the problem of the mūṭipani disappearing. We have to learn to give again. We have to marry trees again.

I wondered: What do dense fog, the disappearing mūṭipani, the kōlam, generosity, and tree marriage have in common? I began to decipher the puzzle when she spoke about the disappearance of the mūṭipani in the sky: she was referring to the depletion of the ozone layer. She saw this depletion, as well as the kōlam disappearing, as indicators of the illness of the entire planet, which is sickly, suffocating, infertile, and increasingly inhospitable for life. All of this, Saroja contends, is a result of an ungenerous attitude: the "dense fog" or the ozone layer is collapsing because of our declining levels of generosity toward one another.[2]

Saroja brings the kōlam into this, too. In her view, the kōlam is primarily an expression of generosity and hospitality, a visual living metaphor for the very qualities that are disappearing. The kōlam, besides being a message to the community about the household, is made with materials that are actually food. The design is drawn with ground rice flour. Throughout the day, it feeds the small creatures of the earth. Saroja's solution to the dissolution of the kōlam tradition and to the disappearance of the ozone layer is "marrying trees." We will discuss this later, but for now let's just say that marrying a tree represents a way of restoring the earth by establishing relationships with the powerful, creative, and auspicious forces of trees. Perhaps trees serve as an ultimate personification of giving, an enactment of the ideal of generosity in everyday life, just as the kōlam does.

This chapter explores the next level of my theory of embedded ecologies, which I described in the previous chapter. This theory, in teasing out the threads of a subtle and complex relationship between the cultural and natural worlds, tries to provide a lens through which a culture can understand and act on the perception of the natural world. How is the natural world perceived, articulated, and framed through cultural and religious knowledge in Tamil Nadu, and in a broader view the rest of India, through what we call "indigenous" or nature-based religions?[3]

I have selected and deciphered three interrelated ritual acts that represent the significance of the reciprocal generosity between nature and culture: creating the kōlam, ritually using plants and trees, and marrying trees. What ties the three together is the notion that the auspiciousness of nature can be transferred to humans. In return, humans respect and honor the natural world.

The starting point is the kōlam. A woman creates an intricate pattern on her threshold every morning and "feeds a thousand souls" with the rice flour. In return, the goddess Lakshmi brings good luck into the home and the household's positive karma is increased and balanced. Next comes the second act. We recognize that there are many different plants and trees that play a critical ritual role in removing our afflictions and taking away suffering. And finally, we adore and marry the tree so that it takes away the suffering caused by not finding a mate or not having children; the trees transfer their regenerating power to us. Each of these ritual acts illustrates the interplay between the natural and cultural worlds as social exchanges.

Human beings enjoy each other in relationships that are based on deference, respect, admiration, and above all ritual exchange—for instance, bringing a gift when you are a guest. The people of Tamil Nadu have similar ritualistic relationships with objects and phenomena in the natural world as they do with people. In a world where, as Saroja says, "We are losing the ability to give to each other," these three rituals point to a kind of lived practice of generosity in the community. When rituals like these die or lose their poignancy, I realized that we can easily forget the real and powerful significance of generosity in the community. It made me see how much I had lost the practice of giving in my own life.

Feeding a Thousand Souls

The first ritual we will discuss is the making of the kōlam. Janaki, an elderly woman with her hair rolled up casually in a bun at the nape of her neck and a small garland of woven jasmine flowers circled around her bun, brought this to my attention when she bemoaned the change from the use of rice flour to that of stone powder, plastic stick-ons, or acrylic paint, which some modern women employ when drawing the kōlam:

> We do not know why we do the kōlam anymore. We have forgotten. If we had not, we would not now make it out of plastic or white stone powder. The materials we used to use were meant to be consumed by the creatures of the earth. Now everything is modern, modern, modern. One of the main reasons we made the kōlam with rice flour was to feed a thousand souls every day. But who can feed so many people-souls? Only kings and very wealthy people can actually fulfill this kind of obligation. Instead, ordinary people like us do the kōlam. You see ants, birds, worms, insects, and maggots—all are invited to come and eat the kōlam. The knowledge of why we always used rice flour has been lost. If we remembered, we wouldn't be using plastic or stone. The idea of giving to others is being slowly forgotten. How ungenerous we are becoming!

Janaki's sadness at the loss of meaning surrounding the kōlam practice was echoed by many other women in their response to the coming of modern materials. An individual woman's, and by extension her household's generosity of spirit toward human and non-human souls has always been valued and made visible, publicly, through these ritual blessing designs. Gradually, the design is carried away by the feet of passersby, but it also serves as a feeder of sorts for small animals, including birds, ants, worms, and insects. In this way, the kōlam disappears a few hours after it is made, which it was always meant to do. Doing the kōlam is an act of sharing, which is by nature ephemeral. Giving is ephemeral. It is the movement of a gift from one to another. *When the kōlam loses its nature of being a daily offering, it loses its ability to give.*

As we know, every religious tradition has its own moral accounting system. In Hinduism, karma is a kind of moral accounting concept capturing the notion that every action has a ripple effect, whether the consequences were intended or not. Human beings are not like plants. We move around. We do things. And those activities often have negative consequences. When a Hindu woman "feeds a thousand souls" through making the kōlam the first thing in the morning, she is compensating for the negative actions she will commit later in the day, or may have committed the previous day, the previous month, or year, or any time after her birth.

Feeding a guest is part of the same ritual act. This is why, throughout India, there is such a huge emphasis on feeding a guest in your house, someone who is a complete stranger. This is not necessarily networking; there can be little immediate direct self-interest in completing the act. The only long-term value to the woman householder can be that she is fulfilling her and her household's larger karmic obligation. It is as if she is constantly pumping positive karmic value into the universe. The guest ritual, however, only feeds human souls. The kōlam ritual feeds animal souls, and in Hinduism, this seems to have a similar ritual karmic benefit.[4]

In fact, the kōlam's gradual disappearance over the course of the day is the result of small birds, ants, and insects grazing on the rice flour. A few hours after a kōlam is made, pieces of it disappear as if it had been bitten into—and indeed it has. Strange breathing holes appear in the surface of the dirt, which are the burrowing holes of tiny creatures that pop up so they can dine on the kōlam. In return for this act of generosity to the small creatures, gods and goddesses protect the household. As the kōlam is dispersed, it signifies the departure of the gods or goddesses who had been hosted there. In fact, gods and goddesses are said to dwell in the very acts of generosity.

The divine spirits are invited for the honoring ritual. If they do come, they do not stay once the ritual is over, for they have other things to do. There is, on the part of humans, a continual need to attract the attention of the divine through various acts of ritual generosity. This reflects another aspect of embedded ecologies. It is reflected in the idea that these rituals are seen as a way of expressing reciprocal generosity between nature and culture. We will pick up this thread of "feeding a thousand souls" in more detail in the next chapter.

Generating Auspiciousness from Plants and Trees

The second example of embedded ecologies is the generation and transfer of auspiciousness between the plant/tree world and the human world. Beyond the kōlam, there is another way of seeing reciprocal generosity: through rituals that incorporate trees and plants. We will see how four particular trees and plants—coconuts, mangos, bananas, and figs—figure prominently in life, marriage, and death rituals.[5] We will then examine how these rituals act as a metaphorical transference between the worlds of plants and humans.

When I first moved to the outskirts of Madurai, I was introduced to a Tamil man, Aiyaswamy, who was known throughout the area as an astrologer. Yet, as I was to find out, he was also thoroughly versed in the meaning and significance of the kōlam. The first day I went to see him I hired an auto rickshaw to travel over the bumpy roads to reach his village. I noticed that people smiled as they directed me to his house. When I got there, I was astounded to see a long line of people waiting to get their fortunes told by him. I waited along with everyone else for hours. Once I told him that I had come to see him not to have my fortunes told but to learn about the kōlam, his eyes lit up. He finished his clients for the day, and then shared his knowledge with me for an entire week. I was honored beyond words by his generosity. Ultimately I thanked him by preparing him a meal in the traditional way—serving him first and then eating myself, a special offering called *parimāṟuthal,* a gift of giving full attention to someone else while serving them food.

Aiyaswamy's many gifts of knowledge are scattered throughout this book. He explained to me the connection between auspiciousness and the plant/tree world. Not only was he a well-known astrologer, he was also an actor in a drama troupe and served the Madurai community in multiple roles. For me, it was his expertise in Sanskrit and traditional Tamil science and art forms that was most intriguing. A conversation about the meaning of a tree in front of a temple led to reflections about it being an act in which one generates and reflects auspiciousness, which then led to the presence of divine residency in trees, and then to the reproductive metaphors associated with plants. This was, at first, perplexing for me and may be for you as well. But bear with me: what he teases out are insights that compare metaphorically the kōlam's ability to generate auspiciousness with that very same auspiciousness generated by plants and trees that is transferred to humans. Below I offer, to the extent that I can, a fuller sense of the conversation, which also reveals how botanical knowledge is embedded and understood within ritual contexts through the binary opposition of auspiciousness and inauspiciousness. What these rituals have in common, I believe, is that they are rituals of desire—for birth, marriage, or the release of the soul after death. This first simple question prompted him to share surprising knowledge on the kōlam.

Vijaya: What is the relationship between a temple and the kōlam?

Aiyaswamy: The kōlam has the ability to "indicate" that a visēśam [celebration, festivity] is happening inside the temple. Now, ordinarily women will be putting the kōlam on the house, but when festivals come, that very same

> kōlam becomes a huge "size." Then, today, you know that there is something or other—a festivity—because you have put a huge decorative kōlam on your house.
>
> On the day of Thai Pongal [an annual festival], the whole street will have kōlams made on it. It is the idea of visēśam. That is the key idea. It is just like the mango leaf garland we put on the doorway to indicate the idea of a celebration. And just like the banana tree on the threshold of a house, you know something big is happening in that house—a wedding or birth. Or the coconut palmyra leaves we put on the threshold. Or the use of coconut. That same coconut tree, that coconut, or mattai, is used for death.

The *mattai* is the outside layer of the coconut. Aiyaswamy explains that the kōlam, along with the mango leaf garland curved in a half-moon shape on the top threshold of a doorway and the banana trees on each side of the house, is a kind of outside public indicator that magnifies auspiciousness. He went on to discuss the parallel ways in which a mango leaf garland, the coconut palmyra leaves placed against the walls, and two young banana trees on either side of the doorway all help to create a four-sided frame of auspiciousness, each magnifying the auspiciousness of the next edge. The mango leaf garland enlarges the kōlam by drawing the eye from the ground up to the top threshold. The coconut palmyra leaves expand the banana trees, and so on. You know from the visual display of all these elements simultaneously that a birth, a first birthday, a coming-of-age ceremony, or a wedding is going on inside the house.

He went on to say that the same coconut that is used to indicate a heightened sense of auspiciousness (as is associated with a wedding or birth) can also indicate inauspiciousness (as is associated with death). That surprised and confused me. When I asked him how it connected to death, he answered: "On the 10th day after someone dies, they use the coconut mattai [to communicate that there has been a death]. The coconut tree has borne a seed." He was referring to the ritual preparation of the body for cremation, a ceremony so private that if a woman is allowed in at all, she must be postmenopausal.

He went on: "They open it [the coconut] and then, they put . . . the āvi, the spirit of [he coughs to indicate that he does not want to say 'the dead man'] into it. Below the coconut is a special [miniature] building made with coconut fronds, with one opening [that has been] constructed for the soul [to enter]."

This reminded me of the work of cultural anthropologist Diane Mines, who posited that death separates the spirit from the gross body, the gross body from the family, and sometimes families from each other. The spirit, however, can be united with a new subtle body that has been made for it by the living and, through it, can join the ancestors. Later, it can take a rebirth in another earthly gross body (Mines 1990).

Along the same lines, what struck me in Aiyaswamy's description and analysis were the ways in which the spirit associated with the actual body can be seen as separate. After death, it is carefully released from the present body by creating another temporary shelter for it, the coconut frond structure; the soul is led into that coconut on its way to the next reincarnation or bodily form. The coconut and the frond structure are seen as a midway place; they receive the spirit of the deceased person before it rejoins the ancestors. What I found interesting was how the coconut could indicate a heightened sense of either auspiciousness or inauspiciousness (as elaborated in Chapter 4), depending on the ritual context. I pursued this thought with Aiyaswamy:

Vijaya: Then coconuts are used for showing states of mangalam [auspiciousness] and amangalam [inauspiciousness]. Why do we use auspicious objects for indicating inauspicious events? That does not make sense, does it?

Aiyaswamy: Why do you say this—aren't you listening? [He scolds me and continues, emphasizing for extra measure.] I told you, we use the coconut mattai for death *and* for weddings.

Vijaya: [persisting] But why?

Aiyaswamy: [impatiently] Because we use it in a different form. It is the same thing in different form. When we use it to indicate mangalam [auspicious] objects, then its alangāram [decoration] is quite different, so it has a different set of meanings. For amangalam [inauspicious] things it is, again, a different alangāram. That is why decoration is so important. That is how you know what is happening around you. How else would you know [what is going on with other people around you?]

I was beginning to understand the great misconception that I and other people may have about decoration and its importance within a highly ritualized culture, of how visually dense surfaces indicate what is happening inside a household externally to passersby and to the community at large, whether all is well or whether suffering is going on inside the house. In fact, decoration is central for a society to show what is happening inside itself. It helps the community know how to respond to its members' good or bad news. I continued to question him.

Vijaya: What is the mattai?

Aiyaswamy: The mattai of the coconut is the space that emerges, where the raw coconut grows. It is the closed stamen of the coconut, the husk that used to be used for fuel. We also use the braid of coconut fiber. They shake the branches the same way corn is shucked, to separate the outside skin from the nut. In villages, they put the nut in water. After a death, they take the soul into the

> coconut frame reciting mantras. This is what we have done for paramparāya [generations].
>
> You see, our aitīkam [tradition] here in this land is that the coconut tree is the kalpaviruśam [wish-fulfilling tree]—a tree that fulfills all your desires. The history is that the kalpaviruśam is from the world of the gods. We believe that all the gods live or take up kudi [temporary residence] there in the coconut tree and the banana tree.[6]
>
> For example, if we take a marriage—if someone has not been able to get married and they are already 30—then we think that there is a dōsam [transgression, disorder, illness, sin preventing the event]. And we will go to the astrologer [to find out how to fix this problem]. But, second, we might think that [maybe there is a reason for this fate], that the person perhaps should not get married after all, because if she does, then her husband's life . . . [He is reluctant to say more and falls silent to make sure I understand that he is implying that the husband's life would be cut short. Finally, he continues softly]. The same thing can happen to a man as well.
>
> If there is such a belief, then they will arrange a marriage with the banana tree for the first marriage. The banana tree is made into a woman and the tāli [wedding pendant][7] is tied onto the [femalized] tree to take the dōsam away [thereby preventing the terrible fate that presumably was waiting for the male human groom]. Then, the man can be married to a woman [or vice versa]. We tie the tāli on the woman or the man, making that tree the man or woman, and afterwards that tree is cut down, so that it has died instead of the man or woman who was supposed to die.

There is a subtle difference between this process and the tree ceremony described in the section following this one. Here, the tree—the beneficent plant—actually gives its life so the person can change his or her fate. In some ways, this is parallel to the Christian theological explanation of Jesus dying to take on the sins of humanity. In the following ritual, the tree becomes the mate to remove bad luck. He continues:

> Then they conduct a second wedding [with a person this time, and now the couple has escaped the fate that the tree has taken with it to the grave]. The power [to give a man long life] that is in the female is [also considered to be] in the banana tree. Small containers, or thonnais, are made [of banana leaves] to hold the ghee during a hōmam or yāham [fire ceremony]. Have you seen those [containers]?

He is saying that the small containers used to hold ghee during the hōmam or yāham fire ceremony are made of banana leaves. From ancient times during ceremonies, ghee, or melted butter, has been dispensed, one teaspoon at a time, and thrown into the fire. The oil in the butter feeds the fire, and thus feeds the fire god Agni, who is the communicator between the heavens and the earth.

Vijaya: [I nod, indicating I have seen them.] Why the banana leaf'?

Aiyaswamy: Because only in the banana leaf are there no kulais—divisions. The other leaves have parts or sections. We can only use plants without divisions for such auspicious occasions. When the leaves separate, it is like becoming a family. Father, then son, then younger brother, then younger sister; then the family becomes separated into individuals.

I could only speculate as to what he meant by this. The significance of there being no divisions in the leaf has to do with the idea that in a marriage, two people become one. Once the married couple generates a family, however, individuation occurs. The "non-individuated" banana leaf, then, signifies union because it has a unitary shape. Aiyaswamy went on to draw distinctions among different trees, making the correlation between the leaves of the tree and the fruit it produces. I guessed that this was important because the characteristics of the plant must match the desires of the person taking part in the ritual:

> At the same time, if there is only one child, then people will say that, like a banana tree, he has only one leaf—only one son. The coconut leaf, though, has divisions. The vēppa maram [margosa tree] survives on its own. If you chop down a vēppa tree, then it will grow again on its own. A coconut tree is not like that. The banana tree only produces in one batch. It bears only one kulai [litter]. And bamboo, too. The coconut seeds are not many, just one seed [though at times they can appear as clusters].

Banana trees produce clusters of bananas in multiple tiers of production, clearly symbolic of a natural abundance. Coconut trees appear to produce coconut seeds, one at a time. Though they may appear as clusters, they are cut off one by one.

Though I didn't understand everything Aiyaswamy was telling me, later I went over it again and again. I became keenly aware of the subtlety with which the morphological nature of plant species is perceived through the lens of a religious culture, the ways that distinctions in plant forms, and the meaning of those distinctions, are embedded with a religious morphology of auspiciousness. Banana trees and coconut trees are sometimes seen as auspicious and at other times as inauspicious.

Fertility and reproduction are "read into" plant morphologies as embedded metaphors. The theme of the conversation with this remarkable man seems to have been that the reproductive characteristics of trees represent auspicious or potentially reproductive states in humans. Banana and coconut trees are believed to come from heaven and to be inhabited by various gods and goddesses. They are considered abundant because they reproduce their fruits in kulais (clusters, bunches), rather than one at a time, as humans do with human reproduction, the exception being twins, triplets, and so on. The coconut frond is also considered auspicious, because it is an individually fragmented or divided leaf and therefore is related to the abundance of reproduction akin to the reproduction of kinship—of multiple siblings and an incorporation of new in-laws, new births, and new adoptees into the larger family and kinship network. The type of auspiciousness in these trees is directly related to their discernible reproductive characteristics. Leaves, whether single-planed like the banana leaf or multiply divided like the coconut frond, are further distinguished by the types of auspiciousness with which one wants to be associated or desires that one wants to be fulfilled. For example, one wants to transfer the properties of many seeds or of one seed at a time. Maybe the metaphors of reproduction translate directly from the observable botanical characteristics of the plants themselves. The wished-for, the hoped-for, the prayed-for desires are themselves visualized in botanical terms.[8] Trees and plants are imagined into Hindu rituals and we can begin to understand how and why some of these trees and plants can even marry human beings.[9]

"We Have to Marry Trees Again"

Now we move to a more detailed examination of the phenomena that Saroja mentioned at the beginning of the chapter as the two solutions to global warming: tree marriage and learning to give again. When Saroja said, "We have to marry trees again," and Aiyaswamy referred to the tree marriage ritual, I remembered another day long before that one where I had heard that expression. It was the spring of 1990, in the semirural, semiurban outskirts of the old city of Madurai in southern India. During one of my interviews on the kōlam, I had heard about a wedding taking place there. The young woman I spoke to suddenly burst out in the middle of our smoothly running conversation with an incongruous statement: "The kōlam removes suffering. It is a carrier of generosity, dānam, just like with the wedding of a tree."

I exclaimed quickly, "A wedding to a tree! What is that? When does that happen? Does it happen often?"

She slowly explained to me as if I were a blind woman who could not see what was clearly in front of her eyes:

> People suffer. There are times when suffering comes at us suddenly and we do not know how to handle the enormity of it. And that is when we marry trees. Usually it is when someone cannot find a mate and there are a lot of obstacles in their path. Each man or woman they see, it does not work out for them. So, then, we know that there is something about the life path of the person that is preventing them from marrying a human person. So, we arrange the marriage of that person to a tree instead, and then we pray that the tree will take on the burdens of that human being and therefore release that person from their suffering. Then the human person is free to marry someone else. Usually it works out that way. Do you understand? There is someone who is getting married to a tree tomorrow. Do you want to come?

I nodded quickly, "Yes, I would like to come." She took me, then, to the spot where the ceremony would take place.

The next day I arrived at the small glade of trees set within the apartment complex and went to the spot under the pipal tree (a kind of Indian fig tree, commonly called Bo tree in English and *araca maram* in Tamil). The tree was large, with an enormous canopy, providing cooling, dappled shade in the high heat of the noonday sun. It was gaily decorated with marigold garlands, and gigantic kōlams had been made on the earth at the base of the tree. The ritual objects were beginning to be organized and placed in front of it in a semicircle, and in an hour the formal aspects of the ritual began. A crowd had gathered, about 50 guests.

The man that the ceremony was for was dressed as a bridegroom. He had been unmarried for a long time, causing stress to his immediate family and kin. Food for a small feast after the ritual was already cooking outdoors. The priest sat near the tree, dark black hair framing his face, with a beard thickly flowing from his chin. His eyes were focused and serious, intent on the ritual being completed properly. He was setting up the fire ritual, with bricks outlining an enclosure that was about two feet square.

The finely adorned groom was called to sit on the kōlam near the tree. His face did not reflect the usual sunny disposition of a groom-like state, but rather a kind of depressive melancholy. He looked forlorn and hopeless, after all the failures he had already gone through to find a bride. He sat still as a stone, almost as if he were not feeling all the gathered energies around him. He did not resist, clearly willing to be moved here and there by the priest and the women helping with the ceremony who were attempting to find the right place for him to sit in relation to the tree. In this ceremony, the tree was the bride. The two had to ask themselves, which was the front of the bride, which was the back? What was the best place to sit to avoid the roar of traffic nearby?

It was going to be a long ceremony, so where was the most comfortable place to seat guests?

The groom, meanwhile, was passive, almost as if he was not engaged in the process at all. He had already given up any notion that this was going to work. The family sat near him, active, bustling around, handing the priest the appropriate ritual objects as he asked for them—a new brass bowl, flowers, and some kindling sticks for keeping the fire aflame. Meanwhile, wedding guests had gathered around the tree. The priest began to chant, which lasted some hours. As he chanted, flames licked around the large pieces of wood and the heavy smoke rose in front of us.

We, the audience, witnessed the exchange of garlands between the groom and the tree bride. In traditional Hindu weddings, the couple plays a number of games, which symbolize the playfulness and joy that everyone hopes will infuse their marriage. Keep in mind that these two people often have never met each other, so the games also help them get acquainted. In the tree ceremony, this process is simulated. The priest takes on the role of the bride, since the tree cannot move around and play. At one point in this ceremony, there was an exchange of garlands—a symbolic representation of the wedding. Here, the priest guided the garland back and forth between the groom and the tree bride. Some hours later, the tree bride and the groom were designated married and were then fêted. A heaped plate of freshly cooked food and sweets was laid out in front of the tree and an equivalent plate in front of the seated groom. Everyone then sat on the ground and ate a feast. The wedding was over an hour or so later, after all the guests had been fed and they were satisfied. In this ritual, the pipal tree was not cut, as in Aiyaswamy's earlier description.

At the time, I was puzzled, and only years later did I begin to unravel some of this ceremony's many meanings. Conducting rituals with trees is part of the repertoire of solutions offered to families in the throes of suffering. Since trees, like humans, are seen as male or female, the tree selected would be of the opposite gender from the afflicted individual. If a person is continually afflicted by illness or is unable to marry by the age of 30, or if a married couple find themselves infertile, it is suspected that they are under some kind of dōsam (hardship). The word *dōsam* is commonly used to explain a string of personal or familial disasters that form obstacles to the fulfillment of one's desires; they cause a diminishing of literal and metaphorical auspiciousness in the family, a kind of temporary or long-term marring of one's destiny, akin to an eclipse of the sun.

Suffering of this sort within a community is sometimes attributed to the deterioration or souring of relationships between the natural and human cultural worlds. In fact, it is believed that ignoring these relationships can cause inauspicious states such as illness, poverty, infertility, or death. For the individual or community to become whole, healthy, or prosperous, the atrophied relationships with the natural world must be repaired. The ritual with a tree is one possible solution, both a symbolic and a literal reminder of our "kinship" with the natural world. It is integral to healing an unfulfilled life. This may be a key to understanding a tree marriage.

In general, the ritual of arranged marriages in India is used to cement the bonds between separate families. Establishing relationships with the natural world is important for the family's survival, just as the marriage between humans is. It is believed that trees have an enormous capacity to absorb suffering, since they have an abundance of auspiciousness, goodwill, and generosity. As part of the greater natural world, their sacredness is inherently more encompassing than that of humans. Sridhara S. Battar, a priest at the Siva Vishnu Temple in Livermore, California, said, "According to Indian philosophy, a tree is the only natural object that can 'bear the obstacles of man' because it is known 'to be a part of god.'" Therefore, if the ritual with a tree is arranged first, the tree will bear the burden of human suffering and, in a sense, transform the suffering and inauspiciousness into auspiciousness.

If the problem is an inability to find a mate, then a tree marriage will be conducted. When you marry a tree, the tree immediately becomes the person's family. Human mates in various wedding ceremonies around the world will use phrases like "for better or for worse," indicating that one willingly takes on the other person's suffering and carries the burdens with him or her. Likewise, in this Hindu ritual, the tree takes on the burden of its mate.

If the problem is infertility, the couple can circle a tree; then the tree's natural fecundity will be partly transferred to them. In fact, my parents circled many sacred, highly auspicious trees during their six-year period of infertility before they had me. In this South Asian worldview, fertility in plants is believed to encourage fertility in humans, just as the generosity or auspiciousness embedded in the kōlams evokes generosity in the household and the community at large. Using plants in multiple ritual contexts for their reproductive qualities is believed to bring about the fruition of one's desires. It is as if the plants, in the flowering of their fertility, are bringing about the fulfillment of their own desires. Establishing a close relationship with plants, then, expands your own potential to fulfill your desires, whether for reproduction or marriage. An ability to reproduce is linked with the ability to give. The ability to reproduce conveys the presence of the divine and is a sign of the divinity's visible generosity.

In many ways, the same ideas of kinship are illustrated through the kōlam when women say, "We make the kōlam to remove suffering or to prevent suffering from entering the home." The woman of the house is making this creation first thing in the morning to protect her family and immediate kin. When the woman says, "We make the kōlam as a way to feed a thousand souls," she is thinking of all the creatures living around her household as extended kin. These sorts of ritual drawings echo the desire for a more intimate kinship with the natural world. It is auspiciousness itself, whether accrued through ritual marriage to a tree, or by feeding a thousand souls every day, that enables the Tamil to get by for yet another day, in the midst of suffering.[10]

Mutual Generosity, Auspiciousness, and Fertility

Establishing relationships with the natural world is a necessary component of relationships in the social and cultural worlds. A ritual might involve creating the kōlam, invoking the goddesses Lakshmi, Bhūdevi, or Ganga; generating auspiciousness through plants and trees; or marrying a tree so it takes on your burden. The kōlam and its many counterparts belong to a category that I call "rituals of generosity."

Through the form of *pūja*, or ritual offerings, one enacts the hope for a particular type of relationship with the divinities. In evoking a generous heart, rituals of generosity circumscribe human relationships in both cultural and natural contexts. According to the classical Tamil text the *Tirukkural*, giving hospitality from the household to those who ask is one of the ways of attracting the goddess of prosperity. According to a proverb in a section of the *Tirukkural* called "An Open House," "The Goddess of Prosperity will be gladdened in heart and linger in the house of the man whose smiling face welcomes those who seek hospitality" (Rajagopalachari: 10–11).

We have seen that the kōlam establishes a particular type of sacred relationship between the human and natural worlds at thresholds. And we have seen how divine residency establishes relationships of generosity with trees. These examples suggest an interesting congruence between ritual form and intention. As in any social exchange, these relationships are predicated on the expectation of *mutual* ritual generosity—that is, one gives freely and then receives gifts in return. Just as we can have generous relationships with human beings, so humans can have generous relationships with trees, rocks, rivers, and other aspects of the natural world.

The kōlam is a ritual act that physically embodies blessings, or "positive intentionalities," reducing the accumulation of negative intentionalities such as jealousy, envy, or greed. The positive intentionalities travel from the women's hands, through the kōlam, through the feet of those passing through its energy field, into their bodies. With the kōlam, women's sphere of auspicious power moves in two directions: outward to the world beyond the threshold, and inward to the home, where it contributes to its stability. Making the kōlam is like raising the sail on a ship for that day, enabling it to leap forward on its course with a strong tailwind. In this way, both the tangible kōlam and the auspicious effects of its creation are carried into the larger world.

In an environment of scarcity, where the next meal might be just out of reach, where the world appears capricious and disorderly and death strikes frequently and brutally, where infertility is a source of private and public grief and child mortality rates are high, reality takes on a different cast from a culture that is comfortably secure. Life is seen as something precious and rare, like the unanticipated arrival of good fortune. The cruelty and heartlessness in oneself and others must be faced, since immoral behavior is seen as the cause of poverty, misfortune, and other forms of inauspiciousness.

In this context, acts of sacredness, as well as faith in divine relationships, signify the courage to go up against despair and to be open to the hope of regeneration from the brutalities inflicted by nature and other humans. In making the kōlam, the hope is that the auspicious power embedded in the rice flour and invoked by the ritual will be transferred to the community, thereby generating abundance and good will.

Calling upon the divine to inhabit trees or thresholds—whether the fig, the coconut, the banana, or the mango—is part of the larger social fabric of "positive intentionalities" in Hindu popular life. Such acts of generosity in the face of suffering and scarcity are imbued with spirit and energy, and acts of goodness and piety become "weapons of the weak" (Scott 1985). Thus, positive intentionalities can be seen as manifestations of creativity within the larger social arena.

Similar to that of the kōlam, the motivation for conducting marriages with trees is the desire to create relationships with auspicious elements in the natural world. Auspiciousness can be linked with the ritual principle of productivity and reproductivity, or generation and regeneration. "Rituals of generosity" are established at auspicious sites, such as trees and rivers, using auspicious powders like kumkum and turmeric. These rituals enable one to gain fertility or potentially fertile states found in marriage and pregnancy. Regardless of whether the association is within the "natural" or the "cultural" realm, the auspicious forces are transferred to the individual through rituals of generosity. This mutually reinforcing relationship is best conveyed through the description of a Balinese shaman, who, according to David Abram:

> ... acts as an intermediary between the human community and the larger ecological field, ensuring that there is an appropriate flow of nourishment, not just from the landscape to the human inhabitants, but from the human community back to the local earth. By his constant rituals, trances, ecstasies, and "journeys," he ensures that the relation between human society and the larger society of beings is balanced and reciprocal, and that the village never takes more from the living land than it returns to it—not just materially but with prayers, propitiations, and praise. The scale of a harvest or the size of a hunt are always negotiated

> between the tribal community and the natural world that it inhabits. To some extent every adult in the community is engaged in this process of listening and attuning to the other presences that surround and influence daily life. (1996, 7)

In a similar way, the Tamil woman negotiates for her community the webs of generosity between the natural and cultural realms through the practice of making the kōlam.

The Coming of the Refrigerator

Sometimes the rituals of generosity, and the willingness to be beneficent in modern life, radically shift when one least expects it.

On one hot afternoon, I sat on my balcony observing the street I lived on in the outskirts of Madurai. It was not unusual to see both men and women traveling throughout the neighborhood streets, asking for food at each house. Sometimes, one could hear in the distance a voice raised in entreaty—"Amma, Amma" [Mother, Mother]—as a figure approached a doorway. Occasionally these men and women were dressed in saffron clothes, which meant they belonged to a religious order, but just as often they were dressed in tattered clothes, which meant that they were not saints but were elderly or widows or just needed a meal.

In most households, meals were still prepared fresh; it was an enormous amount of work for the woman of the house. Simply making idlis, a common food combining fermented rice and lentils, could take many hours. First the woman hand-grinds raw rice into flour paste using a stone and water. Then she lets it rise for hours. Finally she steams the rice paste in a steamer covered with cheesecloth. From morning to late in the evening, the sounds of a meal being prepared could be heard from the street: pounding, shredding, slicing, rolling, and boiling. According to custom, the household usually cooked an extra person's meal beyond what the family needed.

Whenever a beggar would come to the door, it was customary to give some rice, lentils, and vegetables, sometimes cooked and sometimes raw. In order not to waste the leftover cooked food, there was a concerted effort to find a beggar to give the leftovers to. From my upper balcony, I would hear mothers calling their daughters to go down the street and bring back a beggar to feed so that no food would go to waste. Consequently, beggars were in demand, morally and physically, to soak up the excess supplies. Lakshmi is said to be embedded in every grain of rice, so if you wasted food, it was as if you were wasting god. The concept was offensive.

Then one day, something unexpected happened: a refrigerator arrived at my neighbor's house. It was a big moment. The neighbors from several nearby houses gathered together and shared in the festivities and joys of the first refrigerator coming into the area.

Some weeks later I observed the following scene. A beggar arrived at the door of the neighbor who had just bought the refrigerator. Instead of the usual hands offering a bowl with food, an annoyed voice issued from the doorway: "Shoo, shoo, shoo, go away, go away. Why are you people always coming around here?"

I was surprised as I listened to the tone of the voice, which was not magnanimous, and I realized that a woman who owns a refrigerator has a different relationship to leftovers than one who doesn't. Food that was once perishable could now be preserved rather than given to a wandering beggar or holy person. The very concept of waste as it relates to food and notions of generosity undergoes a dramatic change with the coming of a refrigerator. Rituals of generosity, therefore, also change. The woman will hold on to surplus food and store it rather than letting it move through the household and beyond the individual household.

This story harkens back to the beginning of this chapter, when Saroja was bemoaning the loss of generosity in human beings and the resulting decrease in the protective shield of the ozone layer. How ironic that a refrigerator, which tears a hole in a social fabric that is embedded with generosity—a social order that has existed for generations—is the same tool that produces chemicals that rip holes in the ozone in our atmosphere, reducing our ability to protect ourselves from skin cancer and other ailments.

The kōlam reflects a time when it was still a moral duty to respond to the needs of a stranger within the diameter of your gaze. In modern life, we have been trained to turn our gaze away from the stranger in need. In the 1990s, as modernity as we know it became more and more visible in India, villages became less and less porous to outsiders and strangers. These previously porous threshold areas, porches, or thinnais became closed, privatized, locked, and boarded up. The outsider and the stranger were considered to be more of a threat, a possible thief—and perhaps this was somewhat true due to the increasing economic inequality. In earlier forms of Hinduism there was a belief that the stranger could be a god or goddess in disguise, but this radically changed in the 1990s. The same belief was true historically in Christianity, that the stranger at the door could be Christ, but this perception too changed radically sometime after World War II in the United States. I have heard many Jewish and Christian friends who grew up in the 1930s in the United States say that their grandparents would cook enough so that they could feed a stranger who might knock on the door.

In researching this chapter, I was startled to find so much resonance between the kōlam, trees and the generosity of plants. Deep within the Tamil culture, the kōlam binds together a rich multitude of concepts and rituals that echo each other. The hidden meaning is understood often without being articulated, so for me to discover it was revelatory. Each ritual, no matter how ordinary, is actually full of rich metaphors and has the power to orient the person in a moral and ethical way. The kōlam, as the first ritual act of the day, sets up a ritual of generosity as an orientation to the day. Of course, not every woman who makes a kōlam every day is always generous to her neighbor or a stranger who comes to her for help, but it provides a compass of sorts, a way of guiding her behavior toward a certain ideal of generosity.

11

Feeding a Thousand Souls

A Ritual of Generosity

O wonderful! O wonderful! O wonderful!
I am food! I am food! I am food!
I eat food! I eat food! I eat food!
My name never dies, never dies, never dies!
I was born first in the first of the worlds,
Earlier than the gods, in the belly of what has no death!
Whoever gives me away has helped me the most!
I, who am food, eat the eater of food!
I have overcome this world!
He who knows this shines like the sun.
Such are the laws of the mystery!

—*Taitttīri-ya Upanishad* (Hyde 2007)

Often, in the middle of our conversations, Tamil women would look at me piercingly and state emphatically: "You know, the *real* reason we make the kōlam is to feed a thousand souls." The rushed intensity of their voice implied that they were sharing a hidden deeper truth to the ritual that they expected me never to have heard before, a secret underlying reason lost in time. Because so many women repeated this statement, I became curious as to what it meant. Why was the kōlam now being made of stone flour? It was cheaper than the rice flour, yes, but it was not edible as the rice flour had been before. Why were plastic stick-on kōlams that were placed on the marble thresholds of modern condominiums so popular today? "Didn't the younger women know?" the elderly women constantly complained and scolded. I have circled around this fact several times in previous chapters. In this chapter I will look more closely at the phrase "feed a thousand souls" and its implications.[1]

In the previous chapter we explored rituals of generosity between "nature" and "culture" in three different acts: creating the kōlam, ritually using plants and trees, and marrying trees. We also discussed briefly the idea of "feeding a thousand souls," as the rice-flour kōlams do feed small animals such as ants, bugs, worms, insects, and birds throughout the day as the kōlam disintegrates into the soil (Figures 11.1a, b).

(a) (b)

Figure 11.1a,b Crows eating rice on the ground, Thanjavur.

Although many Tamil women told me that every Hindu is required to feed a thousand souls as a part of his or her daily karmic obligation, very few humans have the resources to feed a thousand human souls. As feeding a thousand animal souls also fulfills this daily obligation, making the kōlam can satisfy this requirement. But why feed a thousand souls in the first place? I discovered three significant clues to the underlying significance of this phrase and how it relates to the kōlam.

Three Clues

The first clue I found was in trying to answer two related questions: (1) Where does this phrase appear in Tamil oral narratives, in contexts other than the kōlam? and (2) Where does it appear in ancient Hindu literature? I met a remarkable elderly woman named Kannamma in the beautiful town of Srivilliputtur. Her gray hair was tied up in a loose bun at the nape of her neck, her face was round and alert, and her sari wrapped in a highly orthodox style of nine yards, resembling a pair of loose pants. We had the following conversation about the concept of *annadānam*, or the generosity of giving food:

Kannamma: . . . there is a heavenly divine body-being called Kethu [one of the nine heavenly astronomical forces].[2] They say that to honor this Kethu, . . . you need to give *annadānam*, you need to give food away at the ocean's edge.

Vijaya: Why the ocean's edge?

Kannamma: Because the ocean's edge is considered to be the most powerful place . . . Because all the sacred waters gather into the ocean . . . You don't have to make a special pilgrimage to the Ganges River because even the Ganges river ultimately joins the ocean . . . You need to feed rice to a thousand people. Those who can do this, do. Those who cannot, what are they to do?

Kannamma's narrative implies that giving rice away to a thousand human beings at the ocean's edge is one of the highest values of dharma. In order to alleviate the negative forces of Kethu, similar to Saturn's malevolent forces, *annadānam* is required. It is not a simple commitment and ritual. This vow, to feed a thousand people at the sea to Kethu, is often performed when a family is suffering or undergoing a series of unexpected hardships.[3] This ritual action could just as well have been oriented to any of the other nine heavenly bodies, such as Rāghu or Shani (Saturn) or even the sun itself (see Chapter 6 for designs specifically attributed to the nine heavenly forces). The feelings of awe and mystery, of fear and respect, of attribution and negativity, of overwhelming power, are often assigned to these nine heavenly bodies to varying degrees. Here in Kannamma's narrative, it seems that Kethu is the focus of awe whose negative effects need to be balanced by the positive karma of feeding a thousand souls.

What is also interesting is that Kannamma says that the ocean is the most sacred place for this ritual, as many sacred rivers flow into it, including the most sacred river of all: the Ganges. Curiously, many Tamil women had explained to me that stepping on the kōlam at the threshold of the house in the early morning was like stepping into the Ganges, and was equivalent to going to a pilgrimage there, one of the highest karmic ritual acts in Hinduism. I did not understand this idea until I placed it against Kannamma's earlier statement. If, indeed, stepping on the kōlam is akin to stepping into the Ganges, it makes sense that for Tamil Hindu women feeding and satisfying the hunger of a thousand animals' lives and souls every single morning through the kōlam is as if they are doing this action at the ocean's edge where the Ganges joins it.[4] This simple ritual act of making the kōlam then becomes equivalent to the moral ecology of one of the highest dharmic acts in Hinduism.[5]

Feeding a thousand souls does not have to be seen as a daily burden. For instance, in Madurai, a well-known and respected priest and astrologer, Thyāgarājabhāgavatār, told me a way to easily "feed a thousand souls":

> Take rice, grind it well, add sesame seeds and a bit of *jaggery* [unrefined whole cane sugar]. Mix this flour, then, make a kōlam with this wet mixture. Wherever ants smell the sweetness of the rice, they will come from far and wide. The ants will eat and eat the rice. If a thousand ants take the rice, and fill their stomachs with it, it is [equal to] feeding a thousand lives and souls.

He told me this with a grin, suggesting that a kōlam made of sugar will ensure that you attract the actual number of a thousand ant souls.

What we can see from this clue is that the kōlam is not the only context where "feeding a thousand souls" is mentioned; it is also said in the context of feeding a thousand human souls at the ocean's edge to honor Kethu or the other astrological forces. We can see here that the idea of "feeding a thousand souls" is highly significant in the oral tradition.

In the literary and religious corpus, it was much more challenging to find this phrase. Though I could not find the exact phrase "feeding a thousand souls" in religious texts, I did find something close. It was in Patrick Olivelle's (2005) critical edition and translation of *Manu's Code of Law*, an ancient Sanskrit treatise on Hindu law. Here, he refers to "a man who is given a thousand." This appears in the context of a list of persons "who purify those alongside whom they eat" (118).[6] According to Olivelle, when the noun is unspecified, "cows, the paradigmatic gift, are understood." But here it is said to refer to either feeding a thousand Brahmins or giving a thousand gold coins (265, note 3.186). Though this kind of ancient gift does not refer specifically to a thousand souls, matching what the elderly kōlam-makers told me, it is striking that it *does* refer to feeding a thousand Brahmins. It is conceivable that over time this kind of prescription changed slowly from feeding a thousand Brahmins to feeding a thousand souls, making the act of generosity much more accessible and possible, especially on a daily basis. The fact that it refers to the number "a thousand" gives us a sense that the number alone is significant in ancient Hindu understandings of gift-giving.

A second clue I discovered was that the daily ritual sacrifices of a householder have a close relationship to the functions of the kōlam. One of the requirements of a human being living by the code of dharma is to perform five sacrifices, or offerings, every day. According to the Dharma Sūtras these five sacrifices are as follows:

> Take out shares for the *bhūtas* every day. That constitutes *bhūtayajña*. Give away food everyday till the pot is exhausted. That constitutes *manuṣyayajña*. Give away food for the sake of the ancestors everyday till the pot is exhausted. That constitutes *pitṛyajña*. Give into the fire till the wood is all consumed. That constitutes *devayajña* . . . and *nṛyajña*, offering reverential hospitality to the guests. (Bajāj and Śrīnivās 1996: 77–82)[7]

To clarify, the first sacrifice is to feed the animals, or *bhūtas*. The second is to give food away until there is none left. The third is to feed the ancestors. The fourth is to feed the gods and goddesses; this is performed through feeding wood to the fire god, Agni, who takes the prayer-filled messages to the heavens. The fifth is offering hospitality to unexpected guests. The kōlam fulfills three of these five sacrifices: feeding animals, providing offerings to the gods and goddesses (Lakshmi, Bhūdevi, Tulasi, Ganesh), and feeding unexpected guests.

The second clue leads us to the idea that these sacrifices are performed to relieve certain debts that human beings are born with. The ultimate absolution of these debts (three, four, or five, depending on the text) does not occur until death, but there are ways to alleviate that debt on a daily basis. According to various ancient Sanskrit dharmic texts, every human being is born with at least three debts: debts to the gods and goddesses, to the teachers, and to the parents (Olivelle 2005: 277–278, note 4.257). In some versions, the fourth debt is a debt of hospitality to humans; this could match the fifth sacrifice to feed unexpected strangers (mentioned earlier). Nath (1987) adds a different fourth debt, which is to all living creatures (37), which could match the first sacrifice to the animals. Olivelle (1993) imputes a fifth debt; this combines hospitality to animals and humans, broadening the category to include human and non-human strangers. As he notes, "The sacrifice to the *bhūtas* is something completely new [in the Mahabharata]. It appears to be an extension of the debt of hospitality from human to non-human beings" (54). He explains in more detail:

> The reason given by Manu for these sacrifices reveals the growing importance of the ethics of non-injury (*ahimśa*): "A householder has five slaughterhouses—the hearth, the grinding stone, the broom, the mortar and pestle, the water pot—by using which he is bound. In order to expiate successively (the offenses committed by means) of all these, the great sages have prescribed for householders the daily (performances of the five) great sacrifices." (54, note 78)

These five householder slaughterhouses reflect the deeper human need to assault and murder the non-human animals (visible and invisible) residing in and around those tools. They embody the survival necessity to use these tools to run a household. In the hearth, for example, even starting a fire in order to stay warm against the cold and to cook your daily food kills microscopic and macroscopic creatures in your vicinity. The same holds true for the grinding stone, the broom, the mortar and pestle, and the water pot. Those creatures we kill, we are responsible for in karmic terms. The simple act of setting up and running a household enabled the destruction of non-human animals. This was considered a tremendously negative karmic offense, and the five great sacrifices alleviate these daily killings.

The kōlam is then one significant way for a female householder to alleviate her individual and household debts and simultaneously perform one or more of the five great sacrifices. The clearest connection between the five sacrifices and the kōlam appears to be the sacrifice done for animals. There is a complicated sense of understanding in these texts in which the world of non-human beings is believed to actually live off the karmic residue of the householder's actions:

> Cats, mice, dogs, pigs, parrots, pigeons, crows, reptiles of all kinds, the bevies of birds and herds of animals that live in the forest, and also the hundreds and thousands of moving and unmoving creatures of diverse kinds that live in the house, the field or the burrow, all of them, O devi, live off what the *gṛastha,* or householder, earns through his karma, his actions. (Bajāj and Śrīnivās 1996: 75)

Does this mean that the animals live directly off the karma accrued by the householder through the benefits of his householding? In a literal sense or a metaphorical sense? How does this benefit balance against the killing referred to earlier? I'm not sure I understand this as well as I would like to. There is an intimate relationship between animals and human beings, as fulfilling your duty actually feeds them, both literally and metaphorically. The kōlam therefore is a symbolic remnant of the relationship among a householder, his or her actions, and the wider context of the sheer existence and survival of all animals.

The second clue becomes richer and richer. Because of this relationship with animals, there are several different rituals you can perform to alleviate your debt to them. There is the *bhūtayajña,* the ritual act of giving to small animals, mentioned earlier in the context of the five sacrifices. Other rituals are found in Kane's *History of Dharmaśāstra* (1962–1975). The first refers to a *bali,* or gift, that is often offered on the ground. First, the area is "to be wiped with the hand and sprinkled with water, and then the *bali* is to be put down" (745–7). This ancient ritual is related to the *Baliharana,* a ritual sacrifice that is "performed to the waters, to herbs and trees, to the house, to the domestic deities, to the deities of the ground (on which the house is built) among others" (745–7). Kane provides more detail: *Baliharana,* if done in the morning, is performed to "day-walking beings" and if done at night is performed to "night-walking beings" (112). In another ritual that Kane describes, *vaiśvadeva,* food is offered on the ground to dogs, crows, birds, and so forth (746–7).[8]

The kōlam is perhaps a way to incorporate one or more of these rituals to animals. For example, the kōlam is performed after the ground is sprinkled with water and, indeed, is offered on the ground. It is also addressed to the deities on the ground such as Bhūdevi. In my mother's time, the kōlam was done in the evening as well as the morning, so it was consumed by both day-walking and night-walking beings. The kōlam is seen as food for animals. So it fits!

This second clue gives us some insights into the question of why we should feed a thousand souls in the first place. The offering of rice flour "to feed a thousand souls" on the ground that constitutes the very making of the kōlam closely fulfills several of the five debts and sacrifices, particularly the debt and sacrifice to animals. The daily feeding of a thousand souls goes some way toward providing daily relief to the extensive and irreconcilable debts accrued by being born a human being and setting up a household, all of which entails daily and continued acts of violence. Because there is such a severe debt that cannot be eradicated in one's lifetime, it makes sense that a great sacrifice is also required, even one so stringent as feeding a thousand souls.[9] This gives us a sense of the power of the kōlam as a ritual act.

The third clue is related to the duty of the householder to give food and hospitality in a disciplined way. As mentioned in Chapter 3, the kōlam is a sign of exteriorized hospitality and letting the world know that the house is overflowing in generosity and gratitude and therefore capable of feeding unexpected guests, a generator of auspiciousness. In the following story from the Mahabharata,[10] we clearly see the value of *disciplined giving* of food, to known and unknown guests, whether one is a rich or poor householder. According to traditional Hindu texts and oral knowledge, there are four stages to a Hindu life: student, householder, forest dweller, and ascetic. The householder, the second stage, is considered to be an exemplary figure, as he is the one who economically supports the other three stages. The members of the household are expected to work and create a surplus for this reason, so they can perform the multiple rituals of hospitality that being a householder entails.[11] Jitendra Bajāj and Maṇḍayam Doḍḍamane Śrīnivās, in their excellent book *Annam Bahu Kurvīta: Recollecting the Indian Discipline of Growing and Sharing Food in Plenty,* describe the duties of a Hindu householder, whether a wealthy king or a very poor man.[12] The ritual act of giving food, or *annadānamāhatmya,* is one of the central duties of any established household (*anna* means food, *dāna* means giving, and *māhatmya* means the greatness of). This ritual duty is expressed by Krishna in the Mahabharata in the following context.

Yudhishthira and the Pandavas had won the enormous civil war against their uncle, Dhritarashtra, and his 100 sons. However, they were deeply sad at the tremendous loss of life of their side of the family as well as their teachers and friends on the other side. Yudhishthira, the eldest of the five brothers, was deeply depressed and was unable to do anything. Finally, Krishna tells him that while he is lost and immersed in his memories of these battles, there is a much bigger battle he needs to think about within his own mind, which no one can help him with. This battle is to pull himself out of his depression. To win this internal war, Krishna advises him to concentrate his energies on a *mahāyajna* , or a great sacrifice. He is to invite all the kings he conquered, all the kings who had assisted him, and all the people from conquered lands for a feast lasting an entire year. This grand feeding would alleviate some of the sins from the killings during the war. Krishna assists him in conducting this ritual, and everybody who comes is fed and satisfied (45–50).

After this is done, he asks Krishna for instructions on dharma. Krishna says the essence of this teaching is in the following: "The world, both animate and inanimate, is sustained by food . . . The giver of food is the giver of life and indeed of everything else. Therefore, one who is desirous of well-being in this world and beyond should make special endeavor to give food" (2–3). Krishna, in the next 15 verses, lays out the centrality of the giving of food in the life of a householder and the greatness of food and its emergence "out of the vital essences of earth and its intimate connection with all life" (2). Krishna says,

> Those who partake of the leftovers of *yajña*—those who eat after having offered proper shares to all others and all of nature—are the virtuous. They are cleansed of all sins. Those who cook for themselves alone are the sinners: in eating alone they partake only of sin. . . . All beings are

> formed of *anna; anna* arises from the rains; rains arise from *yajña*; and *yajña* arises from karma, action. (8)

Anna is food and *yajña* is sacrifice and the offering of food. By feeding people for an entire year, Yudhishthira cleansed himself of his sins from the war, according to Krishna.

At the end of this *yajña,* when mountains of grains and rivers of ghee were consumed, and kings all over the world were served for days and months together, a mongoose rose up, growled fiercely, and said that this *mahāyajna* does not come close to the generosity of others. The person who exceeded this sacrifice was a generous resident of Kuruksetra who gave away one single measure of roasted grain (64–5). This man was a Brahmin and he earned his living by *uñchavṛtti,* or gathering the leftover grains from harvesting fields and marketplaces to feed his wife, son, and sister-in-law, a conscious reaching into the commons for everyday sustenance. This gathering for food in the commons created less of a karmic cost to him and his family. They ate only once a day, and if they couldn't gather any food that day, they didn't eat. At some point, there was a great famine in that land, so they began to starve. Finally, after weeks of searching, they found one measure of barley, which they brought home, roasted, and divided into four quarters.

Before they began eating, there was a knock on the door and an unknown guest arrived. They greeted him with great pleasure and delight and welcomed him into their little mud house. The householder offered the guest his quarter of the roasted grain. The guest ate that quarter but still looked hungry and so the wife offered the guest her quarter. The guest was still not satisfied, so the son offered his quarter, and then later the daughter-in-law offered her quarter until the guest was finally satisfied. The guest turned out to be the god Dharma himself who had come in human form to test the family. The householder had fulfilled the dharma of *annadāna,* "to the discipline of satisfying the hungry before eating for oneself," (64) and so a chariot appeared to take them all to heaven.

The mongoose witnessed these events and touched some of the grains that had fallen from the chariot as it was ascending. These fallen grains turned the mongoose's head and half of his body into gold. Since then, he had been attending many other feasts to see if he could turn the rest of his body into gold. But because he did not turn into gold at Yudhishthira's feast, he knew that the dharmic value of the food sacrifice of the poor Brahmin was much greater than Yudhishthira's feeding of so many people for an entire year (64–65).

This brings us back to the third clue of the householder, whether a king or a poor Brahmin, having a duty to provide *disciplined hospitality* to strangers. The female householder relieves the negative karmic actions of her life by feeding others through the making of the kōlam. The logic in Yudhishthira's story is that the kings and the rich have a duty to give of their abundance to those who are in need and satisfy their hunger so that no one in the society is left hungry. The mongoose's tale inside the story of Yudhishthira's feast reveals, though, that the duty of sharing food with strangers is not just the responsibility of the king and the rich. *Every* householder is obligated to give to strangers if given the opportunity before taking food himself or herself. That seems to be a classic textual precept for right living as a Hindu householder.[13]

Beyond this precept, the householder's disciplined action of giving away food even in the harshest circumstances is of great karmic benefit. The poor family's generosity is of greater karmic value than Yudhishthira, who fed thousands of people over an entire year. The reason Yudhishthira fed so many people was to relieve the karmic debt of killing his guests' relatives and to unify the country after a major civil war. As a king, he could easily afford such a feast. Yet the poor family gave all that they had, even if it meant further starving themselves, to feed an unexpected and unknown stranger at their door. This had greater karmic value because of the importance in the Dharmaśāstras of feeding the *atithi*, or the unexpected stranger guest:

> It is such an uninvited and unacquainted one who must be welcomed with great ceremony and offered food with reverence. This is a discipline enjoined upon all *gṛhastas* (householders), even those who live in great austerity themselves. . . . And, the main qualification of an *atithi* is that there is no permanence to his coming and going, and he is someone who is not even remotely known or related to the host. He comes unknown, uninvited and unexpected. (Bajāj and Śrīnivās 1996: 92)

In fact, by his or her very actions of ritual generosity, the householder is considered to be, in Hindu religious or philosophical terms, an expression of the highest good. A householder is like a great tree that provides sustenance to all who seek his or her help. So this act of feeding a thousand souls, of feeding a thousand strangers, is the epitome of ritual generosity—of feeding others before you feed yourself, of feeding others before they even come to ask you for food, of feeding in a disciplined way, of expressing hospitality.[14]

Generosity of the First Instance

Another important aspect of the discipline of giving food I discovered was the idea of generosity of the *first instance*, where giving before being asked is of more value than giving because you were given to (that is, through reciprocity). It always puzzled me why the kōlam is always done as the *first* ritual act of the day, for most Hindu rituals require a purification bath before being performed. A female householder rises from her bed, a highly polluted context given the nature of a marital bed and the implied sexuality contained within it. She then immediately creates the kōlam, *even before* her daily bath (mentioned in Chapter 4). The kōlam seems to be done with a sense of urgency; there is no time even for a ritual purification bath. One reason could be that the notion of auspiciousness is more important than the notion of ritual purity.[15] But another reason could be that the kōlam is a daily ritual performance that demonstrates the idea of giving first, before anyone else has a chance to give to you. The kōlam could then be a daily embodiment of the "first instance" of feeding a thousand souls, so it is not seen as reciprocal giving.

According to the well-known *Tirukkural*, an ancient Tamil collection of proverbs, "The good deed that is done not in return, but in the *first instance*, is more precious than anything in this world or beyond. Nothing can repay that act. What is done in return for something previously done can never be as great as the deed born out of sheer generosity, be it ever so small by itself . . . It is above every other kinds of goodness" (Rajagopalachari 1981: 14). As a first ritual act of the day, the kōlam can be seen clearly as something given "to feed a thousand souls" as the very "first instance." This would therefore increase a female householder's karma accounting for the day. Perhaps that is why there seems to be a sense of urgency to perform the kōlam before doing anything else. This would directly increase the karmic repayment of the initial debts of being a householder. So "feeding a thousand souls" is a direct example of generosity of the first instance and gives the female householder maximum ritual debt relief.

At the other end of the day, the disciplined giving of the household does not stop. As Manu states, "in no case a guest who arrives after sunset should be turned away or allowed to sleep unfed" (Bajāj and Śrīnivās 1996: 93). I concluded that this must be why, according to many elderly women, the kōlam used to be done twice a day—at sunrise and sunset. Just as the morning kōlam should be completed before the first rays of the sun touch the front threshold of the house, so, too, the evening kōlam should be completed before the last rays of the sun touch the front threshold of the house. Though I had seen the kōlam being created at sunset several times, I never understood until now why, except for the more common explanation that it was a way to say goodbye to Lakshmi and to welcome her sister, the goddess Mūdevi. This is yet another explanation, that no human or animal should go to sleep without being fed at night. So the injunction to feed a thousand souls as the first instance of the day also links to disciplined giving as the first instance of the night.

The story of the half-golden mongoose reveals the multifaceted nature of disciplined giving. Disciplined giving entails a general duty to give food and hospitality, whether you are rich or poor. The moral value depends on the proportion of what you give compared to what you have, not on the actual amount that you give. The karmic value increases when you give food to an unexpected and unknown guest and when you give food at the beginning and the end of the day, as the first and last instance. The kōlam creatively addresses these facets of disciplined giving by symbolizing and fulfilling the moral duty of giving away food. It also symbolizes and fulfills the act of giving food to an unexpected stranger. Lastly, it is an enactment of the first and last instance. The act of "feeding a thousand souls" is a disciplined way to give, and the kōlam is a personification of this discipline.

The three clues I have discussed are intimately related to the idea of hospitality and require an understanding of the role of giving food. In addition, the role of the householder, the discipline of giving as an integral part of householding, the first instance, the five sacrifices, and the five debts critically map these wider ritual contexts and reveal an array of insights. In the first clue, we saw that this phrase appears outside of the context of the kōlam in Tamil women's oral narratives in reference to another god, Kethu. The related phrase, "the giving of a thousand," can be found in ancient Sanskrit religious literature, showing that the idea of giving a thousand is important in and of itself in Hindu ritual understanding. In the second clue, we looked at the five sacrifices and saw how the moral duty of the kōlam embedded in the phrase "feeding a thousand souls" could be a way to alleviate three of the five debts human beings are born with. The third clue provided a critical understanding of disciplined giving in the story of the half-golden mongoose that parallels the way in which the feeding of a thousand souls functions in the understanding of the kōlam.

For many of the women I talked with, making the kōlam to feed a thousand souls seemed to be an implicit code of dharma. Dharma is one of the key concepts in Hinduism, and though it is a difficult concept to translate into English, it has a sense of maintaining the social order, keeping the ritual life going, and fulfilling your duty. A broader definition of dharma includes within it a sense of piety; Olivelle (1999: xxi) states that dharma indicates "all the rules of behavior, including moral and religious behavior that a community recognizes as binding on its members."[16] These rules of behavior can be found within wide-ranging dharmic texts, both literary and oral.

Underlying these three clues is a basic dharmic injunction to give food away, which is found throughout written and oral Hindu literature. Krishna himself says that he *is* food, and he will not come to you unless you give him away in the form of food. He says, "The one who gives me is in fact the one who obtains me. On the other hand, the one who does not give is consumed by me. I am the *annadevatā*, I eat the one who does not give *anna*" (Bajāj and Śrīnivās

1996: 132). The threat that if you do not give food away, you will be eaten by Krishna himself serves as a not-so-gentle reminder of the dire consequences of not following such a basic dharmic concept as giving away food. The kōlam is an elegant and practical way of fulfilling this obligation. For me, these dharmic nuances surrounding this important act of ritually giving food away to strangers are some of the most profoundly moving understandings that emerged from my exploration of the kōlam.

12

Endings

I approached this research project as a secular humanist, an intellectual, a feminist, and an environmentalist. Initially, my intention was to look at this ritual for its symbolic, mythic, and cultural meanings, especially for women. I was deeply skeptical of the moral claims of religion, and was just as surprised to see this kind of moral grounding in a ritual that on the outside seemed so fun, playful, and ephemeral. And yet underneath these lighter aspects was a serious core. My task became to uncover layers of meaning around this folk art ritual. Most of the preceding chapters had a focus of inquiry that circled around a particular aspect of what Tamil women taught me; these were centered around the most common conversations I had with them throughout my intermittent formal research from 1987 to 1999. These dialogues and narratives focused on critical aspects of the kōlam, such as rituals, origins, thresholds, competitions, embedded ecologies, and tree marriages. What emerged in the post-fieldwork phase of organizing the research and writing this book were three further layers of understanding: (1) certain perceivable rivers of patterns in the designs, (2) mathematics, and (3) rituals of generosity and hospitality. What has been most surprising is how many disciplines the study of the kōlam has pulled me directly into. I was forced to plunge into disciplines as various as aesthetics and art history; ancient, medieval, and contemporary Tamil literature and ancient Sanskrit literature; anthropology, ethnography, and even mathematics.

Throughout this process, I slowly began to appreciate how folk religious art has embedded within it moral values, which in turn shape communities and their behaviors. The kōlam is in fact a rich, extensive metaphor for Tamil cultural values. I began to see the kōlam as a tapestry that weaves together different threads of knowledge reflecting the behavior of society at large, such as generosity to strangers. This stunned me. I simply did not expect this amount of embedded knowledge in the kōlam.

Similarly, other ritual practices may very well have concepts, practices, and philosophies layered through them. Whether it is other Hindu women's rituals, or other Hindu rituals, or any other ritual of any other religion, I can now easily imagine a parallel unpacking of complex layers of moral and ethical understandings. These nets of understandings surround that ritual and are embedded within it.

Writing this book has been a very long, difficult process. For me the kōlam is not merely a passing research interest; I am convinced that it will entrance me for the rest of my life. Only when I realized that this book could never tell the complete story of the kōlam, and would always be just a partial rendition, could I acquire the freedom to finish the book. Another reason was my struggle to find my voice as a writer. I was torn between using a clean-cut scholarly voice versus a more muddling and open personal one. Most of all, I feared that using only a scholarly voice would be distancing and would leave out the potential audience of the very Tamil women who had taught me so much. I wanted them to be able to see themselves in the book and to feel a resonance with its themes. A third reason is due to a 15-year-long string of bad luck in my life: the near-fatal loss of a twin pregnancy and six months of accompanying bed rest; a near-deadly car accident with an 18-wheel semi-truck that resulted in a two-year recovery process; the constant severe ill health of an immediate family member that was a five-year preoccupation; my father's illness and death and the subsequent grief, all lasting two years; an assault by a homeless man; and a series of health-related personal setbacks that seemed interminable and too numerous to even list. When I finally had one year without any obstacles, I was able to finish the book.

Looking back now, I can see how this *longue durée* made me more deeply aware of the philosophical and emotional resonances that women had tried to teach me but that I had failed to understand throughout the research process. When I began this research, I was in my late 20s; by the time I finished my formal research and my Ph.D., I was into my mid-30s. Soon after, I experienced a severe five-year period of infertility. Over the next decade, I began teaching, received tenure, and had twin girls. It took me a long time to realize the significance of certain key aspects of the kōlam, such as showing gratitude, increasing fertility, representing a continued state of well-being or auspiciousness, calling for good luck, and sending positive intentions out into the world. As I entered mid-life and realized that I could not take for granted the continuation of a secure everyday life, my understanding was far different from what it had been as a beginning graduate student/scholar in her late 20s.

The foundation of these realizations was that I needed to be active in desiring auspiciousness to even have a chance at attaining it. To remember that performing the kōlam is in fact a way of both beckoning Lakshmi and displaying that quality in the public gaze. I sensed that being able to mark each day with a kōlam as an announcement of a continued state of good health and auspiciousness, was in fact, a significant way of stating your desire for increased fertility and calling out for good luck. Women implied that if you do not appreciate or feel gratitude when things are going well, then life's challenges will become even more difficult when they do inevitably come along. The kōlam was a way of dealing with suffering as well as a way to actively desire nonsuffering.

At the core of this daily practice are Tamil women themselves who exercise their ritual and secular powers through the cultural and religious reproduction of values, concerns, and imaginations that are practiced in the public arena. The kōlam is a powerful vehicle for Tamil women's self-expression, a central metaphor and symbol for creativity. It evokes an entire way of being in the world; it articulates desires, concerns, sensibilities, and suffering, and ultimately it affirms the power of women's blessings to create a desired reality: a healthy, happy household.

I began this book with stories from my childhood and early adulthood, each story hinting at the origins of my interest in the kōlam. I end this book with stories from the middle of my life, each story illuminating a personal epiphany about the kōlam. They offer glimpses of my slow realization that the kōlam was no longer something I looked at from the perspective of a scholar; rather, it gave me epiphanies from the inside out. These stories, when they occurred, startled me and brought me face to face with the realization that the kōlam is still very much alive in many unexpected contexts, from California to India.

Kōlam Competition in California

In the middle of January 2004, I decided to do some follow-up ethnography with the kōlam in northern California. I attended a kōlam competition in Fremont, California, a city with a high population of diasporic Indian-Americans. The context was a Pongal Rice Festival celebration hosted by the local Tamil Manram, a community organization focused on the cultivation of Tamil culture. I had attended similar Pongal celebrations nearly every year between 1987 and 1994 in India as these festivals represented the heyday of kōlam-making, but this was the first time I had attended one in northern California. I had never tried to do fieldwork in the United States before. I brought with me my three-and-a-half-year-old twin children, Uma and Jaya; my American husband, who is of Norwegian-Swedish descent; and my parents, who were visiting from their home in suburban Maryland. We entered the large auditorium of the middle school, filled with noisy pools of commotion, and the organizers tried to steer us to different competitions, among them the kōlam competition.

Right away, I noticed many unusual aspects of this kōlam competition. The drawings were done on paper with colored pencils and pens in people's homes, brought to the site and taped on the walls; they were not done on actual marked floor areas as they are usually done in kōlam competitions in Tamil Nadu. I wondered if that had to do with some of the rules against marking up spaces with colored powders in a rented middle school auditorium, and how hard it would be, after the event, to wipe away the rice powders and colored powders from the finished wood flooring.

I watched other people's children and my own as they became mesmerized by the kōlam. They were drawn somehow to these designs on the wall, made by their older sisters, mothers, aunts, and grandmothers. The sheer fun of it, I could see, flowed over in women's faces. My children clambered onto my body, demanding, "Teach me the kōlam! When are you going to teach us the kōlam?" They were excited by everyone else's love of the kōlam. I watched my mother's eyes light up as she came to each kōlam design and analyzed it. "That lotus flower is a bit loose," she would say. "See how that is imbalanced in the right corner." She would point to the lined figures and say, "Now this one is really beautiful; see how the lines are balanced cleanly." She would laugh if she found a funny one. There was not a set of invited judges as there would have been at an Indian competition. Here, the audience members themselves were the judges and were encouraged to do a written evaluation of each kōlam entry.

I looked into the faces of the Tamil women there; they had emigrated from Madurai, Tirunelveli, Thanjavur, Chennai, Coimbatore, and so many of the other places in Tamil Nadu I had lived in and visited. I realized how close the immigrant remains to her native place. The women had experienced kōlams in India in these particular bodies and were literally carriers of the tradition, as was my mother. At that moment, I became much more interested in the transmission of the kōlam: How will it live in this land that is so different from its native place? The buzz around the kōlam in this middle school was encouraging: there was still a deep, engaged interest. I realized that we were all body carriers of memories of place, of habits of mind, of drawing designs, of kōlams. I looked at these grandmothers' faces; they resembled those I had been with all over Tamil Nadu. I felt almost at home again, as if I were back in India.

Stepping on a Thousand Good Lucks

In the middle of July 2005, my mother took an entire morning to draw a huge kōlam in a side patio of our home. Our children watched rapturously, squatting, aged four and a half by then and still as a leaf on a windless day. They watched, awed by this grand, room-size kōlam coming into being, layer after layer of wet rice flour flowing evenly out of my mother's hands, and by the hours and hours of quiet, steady, almost meditation-like movements it took her. "There is a lotus flower," "a lamp," "a mango leaf," "a step," "a banana-laden stem," they would whisper to each other, having heard my mother tell what it was the first time she drew it (Figure 12.1). They talked about this gigantic kōlam over the next year, as it faded from view through the next rain-laden northern California winter. A few months later, I took my children to India for the first time. Seeing kōlams there all over Tamil Nadu, Jaya remarked with a big grin, "Amma, it is like stepping on a thousand good lucks!"

And it is! The reason for making the kōlam, I thought to myself, is to alleviate women's greatest fears: failure, infertility, luck falling on them badly, poverty striking them out of the blue, losing everything they have. They believed if they made the kōlam, they would keep these awful happenings at bay. By calling on the goddess every morning, by gifting her with a drawing embedded with their desires, by feeding other souls first before feeding themselves and their family, by asking for the forgiveness of the earth goddess for walking on her and abusing her throughout the day, by calling on the goddess of luck herself to come and visit them, Tamil women believed that the kōlam was a visible sign every single morning of their prayers. What does it mean now? That we need whatever luck we can get, that we need our desires fulfilled, and that we need to keep working at it with the fullest of intentions.

Figure 12.1 Pichammal Nagarajan's kōlam with Jaya and Uma, San Francisco Bay area. Photo by Jonathan Chester.

Chariot Festival

In December 2010 I was in Chidambaram, a small temple town south of Pondicherry in southern India where the famous icon of the Dancing Shiva originates.[1] I was there working on a project on sacred mangroves and the commons. My cousin-brother invited us to attend the Chariot Ratha festival. I stood in the throng-filled street where the huge, mobile images of the Dancing Siva, Parvathi (Siva's wife, a gentler version of Kali), and their sons Ganesh (the elephant-headed god) and Murugan (a six-faced god) were being pulled slowly by thick rope by hundreds of people.

The chariot was huge, its wheels reminiscent of the chariots I had seen in films of the grand chariot festival in Puri, Orissa, with the god Jagannath. Here there were five chariots, and in front of the first chariot with the Dancing Shiva were at least 50 women making kōlams right in front of the huge rolling chariot. It was one of the most amazing sights I had ever seen. I was thrilled by the speed of the women's hands moving across the ground and impressed by the concentration in their faces. The kōlams seemed so alive in their hands, the drawings emerging almost as visual sculptural forms, akin to the Dancing Shiva. The women, too, seemed to be dancing, positioned this way and that, bending at the waist, arms stretched outward, creating magnificent kōlams in the path of the gigantic moving chariots. They were drawn with such intensity; yet they were going to disappear momentarily. It caught, for me, all that was essential in the kōlam: the creating of a carpet of auspiciousness, so that even the ordinary profane street became charged with sacrality in the wake of the dozens of women creating kōlams in the path of the five huge chariots carrying gods and goddesses. It happened two times a year, the circling of the chariots through the city of Chidambaram, and we felt so lucky to have witnessed such an event.

I had not expected to see the kōlam in a new context, and it galvanized my work to see that this ritual is still playing such a significant cultural role in India despite how quickly India is becoming modern. I have seen the kōlam change drastically; at the beginning of my research in the late 1980s, the kōlam was performed frequently and was much more widespread. By the late 1990s, the kōlams were smaller and were being done less frequently; they were slowly losing their everyday character, especially in modern, bustling cosmopolitan cities. And yet the fact that such an ancient ritual practice was still thriving moved me. It was as if we had entered a slip of time, watching this kind of ritual practice going on in the streets, in full view of the public, integrated into the larger ritual structure of the event. It is no longer only a domestic ritual at the home.

Teaching Compassion

In the spring of 2011, I received an unexpected invitation from my children's school to perform the kōlam at the TedX Conference "Teaching Compassion: Making Change Happen." I was deeply ambivalent about doing a kōlam in a non-ritual context and asked my mother for advice. She replied, "What is the conference on?" I said, "To celebrate compassion and to educate teachers, K-12, about different ways of bringing compassion into the classroom." She was silent for a few minutes, then responded: "I think it would be fine to make a kōlam there because one of the main reasons people do it is to feed a thousand souls." I felt an intense relief after she said that. The implication in her words was that the practice of the kōlam was strong enough to withstand being performed in a non-ritual context. The kōlam was way bigger than a conference, and she seemed not to worry about it changing even if it did. My primary anxiety was that the kōlam would be affected by its secularization.

I organized a few women and my mother to draw kōlams at the conference, which took place at a huge converted Ford Motor plant. The plant was at the end of a harbor in the industrial city of Richmond, California, and was one of the biggest buildings I'd ever been in. It had many skylights and large windows and could fit hundreds of people. Within a few hours, glimmering lustrous rice-flour drawings covered the floors of the inside and the outside of the large threshold area. The women drawing the kōlams were delighted to have so much space; they couldn't even cover all the floors because the plant was so immense. It was the perfect stage for the kōlam and made the former factory seem like a grand temple. This was one of the most spectacular contexts I had ever seen the kōlam in. Having the kōlam performed here did not feel as alien as I thought it would. Attendees watched women creating the kōlams and marveled at their intricacy, delicacy, skill, and ephemerality.

During the conference I spoke about the kōlam, setting it in its thick material and philosophical contexts in India and America. This gave the audience a richer experience than just seeing it on a purely aesthetic level. I still felt ambivalent about transferring what was a religious ritual into a purely secular context, as if I were violating the kōlam at a deeply foundational level. I wondered if the multiple meanings would be stripped away when it was placed in a non-ritual context. Every time someone would ask me if it was all right to make the kōlam in front of their own doorstep, even if they had not been raised in that tradition, I felt this conflict. It reminded me of the controversy when Madonna began wearing a bindi at her concerts in the 1990s, or seeing figures of Hindu gods and goddesses on children's lunchboxes. When does engaging a tradition become a way to support those within it and when does it wear away the meanings of a tradition? I did not and still do not know the answers to these questions. Yet I was very moved by the audience's responses to the kōlam, which ranged from curiosity to awe that such a tradition even existed. I came away with a renewed sense of the multiple homes the kōlam could have in America. Yet the deep tension remained.

The audience's responses reminded me of the time, many years prior, when my mother and I presented the kōlam to hundreds of people every day at the Smithsonian for the *Festival of India* (see Chapter 1). There, too, the audience inspired me with their intrigued amazement, which was a catalyst to beginning my own research.

I woke up the children early one Saturday morning. It was Deepavali (Diwali), 2013. We swept the dirt, leaves, and pebbles from the front threshold of our home. Then we all sprinkled water on the pavement and resisted getting into a water fight. Even though it was November and a chilly fall, we all squatted down in bare feet. With our thumbs and our first two fingers, we scooped pinches of rice flour from the small *kinnams*, stainless steel bowls that normally hold food, and began creating big kōlams. The designs looked thick and bold. We were comfortable with each other, my 13-year-old children and I. The rice flour seemed to flow from our hands. We were absorbed in what we were doing, in near silence, just hearing the sounds of our fingers drawing on the ground, listening to the early morning sounds of birds in the tall sycamore tree stretched benevolently above us. Concentrating intensely, it was nearly an hour before we thought we were done. The kōlam glistened on the wet pavement. From that point onward, it was as if we were bound together into one cloth.

People often ask if the tradition of the kōlam is still alive. It is alive in California, in Maryland, and all over the United States. It is alive in India, in Chennai, in New Delhi, in Chidambaram, in small towns, big towns, metropolitan cities, rural villages, urban and suburban neighborhoods, modern and traditional households.[2] It is alive at celebrations of Diwali and major Hindu festivals, Hindu temples, Hindu weddings. The kōlam is very much alive.

A pitch-black silence. A sari rustling in the mild early morning breeze. It is 5 a.m., the time of the Brahma muhurta, the face of Brahma, the god of creation and beginnings. The sun's slivers of light have not yet pierced the stars. Not even a shadow. A woman emerges from the doorway, with a bucket of cow dung water, and starts showering the entryway. It sounds like a cloud pouring rain. Holding a coconut shell filled with rice powder in her hand, she bends down, drawing in the darkness as if it were broad daylight.

sarvamangalam.
May there be well-being for all.

NOTES

Chapter 1

1. *Sombērithananam* (sluggishness and idleness) is opposed to *curucuruppu* (alertness and activity). "Don't just sit there staring looking like Mūdevi, get up and move," is often an admonishment used to get young girls up and about in household work and schoolwork. Bhūdevi is also constantly used in everyday discourse to describe a woman's behavior: "she has the patience of Bhūdevi" or "she has the ability to bear such burdens of life."
2. See Leslie (1992) and Narayan (1989: 221–4) for brief but interesting descriptions and narrations of the tense relationship between Lakshmi and Mūdevi.
3. See also Ilich and Sanders (1988) for understanding how history and technology shapes literacy and orality.
4. Pichammal Nagarajan created kōlam patterns at many sites, including the following: Children's Museum, Washington D.C. in 1986; Healing Arts Center, Stinson Beach, California, in 1990; Million Man March on the Mall, Washington D.C. in 1995; Painted Prayers Exhibition, Arthur M. Sackler Gallery of Art, Smithsonian Institution, Washington D.C. in 1995 (Stonesifer 1995); Museum of International Folk Art, Santa Fe, New Mexico, in 2006; TedX Golden Gate ED Compassion in Education Conference, UC Berkeley Greater Good Science Center, Richmond, California, in 2011 (Nagarajan 2011); and DASER, D.C. Arts and Sciences Rendezvous, Washington D.C. in 2015 (Nagarajan 2015).
5. Borden (1989). See especially Ramanujan's "Classics Lost and Found" (1999 [1989]), a poignant tale of the discovery of ancient Tamil poems by the 19th-century savant, A. V. Swaminathan Iyer. Ramanujan's intertwining of his relationship with ancient Tamil poetry and his calling as a contemporary poet is a moving tribute to the ways in which the past interlopes with our own present. See also Mookerjee (1998 [1985]) for an evocative visual exploration of Indian folk arts.
6. As mentioned earlier, throughout the rural and urban landscapes of India, many different forms "are known under different names in the different parts of the country: . . . *sathya* in Saurashtra, *aripan* or *aypan* in Bhiar, *aipan* in the Kumaon, *ālpanā* in Bengal, *jhunti* in Orissa, *caukā rangāna* or *cauk pūrna* or *sonarakhna* in Uttar Pradesh" (Kramrisch 1985: 247). This article remains one of the best surveys of women's ritual arts in India (247–254). Kramrisch links these designs with other forms of Indian art and design cultures. Within the Sanskrit traditions, there is the *dhūli chitrā, yantras,* and *mandalas*; these are related as kin, but not equivalent forms to the explicitly women's ritual traditions mentioned earlier.

Chapter 2

1. Tamil Sangams are local community organizations that explicitly stimulate the development of Tamil language and culture, both inside and outside Tamil Nadu. Wherever Tamil people have migrated throughout the world, they have founded these Tamil Sangam organizations, which have thrived as community centers, whether in Malaysia, Washington D.C., or San Francisco.
2. For a beautiful rendition and translation of Shaivite poems, see Peterson 1989. For the mythological underpinning of Tamil temples, see Shulman 1980.
3. Ādivāsis constituted 8 percent (over 104 million) of the nation's total population according to the Ministry of Tribal Affairs, Government of India, 2011.
4. For an art historical perspective, see the pioneering 1929 work by Coomaraswamy. For a more recent comprehensive literary analysis of sacred trees in India, see the thorough and excellent 2005 book by Nugteren. For a deeper look into Rajasthan and northern India, see Gold and Gular (2002). For an anthropological and literary understanding of sacred trees in northern India, see Haberman (2013). Haberman concentrates on the three most popular sacred trees: the pipal, the neem, and the banyan trees. For a deeper understanding of the politics around sacred groves in southern India, see Kent (2013).
5. I am using *alis* here as that was the Tamil word used during my earlier fieldwork times. I am aware of the changes in nomenclature and I allude to them here.
6. The most important book locating Chandralekha historically, biographically, and choreographically is Bharucha (1995). See also Kothari (1995). For a comparative theoretical analysis of two different radical choreographers, see the excellent 2004 book by Chatterjee. See also the beautiful interview (her last) by her companion, Sadanand Menon (2010).
7. Thanks to Mark Morris Dance Company, who kindly sent me the video version of the performance (2002).
8. Philpose 2011.
9. Most of the names of the people in this study have been changed to reflect a synthesis of voices and to protect the identities, as per the tradition of ethnographic practice.
10. The whole concept of fieldwork was somewhat problematic for me since I did not identify myself in the role of "professional stranger." Venturing into the field was a more familiar experience than I had expected it to be, and I felt simply as if I were returning to another home. The "field," in the sense in which anthropologists traditionally use the term, is one with which I have always felt uncomfortable, as it necessitates a distance of which I am incapable. I am not alone: I join many within anthropology and religious studies who have offered highly nuanced and compelling understandings of their reflexive positions, and I feel deep kinship with those who speak of "crossing over." The "field" of India was a return to my first home, the country my parents chose to leave, first when I was five, then again when I was 11, at which time I became a permanent alien resident in the United States. At that moment, America was the "field" in which I saw exotic, strange customs wherever I looked. But as I grew into a teenager I became more and more comfortable with my adopted home and its customs, reducing the perception of distance embedded in the word "field."
11. All these experiences have made me particularly conscious of two processes of translation: (1) the ways in which Tamil concepts translate into English and (2) the ways in which English concepts are used to discuss Tamil concepts. Tamil and English differ considerably in quality and texture. In general, the vernacular cadences and rhythms of the Tamil language are difficult to translate into English. I have encountered three basic challenges in this process of translation. First, conceptual structures in Tamil are simply not there in English. Second, women's tones of voice and expressiveness are both matter-of-fact and playful, and it is very hard to make English dance in the particular ways that Tamil dances. Third, many Tamil women believe and act out of a foundational faith, and this quality is very difficult to convey in a secular humanistic discourse. In English, from a secular humanist perspective, an ordinary Tamil comment may seem "superstitious," "unbelievable," or even a kind of Marquesian "fantastical" statement. For example, the notion that cow dung acts as a purifier is a widely held belief; to question it would seem ludicrous to most Tamils, whether they are "educated" or not—yet to name it in this kind of narrative makes me feel uncomfortable, as if I am saying

something not "true" or provable in a scientific way. These challenges pushed and pulled at this very text.

Often it seemed to me that the words of many Tamil women reminded me of a favorite African American writer of mine who lived in the middle of the earlier part of the last century, Zora Neale Hurston. Both had the same earthiness, sassiness, and forthrightness, which we find in her characterization of southern African American women. In this book, I hope I have been able to convey some of the same warmth, intimacy, and liveliness of my encounters that were vividly present for me while I was in India.

12. An earlier draft of this fieldwork event was published in Nagarajan (1994).

Chapter 3

1. For this reason, in this book I have respected women's own reluctance to attach their name to the kōlams they create.
2. As a contemporary extension of the influence of the kōlam in creating an impression of the kōlam-maker, some Tamil films use the motif of the heroine's beautiful kōlam in attracting the male gaze of the hero. The romance is either initiated by a strikingly beautiful kōlam or sustained during the nocturnal hours when a kōlam is being made by the heroine, in apparent safety and half-seclusion. Interestingly, it has become a site for serenading the heroine and in moving the narrative toward modern "love" marriages as opposed to arranged marriages.
3. This respect for rice, and indeed worship of it, is not unique to Tamil Nadu; many other cultures that have rice at the center of their economic livelihood also attach symbolic valences to rice. See especially Ohnuki-Tierney (1993).
4. For a beautiful, evocative rendition of women's ritual folktales in Kangra, in the Himalayan foothills, see Narayan in collaboration with Sood (1997). For a brilliant, provocative, and theoretically nuanced exploration of feminism and ethnography, see Vishweswaran (1994).
5. See Daniel (1984) for an elaboration of this very important concept of *sontha oor*. An important question that Tamils often ask is: What is your origin village; where did you or your family come from? This may help locate the qualities of the particular soil you are descended from and the shared substance of origin.
6. In Tamil the word is *dṛṣṭi*, or "eye," "sight," "evil eye," "to look," or "to concoct." Related concepts include *dṛṣṭi-k-kuṟaivu*, or "defective sight"; *dṛṣṭi-kāḷi* is to dispel the supposed effects of the evil eye by ceremonial rites. Another word, *dṛṣṭi-tōṣam*, indicates "the effect of the evil eye" and "pollution by sight." Interestingly, another related word is *tiruṣṇai*, or "desire" and "lust" (*Tamil Lexicon* 1982). A brilliant article (Dean 2013) explains the increasing prevalence of the evil eye in Tamil Nadu, growing along with increasing affluence, aspiration, and consumerism. For a detailed case-study approach to the exploration of the evil eye as a global phenomenon that is abundant across multiple cultures and religions, see Dundes (1992) and Maloney (1976). For Italian American understandings of this practice, see Sciorra (2011). For a fuller treatment of the evil eye with its archaic language and expressions in Scotland, see McLagen (1902). For a brief but intriguing psychological exploration of the role of envy with the increasing prevalence of social hierarchy, see Berger (2013).
7. "The Ganga and the Rivers of India" (131–189), a chapter in Eck (2012) devoted to the riverine landscapes throughout India, explores the multiple ways in which the Ganga holds the multitude of other sacred Indian rivers within itself; simultaneously, the Ganga flows through the other sacred Indian rivers. This implicit reciprocity, Eck argues, grids the imagination of multiplicity of sacrality mapped out on the Indian subcontinent.
8. The kōlam still maintains a ritual rhythm that reflects the diverse Hindu calendars. One of the signs of British colonialism in India was the British imposition of a Sunday holiday in Bombay in 1836. This disrupted the agricultural cycle of time, which involved intensive bouts of work during certain periods of planting, transplanting, and harvesting and long periods of rest where leisurely pursuits were maintained, including seasonal ritual cycles (from personal conversation with Dr. C. V. Seshadiri). See also Seshadiri (1993).
9. Margaḷi is considered to be the month that bridges a day in the life of a divinity. In other words, one year in human experience is the equivalent of one day in the community of gods and goddesses, and Mārkaḷi marks the start of a new day. There has been debate as to whether

the coming of Pongal, which marks the end of Mārkaḷi in the middle of January, was originally a winter solstice festival that subsequently slipped from its original mooring date (the astrological calendar has not been adjusted over the centuries).

10. Rice, sugarcane, and bananas are especially venerated at this time. Even the poorest household invests in the necessary resources to celebrate properly, cleaning the entire house inside and out, whitewashing the walls, cleaning the floors, and throwing out old belongings to usher in the new year.
11. Other "threshold rituals" include stringing mango leaves on the outer doorways to indicate an auspicious event inside the house, removing obstacles, and performing any ritual involving the god Ganesh. Even saying goodbye on the threshold is ritualized; for example, in many communities within Tamil Nadu it is preferable to say, "I am going and returning" (*peytu varrain*) rather than "I am going," because those words are considered to signify death.
12. The cultural awareness of thresholds is revealed in images of divinity such as yaskshis and yakshas on the thresholds of temples throughout Hindu and Buddhist shrines.
13. It is interesting to note that in contrast to the kōlam, which signifies in a metaphorical and literal sense an auspicious passage for the person leaving the house, there are rituals of first entry into a house. For example, according to the Māyamata, an Indian treatise on architecture, once a new house is finished, the first entry is ritualized. "The entry into a house is made only when it is finished; there should be no hurry to enter an unfinished house; tardiness in entering a finished house means that none but the hosts of deities and spirits will establish themselves there . . . the house is to be entered in an auspicious way at the precisely suitable moment of an auspicious hour in a half day which accords with the horoscope, an auspicious day in an [auspicious] fortnight of an auspicious month." (Dagens 1995 [1985]: 253).
14. For an engaging and lucid analysis of thresholds of ritual time, of birth, life, and death, See Gennep (1960 [1908]). He explains the three stages: "rites of separation from a previous world, preliminal rites, those executed during the transitional stage liminal (or threshold) rites, and the ceremonies of incorporation into the new world post-liminal rites. . . . When 'guardians of the threshold' take on monumental proportions . . . they push the door and the threshold into the background; prayers and sacrifices are addressed to the guardians alone. A rite of spatial passage has become a rite of spiritual passage. The act of passing no longer accomplishes the passage; a personified power insures it through spiritual means . . . Rites of entering a house, a temple, and so forth, have their counterparts in rites of exit . . . At the time of Mohammed, the Arabs stroked the household god when entering and leaving, so that the same gesture was a rite of incorporation or a rite of separation, depending on the case. In the same way, whenever an Orthodox Jew passes through the main door of a house, a finger of his right hand touches the mezuzah, a casket attached to the doorpost" (21–25). This work is extended in Turner (1969).
15. For a detailed understanding of the ways in which the Tamil ideas of land (*oor*) are intertwined with senses of self and identity, see Daniel (1984). For a provocative analysis of the ways in which medieval textual understandings of bhakti literature have physical, psychological, and cultural reinterpretations in contemporary Tamil society, see Trawick (1994). For a fascinating analysis of Tamil ritual possession and its relation to a sense of the self, see Nabokov (2000).
16. See the folklorist and filmmaker Les Blank's film *Gap-Toothed Women* (1987) for a short clip of a kōlam being made in California.
17. Chatterji (1948). See also Chitrangsu Institute of Art & Handicraft (1994); Das Gupta (1960); Gupta (1983); and "Reviving Hindu Tradition Through Alpana" (2009). For a broader view of how Indian art engaged with Western notions of aesthetics see Guha-Thakurta (1992).
18. In October 2013, a conference entitled *From Floor to Ceiling: A Symposium on South Asian Floor-Drawings and Murals* was held at the University of Westminster, London. Organized by Dr. Aurogeeta Das, it brought together leading scholars who were researching various Indian ephemeral ritual arts. This unique conference brought together presentations on the kōlam; muggu; Maithili wall paintings; Santal painting and plastering practices; Caa-Cin, a door-painting tradition in Nepal; Haryana's wall painting tradition; and many more. See http://www.westminster.ac.uk/india-media/events/from-floor-to-ceiling for details on speakers

and topics. For a photographic general introduction, see Mookerjee (1994, 1988) and Huyler (1994). See also Pearson (1996).

19. See Layard (1937). He narrates C. N. Deedes' introduction to the labyrinths connected with the royal tombs of Egypt, where the object of the labyrinth was (1) to exclude the uninitiated from participating in the life after death and (2) to prevent inauspicious and unlucky influences from entering. He elaborates on the labyrinth ritual dance, involving the drawing of labyrinths in the sand, practiced in the Melanesian island of Malekula. Here it is a part of a mortuary rite involving the concept of life after death. Subsequently, he concludes that similar designs are now made by native Indians as games of skill. In the book *Rangoli* by Panditin Godavaribai, published in 1867 in Mumbai, the drawing of the Chakravyuha motif being used as a game is mentioned. See also Brooke (1953); Durai (1929); and Bonnerjea (1933).

Chapter 4

1. For men there are various counterparts to the pottu, or other parallel forehead marks, although they take different forms and reveal other kinds of knowledge.
2. For Tamil understandings of the different kinds of love, kinship and childhood, see Trawick (1994), an exquisite ethnography of literature embedded in everyday life. Interestingly, she mentions the kōlam as an echo of the bilateral cross-cousin marriage pattern found in Tamil culture. For a detailed exploration of the thali, the necklace worn after marriage as a sign of marriage and the heightened state of auspiciousness of a married woman, see Reynolds (1978).
3. I wish to thank her in this special acknowledgment for her help in untangling the many intertwined issues in this chapter. In terms of Islam, there is a wave of feminist anthropological work, which may impinge on how we understand Hinduism and feminism in a contemporary society. See Lila Abu-Lughod's beautiful exploration of women's spaces and ritual powers and the complexity of understanding such subjects in her *Veiled Sentiments: Honor and Poetry in a Bedouin Society* (1986). This book had a deep influence on my own work and thinking. Her own bifurcated American cultural identity made a major contribution to the reflexive turn in anthropological theory in the 1980s and 1990s. Another of her books, *Writing Women's Worlds: Bedouin Stories* (1993), also had a deep influence on my own work. For more recent turns in understanding Islamic feminist theoretical nuances of seeing Islamic women embedded deeply within the contemporary world, see Mahmood (2005). See also the brilliant exploration and critical close reexamination of feminist theoreticians in Hidayatullah (2014).
4. See Nabokov (2000). See Hancock (1999) for her extensive ethnographic description and analysis of rituals of Brahmin women in Chennai, Tamil Nadu. Another ethnographic analysis of south Indian women's rituals that probes the role of symbolism in Karnataka is Hanchett (1988). For the role of fasts in women's ritual lives in Varanasi in northern India, see Pearson (1996).
5. Hart (1973, 1979); Daniel (1984); Wadley (1991); Snow (1991). There are numerous stories of the powers of chaste Tamil women. In the ancient classical Tamil text *Shilapadikaram*, Kannagi sets fire to the town of Madurai because of the injustice done to her husband by the king. It is because of her very chastity, loyalty, and devotion that her ritual power ignites the town and burns it down. See Adigal 2009 (1965). For a nuanced reading of the historical and literary context of Tamil understandings of chastity, see the excellent and informative Monius (2001), where she traces "the importance of virtue (kaṟpu) to the maintenance of social and cosmic order" (14) in the ancient story of Manimēkalai.
6. For example, a large kōlam outlined in red kavi signifies the highest degree of auspiciousness (first menstruation, marriage, childbirth) in an upper-caste household.
7. See the exquisite and beautiful translations of A. K. Ramanujan (1975 [1967], 1985) and his collected essays. He was a most remarkable poet, scholar, and human being.
8. Douglas (2002 [1966]) was one of the first scholars to draw the distinctions among dirt, pollution, and waste in sociological, religious, and environmental terms. In analyzing the nature of taboos and prohibitions, she delved into the Western and Christian roots of the word "pollution." For some other critically important texts on the complex paradoxes with which

to read menstrual and ritual pollution practices around the world, see Buckley (1988) and Douglas (2002). Buckley (1988) lays out the deep ambiguity between women's power and menstrual ritual pollution throughout the world. This was the first time I found my own ambivalent experiences with menstrual pollution reflected in a scholarly text. He presents many examples of how the experience of menstruation and the taboos traditionally associated with it have both given power to women and taken power away.

9. The Tamil word for dancing girl/prostitute, *dēvadāsi*, straddles the world of the betwixt and between, considered both auspicious and impure. Apffell-Marglin (1985) has elaborated brilliantly on this complex paradox. See Soneji (2012).
10. I would like to thank Frederique Apffell-Marglin here for this important insight.
11. I wish to thank Frederique Apffell-Marglin for extended conversations regarding this conundrum of the ambivalence latent in the kōlam and for her help in unwinding this particularly difficult paradox. See Apffell-Marglin (2012), which focuses on menstruating goddesses, for groundbreaking scholarship on Hinduism, female ritual power, and auspiciousness.
12. See Rudolph (1987) for a glimpse of an entire country on the move ritually working on bringing Lakshmi into their households, prefiguring an increase in middle-class wealth, though the poor still are the majority. It is even more of a challenge for the poor and unconnected to make it into the middle class as class segregation increases. See Rhodes (2012) for a brilliant evocation of the layers of the goddess Lakshmi in Indian society.

Chapter 5

1. See Cutler's (1987: 8) introduction on the Tamil Bhakti saints of both Vaishnavite and Shaivite persuasions. For a Shaivite perspective on bhakti in Tamil Nadu, see Ramanujan (1985); Peterson (1989); and Yocum (1982). For a wider perspective on the India-wide phenomenon of the bhakti movement, see Hawley (2005) and Hess (2002, 2015).
2. Though there are many references to the word *kōlam* in the ancient classical Tamil literature of the third century BCE to the fifth century CE (what is called the literature of the classical Sangam age), none of them seem, in my close examination, to be referencing specifically the kōlam of the ritual designs; rather, they refer to the other meanings of the Tamil word *kōlam*: beauty, form, and disguise (*Tamil Lexicon* 1982). Āṇṭāḷ may not actually have been the first Tamil woman to create the ritual practice of the kōlam as an offering to Vishnu, as the practice seems to refer to something ordinary, not extraordinarily inventive or new. See the excellent translation and interpretation of both of these poems and their multilayered interpretations by Venkatesan (2010). I wish to especially thank Professors Kausalya Hart, George Hart, and S. Bharathy at UC Berkeley for their special assistance on this translation and interpretation during the penultimate revision of this section. I wish to thank Professors George and Kausalya Hart for the deeper work of translations of these poems and many others, especially during the many Tamil classes I was privileged to take while they were teaching at UC Berkeley. That Tamil translation work provides the foundational basis of this chapter, though I have used none of my own translations in this chapter. It allowed me to follow Dehejia's and Venketesan's translations and examine several commentaries in order to reach the conclusions I arrived at in this chapter.
3. For an excellent recent translation of both of Āṇṭāḷ's poems, see Venketesan (2010). For an excellent introduction to Āṇṭāḷ and her poetry, see Dehejia (1990) and Āṇṭāḷ (1979). See Narayanan (1999, 1995, 1994, 1987) for notions of devotion in Srivaishnava literature and commentary traditions. For recent commentaries in English and Tamil on Āṇṭāḷ's poetics and social context, see Āṇṭāḷ (1976, 1987, 1989). For a detailed guide to the Sri Āṇṭāḷ Temple in Srīvilliputtūr, see Kaliyanam (1971). For detailed explications of one of her most popularly known songs, see Iyengar (1961); Simha (1982); and Filliozat (1972). For an elaborate exegesis of Āṇṭāḷ's other popular work, see *Nācchiyār Thirumoḻi* (1966). For understanding Āṇṭāḷ as a child, see Naidu (1968).
4. Cutler (1987) briefly refers to Āṇṭāḷ's ambivalent position as a "saint" in the canon of Vaishnavite Bhakti poets. According to Cutler, she is not always included in the canon because "she is considered to be an incarnation of the goddess Earth (Bhūdevi)" (13).

5. On the use of folk narratives in elucidating aspects of a religious tradition, see Narayan (1989), where she teases apart in a lively way one saintly storyteller's tales of saints and scoundrels. This work brings out the multiple complexities of audience, storyteller, and observer interactions.
6. See Venketesan (2010: 6) and the first two chapters of Dehejia (1990).
7. In the Bhakti tradition in Tamil Nadu, the only other female saint is the Shaivite Karaiikal Ammaiyal. See Craddock (2010) for a thoughtful translation.
8. Āṇṭāḷ's name is derived from the word *āntu*, meaning "to rule." However, it is usually referred to in the context of a king's rule. It is interesting to note that the name attributed to a woman saint means "to rule." For an understanding of the relationships between the notions of the king, woman, and power in ancient Tamil culture, see Hart (1973, 1975, 1979).
9. I have condensed the stories into a singular narrative.
10. Since Āṇṭāḷ was adopted, her caste origin is unclear.
11. In the common ritual paradigm, devotees receive the flower garland as prasād. Prasād generally refers to blessed objects that are, in turn, given to devotees, including food, kumkum, flowers, and cloth. Denotatively, the prasād means "clearness" and "grace." The prasād is not received until after it has been offered at the pujā, the most common worship ceremony in Hinduism. If the prasād has been tasted, smelled, worn, or consumed before the offering in any way, then the object is no longer eligible to be blessed because it has been ritually polluted.
12. Āṇṭāḷ is not the only Tamil saint who wins the love of God through transgression. Another famous saint was the Shaivite Nandanār, an untouchable who offered "polluted" substances, such as meat and alcohol. In another transgression story, the wife of the Brahmin Nila-nakkar spat on the linga out of a desire to protect it from a falling spider. For these and other examples, see Dehejia's (1988) chapter on "The Cult of Saints."
13. Another contradiction to the mainstream belief system is the offering of ritually polluted substances to the divine in tantric rituals.
14. In conversation with Kausalya and George Hart (2015).
15. The reach of the *Tiruppāvais* was earlier limited to mostly Vaishnava sects, but it has recently become much more widely available through the proliferation of radio, TV, and the internet. It has become identified as more Tamil, just as the kōlam has come to the forefront because of the increasing circulation of modern print and digital media.
16. I wish to thank the brilliant lecturer Mrs. Kausalya Hart, who guided me in this task.
17. See also the section entitled "Kōlam: The Reality at the Threshold" (3–12) for a lovely philosophical elaboration on the significance of the kōlam and the threshold in Tamil culture. This tale is from Ellappayiṉār's 16th-century text, *Aruṇācalapurāṇam*. This reference is also cited by Ascher in her "Figures on the Threshold" article.

Chapter 6

1. These labyrinth kōlams are the focus in the field of folklore (Brooke 1953; Layard 1937). According to Tadvalkar (2012), "Another reference in this regard is an old rangoli book published in Mumbai in 1867, consisting of rangoli designs with the names and description of each design. In this book, the writer Godavaribai Panditin refers to a kōlam pattern as 'Telangi bhool' which means 'a maze or a mysterious diagram' from Telangana." This refers to the chapbook by Godavaribai Panditin, Rangavallika, Part 1 (Trimbak Janardan Gurjar, Mumbai, 1st ed., 1867). I have not been able to locate it, but it has been referred to both by Layard (1937) and Tadvalkar (2012). It is interesting to note that these chapbooks were important enough to be a part of the earliest publishing history of typeset books in India.
2. For a detailed examination of the temples themselves, see the excellent Raghavan and Narayan (2005).
3. Saroja (1992, 116–117). See also V. Saroja's excellent and thorough Ph.D. dissertation on the kōlam (1988). See also Balu; Pirasuram (1986, 1989 [1980]); Krishnamurthy (1986); Saraswathi and Vijayalakshmi (1991); Illustration by Ramnarayan, Gowri (2007).
4. Thanks to Omar Khan for giving me permission to use this postcard.
5. From the Roja Mutthiah Library collections in Chennai (Rangaswamy Mudaliyar 1928).

6. Chandralekha, in personal conversation with Vijaya Nagarajan, March 1993, Chennai. I met Chandralekha in January 1988 through my friend Parimala, and we hit it off immediately. From 1988 to 2005, we met as often as we could. For many years, she provided a beautiful space of hospitality for me in India, a home away from home where I saw her work with her dancers in her beautiful open-to-the-sky theater in Chennai. Here I saw many of her choreographies as they were being developed. In 1991, as a community organizer and co-Director of the Institute for the Study of Natural & Cultural Resources, we, Lee Swenson and I, helped bring her and her entire troupe to Sicily for the GAIA conference and was instrumental in nominating her for the prestigious GAIA award she received there (September 1991). In 1992, we brought her with other activists and artists to a 10-day traveling seminar-workshop I helped organize with Lee Swenson, W. S. Merwin, and Paula Merwin on *Language, Land and Water in Hawaii* with Rina Swentzell, Tryone Cashman, Margaret Schink, and others (August 1992). In 1993, we brought her to a 10-day seminar-workshop, *On The Commons*, we, Lee Swenson and I, co-organized with Lexi Rome and Kate Strasburg in Montana. We brought together Dashrat Patel, Malcolm Margolin, Rueben Margolin, John McKnight, Wolfgang Sachs, W. S. Merwin and Paula Merwin, and Terry Tempest Williams. In 1997, we brought Chandralekha to Berkeley with Sadanand Menon for a symposium, *Wise, Working Women*, with Maxine Hong Kingston, Grace Paley, and Terry Tempest Williams (December 1997). Over those years I met her and her dance troupe in Frankfurt (1995) and New York City (1998). Throughout this period, I saw most of her dance productions.
7. A few women referred to something mysterious and baffling: that Bharatanatyam dancers actually performed the kōlam with their feet while they were dancing. M. S. Subhalakshmi confirmed that she had done this herself when she was a child learning how to dance in Madurai in the 1930s.

Chapter 7

1. I was awarded the Kathryn Green Fund Fellowship Award for the Djerassi Foundation Resident Artists Program, 2013, and this opportunity was critical in formulating, analyzing, and understanding these challenging materials. This chapter is also based on a constellation of invited lectures. I want to thank foremost Piero Scaruffi, who was incredibly encouraging and supportive. The first and most important was "Embedded Mathematics in Women's Ritual Art from South India," for LASER (Leonardo Art Science Evening Rendezvous) at the University of San Francisco, September 2012; Stanford University, California, April 2013; and UC Berkeley, June 2013. Then, I want to thank Aurogeeta Das, who invited me to the wonderful *Symposium on South Asian Floor-Drawings and Murals* at the Center for Research and Education in Art and Media and South Asian Arts Groups, University of Westminster, London, October 25–27, 2013. The next critical site was at the National Academy of Sciences in Washington D. C. in March 2013 (thanks to J. D. Talasek for inviting my mother and me there); DC Art Science Evening Rendezvous, DASER. Finally, the Department of Theology and Religious Studies Colloquium at University of San Francisco was critical in helping me initially formulate my thoughts in September 2012.
2. I had heard a brilliant paper on the kōlam and mathematics by the anthropologist E. Valentine Daniel (1986).
3. Dr. C. V. Seshadiri was, until his untimely accidental death in 1995, one of the leading philosopher-scientists in India, a Gandhian who founded a remarkable alternative technology center, the Murugappa Chettiar Research Center—Photosynthesis and Energy Division in the village of Tharamani in 1976, then just outside Madras. Here some of the earliest research into solar energy, biogas plants, traditional boats, nutritional algae, organic food (vegetable gardens and rice), and windmills was conducted. This chapter is dedicated to his memory. This chapter is also dedicated to my father, Mr. Rettakudi G. Nagarajan, who instilled in me early on a love of mathematics and all things mathematical.
4. See Marcia Ascher's excellent article summarizing mathematicians' understandings of the kōlam (2002c). In Ascher (2002a) she lays out the structuring of time, the logic of divination, and models and maps. See especially Chapter 6, "Figures on the Threshold" (161–89); it has a summary and analysis of much of the key literature on kōlam and mathematics.

See also her 1991 survey of ethnomathematics around the world. This book lays the foundation of ethnomathematics; in one of the chapters, she explores the tracing of graphs in the sand in Angola called *sona* and *lusona*, which are very similar in graphical structure to the pulli kōlams; these diagrams are called by names such as a leopard with his cubs, Muyombo trees, a small animal that lives in a tree hold and pierces the intestines, the marks on the ground left by a chicken when it is chased, fire, and so forth (39–45). Ascher's deep theoretical work has profoundly shaped the ways in which kōlam has been viewed in the field of mathematics and computer science. Her articles and books are major reference points in this chapter and I am extremely grateful for her intensive and careful work in understanding and translating what the kōlam means mathematically. For a broader examination of the ways in which elemental discoveries in Western traditions of mathematics have been intertwined with non-Western traditions of mathematics, see George Joseph's profound 1991 book, in which he traces the multiple ways in which ritual mathematics in non-European contexts has influenced general Western mathematical theory throughout history. Recently, Sunita Vatuk (2012) has been exploring the intersection between mathematics and the kōlam in a more systematic way.

5. By no means is this chapter meant to be comprehensive. We still need a major work summarizing the mathematical properties of kōlam. This chapter is just a brief introduction to this vast body of work. See also Waring (2012) and Mall (2007).
6. For those pursuing kōlam research in the future, this would be an interestingly line of inquiry to pursue. How did women themselves rank the value of each kind of kōlam? Did this have any relationship to class, caste, language, region, or other variables?
7. According to Jablan, the symbolic meaning of point includes the "primeval element, beginning, and kernel; . . . the symbol of the beginning (grain of seed) and of the end (grain of dust); it represents the smallest substance . . . The point is in fact imaginary: it occupies no space" (Jablan 2002: 262). For a fascinating overview of the theory of symmetry and ornamental art, especially in tilings, Celtic art, and knot designs, see Jablan (2002), Chapter 5 ("The Theory of Symmetry and Ornamental Art," 243–266) and Chapter 6 ("Modularity in Art," 267–302). For a deeper exploration of symmetry in mathematics, art, and nature, see Field and Golubitsky (2009) and Hargittai and Hargittai (1994).
8. See William Jackson's website: http://liberalarts.iupui.edu/~wijackso/tempfrac/. See also Jackson (2004).
9. I wish to thank my children, Jaya and Uma, for helping explain what this means to me.
10. The kōlam is such a critical area of inquiry that in November 2006, in Osaka, Japan, an entire international conference was devoted to its designs. Many leading mathematicians and scientists who have been focusing on it as a site of research gathered from around the world to share ideas. See http://wwwsoc.nii.ac.jp/form/62th-sympo-kolam.htm. In addition, there are now numerous websites devoted to the kōlam designs and millions of citations when one simply Googles the world *kōlam*.
11. He even attempts a classification system: finite matrix kōlams, regular matrix kōlams, pattern languages, and array kōlams. See Asher (2002a, 2002c). See also Siromoney et al. (1972, 1973, 1974) for more detailed explanations and elaborations. See also Subramanian et al. (2006); Narasimhan (1989); and Vatuk (2012).
12. For example, see Ascher (2002a: 184, Stage 1, Stage 2, Stage 3).
13. For a summary of the deeper understanding of picture languages and array grammars, see the excellent and thorough Ascher (2002a, 2002b). See Siromoney (1978, 1986) and Siromoney et al. (1989) for a direct perspective from computer science and mathematics. See also Ehrig et al. (2008).
14. The kōlam took up a 6,600-square-foot area, took five hours to make (from 7 a.m. to noon)) and used 150 kg of white stone powder.
15. According to Lakoff and Nunez, "The Basic Metaphor of Infinity," a single general conceptual metaphor that accounts for multiple mathematical understandings of infinity, has large implications in terms of iterative processes, potential and actual notions of infinity, and how these ideas apply in geometry and induction. See especially Part III: "The Embodiment of Infinity" (155–258) and especially Chapter 8 (155–80). For cross-cultural explorations of the notions of infinity, see Mimica (1988).

16. It is difficult not to note the extraordinary mathematical achievements of the Tamil mathematician Srinivas Ramanujan, who worked with the concept of infinity in the context of number theory and who treated his mathematical powers as a gift from the goddess, and mathematics itself as sacred. In *The Man Who Knew Infinity* (1992), a remarkable biography of Ramanujan, Robert Kanigal says that he "all his life believed in the . . . landscape of the Infinite, in realms both mathematical and spiritual" (7). It is striking that similar to Ramanujan's insights into the nature of infinity, Tamil women seem to intuitively grasp the infinite reach of their kōlams as the dots extend outward into space. I did not find any explicit connection between the kōlam and Ramanujan's mathematical intuitions in his papers at Cambridge University, but one can imagine that the kōlam may have had an influence on him as his mother must have done the kōlams regularly in Kumbakonam, the town where he grew up. Given his adoration of his mother and the goddess of mathematics, I would like to think that he may have been influenced at the subconscious level by geometric patterns found in the kōlam that evoke infinity. See also the film version of Kanigal's book, *The Man Who Knew Infinity* (2016), directed by Matt Brown.
17. Chandralekha, conversation with Vijaya Nagarajan, March 1993, Chennai.

Chapter 8

1. An earlier draft of this chapter was published as Nagarajan (2001).
2. I am grateful to Professor Paula Richman, who took the time out of her busy schedule in early January 1994 to meet me while I was in Madras. She encouraged me to follow the thread of these kōlam competitions. I went to at least six of them during the last six weeks in Thirunelveli, Salem, Coimbatore, and Madurai and observed them in abundance in women's magazines and newspapers. In the winter of 1998–1999, I went to a kōlam competition sponsored by the Thanjavur Art College, where there were many more male judges and some professors from local art colleges, and one of the winning designs was an illustration of ballroom dancing of the hero and heroine from the then-popular film "Titanic." There was little debate about the nature of the kōlam; here, it seemed the painting-style kōlam won the day. I am not sure whether this shift was historical and was happening throughout Tamil Nadu, or whether this was attributable to a local permutation. This chapter could easily have turned into an entire book, as there seemed an infinite number of kōlam competitions.
3. My current research extends the understanding of the commons by looking closely at what I term "the languages of the commons." The kōlam in its own way is a kind of a language of the commons in Tamil Nadu. The kōlam, too, illustrates the distinction between public and private space. It is one of the markers of the commons, a ritual art form that provides a porous divider between the public and the private, the family from the community, the sacred from the profane, the special and the reverent from the everyday. In yet another profound way, it also makes the everyday reverent.
4. See Barnard Bate's excellent study on the Tamil debating tradition, the pattimanrams, in his 2009 book. See Seizer (2005).
5. Visālakshi does not train the children in just the songs of the Vaishnavite saint Āṇṭāḷ; she also teaches the Shaivite male saint Manikkavacagar's *Thiruvācagam*, which also has a special place during this month. However, this chapter will not deal with Manikkavacagar's work. For an elaboration of Manikkavacagar and his poetry, see Yocum (1982).
6. There was debate among the judges as to the age at which a girl was required to enter the women's division—that is, when her skill had reached such a level that it was no longer considered fair for her to compete with the children. The age decided upon was 14. For the most part, the judges knew when a girl was 14 because they had known her all her life. If she falsely entered a lower age to have a better chance at winning a prize, her name would immediately be whisked to the adult women's section and her chances of winning would be lost.
7. One of women's expressive traditions in northern India, the rangōli is a ritual art parallel to the kōlam. The word "rang" means color in Hindi and refers to the most significant aspect of these designs, which is their bright colorfulness.
8. Sumathi Ramaswamy (1997) has explored brilliantly the multiple historical attachments and drives Tamils have toward their Tamil language.

9. It has become a trend in recent competitions to write down the names of the makers alongside their kōlams in order to identify the competitors.

Chapter 9

1. An earlier draft of this chapter was published as Nagarajan (1998).
2. I wish to thank Ann Gold, Ramchandra Guha, Wolfgang Sachs, Lance Nelson, and Christopher Chapple for encouragement, support, and critical readings of this chapter along the path of its development.
3. For a broad introduction to the incarnation of Vishnu as Varāha, see Nagar (1993). For a fascinating explanation of the image of the earth being transmogrified from a beautiful goddess to a cartographic globe held aloft by Varāha, see Ramaswamy (2007). She states, "modern mapped knowledge is hijacked to ensure the survival of the gods . . . the visual image of Earth as an impersonal spherical globe rather than a sentient female or even an animated entity" (28). It remains to be seen how this transformation would affect Hindus' perception of the earth itself—of nature embodied by the goddess earth. See also Chapple and Dwivedi (2011).
4. I am looking at this phenomenologically and how this belief operates ecologically. As far as the feminist issues this gendered earth brings up, that is another matter and cannot be discussed in full here.
5. I am grateful to Bob Goldman at UC Berkeley for this insight.
6. It is interesting to note here a comparison between hunting cultures and the prayers that hunters make before and after the hunt, in a spirit of both thankfulness and forgiveness. This highlights the question: What do we mean by the very notion of "ecological"? It could mean the idea of a balanced population/resources continuum or some other imaginations of this relationship. See Richard K. Nelson's fascinating and rich repertoire of excellent books (1983, 1986, 1989, 1997) tracing the embedded relationships that the Koyukon people have with their environment, especially in the realm of hunting animals. For a complex rendering of embedded relationships of Euro-American discourses about deer, see Nelson (1997).
7. See Patton's brilliant and compelling treatise on a variation of this important theme in ancient Greek mythology in her 2006 book. See Eck (1982a, 1982b) and Darian (1978). For a thorough understanding of the religious meanings of rivers in Maharashtra and especially their feminine qualities, see the excellent Feldhaus (1995). See Baviskar (2003) for a beautiful rendering of the magnificence of Indian rivers in poetics, ecology, and religiosity.
8. For an excellent examination of anthropological theories of pollution, see the classics Buckley (1988) and Douglas 2002 (1966).
9. For a complex reading of the ways in which wilderness interlaces with cultural imaginations of nature and culture, see William Cronon's brilliant collection of articles (1996). See Swearer's more recent collection of engaging articles on the concept of ecologies of flourishing for all (2011). Three important critical recent works dealing with Native American ecological knowledge are Menzies (2006), Slater (2002), and Anderson (2005). For the multiple stories involving wood and civilization across five cultures and five thousand years, see Perlin (2005 [1989]).
10. I remember first thinking of this term during my talk "Hosting the Divine: Ganges, Cowdung and Other Everyday Ecolog(ies) of the Imagination" at UC Berkeley on May 10, 1995, as part of a series on *The Himalayan Experience* organized by Meenu Singh.
11. Ironically, after the start of the Iraq war in 2003 and the media coverage from reporters who were embedded within the troops, the whole notion of embeddedness became more familiar to the public as a whole.
12. For a fascinating inquiry into another aspect of embedded ecologies, see DeLoughrey and Handley (2011).
13. For religious constitution of rivers, see especially Eck (1982) on the Ganges as a goddess and see Feldhaus (1995) for an ethnographic and textual exploration of rivers as women and female goddesses in Maharashtra. See Eck's (2012) excellent and brilliant comprehensive work. See David Haberman's (2006) rich, textual and ethnographic work on the Yamuna

river. For sacred plants, trees, and forests, see Narayan (1997, 1995) and Pintchman (2005); Gold (2001); Haberman (2013); Kent (2013); and Nugteren (2005).

14. For a fascinating exploration of ritual, see Humphrey (1994: vii). She begins with a description of a seemingly ambiguous stance toward ritual: "we grew increasingly puzzled: what were these 'meanings' which seems so weighty in import, and yet so lightly and variously applied?" Humphreys delves into a theory of ritual action that captures its nondogmatic and playful side. See also Bell (1992) for an excellent overview of the ritual literature.
15. See Stanley (1977) for another kind of intermittent sacrality, here defined by both time and space.
16. One of the most fascinating sites of inquiry is pilgrimage to natural places. See Eck (1982a, 2012) and Haberman (1994).
17. See Douglas 2002 (1966) and Ortner (1974: 72) for important theoretical discussions of pollution, taboo and the feminization of the nature and culture distinction. According to Ortner, "the categories of 'nature' and 'culture' are of course conceptual categories—one can find no boundary out in the actual world between the two states or realms of being. And there is no question that some cultures articulate a much stronger opposition between the two categories than others—it has even been argued that primitive peoples (some or all) do not see or intuit any distinction between the human cultural state and the state of nature at all. Yet I would maintain that the universality of ritual betokens an assertion in all human cultures of the specifically human ability to act upon and regulate, rather than passively move with and be moved by, the givens of natural existence. In ritual, the purposive manipulation of given forms toward regulating and sustaining order, every culture asserts that proper relations between human existence and natural forces depend upon culture's employing its special powers to regulate the overall processes of the world and life." See Grimes (2006: 131–46) for a careful distinction between ritual and ecology and its creation of cosmological orientations.
18. For a general overview of ecology and religion, see Kinsley (1995). For particular ethnographies of religions to specific places, see for Northern California, Margolin (1978); for Alaska, see Nelson (1983); for South Asia, see Zimmerman (1987).
19. Schama recognizes the historicity of the perception of the environment in the American environmental movement. He refers to American environmentalists' desire to have the landscape be emptied of humans, to be pure and preserved, in order to save the environment. In the late 19th century, this movement was able to save Yosemite in California, but only at the cost of removing the indigenous peoples already living there. Early environmentalists did not see the removal of indigenous peoples as inimical to the environmental movement. Similarly, the sacred *tulasi* plant represents for Shiva a way of seeing the world that is automatically believed to be conservation-oriented. Here, too, the complexity of assumptions tied to this belief is not clear.
20. Furthermore, in this text Shiva fails to draw sufficient distinctions between Hinduism and other religious communities within India. India is made equivalent to Hinduism and vice versa. Certain aspects of isolated pieces of classical Hindu myths are, moreover, essentialized to represent all of Hinduism.
21. In the specific example of the Ganges watershed, two large dams built by the British colonialists in the 1860s significantly altered the quality and quantity of water flowing downstream. The population explosion is another factor contributing to the change in scale of pollution and its effects.
22. For beautiful stories about the tulsi plant see Narayan (1995a, 1997).
23. See Worster (1977), Devall and Sessions (1985), Chapple (1993), and Schama (1995) for an introduction to this field. See also Arnold and Guha (1995) for an extended introduction to the environmental history of South Asia. For important insights into the relationship between knowledge and environmental destruction, see Banuri (1993).
24. For a brilliant description and poetic analysis of Tamil notions of landscape, see Ramanujan (1994, 1985: 229–317). See Kellert (1993) for elaborate deliberations on the relations between ethics, economics, and ecology and Kellert (2010) for the ways in which human values shape the human perception of the natural world.
25. For a fascinating pamphlet on the complex relationship between "faith" and "reason" in the recent Indian context, see Bharucha (1993).

26. Several major movements come to mind: in Vrindavan, the reforestation campaign; the Swatcha Ganga Campaign in Banaras to clean the river Ganga; and in the foothills of the Himalayas, the Chipko movement to plant trees and prevent deforestation. See the excellent book by Baviskar (2003).
27. The complexity of ecological themes embedded within cultural traditions is explored deeply in the following works. In South Asia, Zimmerman (1987) provides an excellent exposition of the notion of "jungle," both in the Indian landscape and in Indian medicine. His comparison and analysis of categories that flow back and forth between the body and the landscape remains one of the key contributions to "embedded ecologies." Reichel-Dolmatoff (1996) offers a remarkable testimonial to a carefully researched and lived understanding of the Amazon Tukano people. He is concerned with "meaning, with the ways in which the Indians interpret their lives and their environments . . . Meaning can be found in attitudes and daily conversations, in myths and spells, in the manner in which people describe events and emotions, or in the words they use to explain rules of behavior, the do's and don'ts of everyday existence" (7). See Guss (1989) for a story that begins with basketry and ends with cosmology among the Yekuana in Venezuela. Jackson (1995) offers a meditation on the aboriginal understanding of home and the world within a landscape. Lansing (1991) and Evers (1987) provide other examples: water tanks in Bali and deer songs among the Yaqui in the southwestern United States.

Chapter 10

1. *Tamil Lexicon*, Madras (1982: 1859–1860; 2119–2120) for epigraph at beginning of chapter. For an earlier version of this chapter see Nagarajan (2000).
2. For a profound and deep understanding of the relationship amongst hospitality, charity, and the Christian Church throughout history, see the work of Ivan Illich. Cayley (2005) examines closely the historical development of the Christian notion of individualized or familiar hospitality to the stranger to its transformation of serving strangers in institutionalized forms, such as hostels, hospitals, and hotels. See also Cayley (1992). Illich's own works include his many books (1969, 1973, 1974, and 1987).
3. For an elaboration of the concept of moral ecology, see Gold and Gujar (2002). For a profound understanding of ritual ecology, see Apfell-Marglin (2012).
4. Thanks to David Shulman, Wendy Doniger, Martha Selby, Patrick Olivelle, Lawrence Cohen, and several priests at the Siva-Vishnu Temple in Lanham, Maryland, for responding quickly to my requests about possible literary sources for the oral reference to "feeding a thousand souls."
5. This section I dedicate to the author Michael Pollan. I recommend highly his excellent and provocative 2001 book, which propelled and shaped this section.
6. In everyday Tamil discourse, the word *kudi* often implies a kind of rented situation. For example, kudi literally refers to subjects, citizens, family, house, and residence. In addition, it means "to occupy, to take possession of the mind as a deity." A frequent referent to the residency of a divinity, kudi is often used in the context of kudi irukkuruthu, or "being housed."
7. The tāli is usually a gold necklace with a pendant that is given to the wife upon the completion of the marriage rite. The pendant's ornate symbols often depict each household's god or goddess, symbolizing the unification of the two families. One can often guess the caste, class, and region of the wearer from the design motifs.
8. It is reminiscent of George Lakoff and Mark Johnson's 1980 classic. See also Lakoff (1990), another provocative work on metaphor theory and what belongs with what.
9. For a wonderfully researched ethnography on the relationship between trees and Hindus in North India, see Haberman (2013). For the complexity of relationships between sacred groves and environmentalists in Tamil Nadu, see Kent (2013). For more on tree weddings in North India, see Penkower and Pintchman (2014).
10. Indian Americans also perform tree marriages. They return to their home village in India to fix a marital situation that has been deemed extremely unlucky (e.g., divorce, death). This phenomenon is not limited to Tamil Nadu but can also found in Gujarat.

Chapter 11

1. I wish to thank my dear friend in Chennai, Parimala Rao, for helping me solve the problem of this chapter. She introduced me to Bhamini Narayan and Amrita Narayan, who showed me the important book by Bajāj and Śrīnivās (1996). I presented earlier versions of this chapter at the TedX Golden Gate ED event in Richmond, California, on June 11, 2011; at the 22nd Annual Bioneers Conference, San Raphael, California, October 14–16, 2011; and at the Eighth Annual Tamil Conference, Berkeley, California, April 20, 2011.
2. Kethu is one of the nine heavenly forces or *navagrahas*; the nine comprise the five visible planets (Mercury, Venus, Mars, Jupiter, Saturn) and the four forces that are said to influence the earth in the solar system (the Sun, the Moon, Rāghu [the ascending lunar mode], and Kethu [the descending lunar mode]). The lunar modes are the points of intersection of the orbital paths of the sun and the moon. Kethu is the descending lunar mode, when the moon on its orbit crosses south of the path of the sun as seen from earth (elliptic). These nine astronomical forces are said to be strong forces that influence individual lives; they can be positive or negative.
3. Thank you to Martha Selby, Patrick Olivelle, Robert Goldman, Wendy Doniger, and Laurence Cohen for their help in locating clues to this phenomenon.
4. One elderly woman, Lakshmi, even told me you had to feed ten thousand people by the sea if you are serious about expressing generosity to strangers. This seemed to be the most challenging way to fulfill this requirement.
5. For an elaboration on the term "moral ecology" see Gold (1998).
6. Some of the other persons in this category are men who are well versed in the Vedas and men who are 100 years old, among others (Olivelle 2005: 118).
7. Another context in which this becomes important is among elderly Indian American immigrants. See Mazumdar and Shampa (2005).
8. Olivelle (1999) expounds on four different surviving texts ascribed to four individual authors: Āpastamba, Gautama, Baudhāyana, and Vasiṣṭha (xxv). If we look at these four authors' texts more closely, we find some further elaborations of the notion of household sacrifice and feeding strangers. Āpastamba says, "The ground where each Bali offering is made should be consecrated. He should sweep the area with his hand, sprinkling water on it, put down the offering, and then sprinkle water all around" (46). He adds the extension of these offerings at the threshold at the front doorway: "If a man makes these offerings steadfastly in the prescribed manner, he obtains heaven forever, as well as prosperity" (46). Under the section "Distribution of Food and Reception of Guests," he advises: "He should always feed his guests first . . . The master and mistress should never rebuff anyone who comes asking for food at the proper time . . . A couple who acts this way wins a world without end." Gautama says it more pithily: "Oblations are offered also to the *Maruts* at the doors to the house . . . to the guardian deities of the house . . . and to night-stalkers in the evening." About feeding guests, Bauhāyana states: "Every day he should pay homage, even it is just with some flowers. In this way he fulfills that Bali sacrifice to beings" (192). Vasiṣṭha says something contradictory: "Even a rich man should not indulge in feeding a large number" (276). He argues that feeding too large a number decreases the quality of the sacrifice; you are better off to feed one person really well.
9. Thanks to Bethany Schmid for this idea.
10. The Mahabharata, one of the two great epics of ancient India, is the story of Krishna. One of the highlights of this story is the battle between the Pandavas, the five brothers on one side of the family, and their cousins, Duryōdhana and his 100 brothers. For more insight, see Bajāj and Śrīnivās (1996: 109–20).
11. Rajagopalachari (1981) has translated a collection of ancient proverbs, the *Kural*, that have influenced Tamil culture deeply throughout the past 2,000 years. It has sections on virtue, wealth, and love. See also Sundaram (1989).
12. This book explains clearly the centrality of the greatness of food and the giving of food in the Hindu epics the Ramayana and the Mahabharata, as well as the dharmaśāstras and the gṛhastras. It also explains the political manifestation and political centrality in the giving of food in the *chatrams* of Thanjavur, an institution of hospitality run by the queen as recently

as the late 18th century. It briefly traces the collapse of the kingly discipline to feed strangers with the onset of British colonialism. Jamison (1996) provides an excellent exploration of the ancient Vedic construction of the relationship between hospitality and the wife's ritual power.

13. There is a close parallel in Christianity. As Jesus sits opposite the temple treasury, watching the crowds putting in enormous amounts of money, he witnesses a poor widow offering two copper coins, adding up to a penny. "And he called his disciples to him and said to them, "Truly, I say to you, this poor widow has put in more than all those who are contributing to the treasury. For they all contributed out of their abundance; but she out of her poverty has put in everything she had, her whole living" (Mark 12:41–44, Revised Standard Version of the *Bible*). Thanks to the *Book Writing World* writing group and especially Leah for telling me about this story. The Greek tradition of hospitality to the stranger, *xenia*, could also be relevant here, though that tradition is broader than serving food; it also includes giving clothes and a bath. (from personal conversation with Leah Gibson Page). Also, see the delightful article by O'Gorman (2003) on the ancient origins of hospitality in ancient Greece and Rome.
14. The story reveals a metonymic congruence between the king and the householder. The king and queen are the householders of the kingdom and the householders are the king and queen of the household. In a way, women householders, in performing the kōlam, are implying that in the sum of all these kinds of small actions, the woman householder is the dharmic equivalent to the power of the king. It is a question of scale, rather than different kinds of being. A similar argument is made by Apfell-Marglin (1985).
15. I want to thank Frederique Marglin for helping me understand this.
16. Other texts I consulted that were very helpful in my thinking through concepts of dharma were Gupta (2004); Hiltebeitel (2011); and Olivelle (2004). Theorization about the notion of the gift has been a recurring theme in anthropology and literature. For a brilliant analysis of the idea of the "gift" in creativity and art, see Hyde's classic work (2007 [1979]).

Chapter 12

1. I was working on my next research project, which is on sacred arborality in Tamil culture, on "treeness," spanning tree temples, sacred groves, temple forests, and mangroves and looking at the thread of the commons through all of them. Just as each divinity has a sacred animal associated with it, so, too, a sacred tree is associated with many of the Hindu divinities. As I was interested in mangroves, and the *thillai* plant is one of the keystone species in the mangrove ecosystem and is the sacred tree associated with the Dancing Shiva, this was the main reason I had gone to the Chidambaram temple several times.
2. The image of a kōlam has been used as a representative of the Institute for South Asia Studies at UC Berkeley for many decades. One of my early research assistants, Arthi Devarajan, shared an evocative video on Facebook called "Beautiful explanation of Hindu custom for Kolam." This short video reveals a philosophical exploration of the kōlam in a voice of a Tamil teenage girl. The link is https://www.facebook.com/MalaysianIndianMatrimonial/videos/791622457626752/?theater.

BIBLIOGRAPHY

Abram, David. 1996. *The Spell of the Sensuous: Perception and Language in a More-Than-Human World.* New York: Pantheon Books.

Abu-Lughod, Lila. 1986. *Veiled Sentiments: Honor and Poetry in a Bedouin Society* Berkeley: University of California Press.

———. 1993. *Writing Women's Worlds: Bedouin Stories.* Berkeley: University of California Press.

Acocella, Joan. 2003 (April 14). "Double Takes: New York premières from Paul Taylor and Mark Morris." *New Yorker.*

Adigal, Ilangô. 2009 (1965). *Shilappadikaram (The Ankle Bracelet),* trans. Alain Daniélou. New York: New Directions.

Alley, Kelley. 2002. *On the Banks of the Ganga: When Wastewater Meets a Sacred River.* Ann Arbor: University of Michigan Press.

Āṇḍāḷ. 1966. *Nācchiyār Thirumoḷi,* 5th part, trans. Annangrāchāriyāṟswami, Parapavahu. Thiruvadipuram: Sri Kanchi Pirathivāthipayangram.

Anderson, M. Kat. 2005. *Tending the Wild: Native American Knowledge and the Management of California's Natural Resources.* Berkeley: University of California Press.

Āṇṭāḷ. 1976. *Antalaruḷicceyta Tiruppāvai.* Madras: Kuvai Publications.

———. 1979. *Consider Our Vow: Translation of Tiruppāvai and Tiruvempāvai into English,* trans. Norman Cutler. Madurai: Muttu Patippakam.

———. 1987. *The Poems of Āṇṭāḷ: Tiruppavai and Nācchiyār Tirumoli,* trans. P. S. Sundaram. Bombay: Ananthacharya Indological Research Institute.

———. 1989. *Tiruppāvai Illustrations: 32 Nineteenth-Century Line Drawings.* Melkote: Tyaga Bharati Music Education Mission.

Apffel-Marglin, Frederique. 1985. *Wives of the God-King: The Rituals of the Devadasis of Puri.* Oxford: Oxford University Press.

———. 2012. *Rhythms of Life: Enacting the World with the Goddesses of India.* New Delhi: Oxford University Press.

Appadurai, Arjun. 1994. "Disjuncture and Difference in the Global Cultural Economy." In *Colonial Discourse and Post-colonial Theory: A Reader,* ed. Patrick Williams and Laura Chrisman. New York: Columbia University Press: 324–339.

Ardener, Shirley. 1993. *Women and space ground rules and social maps.* Oxford: Berg.

Arnold, David, and Ramchandra Guha. 1995. *Nature, Culture, Imperialism: Essays on the Environmental History of South Asia.* Oxford: Oxford University Press.

Ascher, Marcia. 1991. *Ethnomathematics: A Multicultural View of Mathematical Ideas.* New York: Chapman & Hall.

———. 2002a. *Mathematics Elsewhere: An Exploration of Ideas Across Cultures.* Princeton, NJ: Princeton University Press.

———. 2002b. "Figures on the Threshold." In *Mathematics Elsewhere: An Exploration of Ideas Across Cultures* (161–90). Princeton, NJ: Princeton University Press.

———. 2002c. "The Kolam Tradition: A Tradition of Figure-Drawing in Southern India Expresses Mathematical Ideas and Has Attracted the Attention of Computer Science." *American Scientist*. 90(1): 56–63.

Bajāj, Jitendra, and Maṇḍayam Doḍḍamane Śrīnivās. 1996. *Annam Bahu Kurvīta: Recollecting the Indian Discipline of Growing and Sharing Food in Plenty*. Madras: Centre for Policies Studies Madras.

Balu, Surya. n.d. *Pandigaikāla Kōlanga Pūjaiarai Kōlangal Navagraha Kōlangal Alankāra Allaku Kōlangal*. Chennai: Narmatha Pathipokam.

Banks, M. M. 1935. "Tangled Thread Mazes." *Folklore*. 46(1): 78–80.

———. 1937. "Threshold Designs." *Folklore*. 48(3): 268–9.

Banuri, Tariq, and Frederique Apffel-Marglin. 1993. *Who Will Save the Forests? Knowledge, Power and Environmental Destruction*. London: Zed Books.

Bate, Barnard. 2009. *Tamil Oratory and the Dravidian Aesthetic*. New York: Columbia University Press.

Baviskar, Amita. 2003. *Waterlines: The Penguin Book of River Writings*. New Delhi: Penguin Books.

Bell, Catherine. 1992. *Ritual Theory, Ritual Practice*. Oxford: Oxford University Press.

Berger, Allan S. 2013. "The Evil Eye: A Cautious Look." *Journal of Religion and Health*. 52(3): 785–8.

Bharucha, Rustom. 1993. *The Question of Faith*. Madras: Orient Longman.

———. 1995. *Chandralekha: Woman, Dance, Resistance*. New Delhi: Indus.

Blackburn, Stuart and A. K. Ramanujan. 1986. *Another Harmony New Essays on the Folklore of India*. Berkeley: University of California Press.

Blank, Les. 1987. *Gap-Toothed Women*. Directed by Les Blank and Maureen Gosling. Flower Films.

Blier, Suzanne Preston. 1995. *The Anatomy of Architecture: Ontology and Metaphor in Batamaliba Architectural Expression*. Chicago: University of Chicago Press.

Bonnerjea, B. 1933. "Note on Geometrical Ritual Designs in India." *Man*. 3: 163–4.

Borden, Carla. 1989. *Contemporary Indian Tradition: Voices on Culture, Nature and the Challenge of Change*. Washington D.C.: Smithsonian Institution.

Breckenridge, Carol, Ed. 1995. *Consuming Modernity: Public Culture in a South Asian World*. Minneapolis: University of Minnesota Press.

Brooke, S. C. 1953. "The Labyrinth Pattern in India." *Folklore* 64: 463–72.

Brown, Karen McCarthy. 2001 [1991]. *Mama Lola a Vodou Priestess in Brooklyn*. Berkeley: University of California Press

Buckley, Thomas, and Gottlieb, Alma. 1988. *Blood Magic: The Anthropology of Menstruation*. Berkeley: University of California Press.

Bynum, Caroline Walker. 1991. *Fragmentation and Redemption Essays on Gender and the Human Body in Medieval Religion*. London Zone Books.

Carman, John, and Frederique Apffel-Marglin, eds. 1985. *Purity and Auspiciousness in Indian Society*. International Studies in Sociology and Social Anthropology. Leiden: Brill Academic Publisher.

Carman, John, and Vasudha Narayanan. 1989. *The Tamil Veda: Piḻḻāṉ's Interpretation of the Tiruvāymoḻi*. Chicago: University of Chicago Press.

Cayley, David. 1992. *Illich in Conversation*. Toronto: Anansi Press.

———. 2005. *The River North of the Future: The Testament of Ivan Illich as Told to David Cayley*. Foreword by Charles Taylor. Toronto: Anansi Press.

Chandralekha, Dashrat Patel, and Sadhanand Menon. 1985. *Angika: Traditions of Dance and Body Language in India*. Madras: SKILLS.

Chapple, Christopher K. 1993. *Nonviolence to Animals, Earth, and Self in Asian Traditions*. Albany: State University of New York Press.

Chapple, Christopher K., and O. P. Dwivedi. 2011. *In Praise of Mother Earth: The Pṛthivī Sūkta of the Atharva Veda*. Los Angeles: Marymount Institute Press.

Chapple, Christopher K., and Mary E. Tucker, eds. 2001. *Hinduism and Ecology: The Intersection of Earth, Sky, and Water.* Cambridge, MA: Harvard University Press.

Chatterjee, Ananya. 2004. *Butting Out: Reading Resistive Choreographies Through Works by Jawole Willa Jo Zollar and Chandralekha.* Middletown, CT: Wesleyan University Press.

Chatterji, Tapanmohan, Tarakchadra Das, and Abanindranath Tagore. 1948. *Bāṅglār Brata.* Calcutta: Orient Longmans.

Chenulu, Syamala. 2007. "Teaching Mathematics Through the Art of Kolam." *Mathematics Teaching in the Middle School.* 12(8): 422–8. National Council of Teachers of Mathematics. http://www.jstor.org/stable/41182455.

Chitrangsu Institute of Art & Handicraft. 1994. *Alpana of Santiniketan School.* Calcutta: Calcutta Publication Dept.

Clifford, James. 1993. "On Collecting Art and Culture." *The Cultural Studies Reader*, ed. Simon During. New York: Routledge: 49–73.

"College Organises a Special Painting Exhibition." 2009 (Aug. 14). *The Hindu.* http://www.thehindu.com/todays-paper/tp-national/tp-tamilnadu/college-organises-a-special-painting-exhibition/article205246.ece.

Coomaraswamy, Ananda. 1929. *Yaksas.* Washington D.C.: Smithsonian Institute/Freer Gallery of Art.

Craddock, Elaine. 2010. *Siva's Demon Devotee: Karaikkal Ammaiyar.* New York: SUNY Press.

Cronon, William. 1996. *Uncommon Ground: Rethinking the Human Place in Nature.* New York: W.W. Norton & Company.

Cutler, Norman. 1987. *Songs of Experience: The Poetics of Tamil Devotion.* Religion in Asia and Africa. Bloomington: Indiana University Press.

Dagens, Bruno. 1995 (1985). *Mayamata: An Indian Treatise on Housing Architecture and Iconography.* New Delhi: Sitaram Bhartia Institute of Science and Research.

Daniel, Valentine E. 1984. *Fluid Signs: Being a Person the Tamil Way.* Berkeley: University of California Press.

———. 1986. "Decoding Kolam." Paper presented at the 15th Annual Conference of South Asia, Madison, WI, November 7–9.

Darian, Steven G. 1978. *The Ganges in Myth and History.* Honolulu: University Press of Hawaii.

Darvas, György. 2007. *Symmetry: Cultural-Historical and Ontological Aspects of Science-Arts Relations: The Natural and Man-made World in an Interdisciplinary Approach.* Basel: Birkhäuser.

Das, Aurogeeta. 2011. "Exploring Traditional and Metropolitan Indian Arts Using the Muggu Tradition as a Case Study." Ph.D. diss., University of Westminster.

———, co-organizer. 2013. "From Floor to Ceiling: A Symposium on South Asian Floor-Drawings and Murals." Conference, University of Westminster, London, October 25–26.

Das, Veena. 1995. *Critical Events: An Anthropological Perspective on Contemporary India.* New York: Oxford University Press.

Das Gupta, S. 1960. *Alpana.* Delhi: Publications Division, Ministry of Information and Broadcasting, Govt. of India.

Dean, Melanie. 2013. "From 'Evil Eye' Anxiety to the Desirability of Envy: Status, Consumption and the Politics of Visibility in Urban South India." *Contributions to Indian Sociology.* 47(2): 185–216.

Deedes, C. N. 1935. *The Labyrinth*, ed. S. H. Hooke. New York: The Macmillan Co.

Dehejia, Vidya. 1988. *Slaves of the Lord: The Path of the Tamil Saints.* New Delhi: Munshiram Manoharlal.

———. 1990. *Āṇṭāḷ and Her Path of Love: Poems of a Woman Saint from South India.* Albany: State University of New York Press.

DeLoughrey, Elizabeth, and George B. Handley, eds. 2011. *Postcolonial Ecologies: Literatures of the Environment.* New York: Oxford University Press.

Devall, Bill, and George Sessions. 1985. *Deep Ecology: Living as If Nature Mattered.* Salt Lake City: Peregrine Smith Books.

Dohmen, Renate. 2001. "Happy Homes and the Indian Nation." *Journal of Design History.* 14(2): 129–39.

———. 2004. "The Home in the World: Women, Threshold Designs and Performative Relations in Contemporary Tamil Nadu, South India." *Cultural Geographies.* 11: 7–25.

Doniger, Wendy. 1991. *The Laws of Manu.* New Delhi: Penguin Books.

Douglas, Mary. 2002 (1966). *Purity and Danger: An Analysis of the Concepts of Pollution and Taboo.* London: Routledge.

Dumont, Louis. 1970. *Religion, Politics and History in India.* Paris: Mouton.

———. 1980. *Homo Hierarchicus: The Caste System and Its Implications.* Chicago: University of Chicago Press.

Dundes, Alan. 1966. "Metafolklore and Oral Literary Criticism." *Monist.* 60: 505–16.

———. 1992. *The Evil Eye: A Casebook.* Madison: University of Wisconsin Press.

———. 2005. "Folkloristics in the Twenty-First Century (AFS Invited Presidential Plenary Address, 2004)." *Journal of American Folklore.* 118(470): 385–408. http://dx.doi.org/10.1353/jaf.2005.0044.

Dunning, Jennifer. 2007 (Jan. 7). "Chandralekha, 79, Dancer Who Blended Indian Forms, Dies." *New York Times.* http://www.nytimes.com/2007/01/07/arts/ 07chandralekha.html?_r=0.

Durai, H. G. 1929. "Preliminary Note on Geometrical Diagrams (Kolam) from the Madras Presidency." *Man.* 29: 77.

Eck, Diana. 1981. "India's 'Tīrthas': 'Crossings' in Sacred Geography." In *History of Religions.* Chicago: University of Chicago Press: 323–344.

———. 1982a. *Banaras: City of Light.* New York: Knopf, Inc.

———. 1982b. "Ganga: The Goddess in Hindu Sacred Geography." In *The Divine Consort: Radha and the Goddesses of India,* ed. John Stratton Hawley and Donna Marie Wulff (166–83). Boston: Beacon Press.

———. 1985. *Darsan: Seeing the Divine in India.* Chambersburg, PA: Anima Books.

———. 2012. *India: A Sacred Geography.* New York: Harmony, Random House.

Ehrig, Hartmut, Manfred Nagl, Grzegorz Rozenberg, and Azriel Rosenfeld. 2008. "Graph-Grammars and Their Application to Computer Science." Presented at the 3rd International Workshop, Warrenton, VA, June 13.

Evers, Larry, and Felipe S. Molina. 1987. *Yaqui Deer Songs: Maso Bwikam, A Native American Poetry.* Tucson: Sun Tracks and University of Arizona Press.

Feldhaus, Anne. 1995. *Water and Womanhood: Religious Meanings of Rivers in Maharashtra.* Oxford: Oxford University Press.

Fernandez, Charles. 2010 (March 3). "Malaysia Kolam Creates Record." *The Star Online.* http://thestar.com.my/metro/story.asp?file=/2010/3/3/central/ 5767479&sec=central.

Field, Mike, and Golubitsky, Martin. 2009. *Symmetry in Chaos: A Search for Patterns in Mathematics, Art, and Nature* (2nd ed.). Philadelphia: Society for Industrial and Applied Mathematics.

Freitag, Sandra. 1989. *Collective Action and Community: Public Arenas and the Emergence of Communalism in North India.* Berkeley: University of California Press.

Filliozat, Jeans, trans. 1972. *Un Texte Tamoul de Devotion Vishnouite Le Tiruppāvai d' Āṇṭāḷ.* Pondicherry: Institt Françi D'Indologie.

Gennep, Arnold van. 1960 (1908). *The Rites of Passage,* trans. Monika B. Vizedom and Gabrielle L. Caffe. Chicago: University of Chicago Press.

Gerdes, Paulus. 1989. "Reconstruction and Extension of Lost Symmetries: Examples from the Tamil of South India." In *Symmetry 2: Unifying Human Understanding,* ed. Istvan Hargittai (791–813). Oxford: Pergamon Press.

———. 1991. *Lusona: Geometrical Recreations of Africa.* Maputo, Mozambique: Higher Pedagogical Institute.

———. 1992. *African Pythagoras: A Study in Culture and Mathematics Education.* Maputo, Mozambique: Higher Pedagogical Institute.

———. 1995. *Une Tradition Géométrique en Afrique: Les Dessins Sur le Sable, tome 3: Analyse Comparative.* Paris: L'Harmattan.

———. 1996. *Lunda Geometry: Designs, Polyominoes, Patterns, Symmetries*. Maputo, Mozambique: Ethnomathematics Research Project, Higher Pedagogical Institute.

———. 1998. *Women, Art and Geometry in Southern Africa*. Trenton, NJ: Africa World Press.

———. 1999. *Geometry from Africa: Mathematical and Educational Explorations*. Washington D.C.: The Mathematical Association of America.

———. n.d. "From Liki-Designs to Cycle Matrices: The Discovery of Attractive New Symmetries." *Visual Mathematics*. 4(1). http://members.tripod.com/vismath7/gerd/index.html.

Glassie, Henry. 1995. "Tradition." *Journal of American Folklore*. 108(430): 398.

Gold, Ann. 1998. "Sin and Rain: Moral Ecology in Rural North India." In *Purifying the Earthly Body of God: Religion and Ecology in Hindu India*, ed. Lance E. Nelson. Albany: SUNY Press: 165–195.

———. 2001. *Sacred Landscapes and Cultural Politics: Planting a Tree*, ed. Philip P. Arnold. Vitality of Indigenous Religions Series. Aldershot, Hampshire, UK: Ashgate Publishing Company.

Gold, Ann, and Bhoju Ram Gujar. 2002. *In the Time of Trees and Sorrows: Nature, Power and Memory in Rajasthan*. Durham, NC: Duke University Press.

Government of India. 1960. *Alpana*. New Delhi: Publications Division, Ministry of Information and Broadcasting.

———. 1996. *Rangoli Designs in India Part 1*. New Delhi.

Grimes, Ronald L. 2006. *Rite Out of Place: Ritual, Media, and the Arts*. New York: Oxford University Press.

Guha-Thakurta, Tapati. 1992. *The Making of a New 'Indian' Art*. Cambridge, UK: Cambridge University Press.

Gupta, Eva Maria. 1983. *Brata and Ālpanā in Bengalen*. Wiesbaden: Steiner.

Gupta, V. K. 2004. *Kauṭilīya Arthaśāstra (A Legal, Critical, and Analytical Study)*. Delhi: C. P. Gautam.

Guralnik, David B., ed. 1980. *Webster's New World Dictionary of the American Language*. Cleveland, OH: Collins Publishers, Inc.

Guss, David M. 1989. *To Weave and Sing: Art, Symbol and Narrative in the South American Rain Forest*. Berkeley: University of California Press.

Haberman, David. 1994. *Journey Through Twelve Forests*. Oxford: Oxford University Press.

———. 2006. *River of Love in an Age of Pollution: The Yamuna River of Northern India*. Berkeley: University of California Press.

———. 2013. *People Trees: Worship of Trees in Northern India*. New York: Oxford University Press.

Hanchett, Suzanne. 1988. *Coloured Rice: Symbolic Structure in Hindu Family Festivals*. Delhi: Hindustan Pub. Corp.

Hancock, Mary Elizabeth. 1999. *Womanhood in the Making: Domestic Ritual and Public Culture in Urban South India*. Boulder, CO: Westview Press.

Hargittai, Istvan, ed. 1989. *Symmetry 2: Unifying Human Understanding*. New York: Pergamon Press.

Hargittai, Istvan, and Magdolna Hargittai. 1994. *Symmetry: A Unifying Concept*. Bolinas, CA: Shelter Publication, Inc.

Hargittai, Istvan, and T. C. Laurent. 2002. "Symmetrical Explorations Inspired by the Study of African Cultural Activities." *Symmetry 2000, Part I* (75–89). London: Portland Press.

Harrison, Robert. 1992. *Forests: The Shadow of Civilization*. Chicago: University of Chicago Press.

Hart, George L. 1973. "Women and the Sacred in Ancient Tamilnad." *Journal of Asian Studies*. 32: 233–50.

———. 1975. *The Poems of Ancient Tamil, Their Milieu and Their Sanskrit Counterparts*. Berkeley: University of California Press.

———. 1979. *Poets of the Tamil Anthologies: Ancient Poems of Love and War*. Princeton, NJ: Princeton University Press.

Hawley, John. 2005. *Three Bhakti Voices: Mirabai, Surdas, and Kabir in Their Time and Ours*. New Delhi: Oxford University Press.

Hess, Linda. 2015. *Bodies of Son: Kabir Oral Traditions and Performative Worlds in North India*. New York: Oxford University Press.

Hidayatullah, Aysha. 2014. *Feminist Edges of the Qur'an*. New York: Oxford University Press.

Hiltebeitel, Alf. 2011. *Dharma: Its Early History in Law, Religion, and Narrative*. Oxford: Oxford University Press.

The Hindu. "College organizes a special painting exhibition". Special Correspondent. August 14, 2009.

Hornborg, Ann-Christine. 2008. *Mi'kmaq Landscapes: From Animus to Sacred Ecology*. Burlington, VT: Ashgate Publications.

Humphrey, Caroline, and James Laidlaw. 1994. *The Archetypal Actions of Ritual: A Theory of Ritual Illustrated by the Jain Rite of Worship*. Oxford: Clarendon Press.

Huyler, Stephen. 1994. *Painted Prayers: Women's Art in Village India*. London: Thames and Hudson.

Hyde, Lewis. 2007 (1979). *The Gift: Creativity and the Artist in the Modern World*. New York: Random House.

Illich, Ivan. 1969. *Celebration of Awareness: A Call for Institutional Revolution*. New York: Doubleday.

———. 1973. *Tools for Conviviality*. New York: Harper & Row.

———. 1974. *Energy and Equity*. London: Marion Boyars.

———. 1985. *H_2O and the Waters of Forgetfulness: A Historicity of Stuff*. Dallas: Dallas Institute of Humanities.

———. 1987. *Toward a History of Needs*. Berkeley: Heyday Books.

Illich, Ivan, and Barry Sanders. 1988. *ABC: The Alphabetization of the Popular Mind*. San Francisco: North Point Press.

Ishimoto, Yukitaka. 2009. "Solving Infinite Kolam in Knot Theory." GPP Seminar, France, March 13.

Iyengar, Krishnaswamy Srinivasa. 1961. *Tiruppavai Vyakyanam*. Tricchy: Srinivasam Press.

Jablan, Slavik Vlado. 2002. *Symmetry, Ornament and Modularity*. K and E Series on Knots and Everything, Vol. 30. Hackensack, NJ: World Scientific Publication.

Jackson, Michael. 1995. *At Home in the World*. Durham, NC, and London: Duke University Press.

Jackson, William. 2004. *Heaven's Fractal Net: Retrieving Lost Visions in the Humanities*. Bloomington: Indiana University Press.

Jamison, Stephanie W. 1996. *Sacrificed Wife/Sacrificer Wife: Women, Ritual, and Hospitality in Ancient India*. New York: Oxford University Press.

Johnson, Mark, and George Lakoff. 1980. *Metaphors We Live By*. Chicago: University of Chicago Press.

Joseph, George. 1991. *The Crest of the Peacock: Non-European Roots of Mathematics*. Princeton, NJ: Princeton University Press.

Kabir, Linda Beth Hess, and Śukadeva Siṃha. 2002 (1983). *The Bijak of Kabir*. Oxford: Oxford University Press.

Kaliyanam, G. 1971. *Guide and History of Sri Andal Temple*. Srivilliputtur: Sri Nachiar Devasthanam.

Kane, P. V. 1962–75. *History of Dharmaśāstra*. 5 vols. Poona: Bhandarkar Oriental Research Institute.

Kanigal, Robert. 1992. *The Man Who Knew Infinity*. New York: Washington Square Press.

Katz, Victor J. 2002. "Notices of the American Mathematical Society." *Review of Mathematics Elsewhere: An Exploration of Ideas Across Cultures*. Notices of the American Mathematical Society. 50(5): 556–60.

Kellert, Stephen R., and Edward O. Wilson. 1993. *The Biophilia Hypothesis*. Washington D.C.: Island Press.

Kellert, Stephen R., and James Speth, eds. 2010. *The Coming Transformation: Values to Sustain Natural and Human Communities*, ed. Gus Speth. New Haven, CT: Yale University School of Forestry and Environmental Studies.

Kent, Eliza. 2013. *Sacred Groves and Local Gods: Religion and Environmentalism in South India*. New York: Oxford University Press.

Khanna, Madhu. 1979. *Yantra: The Tantric Symbol of Cosmic Unity*. London: Thames and Hudson.

Kinsley, David. 1995. *Ecology and Religion: Ecological Spirituality in Cross-Cultural Perspective*. Englewood Cliffs, NJ: Prentice-Hall.

"'Kolam' draws huge crowd." 2010 (Jan. 7). *The Hindu*. http://www.hindu.com/2010/01/07/stories/2010010750830200.htm.

Kothari, Sunil. 1995. *New Directions in Indian Dance*. National Centre for Performing Arts, Mumbai: Marg Publications.

Kramrisch, Stella. 1983. *Exploring India's Sacred Art*. Philadelphia: University of Pennsylvania Press.

———. 1985. "The Ritual Arts of India." In *Adithi: The Living Arts of India* (247–70). Washington D.C.: Festival of India and Smithsonian Institution Press.

Krishnakumar, P. R. 1992. *An Introduction to the Mysticism of the Sri Chakra*. Chennai: Sri Chakra Foundation.

Krishnamurthy, V. 1986. *Puthir Cinthanai Kanitham*. Chennai: New Century Book House.

Kuliachev, A. P. 1984. "Sriyantra and Its Mathematical Properties." *Indian Journal of History of Science*. 19: 279–92.

Laine, Anna. 2009. "In Conversation with the Kolam Practice: Auspiciousness and Artistic Experiences Among Women in Tamilnadu, South India." Ph.D. diss., University of Gothenburg, Sweden.

Lakoff, George. 1990. *Women, Fire and Dangerous Things: What Categories Reveal About the Mind*. Chicago: University of Chicago Press.

Lakoff, George, and Raphael Nunez. 2000. *Where Mathematics Comes From: How the Embodied Mind Brings Mathematics into Being*. New York: Basic Books.

Lambert, Bruce. 1993 (July 16). "Attipat K. Ramanujan, 64, Poet and Scholar of Indian Literature." *New York Times*. http://www.nytimes.com/1993/07/16/obituaries/attipat-k-ramanujan-64-poet-and-scholar-of-indian-literature.html.

Lansing, J. Stephen. 1991. *Priests and Programmers: Technologies of Power in the Engineered Landscape of Bali*. Princeton, NJ: Princeton University Press.

Layard, J. 1937. "Labyrinth Ritual in South India." *Folklore*. 48: 114–82.

Lazere, Arthur. 2002. "Mark Morris Dance Group: The Silk Road Dance Project: Kolam." *Culturevulture.net*. http://www.culturevulture.net/Dance/MarkMorrisv SilkRoad.htm.

Leslie, Julia. 1989. *The Perfect Wife*. Delhi: Oxford University Press.

———, ed. 1992. "Sri and Jyestha: Ambivalent Role Models for Women." In *Roles and Rituals for Hindu Women*. New Delhi: Motilal Banarsidass.

Mackay, Alan L. 1986. "But What is Symmetry?" *Computer and Mathematics Applications*. 12B(1-2): 19–20.

Madan, T. N. 1987. *Non-Renunciation: Themes and Interpretations of Hindu Culture*. New York: Oxford University Press.

Madvathasan, Mayilai. 1962. *Nālāyira Divyaprabandam*. Madras: Manali Ramakrishna Mudaliyar Specific Endowments.

Mahmood, Saba. 2005. *Politics of Piety: The Islamic Revival and the Feminist Subject*. Princeton, NJ: Princeton University Press.

Malaysian Indian Matrimony. "Beautiful Explanation of Hindu Custom for Kolam." Accessed Jan. 16, 2016. https://www.facebook.com/MalaysianIndianMatrimonial/videos/791622457626752/.

Mall, Amar S. 2007. "Structure, Innovation and Agency in Pattern Construction: The Kōlam of Southern India." In *Creativity and Cultural Improvisation*, ed. Elizabeth Hallam and Tim Ingold (55–78). Oxford: Berg Publishers.

Maloney, C. 1976. *Maloney: The Evil Eye*. New York: Columbia University Press.

Manimēkalai Pirasuram. 1986. *Rangōli Kōlam Pōduvathu Eppadi: Pākam I*. Chennai: Manimēkalai Pirasuram.

———. 1989 (1980). *Vakai Vakaiyana Kōlangal: Pākams 1, 2, and 3*. Chennai: Manimēkalai Pirasuram.

Margolin, Malcolm. 1978. *The Ohlone Way: Indian Life in the San Francisco-Monterey Bay Area*. Berkeley: Heyday Books.

Margolin, Malcolm, Edited with commentary. 1993. *The Way we lived: California Indian stories, songs & reminiscences*. Berkeley: Heyday Books.

Mazumdar, Sanjoy, and Shampa Mazumdar. 2005. "Home in the Context of Religion for Elderly Hindus in India." In *Home and Identity in Late Life: International Perspectives*, ed. Granam D. Rowles and Habib Chaudhury. New York: Springer Publishing Co.

McLagen, Robert. 1902. *Evil Eye in the Western Highlands.* London: Nutt.

Menon, Sadanand. 2007 (Jan. 3). "For Chandralekha, the Body Was Erotic, Sensuous." *Rediff India Abroad.* http://www.rediff.com/news/2007/jan/ 03inter.htm.

———. 2010. "To This Day I Feel That I Touched Time: A Conversation with Chandralekha." *Marg, A Magazine of the Arts.* 61(4). http://www.thefreelibrary.com/A+conversation+with +Chandralekha.-a0249607826.

Menzies, Charles R., ed. 2006. *Traditional Ecological Knowledge and Natural Resource Management.* Lincoln: University of Nebraska Press.

Mimica, Jadran. 1988. *Intimations of Infinity: The Mythopoeia of the Iqwaye Counting and Number System.* Oxford: Berg Publishers, Inc.

Mines, Diane P. 1990. "Hindu Periods of Death 'Impurity.'" *India Through Hindu Categories,* ed. McKim Marriott. New Delhi: Sage.

Mines, Mattison. 1994. *Public Faces, Private Voices: Community and Individuality in South India.* Berkeley: University of California Press.

Ministry of Tribal Affairs, Government of India. 2011. *Scheduled Tribes Data.* Ministry of Tribal Affairs. http://tribal.nic.in/WriteReadData/userfiles/file/Sectio%20 Table/Section1Table.pdf.

Monius, Anne. 2001. *Imagining a Place for Buddhism: Literary Culture and Religious Community in Tamil-Speaking South India.* New York: Oxford University Press.

Mookerjee, Ajit. 1988. *Kali: The Feminine Force.* New York: Destiny Books.

———. 1994. *Tantra Art: Its Philosophy and Physics.* Paris: Rupa & Co.

———. 1998 (1985). *Ritual Art of India.* London: Thames and Hudson.

Morris, Mark. 2002. *Kolam.* Music by Zakir Hussain (arranged by George Brooks); Ethan Iverson. Berkeley, CA: Zellerbach Hall, Cal Performances. DVD. April 20.

Nabokov, Isabelle. 2000. *Religion Against the Self: An Ethnography of Tamil Rituals.* New York: Oxford University Press.

Nagar, Shanti Lal. 1993. *Varaha in Indian Art, Culture and Literature.* New Delhi: Aryan Books International.

Nagarajan, Vijaya. 1993. "Hosting the Divine: The Kolam in Tamil Nadu." In *Mud, Mirror and Thread: Folk Traditions of Rural India,* ed. Nora Fisher: 192–204. Albuquerque: Museum of New Mexico Press.

———. 1994. "A Train and a Threshold." *A Manual of Collected Materials for Combating Sexual Harassment,* ed. Paula Richman (70–71). Chicago: American Institute of Indian Studies.

———. 1995. "Hosting the Divine: Ganges, Cow Dung, and Other Everyday Ecolog(ies) of the Imagination." *The Himalayan Experience.* Host, Meena Singh. UC Berkeley.

———. 1998. "The Earth as Goddess Bhudevi: Towards a Theory of Embedded Ecologies in Folk Hinduism." In *Purifying the Earthly Body of God: Religion and Ecology in Hindu India,* ed. Lance Nelson (269–98). Albany: State University of New York Press.

———. 2000. "Rituals of Embedded Ecologies: Drawing Kolams, Marrying Trees and Generating Auspiciousness." In *Hinduism and Ecology The Intersection of Earth, Sky, and Water,* ed. Christopher Chapple and Mary Evelyn Tucker (453–68). Cambridge, MA: Harvard University Press.

———. 2001. "(In)Corporating Threshold Art: Kolam Competitions, Patronage and Colgate." In *Religions/Globalization: Theories and Cases,* ed. Lois Lorentzen, Dwight Hopkins, David Batstone, and Eduardo Mandieta (161–86). Durham, NC: Duke University Press.

———. 2011. "Feeding a Thousand Souls, Kōlam as a Ritual of Generosity and Compassion." Paper presented at the TEDx Golden Gate ED Conference: Teaching Compassion Makes Us Happier, Smarter, and Healthier. Richmond, CA, June 11.

———. 2011."Feeding a Thousand Souls: Women, Ritual and Ecology." Paper presented at the 22nd Annual Bioneers Conference, San Raphael, CA, October 14–16.

———. 2012."Kōlam: Beauty, Feeding a Thousand Souls, and Generosity." Paper presented at the 8th Annual Tamil Conference, Berkeley, CA, April 20.

———. 2013. "Rangōli and Kōlam." *Sahapedia: An Online Encyclopedia on Indian Culture and Heritage*. Reprinted from K. A. Jacobsen, H. Basu, A. Malinar, and V. Narayanan, eds. (2010), *Encyclopedia of Hinduism*, Vol. II (472–8). Leiden, Netherlands: Brill.

———. 2015. *Mathematics and Kolam, A Woman's Ritual Art Form from Tamil Nadu, India*. Washington D.C.: National Academy of Sciences (DASER, D.C. Arts and Sciences Rendezvous). http://www.cpnas.org/events/daser-031915.html.

Naidu, N. Varadarajulu. 1968. *Sri Āṇṭāḷ Pillaitamil*. Madras: Asian Printers.

Nammāḷvār. 1981. *Hymns for the Drowning: Poems for Viṣṇu*, trans. A. K. Ramanujan. Princeton, NJ: Princeton University Press.

Nandy, Meera. 2003. *Prophets Facing Backwards: Postmodern Critiques of Science and Hindu Nationalism in India*. New Brunswick, NJ: Rutgers University Press.

Narasimhan, R., ed. 1989. *A Perspective in Theoretical Computer Science*. Series in Computer Science. Singapore: World Scientific Publishing Co., Inc.

Narayan, Kirin. 1989. *Storytellers, Saints, and Scoundrels: Folk Narrative in Hindu Religious Teaching*. Philadelphia: University of Pennsylvania Press.

———. 1995a. "How a Girl Became a Sacred Plant." In *Religions of India in Practice*, ed. Donald Lopez (487–94). Princeton, NJ: Princeton University Press.

———. 1995b. "The Practice of Oral Literary Criticism: Women's Songs in Kangra, India." *Journal of American Folklore*. 108:243–64.

———. 1997. "The Sprouting and Uprooting of Saili: The Story of Sacred Tulsi in Kangra." *Manushi: A Journal of Women and Society*. 102: 30–38.

———, in collaboration with Urmila Devi Sood. 1997. *Mondays on the Dark Night of the Moon: Himalayan Foothill Folktales*. New York: Oxford University Press.

Narayanan, Vasudha. 1987. *The Way and the Goal: Expressions of Devotion in Early Śrivaisṇava Commentary*. Washington D.C.: Institute for Vaishnava Studies.

———. 1994. *The Vernacular Veda: Revelation, Recitation, and Ritual*. Columbia: University of South Carolina Press.

———. 1999. "Brimming with Bhakti, Embodiment of Shakti." In *Feminism and World Religions*, ed. Arvind Sharma and Katherine Young (25–77). Albany: State University of New York.

Nath, Vijay. 1987. *Dāna: Gift System in Ancient India: A Socio-Economic Perspective*. New Delhi: Munshiram Manoharlal Publishers Pvt. Ltd.

Nelson, Richard. 1983. *Make Prayers to the Raven*. Chicago: University of Chicago Press.

———. 1986. *Hunters of the Northern Forest: Designs for Survival Among the Alaskan Kutchin*. Chicago: University of Chicago Press.

———. 1989. *The Island Within*. San Francisco: North Point Press.

———. 1997. *Heart and Blood: Living with Deer in America*. New York: Random House.

Nugteren, Albertina. 2005. *Belief, Bounty, and Beauty: Rituals Around Sacred Trees in India*. Leiden: Brill.

O'Gorman, Kevin D. 2005. "Modern Hospitality: Lessons from the Past." *Journal of Hospitality and Tourism Management*. 12(2): 141–51.

Ohnuki-Tierney. 1993. *Rice as Self*. Princeton, NJ: Princeton University Press.

Olivelle, Patrick. 1993. *The Āśrama System: The History and Hermeneutics of a Religious Institution*. Oxford: Oxford University Press.

———, trans. 1999. *Dharmasūtras: The Law Codes of Ancient India, Āpastabma, Gautama, Baudhāyana, and Vasiṣṭha*. Oxford: Oxford University Press.

———, ed. 2004. *Dharma: Studies in its Semantic, Cultural, and Religious History*. Delhi: Motilal Banarsidass Publishers Pvt. Ltd.

———. 2005. *Manu's Code of Law: A Critical Edition and Translation of the Mānava-Dharmaśāstra*. Oxford: Oxford University Press.

Orr, Leslie C. 2000. *Donors, Devotees, and Daughters of God: Temple Women in Medieval Tamilnadu*. Cary, NC: Oxford University Press.

Ortner, Sherry. 1974. "Is Female to Male as Nature Is to Culture?" In *Woman, Culture, and Society*, ed. Michelle Zimbalist Rosaldo and Louise Lamphere. Stanford, CA: Stanford University Press: 67–88.

Oxford English Dictionary. 1987. Definitions of auspicious, fractal, infinity, and symmetry. New Edition. Oxford: Oxford University Press.

Patton, Kimberley. 2006. *The Sea Can Wash Away All Evils: Modern Marine Pollution and the Ancient Cathartic Ocean*. New York: Columbia University Press.

Pearson, Anne Mackenzie. 1996. *Because It Gives Me Peace of Mind: Ritual Fasts in the Religious Lives of Hindu Women*. Albany: State University of New York Press.

Penkower, Linda, and Tracy Pintchman. 2014. "A Tale of Two Weddings: Gendered Performances of Tuls's Marriage to Krsna." *Studies in Comparative Religion*. Columbia: University of South Carolina Press.

Perlin, John. 2005 (1989). *A Forest Journey: The Story of Wood and Civilization*. Woodstock, VT: The Countryman Press.

Peterson, Indira. 1989. *Poems to Siva: The Hymns of the Tamil Saints*. Princeton, NJ: Princeton University Press.

Philipose, Pamela. 2011 (Nov. 3). "Chandralekha's Archive Reveals Story of One of India's Great Modernists." *News Blaze*. http://newsblaze.com/story/20111103113332 iwfs.nb/topstory.html.

Philipose, Pamela. 2011 (Nov. 12). "Dance, as She Saw It." *The Deccan Herald, Women's Feature Service*.

Pillai, Shanmugan, and V. Saroja. 1987. *Kala Aayvil Kōlankal*. Madurai: Ananda Padippakam.

Pintchman, Tracy. 2005. *Guests at God's Wedding: Celebrating Kartik Among the Women of Benares*. New York: SUNY Press.

Pollan, Michael. 2001. *The Botany of Desire: A Plant's Eye View of the World*. New York: Random House.

Polyani, Karl. 1957. *Trade and Market in Early Empires: Economies in History and Theory*. Chicago: Gateway Edition.

Pressman, Edward R., et al (producer), and Matthew Brown (director). 2016. *The Man Who Knew Infinity* [motion picture]. Warner Bros.

Puri, Rajika. 2003. "Kolam by Mark Morris Dance Group Has Its NY Premier at B.A.M." *Narthaki*. http://www.narthaki.com/info/reviews/rev106.html.

Raghavan, Padma, and Savita Narayan. 2005. *Navagraha Temples of Tamil Nadu: Kaveri Delta*. Mumbai: English Edition Publishers and Distributors.

Rajagopalachari, C., trans. 1981. *Kural: The Great Book of Tiru-Valluvar*. Bombay: Bharatiya Vidya Bhavan.

Ramanujan, A. K., trans. 1975 (1967). *The Interior Landscape: Love Poems from a Classical Tamil Anthology*. Bloomington: Indiana University Press.

———, trans. 1985 (1973). *Speaking of Śiva*. Middlesex, UK: Penguin Books.

———, trans. 1985. *Poems of Love and War: from the Eight Anthologies and the Ten Long Poems of Classical Tamil*. Delhi: Oxford University Press.

———. 1999 (1989). "Classics Lost and Found." In *The Collected Essays of A.K. Ramanujan*. New Delhi: Oxford University Press: 194–196.

———. 1999 (1989). "Is There an Indian Way of Thinking?" In *The Collected Essays of A.K. Ramanujan* (41–58). New Delhi: Oxford University Press.

———. 1994 "Some Thoughts on 'Non-Western' Classics, with Indian Examples." *World Literature Today*: 68 .

Ramaswamy, Sumathi. 1997. *Passions of the Tongue: Language Devotion in Tamil India, 1891–1970*. Berkeley: University of California Press.

———. 2007. "Of Gods and Globes: The Territorialisation of Hindu Deities in Popular Visual Culture." In *India's Popular Culture: Iconic Spaces and Fluid Images*, ed. J. Jain. Mumbai: Marg Publications. 19–31.

Ramnarayan, Gowri. 2008. *Grandma's Kōlams*. Chennai: Oxygen Books.

Reichel-Dolmatoff, Gerardo. 1996. *The Forest Within: The World-View of the Tukano Amazonian Indians.* Devon, UK: Themis Books.

"Reviving Hindu Tradition Through Alpana." 2009 (Dec. 12). *The Statesman (India).* Database: NewsBank.

Reynolds, Holly. 1978. "To Keep the Tāli Strong: Women's Rituals in Tamilnad, India." PhD diss., University of Wisconsin-Madison.

Rhodes, Constantina. 2012. *Invoking Lakshmi: The Goddess of Wealth in Song and Ceremony.* New York: SUNY.

Robinson, Thamburaj. 2007. "Extended Pasting Scheme for Kolam Pattern Generation." *Forma.* 22: 55–64.

Rudolph, Lloyd. 1987. *In Pursuit of Lakshmi: The Political Economy of the Indian State.* Chicago: University of Chicago Press.

Sachs, Wolfgang. 1993. *Global Ecology: A New Arena of Political Conflict.* London: Zed Books.

Saksena, Jogendra. 1979. *Art of Rājasthān henna and floor decorations.* Delhi: Sundeep.

———. 1985. *Mandana, a folk art of Rājasthān.* New Delhi: Crafts Museum.

Śaṅkarācārya. 1965. *Saundaryalaharī (The Ocean of Beauty) of Srī Śaṃkarabhagavatpāda,* trans. T. R. Srinivasa Ayyangar and Pandit S. Subrahmanya Sastri. Madras: Theosophical Publishing House.

———. 2000 (1937). *Saundaryalaharī (The Ocean of Beauty) of Srī Śaṃkarabhagavatpāda,* trans. T. R. Srinivasa Ayyangar and Pandit S. Subrahmanya Sastri. Adyar: Theosophical Publication House.

Saraswathi, R. and L. Vijayalakshmi. 1991. *Kotaiwar Idum Kolangal.* Chennai: Lakshmi Nilayam.

Saroja, V. 1988. "Tamil Panpāttil Kōlangal." PhD diss., Madurai Kamaraj University, India.

———. 1992. *Manin Manam.* Madurai: Vanjiko Pathipakan.

Sax, William, ed. 1995. "The Realm of Play and the Sacred Stage." In *Gods at Play: Līlā in South Asia* (177–204). New York: Oxford University Press.

Schama, Simon. 1995. *Landscape and Memory.* New York: Alfred A. Knopf.

Sciorra, Joseph. 2011. *Italian Folk: Vernacular Culture in Italian-American Lives* (190–208). New York: Fordham University Press.

Scott, James. 1985. *Weapons of the Weak: Everyday Forms of Peasant Resistance.* New Haven, CT: Yale University Press.

Seizer, Susan. 2005. *Stigma's of the Tamil Stage: An Ethnography of Special Drama Artists in South India.* Durham, NC: Duke University Press.

Seshadiri, C.V. 1993. *Equity is Good Science: The Equity Papers.* Tharamani, Madras: Shri AMM Murugappa Chettiar Research Centre.

Shankaranarayanan, C. D. 2002. *Nāchiyār Thirumoḷi.* Chennai: Nillai Nilayam.

Shiva, Vandana. 1989. *Staying Alive: Women, Ecology, and Development.* London: Zed Books.

Shulman, David. 1980. *Tamil Temple Myths.* Princeton, NJ: Princeton University Press.

———. 1985. *The King and the Clown in South Indian Myth and Poetry.* Princeton, NJ: Princeton University Press.

Simha, S. L. N. 1982. *Tiruppavai of Goda: Our Lady Saint Andral's Krishna Poem.* Bombay: Ananthacharya Indological Research Institute.

Siromoney, Gift. 1978. "South Indian *Kolam* Patterns." *Kalakshetra Quarterly.* 1(1): 9–14.

———. 1985. *Studies on the Traditional Art of Kōlam.* Madras: Madras Christian College.

———. 1986. "Rosenfeld's Cycle Grammars and *Kolam.*" Presented at the Third International Workshop on Graph Grammars and their applications to Computer Science, Airlie, VA, December 2–6.

Siromoney, Gift, Rani Siromoney, and Kamala Krithivasan. 1972. "Abstract Families of Matrices and Picture Languages." *Computer Graphics and Image Processing.* 1: 284–307.

———. 1973. "Picture Languages with Array Rewriting Rules." *Information and Control.* 22: 447–70.

———. 1974. "Array Grammars and Kolam." *Computer Graphics and Image Processing.* 3: 63–88.

Siromoney, Gift, Rani Siromoney, and T. Robinson. 1989. "Kambi *Kolam* and Cycle Grammars." In *A Perspective in Theoretical Computer Science, Commemorative Volume for Gift Siromoney.* ed. R. Narasimhan (267–300). Singapore: World Scientific Publishing Co.

Slater, Candace. 2002. *Entangled Edens: Visions of the Amazon.* Berkeley: University of California Press.

Society for Science on Form Japan. 2006. "The International Symposium on Katachi*/Form in Folk Art." 62nd Autumn Symposium, Osaka University, November 3–5.

Soneji, Devesh. 2012. *Unfinished Gestures: Devadāsīs, Memory, and Modernity in South India.* Chicago: University of Chicago Press.

Stanley, John. 1977. "Special Time, Special Power: The Fluidity of Power in a Popular Hindu Festival." *Journal of Asian Studies.* 37(1): 27–43.

Stonesifer, Jene. 1995 (Aug. 17). "Domestic Blessings." *Washington Post.* http://www.washingtonpost.com/archive/lifestyle/home-garden//1995/08/17/domestic-blessings/96127ab4-34c9-4e78-9d43-7a86dbf3e56f/.

Subramanian, K. G., K. Rangarajan, and M. Mukund, eds. 2006. *Formal Models, Languages And Applications (Machine Perception and Artificial Intelligence).* Madras: World Scientific Publishing Co., Inc.

Sundaram, P. S., trans. 1989. *Tiruvalluvar: The Kural.* New Delhi: Penguin Books.

Swearer, Donald K., and Susan Lloyd McGarry, eds. 2011. *Ecologies of Human Flourishing.* Cambridge, MA: Harvard University Press.

Tadvalkar, Nayana. 2012. "Ephemeral Floor Art of India: History, Tradition and Continuity." PhD diss., SNDT Women's University. http://hdl.handle.net/10603/4605.

Tagore, Abinindranath. 1921. *L'Alpana on les Decorations Rituelles Au Bengale.* Paris: Editions Bossard.

Tamil Lexicon. 1982. Madras: University of Madras.

Tamilvanan, Lēna. 1990. *Vagai Vagaiyana Kōrangal.* Chennai: Hanimekalai Pirasuram.

Trawick, Peggy. 1994. *Notes on Love in a Tamil Family.* Berkeley: University of California Press.

Turner, Victor. 1969. *The Ritual Process: Structure and anti-structure.* Chicago: Aldine Publishing Co.

Vatuk, Sunita. 2012. "Putting Kolams: Mathematical Thinking in a Women's Art." *Proceedings of Episteme 5, India.* City College of New York, CUNY.

Veeragavācāriyār, Sri Uttamūrthy. 1956. *Āṇṭāḷ: Upaya Vedanta Granta Mālai: Muthal Thiruvanthāthi.* Kanchipuram: Sri Venketeswara Publishers.

Venketesan, Archana. 2010. *The Sacred Garland: Āṇṭāḷ's Tiruppavai and Nacciyar Thirumoli. Translation with Introduction and Commentary.* New York: Oxford University Press.

Vishweswaran, Kamala. 1994. *Fictions of Feminist Ethnography.* Minneapolis: University of Minnesota Press.

Wadley, Susan Snow. 1991. "Paradoxical Powers of Tamil Women." In *Powers of Tamil Women.* Syracuse, NY: Maxwell School of Citizenship and Public Affairs, Syracuse University. http://ehrafworldcultures.yale.edu/document?id=aw16-055.

Waring, Timothy M. 2012. "Sequential Encoding of Tamil Kolam Patterns." *Forma.* 27: 83–92.

White, David Gordon. 1996. *The Alchemical Body: Siddha Traditions in Medieval India.* Chicago: University of Chicago Press.

Wiliam, Eurwyn. 2014. "'To Keep the Devil at Bay'? Ephemeral Floor Decoration in Wales during the Nineteenth and Early Twentieth Centuries." *Folk Life: Journal of Ethnological Studies.* 52(2):152-75.

Williams, Raymond. 1983. *Keywords: A Vocabulary of Culture and Society.* London: Fontana.

Worster, Donald. 1977. *Nature's Economy: A History of Ecological Ideas.* Cambridge, UK: Cambridge University Press.

Yanagisawa, Kiwamu, and Shojiro Nagata. 2007. "Fundamental Study on Design System of Kolam Pattern." *Forma* (22:31–46).

Yocum, Glenn. 1982. *Hymns to the Dancing Siva: A Study of Manikkavacakar's Tiruvacakam.* New Delhi: Heritage.

Zimmerman, Francis. 2011 (1987). *The Jungle and the Aroma of Meats: An Ecological Theme in Hindu Medicine.* Comparative Studies of Health Systems & Medical Care. Berkeley: University of California Press.

In loving memory of
my father, R. G. Nagarajan,
one of my most stalwart and steady supporters

and for those who had deeply supported this work in so many countless ways:

V. S. Naipaul (1932–2018)
Saba Mamood (1962–2018)
Gerardo Marin (1947–2018)
Bokara Legendre (1940–2017)
Isabelle Nabokov (1956–2017)
Paula Merwin (1936–2017)
Barnard Bate (1960–2016)
Doug Tompkins (1943–2015)
Rina Swentzell (1939–2015)
Peter Matthiessen (1927–2014)
Marcia Ascher (1935–2013)
R. G. Nagarajan (1932–2013)
Peter Warshall (1940–2013)
Dashrat Patel (1927–2010)
James D. Houston (1933–2009)
Smitu Kothari (1950–2009)
Aditya Behl (1965–2009)
Grace Paley (1922–2007)
Ramchandra Gandhi (1937–2007)
Chandralekha (1928–2006)
Alan Dundes (1934–2005)
Komul Kothari (1929–2004)
Ivan Illich (1926–2002)
C. V. Seshadiri (1930–1995)
A. K. Ramanujan (1929–1993)
Barbara Stoler Miller (1940–1993)
Stella Kramrisch (1896–1993)

INDEX

Page numbers followed by *t* and *f* denote tables and figures.